Judicial Reforms in India

PUBLISHED BY
ACADEMIC FOUNDATION
IN ASSOCIATION WITH

RAJIV GANDHI INSTITUTE FOR
CONTEMPORARY STUDIES (RGICS)
NEW DELHI

The Rajiv Gandhi Institute for Contemporary Studies (RGICS), New Delhi is part of the Rajiv Gandhi Foundation and functions as a think tank. The target audience of the RGICS includes parliamentarians, legislators and representatives of political parties, public policymakers and their advisers, the intelligentsia, the media and various interest groups. To interface with these groups, RGICS uses different modes of communication like books, monographs, working papers, symposia, discussions, talks and lectures. The RGICS research work is focused on international economic relations, law reforms, IT and economic reforms in India.

THE EDITORS

Arnab Kumar Hazra is a staff consultant to the Asian Development Bank for the India Administration of Justice Project. He has been a Fellow with the Rajiv Gandhi Institute for Contemporary Studies, Delhi; Economic Advisor to the Embassy of the Republic of Korea and Consultant to the National Council of Applied Economic Research, Delhi. He is a professional economist and was educated in St. Xavier's College (Calcutta), and Jawaharlal Nehru University (New Delhi). He has worked and published nationally and internationally in the area of legal reforms. His special interests, besides legal reforms, are in labour laws and natural resource economics.

Bibek Debroy is a professional economist and was educated in Presidency College (Calcutta), Delhi School of Economics and Trinity College (Cambridge). He has worked at Presidency College (Calcutta), Gokhale Institute of Politics and Economics (Pune), Indian Institute of Foreign Trade (Delhi), National Council of Applied Economic Research (Delhi) and as Consultant, Department of Economic Affairs, Ministry of Finance, Government of India. He has been the Director of the Rajiv Gandhi Institute for Contemporary Studies (RGICS), Rajiv Gandhi Foundation, New Delhi. He was also the Director for a project known as LARGE, set up by the Ministry of Finance and UNDP to examine legal reforms. Presently he is Secretary General, PHD Chamber of Commerce and Industry, New Delhi. Bibek Debroy is the author and editor of several books, papers and popular articles and has been consulting editor and columnist with Business Standard. His special interests are international trade (in particular the WTO), law reform and the political economy of liberalisation in India. He has been listed in many bibliographies and has been a member of several government committees.

Judicial Reforms in India

Issues and Aspects

EDITORS:

ARNAB KUMAR HAZRA • BIBEK DEBROY

ACADEMIC FOUNDATION
NEW DELHI

First published in 2007
by

ACADEMIC FOUNDATION
4772-73 / 23 Bharat Ram Road, (23 Ansari Road),
Darya Ganj, New Delhi - 110 002 (India).
Phones : 23245001 / 02 / 03 / 04.
Fax : +91-11-23245005.
E-mail : academic@vsnl.com
www. academicfoundation.com

in association with :

Rajiv Gandhi Institute for Contemporary Studies, New Delhi

Judicial Reforms in India: Issues and Aspects
editors: Arnab Kumar Hazra and Bibek Debroy

ISBN 10: 81-7188-537-3
ISBN 13: 978-81-7188-537-3

Typeset by Italics India, New Delhi.
Printed and bound in India.

Contents

List of Tables, Figures and Appendices

TABLES

FIGURES

APPENDICES

Acknowledgements

The paper "What Can the Rule of Law Variable Tell us about Rule of Law Reforms?" by Kevin E. Davis, was published in the *Michigan Journal of International Law, Volume 26:1,* Fall 2004.

The paper "Delays in the Administration of Justice" by Carl Baar was originally prepared for presentation at the Commonwealth Magistrates and Judges Association Conference, Accra, Ghana, Second Plenary Session, August 2, 2005. Minor revisions were subsequently made on August 8, 2005.

The paper "The Problem of Court Congestion: Evidence from Indian Lower Courts", by Arnab Kumar Hazra and Maja B. Micevska was originally published as *ZEF-Discussion Papers on Development Policy No. 88*, Centre for Development Research, University of Bonn, Germany, July 2004. The version that appears here was presented at The Royal Economic Society Annual Conference, 2004, Swansea, UK, April 5-7, 2004 and 24th Annual Conference of European Public Choice Society, DIW Berlin, Germany, April 15-18, 2004.

The paper "The Reduction of Case Backlog in the Courts: A Framework and Strategy", by Carl Baar and Robert G. Hann of Justice Development International Ltd., was prepared for The Third Biennial Meeting of Commonwealth Judicial Education Institute, hosted by the National Judicial Academy, Bhopal, India on March 14-18, 2005. An earlier version of this paper was prepared for the Social Conflict and Legal Reform Project (SCLR), a joint project of the Government of Jamaica and the Government of Canada (CIDA).

A part of the paper "Crime, Deterrence and the Need for Reforms: An Analysis of Indian States", by Debashis Chakraborty, Arnab Kumar Hazra and Pavel Chakraborty was published in the paper "Institutional Reforms in the Enforcement of Criminal Justice in India", by Arnab Kumar Hazra, in Bibek Debroy (ed.), *Agenda for Improving Governance*, Academic Foundation, New Delhi, February 2004.

Editors/Contributors

Carl Baar is Professor Emeritus, Brock University, St. Catharine's, Ontario, Canada. He is also Adjunct Professor of Political Science, York University, Toronto, Ontario, Canada; and Principal, Justice Development International Ltd.

Amarjit Singh Bedi is an advocate and practices in the Supreme Court of India as well as in the Delhi High Court. He has been associated as a consultant on information technology to the India Administration of Justice Project.

Laveesh Bhandari heads Indicus Analytics, an economics research firm. He completed his Ph.D. in Economics from Boston University in 1996 and his thesis received the Best Thesis in International Economics Award by EXIM Bank of India. He was also awarded the Hite Fellowship for his work on international finance. He began his career as a Consultant for Manhattan (now Brookdale) Funds, New York and joined the National Council of Applied Economic Research (NCAER), New Delhi, as a Senior Economist in 1997. He has taught economics at Boston University and IIT Delhi and was also the Managing Editor of the *Journal of Emerging Market Finance.*

G.C. Bharuka is a former Judge of the High Courts of Karnataka and Patna. Presently he is the Chairman of the E-Committee of the Supreme Court of India, which is in charge of the project to implement ICT in the judiciary. He is the author of the book *Rejuvenating Judicial System through E-Governance & Attitudinal Change*. His specialisation, apart from information technology, is in the areas of intellectual property, commercial contracts, telecommunication, insurance and corporate law.

Debashis Chakraborty is Assistant Professor at the Indian Institute of Foreign Trade, New Delhi. Debashis has been educated at University of Calcutta and Centre for International Trade and Development, JNU. He has earlier worked in Rajiv Gandhi Institute for Contemporary Studies (RGICS), New Delhi as a researcher.

Pavel Chakraborty is Research Associate, Global Agreements of Legislation and Trade, The Energy and Resources Institute (TERI), New Delhi.

Kevin E. Davis is Professor of Law, New York University School of Law, USA. He joined NYU from a professorship at the University of Toronto, and works on commercial and financial law aspects of law and development and related issues of governance. He has particular expertise on Caribbean and small island economies and polities. He is co-author of a major study of these issues with Michael Trebilcock (2005), and has also written an economic analysis of the OECD Anti-Bribery Convention.

Bibek Debroy is Secretary General, PHD Chamber of Commerce and Industry, Delhi. He was earlier Director, Rajiv Gandhi Institute for Contemporary Studies (RGICS), Rajiv Gandhi Foundation, Delhi. He is a professional economist and was educated in Presidency College (Kolkata), Delhi School of Economics and Trinity College (Cambridge). He has worked at Presidency College (Kolkata), Gokhale Institute of Politics and Economics (Pune), Indian Institute of Foreign Trade (Delhi), National Council of Applied Economic Research (Delhi) and as Consultant, Department of Economic Affairs, Ministry of Finance, Government of India. He was also the Director for a project known as LARGE, set up by the Ministry of Finance and UNDP to examine legal reforms. He is the author and editor of several books, papers and popular articles and is also Consulting Editor with *Business Standard*. Bibek Debroy's special interests are international trade (in particular the WTO), law reform and the political economy of liberalisation in India.

Robert G. Hann is an economist and criminologist who has been leading justice-related research and reform projects for over 30 years. As a Principal of Justice Development International Ltd. (JDI) and Robert Hann & Associates Limited, he is currently leading projects to evaluate the pilot family court in Trinidad and Tobago, to develop a strategic plan for the Jamaican Criminal Justice System, to evaluate an alternative model of delivering legal services in criminal cases (in Canada), to develop judicial bench books for cases with self represented accused in civil, family and criminal cases, and to assess alternative governance models for court administration. He has also worked recently in India in the areas of court performance standards, information systems and facilities.

Arnab Kumar Hazra is a staff consultant to the Asian Development Bank for the India Administration of Justice Project. He has been a Fellow with the Rajiv Gandhi Institute for Contemporary Studies, Delhi, Economic Advisor to the Embassy of the Republic of Korea and Consultant to the National Council of Applied Economic Research (NCAER), Delhi. He is a professional economist and was educated in St. Xavier's College (Calcutta) and Jawaharlal Nehru University (New Delhi). He has worked and published nationally and internationally in the area of legal reforms. His special interests, besides legal reforms, are in labour laws and natural resource economics.

Maja B. Micevska is a Senior Researcher at the ESCE, and a Senior Fellow at the Center for Development Research, University of Bonn. She earned her Ph.D. in Economics at Claremont Graduate University. Her main fields of research are development economics, labour economics, population economics, and the economics of transition with a special focus on transition mobilities.

Nandan Nawn is Lecturer at the WB National University of Juridical Sciences, Salt Lake, Kolkata. His area of interests are Environmental Economics, Development Economics and Law and Economics.

Murali Sagi is Director, Information Systems and Strategic Planning, Judicial Commission of New South Wales, Sydney, Australia. He has written and published extensively on the use of information technology in the courts.

Videh Upadhyay is an advocate and practices in the Supreme Court of India. He is a former Visiting Fellow at Centre for Law and Governance, Jawaharlal Nehru University, New Delhi and the

University of California, Berkeley. He is closely associated with United Nations Development Programme (UNDP) and Department for International Development (DFID) India in furthering the area of law reform in the country. He has also recently authored a comprehensive work titled *Public Interest Litigation for the Halsbury's Laws of India.*

Barry Walsh is an international law and justice sector consultant who specialises in court and judicial administration policy development and institutional strengthening. Admitted to the bar of New South Wales in 1985, he has a diploma of law and post graduate qualifications in public sector management and change management. After a long career as a bureaucrat and court administrator in Australia, he has worked in the justice sectors of Papua New Guinea, Indonesia, Nepal and India.

1

Introduction: Issues and Aspects of Judicial Reforms in India

ARNAB KUMAR HAZRA
and BIBEK DEBROY

Economic reforms are driven by the intention of driving up India's GDP growth rates, from the present trend of around 6.5 per cent to 8 per cent plus.[1] In attaining higher GDP growth rates, legal reforms are now recognised as a critical ingredient. In a somewhat belated recognition of the importance of legal reforms, *Economic Survey 2004-2005* has a section on the infrastructure of contract enforcement.[2] The Indian legal infrastructure needed reforms in any case, even if the post-1991 cycle of reforms hadn't been introduced. However, liberalisation provided an additional trigger. The word 'law' has varying interpretations. Consequently, the expression legal reform also needs to be pinned down. There are three layers in legal reform. First, there is an element of statutory law reform and there are three clear elements to statutory law reform: (a) weeding out old and dysfunctional elements in legislation;[3] (b) unification and harmonisation; and (c) reducing state intervention. Second, legal reform has to have an administrative law reform component, meaning the subordinate legislation in the form of rules, regulations, orders and instructions from ministries and government departments. Often, constraints to efficient decision making come about through administrative law, rather than through statutory law and discretion, bribery and rent-seeking are fallouts. Finally, the third element of legal

1. The Tenth Five Year Plan (2002-07) has 8 per cent as a target, while the National Common Minimum Programme (NCMP) talks of 7-8 per cent.

2. *Economic Survey* sets out the reform agenda, especially in its first chapter. Although *Economic Survey* originates with Finance Ministry and Department of Economic Affairs, it is remarkable that legal reforms found no explicit mention earlier, except for references to specific statutes.

3. The earliest Central statutes date back to 1836 and are the Bengal Indigo Contracts Act and the Bengal Districts Act.

reform is what may be called judicial reforms, although swifter dispute resolution and contract enforcement are not exclusively judicial issues.

The Indian judiciary is swamped with a huge number of pending cases. This apparently insurmountable problem increases inefficiencies in the system, apart from placing a question mark over the efficacy over other legal reform measures initiated. This institution has also generally remained outside reform initiatives initiated in India in the last 15 years.[4] Inefficiency in the judicial system also leads to frivolous litigation, with harassment and delays as the primary motive, crowding out genuine litigants and forcing them to seek solutions in a quasi-legal framework.

The benefits of a good judicial system, or conversely the perils of neglecting judicial reforms are many, covering economic, political and social spheres. The importance of the judicial system lies in checking abuses of government power, enforcing property rights, enabling exchanges between private parties and most importantly, upholding the 'rule of law'. A balanced swift, affordable (accessible) and fair justice delivery system besides promoting law and order, aids in the development of markets, investments, including foreign direct investments, and economic growth, and therefore helps in poverty reduction. Legal empowerment seeks to make concrete improvements in people's lives through improved access to legal services and complementary non-legal services. Legal empowerment works to reduce poverty, build civil society, encourage development, and promote human rights. Consequently, neglecting judicial reforms has social, political and economic costs. Good economic policies need strong and accountable institutions to support and implement them. Justice forms the basis of a lasting social order.

There is a genuine need to clear the dockets of the courts. Addressing this need usually involves a multi-pronged strategy, and the entire gamut of the initiatives involved can collectively be categorised under the umbrella called Judicial Reforms. In this volume, when judicial reforms are discussed, the reforms essentially pertain to the District and Subordinate Courts in India. It should be made clear that

4. Arun Jaitley, the former Union Law Minister, commented, "If there is one sector which has kept away from the reforms process it is the administration of Justice", *R. N. Malhotra Memorial Lecture* on "India's Judicial Reforms", India International Centre, New Delhi, February 14, 2001.

the framework of issues and aspects of judicial reforms documented is in no way claimed to be comprehensive. In fact, given the varied character of needs across Indian states, the endeavour is to touch on some of the important and basic issues of judicial reforms in India.

India is the largest democracy in the world, where rule of law exists. The country has a fiercely independent judiciary. There is considerable political stability, as well as freedom of expression, freedom of political association, freedom of political opposition and dissent. The central institutions of the legal system are regarded to be fair.

At the apex of governance lies the Constitution of India and the Preamble to the Constitution. In a sense, the Preamble is above the Constitution in importance, because even though the Constitution can be amended, the basic spirit of the Preamble cannot be changed. Below the Preamble and the Constitution is the 'Legislature' that makes laws through legislation enacted in Parliament or Legislative Assemblies. The Executive or the Bureaucracy, which is the second pillar of India's democracy, enacts a number of rules and regulations, which aids in its functioning. The Judiciary, the third and final pillar of India's democracy, on the one hand, settles disputes between two parties, and on the other hand, interprets laws, rules and regulations made by the legislature and the executive.

The judicial system in India is vertically structured. There are around 12,000 courts—1 Supreme Court, 21 High Courts, 3,150 District Level Courts, 4,816 *Munsif*/Magistrate Courts and 1,964 Magistrate II and equivalent courts. Only 6 of the High Courts have original jurisdiction, that is, civil suits can be directly filed in these courts, provided the monetary value of the suit is above a certain amount. These are the High Courts of Bombay, Calcutta, Delhi, Himachal Pradesh, Jammu and Kashmir and Madras. The minimum monetary values admissible differ among these 6 courts. Other High Courts are Appellate Courts. In states where the High Court does not have original jurisdiction, even disputes involving large sums of money have to go through lower courts, which often do not have requisite expertise to decide on complicated issues. The case eventually goes to the High Court, but only after considerable delay. On the other hand, where High Courts have original jurisdiction, the monetary limit is often so low that far too many cases go straight to already clogged High Courts. However, all High Courts also have additional original jurisdiction under special statutes like, the Representation of the People Act, 1951; Companies Act, 1956; Banking Companies Act, 1949; Indian Divorce Act, 1869; Parsi Marriages and Divorce Act, 1936. Civil and criminal cases are both handled by the same court. For various (mostly non-judicial) reasons, criminal cases get higher priority. Since most civil cases are commercial disputes, this hampers the settlement of economic disputes leading to higher contracting (transaction) costs and general inefficiency of commercial activity. This problem of overlapping functions works in other ways as well. A district magistrate has to deal with land revenue cases and general administration and is very often the appellate authority on criminal cases. There is therefore, no clear distinction across the administrative and judiciary responsibilities of such officials. Add to this overlapping jurisdiction in certain cases. Any judicial reform framework actually needs to target the District and Subordinate courts, for these are the trial courts in India. Apart from these there are also specialised tribunals created under special Acts (for example, the industrial and labour tribunals, consumer courts), *Lok Adalats*, *Gram Nyayalayas*, etc. The tribunals supplement the traditional judicial hierarchy of civil courts, and come into existence through various legislations and enactments. Another aspect that distinguishes the higher judiciary, consisting of the Supreme Court and the High Courts, from lower judiciary is that while one can go to the subordinate judiciary on points of both facts as well as law, the higher courts don't usually entertain cases with points of facts. One can appeal to the higher courts only on points of law. It must be mentioned that Constitutional matters are not within the jurisdiction of the lower judiciary, that is, the District and Subordinate Courts and must go either to the Supreme Court or to the High Court in their writ jurisdiction. The writ in India, as issued by the High Court or the Supreme Court, essentially corresponds to the prerogative writ known to English law and is mainly issued in the field of public law to enforce fundamental rights (in the case of the Supreme Court and the High Courts) and other rights (in the case of the High Courts). In general, a writ can be issued only against the State or a public authority. Although, in theory, writs are extraordinary remedies, however, from the point of view of the volume of litigation and the time taken in courts, their importance is tremendous. The need for invoking this jurisdiction grew largely out of an increased role for the State in the life of the ordinary citizens in independent India.

It is important to point out certain issues related to law reforms first. Foremost among these, is the issue of economic linkage between economic growth and rule of law reforms. The political milieu of a country rests on the 'rule of law' in the land. Within the contours of the 'rule of law,[5] the procedural and institutional characteristics of a country's legal system are of paramount importance. The positive linkage between 'rule of law' and economic growth is perhaps undeniable, especially in developing countries. This is specially embodied in the arguments of the 'New Institutional Economics' school, which emphasises the protection of private property rights and the facilitation and enforcement of long-term contracts as essential ingredients to raising levels of investment and hence economic growth. A number of cross-country econometric studies do provide compelling evidence towards this.[6] In one particularly influential study entitled "Governance Matters",[7] undertaken by Kaufmann, Kraay and Zoido-Lobatón, wherein data (survey based) was divided into six clusters—'voice and accountability', 'political stability', 'government effectiveness', 'regulatory quality', 'rule of law', and 'control of corruption'—the authors created indexes that measure institutional quality along each of these six dimensions, as well as a composite 'governance' index designed to measure the overall quality of governance in a society. They then regressed these indices on three measures of development—per capita GDP, infant mortality and adult literacy. They found strong correlations between their measures of development and their measures of institutional quality. Other studies using fewer measures of institutional quality, and typically

---

5. Thomas Carothers defines 'Rule of Law' as a system in which the laws are public knowledge, are clear in meaning, and apply equally to everyone. They enshrine and uphold the political and civil liberties that have gained status as universal human rights over the last half-century. In particular, anyone accused of a crime has the right to a fair, prompt hearing and is presumed innocent until proved guilty. The central institutions of the legal system, including courts, prosecutors, and police, are reasonably fair, competent, and efficient. Judges are impartial and independent, not subject to political influence or manipulation. Perhaps most important, the government is embedded in a comprehensive legal framework, its officials accept that the law will be applied to their own conduct, and the government seeks to be law-abiding. See Carothers, Thomas (1998). "The Rule of Law Revival", 77, *Foreign Affairs*, p. 95.

6. Daniels, Ronald J., and Michael Trebilcock (2004). "The Political Economy of Rule of Law Reform in Developing Countries", at *www.wdi.bus.umich.edu/global_conf/papers/revised/Trebilcock_Michael.pdf*.

7. Kaufmann, Daniel, Aart Kraay and Pablo Zoido-Lobatón (1999). "Governance Matters", *World Bank Policy Research Working Papers No. 2196*.

focusing exclusively upon measures of economic development, have produced similar results.[8] It now appears to be regarded as a truism that the 'rule of law' is causally related to economic development. The evidence of a negative correlation between residents' perceptions of judicial unpredictability and growth and investment is also robust.[9]

A digression on governance is in order. The expression 'governance' has now become a buzzword. Everyone uses it, without necessarily defining it. At one level, we have a concept of corporate governance, related to efficient management of corporations.[10] That too, has a link with economic development. However, when we normally link governance with economic development, we have in mind what should actually be called public governance, related to the act of governing. Every society has a framework for exercising government functions, through three main organs of State, the legislature, the executive and the judiciary, with divisions between the three enshrined in the Constitution, if there is one. But clearly, governance is more than these formal institutions of government. It is also about decision-making processes and about interactions between civil society and these formal institutions. Having said this, it is not easy to define governance. Three commonly-used definitions will illustrate the point. To the UNDP, "Governance is the system of values, policies and institutions by which a society manages its economic, political and social affairs through interactions within and among the state, civil society and private sector. It is the way a society organises itself to make and implement decisions achieving mutual understanding, agreement and action. It comprises the mechanisms and processes for citizens and groups to articulate their interests, mediate their differences and exercise their legal rights and obligations. It is the rules, institutions and practices that set limits and provide incentives for individuals, organisations and firms. Governance, including its social, political and economic dimensions, operates at every level of human enterprise, be it the household,

---

8. For details, see Daniels, Ronald J., and Michael Trebilcock, *op. cit.*

9. Brunetti Aymo, Gregory Kisunko and Beatrice Weder (1998). "Credibility of Rules and Economic Growth: Evidence from a Worldwide Survey of the Private Sector", 12, *World Bank Economic Review*, p. 353.

10. There is no unique definition of corporate governance either, encompassing, as it does, contracts, incentives, rights and responsibilities across different agents within the corporation and shareholder democracy.

village, municipality, nation, region or globe."[11] For the World Bank, "We define governance as the traditions and institutions by which authority in a country is exercised for the common good. This includes: (i) the process by which those in authority are selected, monitored and replaced, (ii) the capacity of the government to effectively manage its resources and implement sound policies, and (iii) the respect of citizens and the state for the institutions that govern economic and social interactions among them."[12] And finally, for the European Commission, "Governance concerns the state's ability to serve the citizens. It refers to the rules, processes, and behaviours by which interests are articulated, resources are managed, and power is exercised in society. The way public functions are carried out, public resources are managed and public regulatory powers are exercised is the major issue to be addressed in this context. In spite of its open and broad character, governance is a meaningful and practical concept relating to the very basic aspects of the functioning of any society and political and social systems. It can be described as a basic measure of stability and performance of a society. As the concepts of human rights, democratisation and democracy, the rule of law, civil society, decentralised power sharing, and sound public administration, gain importance and relevance as a society develops into a more sophisticated political system, governance evolves into good governance."[13] These definitions may complement one another and even overlap. But they are not identical.

Defining governance may have been difficult, measuring and quantifying it is virtually impossible.[14] Some of these problems are

11. *UNDP Strategy Note on Governance for Human Development*, 2004.

12. World Bank Institute Website, *http://www.worldbank.org/wbi/governance/*

13. *Communication on Governance and Development*, October 2003, COM (03) 615.

14. See, Besancon, M. (2003). "Good Governance Rankings: The Art of Measurement", *World Peace Foundation Report, No. 36*, Cambridge, MA; Sudders, M. and J. Nahem, (2004). *Governance Indicators: A Users' Guide*, UNDP, Oslo; Landman, T. and J. Häusermann, (2002). "Map Making and Analysis of the Main International Initiatives on Developing Indicators on Democracy and Good Governance", University of Essex, Human Rights Centre *Report for the Statistical Office of the Commission of the European Communities (EUROSTAT)*; Kaufmann, D., A. Kraay, and P. Zoido-Lobatón, (2003). "Governance Matters III: Governance Indicators for 1996-2002", *Draft Paper*, World Bank, Washington, D.C.; Hyman, G. and R, Silver (1998). *Handbook of Democracy and Governance Program Indicators*, USAID, Washington, D.C.; Kaufmann, D., A. Kraay, and P. Zoido-Lobatón, (2000). "Governance Matters: From Measurement to Action", *Finance and Development*, 37(2), and Kapoor, I. (2004). "Donor Participatory Governance Evaluation: Initial Trends, Implications, Opportunities, Constraints", *Journal of International Development*, 16 (2), pp.157-170, for excellent discussions of the methodological problems.

the following. First, some governance indicators depend on *de jure* international commitments made by countries and these may have no relation with what actually obtains *de facto*. These are indicators based on ratification of standards, codes or treaties, but monitoring implementation is close to impossible. Second, governance measurement should be based on tangible improvements in outcomes or performance. These are indeed the kinds of indicators one uses in measuring and quantifying economic development. However, governance is a process and quite apart from the problem of differing perceptions about what should be included and what should be excluded in governance, objective data are impossible to obtain. Hence, one relies on subjective responses to questionnaires administered to respondents. Each such survey raises questions about sample designs, sample sizes and even the questions themselves, apart from the issue of inherent subjectivity and a perceptional problem. Third, while on these surveys, there is an issue of converting what is fundamentally an ordinal or ranking response to cardinal values. This is typically done through scores. Fourth, the normative assumptions in questions cannot be ignored. For example, voter turnouts are used as a proxy for democracy, the value judgment being that high voter turnouts are better. But in countries where voting is not compulsory, non-voting also represents a choice. Alternatively, questions may be asked about the period between detention and trial, the value judgment being that the shorter the period, the better. However, justice is also about a fair trial, not just a speedy trial. Fifth, once one has obtained the scores, they must be aggregated to arrive at a composite figure and this requires choice of weighting and differing weights can lead to differing overall results. The point is not to denigrate the use of governance surveys. After all, one is trying to capture something that is difficult to measure. However, most governance surveys tend to gloss over these problems and suggest robustness in governance estimation that simply does not exist.

Among governance surveys, the broadest one is the World Bank's. The World Bank Institute's Governance Matters set of indicators cover six sets of indicators—voice and accountability, political stability and absence of violence, government effectiveness, regulatory quality, rule of law and corruption. These have several sets of figures. But the easiest one to use for illustrative purposes is the percentile rank, indicating the percentage of countries that rank worse than the chosen country. In 2004, among 209 countries, India had a percentile rank of

53.9 per cent for voice and accountability, 24.3 per cent for political stability, 55.8 per cent for government effectiveness, 26.6 per cent for regulatory quality, 50.7 per cent for rule of law and 47.3 per cent for control of corruption. Measurement of economic development is more robust than measurement of governance. And partly as a result of this, there are problems when we attempt to correlate the two. Jeffrey Sachs' recent book has the following:[15] "The point is that virtually all poor countries have governance and corruption indicators that are below those of the high-income countries. Governance and higher incomes go hand in hand not only because good governance raises incomes, but also, and perhaps even more important, because higher income leads to improved governance. As a country's income raises, governance improves for two major reasons. First, a more literate and affluent society is better able to keep the government honest by playing a watchdog role over government processes. Newschapters, television, books, telephones, transport, and now the Internet, all of which are vastly more available in rich countries, enhance this watchdog function and empower civil society. Second, a more affluent society can afford to invest in high-quality governance. When governments are backed by ample tax receipts, the civil service is better educated, extensive computerisation improves information flows, and the public administration is professionally managed." There are two kinds of issues that arise. First, how strong is the correlation between per capita income and governance? There are various indicators of governance, and such strong positive correlations do not characterise all indicators of governance. And this is precisely what Sachs means by arguing that the correlation between governance and economic growth is not all that robust, although a weak correlation does indeed exist. The second issue is an even more important one. Does this correlation establish causation, and if so, in what direction is the causal relationship? Does better governance lead to a benign effect on per capita incomes? Do higher incomes lead to governance improvements? Or is the correlation entirely spurious and are there other factors that lead to improvements in both economic development and governance? Proponents of better governance tend to argue that good governance is good for economic development and over-state their case. The statistical support for such a strong assertion is weak.

---

15. Sachs, Jeffery (2005). *The End of Poverty, Economic Possibilities for Our Time*, The Penguin Press, New York.

It is against this background that the 13 chapters in this volume should be considered. The 2nd chapter is by Kevin Davis and goes back to some of the governance-type issues mentioned earlier. He argues that the recent resurgence of optimism regarding the role of legal reforms in promoting development seems to be based in part on cross-country statistical analyses that purport to show causal relationships between variables measuring characteristics of legal institutions and variables measuring levels of various kinds of development. However, the persuasiveness of these analyses is limited by the quality of the legal data on which they rely. As it turns out, many of the variables that are commonly used to measure respect for the rule of law, and enforcement of property rights and contracts do not capture information capable of shedding light upon the potential impact of purely legal reforms. In some cases, the variables capture the interaction between legal and non-legal features of society. In other cases, they aggregate the effects of a large number of legal institutions. In still other cases, they capture information about features of legal systems that are not amenable to reform.

The 3rd chapter, by Bibek Debroy and Laveesh Bhandari, moves from cross-country to interstate, within India. Cross-country rankings of economic freedom exist. But there are few at sub-regional levels and this is the first attempt to devise a sub-regional ranking for India.[16] Twenty states are ranked, data not being available for others. Of the three broad heads used in the economic freedom rating, one is specifically on legal structure and security of property rights and includes variables like ratio of total value of property recovered to total value of property stolen, violent crimes as a share of total crimes, cases under economic offences as a share of total cases registered, vacant posts in the judiciary as a ratio of total posts sanctioned, percentage of cases where investigations were completed by the police and percentage of cases where trials were completed by courts.

There is a debate as to whether law reform should facilitate market transactions or whether the emphasis should be on promoting good governance and alleviating poverty. Without getting into this debate, there can be no denying the fact that any measure to promote judicial efficiency and reforms increases access to justice.

16. Actually, this is a 2005 and updated version of a similar ranking undertaken by the authors in 2004.

When long-term contracts are not enforceable, firms circumvent the judicial system altogether by vertical and conglomerate integration, turning arms-length transactions into intra-firm ones.[17] This, argues Williamson, results in higher transaction costs and a "low-performance economy".[18] Evidence suggests that well-developed formal mechanisms to enforce contracts make everybody better off. Evidence also shows that greater judicial efficiency may be particularly important for smaller and unaffiliated entrepreneurs and firms. This pattern is also illustrated in a study of the software industry in India.[19] The study shows that young firms are significantly more likely to have fixed-price contracts and to bear the overrun costs in complex contracts. This is not because of inferior product quality. Young firms often outperform established firms in the production of high-quality products. Rather, these findings suggest that the primary beneficiaries of well-functioning commercial courts are new, small firms, unaffiliated with either private business groups or the state, run by those who do not necessarily have established social connections.

The linkage between judicial reforms and economic growth was seen to be positive although casual. Economic growth does in turn help in poverty reduction. Therefore, the linkage with poverty is positive, though more indirect. Nevertheless, as both Eyzaguirre[20] and Blair and Hansen[21] note, inefficiencies in court procedures and management often provide opportunities for rent-seeking by attorneys, judges, and judicial support personnel. Invariably, the poor are at the receiving end of such inefficiencies. The linkage with the poor is therefore more direct. Enforcement of property rights is one of the important functions of a fair and accessible judiciary. In most

17. Messick, Richard (1999). "Judicial Reform and Economic Development: A Survey of the Issues", 14(1), *The World Bank Research Observer*, pp. 117-36.
18. Williamson, E. Oliver (1995). "The Institutions and Governance of Economic Development and Reform", in Michael Bruno and Boris Pleskovic, (eds.), *Proceedings of the Annual World Bank Conference on Development Economics 1994*, World Bank, Washington, D.C.
19. World Bank (1997). *World Development Report 1997: The State in a Changing World*, p. 19, Oxford University Press, New York.
20. Eyzaguirre, Hugo (1996). "Institutions and Economic Development: Judicial Reform in Latin America", *DPP Strategy and Working Paper 103*, Inter-American Development Bank, Washington, D.C.
21. Blair, Harry and Gary Hansen (1994). "Weighing in on the Scales of Justice: Strategic Approaches for Donor-Supported Rule of Law Programs", *Program and Operations Assessment Report 7*, U.S. Agency for International Development, Washington, D.C.

developing countries, where land titles are poorly recorded, the poor with their limited resources find it almost impossible to establish their claims and wade though a treacherous judicial system, with endemic delays. The 4th chapter by Videh Upadhyay illustrates that the poverty of the judicial system is largely explained by the absence of a law from below tradition, spliced with the diminishing tradition of customary law and legal pluralism. Consequently, an assortment of rights has not mitigated poverty. The point is further elaborated with three specific examples of poverty.

The 5th chapter, by Justice G.C. Bharuka, is on access to justice in India. Although other Indian access to justice chapters figure later in the volume, there is a special reason for including this chapter as the first one. It sets out many of the problems that India's citizens identify with and provides the backdrop, including some historical overtones. The point is also made that the judiciary alone cannot solve the backlog problem. In particular, there is an issue of access to financial resources. A pendency figure of 31.2 million on 1st January 2005 is cited, far higher than other pendency figures cited in other chapters in this volume. Clearing this backlog will require an additional 35,000 courts. The point is also made, and this is a point sometimes missed, that the efficiency of alternative dispute resolution (ADR) cannot be gauged in the absence of a strong adjudicatory system.

Having outlined the linkage of judicial reforms with economic growth and access to justice, the volume next turns to aspects in judicial reforms. Aspects within the context of judicial reforms necessitate at least a three-pronged approach.[22] While at one level, there is the aspect of judicial strength, at the second level, there is the critical aspect of judicial or court productivity, and the third level concerns court information technology systems. The strength of a court essentially pertains to its judicial strength, although non-judicial staff and their skill sets are equally important aspects. The main question pertains to the merits of an enhancement of this judicial strength as purely a supply-side solution to clearing pending cases. Court productivity enhancements can happen due to a variety of factors. The first factor pertains to judicial education (through training and continuing education) as a means of increasing judicial efficiency. A second aspect would be better management of court

22. This is not to suggest that these are the only areas requiring reforms, but these are the three most obvious areas and require very little of rule change to affect them, while lying at the heart of judicial reform.

dockets and this forms the heart of judicial reform initiatives. Linked to this is the aspect of alternative dispute resolution (ADR) mechanisms, which if successfully developed and implemented, can take away a huge burden/load from the court dockets. However, the back office functions of a court, like the process serving agency, that are performed by non-legal staff, also need to reform in order to keep pace with their judicial counterparts and forms the last aspect of the court productivity component. Reforms in court administration governance are associated with training of non-judicial staff, better human resource practices, workforce planning and infrastructure planning. Closely associated to caseflow management practices is the aspect of court systems, in particular, the use of information technology by developing or modifying a case management information technology system for courts. This leads to simplified, harmonised and transparent functionalities through which a case proceeds to its logical end. Enhancing IT capabilities help to usher in transparency in processes and court information dissemination. There are also issues that deal exclusively with the criminal justice system—the police and the prosecution. These institutions are in dire need of reform.

The 6th chapter by Carl Baar is like an introductory piece on the aspect of delays in the administration of justice. The chapter focuses on how delay has developed, particularly in the British Commonwealth; the consequences of the extreme delays that afflict many of our courts; and the steps that can and should be taken to reduce case backlogs and establish prompt, fair and accessible trial court practices. However, the most important point that he makes is the feasibility of such reform initiatives. There is also an important distinction between backlog reduction and delay reduction. Resources alone do not reduce delay and most so-called delay reduction projects have actually been backlog reduction efforts. This raises the issue of how delay reduction programmes should be evaluated, since, backlog reduction may lead to continued delays in new cases. Hence, delay reduction strategies should be judged through time-specific disposition rates.

In India, a lack of judges has generally been cited as the main reason for court congestion and delays.[23] Indeed, the number of

23. The number of judges per 100,000 inhabitants ranged from 0.13 in Canada to 23.21 in the Slovak Republic, not showing significant correlation with GDP per capita. It should be noted, however, that for some of the countries, the statistics covered only the federal court system.

judges per capita has been low compared to other countries. For instance, data on 30 selected countries from the World Bank *Justice Sector at a Glance* database indicate that in 2000, the average number of judges per 100,000 inhabitants was 6.38.[24] The corresponding number for India is about 2.7 judges. Moreover, vacancies have been a historical problem. The district and subordinate courts, on an average, have between 10 and 15 per cent of the positions vacant, with some states like Delhi being the worst offenders, with vacancy percentage remaining above 30 consistently in the last 12 years (since data has become available). The situation in the High Courts is marginally worse.

There are two questions that pertain to the relationship between judicial strength, court congestion and judicial reforms in India. The first question that arises, given the backdrop of low judicial strength per capita as well as huge persistent vacancies, is whether there exists a policy for judicial workforce planning and the nature of reform measures that are needed. There are almost no systems in any of the district courts for workforce planning, i.e., concerned with planning for recruitment, career management, personal development or job related skills training, whether for judges or non-judicial staff. The consequence is that decisions about the deployment of staff are made without the benefit of accurate HR records or consideration of the competencies required. There are usually no persons qualified to advise the district court leadership on personnel management or training, either with respect to administrative staff or the judiciary. While establishing a Human Resource Unit and functions in district and subordinate courts throughout the country is an important judicial reform initiative, the process of recruitment also needs careful reconsideration, since the high vacancies is a consistent and persistent problem, which has been observed both across states and across time. The judicial appointment and promotion process in India is *de facto* in the hands of the judiciary, whether the process involves Judges in the High Courts or the District Courts.[25] This

---

24. The actual number of judges is even lower, since the calculation is based on the sanctioned judge strength, not accounting for vacancies.

25. There are five main methods of appointing judges: election, as used in some parts of the United States, political, as used in Australia, fettered political as used in Canada, judicial as used in some civil jurisdictions in Europe and South America and in India, and selection bodies making recommendations to the political appointment authority. These latter selection bodies, often called judicial service commissions, have come in the past half century into common use in many jurisdictions. They vary in their composition, manner of member selection, powers and functions.

judicial control of appointments is unusual in common law jurisdictions outside of the subcontinent. The responsibility for appointments and discipline places an added administrative burden on courts already overburdened with judicial caseload. The fact that recruitment for judicial service officers is highly irregular throughout the country, despite high vacancy rates, indicates the difficulty the High Courts have in finding time for this administrative function. Perhaps the initiation of the recruitment process should not begin from within the judiciary. There should also be a mechanism for judge rostering and workforce planning, making available in advance the knowledge about future vacancies and thereby enabling the process of recruitment to begin automatically. The judiciary in India seems to be quite reluctant to put in place a system of judge rostering. Further, the recruitment process should be an annual exercise. These might seem to be simple steps, but in reality, are huge problems. The second question that arises is whether raising judicial strength is a necessary and sufficient condition to solve the problem of court congestion and thereby render other judicial reform initiatives less significant.

The 7th chapter by Arnab Kumar Hazra and Maja B. Micevska explores the problem of court congestion in Indian lower courts, using several measures to capture court congestion, including caseloads per capita and per judge, the number of cases older than a year, per capita and per judge, and congestion rates calculated as the ratio of cases older than a year to cases disposed. The authors conclude that the Indian state judiciaries differ with respect to the nature and level of congestion. They also identify the reasons why some judiciaries are more congested than others. The results show that the large number of judges per capita is negatively related to congestion rates, while judgeship vacancies have a positive effect on caseloads per judge. Court productivity captured by the clearance rates has a significant and negative effect on both caseloads and congestion rates and seems to be crucial for the effectiveness of congestion-reduction programmes. Finally, judiciaries with lower litigation rates display a relatively better performance with respect to current caseloads, but are not efficient in addressing the real backlogs of cases pending for more than a year. In summary, the chapter demonstrates that 'one-size-fits-all' is wrong. While increasing the number of judges might lead to a reduction in congestion rates, this solution is not likely to contribute to an improvement of the situation in the court systems facing large caseloads. On the other hand, filling of vacancies seems particularly relevant for judiciaries with large caseloads per judge. The clearance rates have a well-defined, negative effect on both caseloads and congestion rates. This suggests that improvements in court productivity are crucial for reducing the congestion in all state judiciaries. Finally, reduction in litigation rates, coupled with an increased emphasis on resolving cases that are pending for a long time, is also likely to assist lower courts in every state to address their backlogs.

Although judicial efficiency (a proxy for court productivity) is not a traditional characteristic of rule of law, it—like judicial independence—is grounded in the ideal of fairness. Protracted case processing times and overburdened administrative staff may lead to resource-privileged individuals dominating the court's time to the detriment of those who have fewer resources with which to exert influence. Those with limited access to justice may resort to extra-legal or illegal means of resolving conflict, such as coercion or physical violence. Hazra and Micevska demonstrate that clearance rates have a significant and negative effect on caseloads per capita and per judge, as well as on congestion rates. This means that court productivity is a very important factor in reducing court backlogs and congestion. The effect on the backlog of cases older than a year is insignificant; indicating that courts are focusing mainly on new cases filed each year and not addressing their pending cases. Essentially, the chapter reveals that improving efficiency of the judiciary, so as to dispose more cases within the same resources, is also important in reducing court congestion and simple supply-side solutions of increasing the number of judges might not entirely solve the problem.

Court productivity can be increased in four ways—through judicial education/training, through better administration of courts in terms of its non-judicial functions, through the increased use of alternative dispute resolution (ADR) mechanisms, and through better case and caseflow management. The aspect of judicial education is very important in the Indian context, but it is too vast a subject to be covered here, given the fact that continuing education and training is quite *ad hoc* in India, with little harmonisation in the curriculum across states; and the judicial academies that impart such programmes are still in the institutional development phase. Better administration of courts in terms of non-judicial functions or court administration and governance-related reforms are equally important. The judicial hierarchy in India has become an administrative hierarchy, meaning that most subordinate courts do not have the managerial skills, personnel, processes and institutions to govern their own affairs. The system of court administration in India also differs from state to state. For example, the numbers of branches in courts differ, or the number and formats of forms any particular branch (say the *Nazarat* or the process serving agency) uses for reporting and record-keeping might differ. Moreover, the recruitment processes for non-judicial courtroom and branch level staffs are *ad hoc*, do not usually mandate predetermined skill-set levels and the educational qualifications required are also quite preliminary. Therefore, reforms in this area need to follow certain basic rules. First, it is essential to perform training needs analysis and design, detailed training programmes for a variety of jobs through a training-of-trainers model, and ensure follow ups in skill-set enhancement requirements from time to time. Basic computer literacy must also be ensured. Second, there is the issue of harmonisation of forms and functions that are a part of the governance process. Third, basic infrastructure support needs to be provided. For example, the process servers need to given motorcycles to deliver summons (in certain states in India they are still expected to deliver on foot). Fourth, courts usually lack the capacity for budget management, audit and information technology-enabled fee management systems. The accounts and budget wing of the courts in almost every state will need substantial capacity-building. Finally, the courts need to develop separate well-equipped and trained wings for human resource, accounts, information technology systems and infrastructure management.

In India there is a debate over the use of ADRs and its efficacy. There can be no doubt that judicious use ADR mechanisms can be an effective tool for clearing the backlog of dockets. However, the ADR mechanism can in no way substitute or even supplement the formal court procedures. While a large number of disputes being resolved through mediation and conciliation is no doubt good and important, it is necessary to create conditions for their effectiveness, which is lacking in the Indian scenario. Cases related to family matters, motor accidents and commercial cases, where parties themselves bind themselves for resolving disputes through arbitration, are some examples where the use of ADRs have been by and large successful in and it is in these areas at least that substantial backlog reduction can be obtained. However, experience in other countries suggests that apart from benefits, there exist several limitations to alternative dispute resolutions. For any successful mechanism, alternative or conventional alike, a number of steps are required to be taken by the State. The present euphoria over *Lok Adalats* (an example of ADR) is exclusive to selected areas. There are also a number of limitations faced by *Lok Adalats* too, like no obligatory mediation (nullifying the advantages of early neutral evaluation in terms of saving time). Again a number of *Lok Adalats* are facing the backlog problem themselves. The 8th chapter by Nandan Nawn is a conceptual and descriptive sketch of ADR mechanisms.

On the other hand, case and caseflow management is an administrative process, which does not directly impact the adjudication of substantive legal or procedural issues. However, case and caseflow management forms the heart of judicial reforms, and this can be more easily discerned and delivered. This has two levels of delivery. At the macro level, one looks at the institutional characteristics of the legal system *vis-à-vis* other legal systems that incorporate best practices within a similar framework. At the micro level, one looks at the strategies for improving efficiency and effectiveness of court processes. The 9th chapter by Barry Walsh looks at the institutional aspects at the macro level of case management. Case management practices and associated expectations of participants in the Indian court system are significantly different from most other countries who have inherited their legal systems from the British; and those differences help to identify the strategies which may be pursued in overcoming the case backlog and delay problem in India. As the chapter clearly demonstrates, there are several issues pertaining from the question of excessive trials in India,[26] to low criminal plea rates,[27] frequent adjournments, fragmented trials as opposed to continuous trials,[28] propensity of

26. In best practice systems, 70 per cent or more of civil disposals can be expected to settle before a trial begins. In Indian trial courts, the settlement of a case by voluntary agreement between the parties is a rarity.

27. Plea rates are the proportion of criminal cases in which the accused person pleads guilty and thereby avoids a trial. Best practice criminal justice systems endeavour to give accused persons ample incentives and opportunities to plead guilty and they do this by usually offering efficient prosecutions that have a high probability of finding of guilt. They provide outcome date certainty and they assure consistency in sentencing.

28. It is widely accepted that continuous trials provide a more efficient way of conducting trials than fragmented trials, as in the former, there appears to be more certainty about the trial completion date and therefore, more inducement for settlement between the parties.

filing of multiple suits in connection to a single case, and the question of recording evidence and the in-built inefficiencies.

The principal micro aspects of caseflow management are brought out in the 10th chapter by Carl Baar and Robert G. Hann and can be summarised in the following way. One of the key technical supports for backlog and delay reduction is reliable statistical information necessary to monitor and evaluate the effectiveness of reform efforts. Automatic generation of these reports in a harmonised format is a key step in designing micro aspects of case management. Another important aspect is the distinction between backlogged cases and pending cases. The former needs to be targeted specifically, through case management techniques like the removal of inactive cases by summary administrative means such as dismissal rules. Related to this, is the issue of time standards and adherence to those. For example, use of specialised tracks with time standards appropriate for those cases and automatic monitoring and generation of appropriate notices to ensure that cases that are outside time standards are identified and acted upon, is an important caseflow management measure. Reduce the amount of judge-time spent on a case by use of caseflow management techniques like removal of unnecessary steps in the court process. There is a need for introduction of new processes to perform key tasks in a more cost-effective manner, like early case conferences in complex cases. One should add to that, smoothing the flow of cases through improvements in core court processes, like differentiated case management, through the use of specialised tracks and a strict adjournment policy that encourages litigants and counsel to be prepared on the date set for them to appear. Then there is the matter of improving the efficiency with which specific processes are performed, like use of video remand instead of transportation to court for hearing bail applications. Finally, one needs clear vision, ownership and leadership by the judiciary in a backlog reduction and judicial reforms programme and more effective planning, management and coordination among courtroom staff, branch level staff and judges.

The trend of the leading courts in the world is to develop a robust case management system that is multi-tiered, multi-platform and web-based. A typical Case Management System (CMS) collects, organises, processes, stores and retrieves information. A CMS can record events from payment of process fee to change of jurisdiction, execution of judgments, etc. The introduction of Information

Technology (IT) can automate the process and help the courts in ways that helps in reducing redundant data entry, delays, improving hearings and trials and improving the quality of sentencing, through providing better information to judges. A fully-developed IT enabled CMS will be able to reduce case delays through more accurate and timely reporting on case status. An automated CMS can improve upon the system of manual files by way of offering real-time updates into the status of cases, and it can generate data for specialists known as Information Analysts (IA) to ascertain the exact bottlenecks in the courts and the various sources of delay. The reasons for case delay may vary from transfer of cases between the courts and jurisdiction or due to non-presence of lawyers. The causes of delay ascertained through use of an automated CMS may pinpoint some defence lawyers who may be using frequent delay tactics or some judges may be inherently slow in disposing cases. The 11th chapter by Murali Sagi brings out the benefits of incorporating an IT system into the courts, as is the best practice worldwide.

An IT-enabled CMS, by international best practice standards, is still quite underdeveloped in the Indian context, barring a couple of states like Karnataka and Delhi. Such a system can make very useful contributions in certain basic fields. The effective use of information technology is brought out in the 12th chapter by Amarjit Singh Bedi. These can be summarised as the following. A fully-automated CMS usually is linked with the process serving branch of the court. The Process Serving Module of a CMS has the ability to track the progress of each individual process issued by the court in each case. The processes can be tracked not only by case, but can only also be tracked by process-server, area, jurisdiction type, etc. Technology can help the judges in better maintaining control of their calendars (cause list) to process a case with more effective hearings and fewer adjournments. One of the major causes of adjournment in the courts is due to the poor level of attendance at court hearings by advocates, witnesses and/or parties. With emerging new technologies such as RFID (Radio Frequency Identification), it is now possible to have embedded chips on the file covers, which will enable RFID readers to track a file, even without opening a file cabinet to know the contents of the files inside. Technology gives options for the courts to be linked *via* Local Area Network (LAN) or Wide Area Network (WAN). LAN/WAN enables the court to keep updating the data from the different courtrooms and the various court-complexes in their jurisdiction.

There is the option to connect courts through wires or use new and emerging technologies such as Wi-Fi and the Wi-Fi Max. Having this in the court implies the ability to trigger reminders and assign actions to other staff. Such a system will be able to generate alerts automatically for the judge and/or court officials, especially for cases that require special attention or accelerated case management, etc. Such a system will enable the introduction of facilities, including e-filing, e-services, e-transaction and substantially benefit the user in reducing his costs, time management (working at convenient hours), bringing in transparency, and improving efficiency. The online payment gateway is also closely linked with Fee Management Systems (manage and record payments into and out of court). The importance of collecting and analysing data cannot be stressed enough. A good case monitoring system enables the court to plan and budget in real-time, improve performance of the court, make events more predictable, improve processes for better control, and helps in administrative decision making. Workload balancing is otherwise done manually and by the District Judge. Setting up a MIS system will enable the Court Administrator to better manage staff and will enable deployment of staff for optimum utilisation.

The poor in India are affected particularly by the lack of reforms in criminal cases. Most judicial reform initiatives deliberately avoid the issues in criminal justice system reforms and police reforms, as they are much more difficult to undertake. The workloads on both the investigating authority (the police) and the dispute resolution authority (the courts) are huge. This has serious implications for justice, especially for the poor. It is now a well-established fact that the jail population of undertrial prisoners is huge. These people, who are locked in a criminal case, are in jail simply because they have not been able to procure bail to come out of the jails. They have not been able to procure bail because they have either been unable to hire a lawyer to do the needful for them, or have been unable to furnish the bail amount. This has happened simply because they are poor. The sole basis for the detention of undertrials is to ensure their appearance in the trial. Consequently, thousands of them, arrested on suspicion of committing crimes (most cases are petty), languish in jails. Many remain in jail for a much longer period than the maximum punishment under the law for the crime committed, due to court congestion. It was found that more than 85 per cent of the prisoners in New Delhi's Tihar Jail were undertrials.[29] An important component of rule of law reforms is access to justice for the poor.

There is a direct linkage between the issue of crime, deterrence and police reforms. The 13th and final chapter, by Debashis Chakraborty, Arnab Kumar Hazra and Pavel Chakraborty, looks into these issues. The criminal justice system in India is becoming progressively ineffective. This situation has been allowed to develop primarily on account of the total apathy and lack of will on the part of all concerned. Laws and procedures are so cumbersome that criminal cases keep accumulating and remain pending for years. The low conviction rate has created a situation so that a resourceful criminal no longer fears punishment. Many cases are pending for over 10 years. The system must recognise the ground realities and not get caught in impractical laws and procedures. A balanced approach towards the rights of the accused and the needs of society should help in devising a system that will deliver justice within a reasonable time-frame. To ensure a better working of the system, The Evidence Act and The Criminal Procedure Code need drastic amendments. It is high time that urgent attention is paid to the resolution of the problems by taking appropriate remedial measures, before the situation deteriorates any further. Immediate remedial measures can essentially be in two directions. The first involves the improvement in the infrastructure requirements and the second involves reforms in the procedural aspects and law. While this second aspect involves legislative interventions, the first essentially pertains to police reforms. This chapter also looks into the role of the police in the context of the criminal justice system and the reforms needed there. Considerable government literature already exists in this regard and there is practically very little to add to them. So in effect, this chapter serves as a survey of the available official literature on police reforms. This is indeed very vital, although most reports are not strictly in the public domain and are quite old too (though extremely relevant). Moreover, it is easier for the government to implement measures that have been suggested by its own machinery.

The 13 chapters included in this volume provide plenty of material for pessimism. But they also indicate directions for reforms and consequent optimism.

29. Government of India (1997). *Report of the Committee on Rationalisation of Classification of Prisoners in Tihar Jail*, New Delhi.

2

What Can the Rule of Law Variable Tell Us About Rule of Law Reforms?

KEVIN E. DAVIS[1]

Introduction

In 2001 per capita income in Haiti was $480, the infant mortality rate was 79 per 1000 live births and the illiteracy rate (age 15 and over) hovered around 50 per cent. By comparison, in the United States, less than two hours flying time away, the per capita income was $34,280, the infant mortality rate was 7 per 1000 live births, and the illiteracy rate was negligible.[2] Understanding the reasons why these sorts of disparities in important measures of development arise and persist, is one of the greatest challenges in all of the social sciences.

For a few brief years in the 1960s and the early 1970s, American legal academics joined with their colleagues in other disciplines to investigate these issues in an exercise now known as the 'law and development' movement. Eventually, however, the principal participants in the exercise became disillusioned and lost their faith in the ability of law, much less legal scholarship, to contribute to development. Thus, the law and development movement in the United States died a noisy and well-documented death.[3]

---

1. This chapter draws upon research conducted with Michael Trebilcock as part of a larger study of the relationship between law and development. I am grateful for helpful comments from GuyLaine Charles, Barry Friedman, Henry Hansmann, Helen Hershkoff, Lewis Kornhauser, Daryl Levinson, Richard Messick, Barry Metzger, Frank Upham, Katrina Wyman and participants in an NYU Institute for Law and Society Brown Bag Luncheon and the Globalization, Law and Development Conference sponsored by the University of Michigan Law School and the William Davidson Institute.

2. World Bank, *World Development Indicators 2003*.

3. Trubek, David M. and Marc Galanter (1974). "Scholars in Self-Estrangement: Some Reflections on the Crisis in Law and Development Studies in the United States", *Wis. L. Rev. 1062*; Brian Z. Tamanaha (1995). The Lessons of Law-and-Development Studies, *89 Am. J. Int'l L. 470* reviewing *Law and Development* (Anthony Carty, ed., vol. 2, 1992); *Law and Crisis in the Third World* (Sammy Adelman and Abdul Paliwala, eds. 1993); John Henry Merryman(1977). *Comparative Law and Social Change: On the Origins, Style, Decline &* "Revival of the Law and Development Movement", 25 *Am. J. Comp. L.* 457.

Between approximately the mid-1970s and the mid-1990s the American legal academy turned its back on development studies. At the same time, mainstream development studies also largely turned its back on law. During this period development issues were viewed as the proper domain of economists and political scientists. The economists largely focused on topics such as interest rates, tariffs, subsidies and wage and price controls. Meanwhile, political scientists focused on meta-issues such as whether developing countries were better off adopting democracy or authoritarianism. Now in the post-Cold War era, the situation is completely different. Both inside and outside the academy, capitalism has triumphed and little or no effort is being made to revive communism. Virtually all attention is now focused upon methods of establishing or enhancing the performance of capitalist economies.

Laws and legal institutions feature prominently in this new intellectual terrain. One reason for this is that economists have become more attuned to the potential economic functions of legal institutions. It is now widely accepted that markets are unlikely to function in the absence of bodies of contract law and systems of property rights (defined broadly to include corporate and commercial law) that encourage exchange and investment, the two main wealth-creating activities in a capitalist system.[4] Similarly, political scientists are now well aware of the fact that the political arrangements that they tend to regard as being characteristic of developed societies—such as democracy, respect for human rights and the welfare state—are almost invariably defined and protected by legal norms and institutions, especially constitutions and the courts that interpret them.[5] These insights have led to a consensus that the overall 'quality' of legal institutions is an important determinant of development.[6] This view is typically expressed in shorthand form by the assertion that the 'rule of law' is an essential pre-condition to development.[7] Motivated by this consensus, multilateral institutions

---

4. Douglass North (1990.) *Institutions, Institutional Change and Economic Performance;* World Bank(1997), *World Development Report 1997: The State in a Changing World.*

5. Mancur Olson (2000). *Power and Prosperity: Outgrowing Communist and Capitalist Dictatorships,* 39 (discussing the role of an independent judiciary in sustaining democracy).

6. World Bank, *supra* note 4; see also, Hernando De Soto(1989). *The Other Path: The Invisible Revolution in the Third World* 185-87.

7. Carothers, Thomas (1998). "The Rule of Law Revival", 77 *Foreign Affairs,* Mar./Apr.at 95; Ibrahim F.I. Shihata(1997), *Complementary Reform: Essays On Legal, Judicial and Other Institutions Reforms Supported by the World Bank.*

and developed countries have invested tremendous amounts of resources in efforts to reform legal institutions in developing countries.[8]

Optimistic claims about the role of legal institutions in achieving development have a long lineage. In fact, most contemporary versions of this theory can be traced back to the turn-of-the-century writings of Max Weber.[9] But theoretical analyses that are sceptical about whether legal institutions play an independent role in achieving development, or any other form of social change, are equally easy to find. For example, Engels understood a society's level of economic development as a factor explaining, rather than being explained by, the characteristics of its laws and legal institutions.[10] Similarly but more recently, in declaring the end of the first law and development movement, Trubek and Galanter questioned whether legal institutions (and in particular the courts) played a central role at all in developing countries.[11]

Given that both optimistic and sceptical claims about law and development seem equally coherent, what explains the recent abundance of optimism? I would suggest that part of the explanation lies in the fact that in recent years the law optimists have achieved a form of methodological superiority over the sceptics by more effectively deploying empirical analyses in support of their claims. Historically, the empirical basis for optimistic claims about the role of law was, at least by the standards of most modern social scientists, shaky. Weber, for example, based his conclusions upon qualitative analyses of a wide range of societies, both historical and contemporary, that were of dubious accuracy. My impression, however, is that the empirical bases for sceptical claims were typically just as anecdotal and subjective.

---

8. Carothers, *supra* note 7.

9. Trubek, David (1972). "Max Weber on Law and the Rise of Capitalism",*Wis. L. Rev. 720*; Tom Ginsburg (2000). "Does Law Matter for Economic Development? Evidence from East Asia", 34 *Law & Soc'y Rev. 829*. See generally Max Weber(1978). *Economy and Society: An Outline of Interpretive Sociology*.

10. Engels, Friedrich (1972)."Speech at the Graveside of Karl Marx", in *The Marx-Engels Reader*, at 603 (Robert C. Tucker ed.).

11. Trubek and Galanter, *supra* note 3. For a more recent example of a sceptical approach to law and development see Frank Upham (2002). "Mythmaking in the Rule of Law Orthodoxy" (Carnegie Endowment for Int'l Peace, Rule of Law Series, *Working Paper No. 30*). For a more extensive discussion of the recent intellectual history of law and development see Kevin Davis and Michael Trebilcock (2004). *The Recent Intellectual History of Law and Development*, (unpublished).

This all changed in the early 1990s, when an intrepid group of economists began to conduct statistical analyses of cross-country data to establish the existence of causal connections between quantitative measures of the characteristics of legal institutions and measures of social and economic development. The most prominent examples of these studies are ones that claim to have found a causal relationship between respect for the rule of law and levels of economic growth.[12] However, other studies have also claimed to find causal relationships between legal variables—by which I mean simply any variable that purports to measure characteristics of a legal system—such as protection of property rights and the enforceability of contracts and various measures of the level of development.[13] Still other studies have established relationships between countries' legal heritage (meaning the historical origins of their legal system) and their levels of economic development.[14]

This literature is often interpreted as providing a strong empirical grounding for optimistic perspectives on law and development.[15] For example, in a well-known series of chapters, Clague, Keefer, Knack, and Olson devised an innovative variable called Contract Intensive Money (CIM) that they claim measures the enforceability of contracts. After conducting a variety of regression analyses and finding a positive relationship between CIM, investment, and growth, the authors go on to state:

"Countries with low CIM (or low scores on other, more subjective measures of contract rights and property security) would be advised to examine closely government policies related to enforcement of contracts between private economic actors and the due process guarantees that governments afford firms and individuals when they create and implement policies."[16]

---

12. Robert J. Barro (1997). *Determinants of Economic Growth: A Cross-Country Empirical Study*; Daniel Kaufmann *et al.* (1999). "Governance Matters", The World Bank, *Policy Research Working Paper No. 2196.*

13. Christopher Clague *et al.* (1997). "Institutions and Economic Performance: Property Rights and Contract Enforcement", in *Institutions and Economic Development: Growth and Governance in Less-Developed and Post-Socialist Countries*, 67-90 (Christopher Clague ed., 1997).

14. Paul Mahoney (2001). G. "The Common Law and Economic Growth: Hayek Might be Right", *30 J. Legal Stud. 503.*

15. For a brief non-technical survey of this literature, see Frank B. Cross (2002). "Law and Economic Growth", *80 Tex. L. Rev. 1737.*

16. Clague Christopher *et al.* (1999). "Contract-Intensive Money", *4 J. Econ. Growth 185*, 205.

This understanding of the significance of cross-country statistical analyses appears to be particularly prevalent within the World Bank.[17] The World Bank has conducted, or at least sponsored, several cross-country statistical analyses of the relationship between legal variables and measures of development. One prominent set of studies uses a large number of subjective measures of institutional quality—meaning data obtained from either polls of country experts or surveys of residents—grouped into six clusters, 'voice and accountability', 'political stability', 'government effectiveness', 'regulatory quality', 'rule of law' (which includes variables measuring respect for property rights), and 'control of corruption'.[18] Other important studies use data derived from surveys of lawyers (the Lex Mundi study) or business enterprises (the World Business Environment Survey) based in the relevant countries.[19] All of these studies generally find positive correlations between the legal variables that they employ and measures of development, and their results are commonly cited in key World Bank publications advocating legal reforms in developing countries.[20] Over the past decade, in a strong display of legal optimism, the World Bank has made significant investments in funding these types of reforms.[21]

Potential Methodological Issues

Statistical analyses that attempt to use legal variables to explain measures of development are open to at least three basic sorts of objections. [22] First, one might question the choice of dependent variable. In other words, one might question whether the variables

---

17. For an articulate statement of the role of empirical analysis as a guide to legal reform see Daniel Kaufmann, "Rethinking Governance: Empirical Lessons Challenge Orthodoxy", *http://www.worldbank.org/wbi/governance/pdf/rethink_gov_stanford.pdf.*

18. Kaufmann *et al., supra* note 11.

19. Acemoglu Daron and Simon Johnson (2004), "Unbundling Institutions" (October 2004), *http://econ-www.mit.edu/faculty/download_pdf.php?id=660.*

20. World Bank, *World Development Report 2002: Building Institutions for Markets,* 19 (2002); World Bank, *World Development Report 2000/2001: Attacking Poverty,* 50, 103 (2000); World Bank, *Doing Business in 2004: Understanding Regulation* (2004).

21. See generally, World Bank(2004). *Initiatives in Legal and Judicial Reform.*

22. "Direct Investment in South Asia", 23 *Legal Studies 649 (2003).* For methodological critiques of studies relying upon other cross-country data on institutional performance see Kurt Weyland, "Good Governance" and Development: A Skeptical View", unpublished manuscript, and Johnston Michael (2002). "Measuring the New Corruption Rankings: Implications for Analysis and Reform", in A. J. Heidenheimer and M. Johnston (eds.), *Political Corruption* (3rd ed.) 865.

chosen to measure the level of development accurately capture all of the features of a society that are relevant to promoting development. For instance, one might argue that a society's per capita income, perhaps the most commonly used measure of development, is a poor measure of whether a society embodies the kind of tolerance, respect, and broadly distributed opportunities for human flourishing that characterise a truly developed society. The focus here is on problems that stem from the legal variables used in these studies and so, although important, this line of argument, which inevitably leads to the controversial question—'What is development?'—will not be pursued here.

A second line of attack would be to question the choice of legal variables and ask whether they actually provide useful information about societies' legal systems. In this context useful information must be defined to mean information that identifies specific aspects of a legal system that are amenable to reforms designed to promote development. No other type of information seems capable of supporting the optimistic claim that it is possible to promote a society's development by modifying specific features of its legal system.

Broadly speaking, there are at least three ways in which a variable that purports to measure characteristics of a legal system might in fact fail to capture useful information of the sort that it purports to capture. First, the variable in question may not refer exclusively to aspects of the legal system. A legal system is typically defined as some sort of combination of norms and personnel, with the relevant norms usually being limited to those that are applied or enforced by agents of the state. At the margins there may be doubt about which norms and which personnel fall within the scope of this definition and thus qualify as part of the legal system, but it is clear that this way of defining a legal system serves to exclude at least some features of a society and its inhabitants. So for example, a variable that essentially measures the wealth of a society does not seem to qualify as a measure of any characteristic of its legal system. Similarly, variables that refer exclusively to characteristics of non-legal norms or non-legal personnel should not qualify as legal variables. Finally, there are some variables—the recurring examples in this context are crime rates—that describe the products of interaction between both legal and non-legal factors. These types of variables are of limited use as guides to legal reform unless it is clear how they respond to purely legal reforms. Of course, variables that do not relate exclusively to the legal system might provide information about the potential effects of non-legal reforms. However, such information is of little use to those who press the claim that legal reforms are of crucial significance or who specialise in conducting legal reforms.

A second reason why a legal variable might prove to be unhelpful is if it lacks clarity. Sometimes this occurs because the variable captures too broad a range of characteristics of a legal system to provide practical guidance for reformers. For example, a variable measuring the 'quality of the legal system' is simply too highly aggregated to be of great assistance to reformers with finite resources. On other occasions the lack of clarity stems from the fact that the label assigned to the variable does not correspond, at least in ordinary usage, to what it in fact measures. This frequently occurs because the variable is labelled to suggest that it captures information about the functioning of a legal system in a broad range of circumstances, such as enforceability of contracts simpliciter, when in fact it captures a much narrower set of information, such as enforceability of government contracts, which is not necessarily representative of the broader set of information.

A third way in which a putative legal variable might prove to be unhelpful to legal reformers is if it refers to aspects of a society that are not amenable to reform. The clearest example of such a variable would be one that captures purely historical information—which cannot be changed—without any analogue in any contemporary society. Whether a legal system can trace its roots back to England or France does not directly reveal anything about the present characteristics of its legal system and so showing an association between French legal heritage and poor development outcomes provides little guidance. Less clear examples would be variables that are theoretically amenable to reform, but in practice can only be manipulated with difficulty. For example, in some societies fundamental constitutional norms are extremely difficult to amend.

A final general approach to challenging optimistic statistical analyses of the role of law in development is to question the inferences about the relationship between law and development that researchers have drawn from their data. For instance, studies of this kind are typically vulnerable to the claim that the observed correlations simply reflect the existence of an as yet unobserved factor that causes both the characteristics of legal institutions and levels of development to vary without implying any causal connection between the latter sets of variables.[23] Another concern is that the researchers have failed to capture important structural features of the relationship between the variables. For example, they might characterise a relationship as linear when it is actually non-linear. It may be the case, for instance, that judicial efficiency matters up to a point, but beyond that point its importance diminishes.

It is possible to criticise the inferences that researchers draw about the relationship between legal systems and development even when they use appropriate data to measure dimensions of both legal systems and development. However, it is often even easier to mount such a critique when they use inappropriate data. For example, one way of misstating the relationship between law and development would be to attribute high levels of development principally to legal reforms when in fact development is explained, at least to some extent, by interactions between the legal system and other aspects of a society such as morality and economic inequality. This type of error is particularly likely to occur if one purports to measure the quality of a legal system by using data that actually captures interactions between the legal system and, for example, inequality.[24]

Illustrations

The methodological concerns raised in the preceding Part are not merely theoretical. In fact, a number of the most commonly used legal variables are vulnerable to complaints that they do not capture useful information or are incapable of supporting inferences about the relationship between law and development.

A. Rule of Law

As mentioned above, a significant number of studies have found what appear to be causal connections between variables that measure respect for the rule of law and measures of social and economic development.[25] The most commonly used source of data on respect

23. See generally, Janine Aron(2000). "Growth and Institutions: A Review of the Evidence", *15 World Bank Research Observer 99*; T.N. Srinivasan and Jagdish Bhagwati (2001). "Outward-Orientation and Development: Are Revisionists Right?" in *Trade Development and Political Economy: Essays in Honour of Anne O. Krueger*, 3, 20-22 (Deepak Lal and Richard H. Snape eds.).

24. For a similar complaint that widely used measures of the quality of political institutions are actually "outcome measures," see Glaeser *et al.*, (2004). "Do Institutions Cause Growth?", *9 J. Econ. Growth 271.*

25. See sources cited *supra* in note 12.

for the rule of law is a private publication known as the International Country Risk Guide (ICRG), which provides quantitative assessments by unidentified experts of the strength of the law and order tradition in various countries.[26] According to the ICRG, the law and order variable is constructed as follows:

> Law and Order are assessed separately, with each sub-component comprising zero to three points. The Law sub-component is an assessment of the strength and impartiality of the legal system, while the Order sub-component is an assessment of popular observance of the law. Thus, a country can enjoy a high rating—three—in terms of its judicial system, but a low rating—one—if it suffers from a very high crime rate or if the law is routinely ignored without effective sanction (for example, widespread illegal strikes).[27]

For our purposes the first point to notice is that this variable clearly includes information about both the behaviour of legal personnel and the behaviour of members of the general public. Consequently, it is difficult to describe this measure of the rule of law as a purely legal variable. This in turn means that studies showing a correlation between the rule of law and development tell us little or nothing about the relationship between the design of a legal system and development outcomes. Given the way that this variable is defined, the widely observed statistical relationship between the rule of law and development may boil down to a relationship between crime rates and development.

Some might argue that crime rates and more generally rates of non-compliance with the law are strongly determined by, and thus represent reasonable proxies for, the presence of specific features in a society's legal system. For example, one might presume that low crime rates in a given society reflect the existence of a harsh criminal code or a large and dedicated police force. Those rates might, however, also reflect the fact that members of the local population are

---

26. The ICRG is one of two sources of cross-country institutional data whose use in published studies is described as 'High' by the World Bank. The other source is Freedom House. However, the Freedom House data being referred to here are on political freedoms and civil liberties, which is not designed to provide exclusively legal information. See World Bank, *Indicators of Governance and Institutional Quality*, *http://www1.worldbank.org/publicsector/indicators.htm#research%20papers.*

27. *International Country Risk Guide*, About ICRG, at *http://www.icrgonline.com/page.aspx?page+icrgmethods#*_The_Composite_Risk.

unusually willing to report crimes, appear as witnesses in legal proceedings and shun offenders, or that they have particularly deep ethical commitments to law abiding behaviour. More generally, prevailing ethical norms and the extent of law-abidingness are likely to depend upon an array of factors such as the strength of families and other informal social networks, the extent of poverty and economic inequality, and the degree to which state officials are perceived as exercising legitimate rather than illegitimate authority. Legal rules and the manner in which they are enforced may influence some or all of these features of a society, but any causal relationships are likely to be subtle, indirect, and context-specific. Theoretically speaking, it is even possible that strengthening laws or improving law enforcement will undermine the ability of moral values and family structures to serve as alternative methods of inducing compliance with the law. Consequently, it is difficult to see how information about a society's crime rates qualifies as a reasonable proxy for information about the characteristics of its legal system.

There is also a second and more subtle reason for believing that the ICRG's rule of law variable captures a combination of legal and non-legal information. This concern stems from the fact that the variable is based on subjective assessments made by individuals who are not necessarily resident in the society to which their assessments pertain. Those assessments will naturally be a function of the information available to the assessors about the phenomena they are assessing. However, the nature of that information may in turn be a function of non-legal variables. Most notably, unless the assessors rely exclusively on first hand observations or official statistics, the nature of the information they obtain about the behaviour of both legal personnel and members of the general public seems likely to depend heavily on the behaviour of the local news media. For example, perceptions of the integrity of state officials will depend in part on the willingness of investigative journalists to uncover political corruption. Similarly, perceptions of the frequency of various types of crimes will typically depend on the media's willingness to report those crimes. In principle, therefore, the apparent connection between low levels of respect for the rule of law and underdevelopment could simply reflect a relationship between aggressive media reporting and underdevelopment.[28] Alternatively, if aggressive media activity is more common in developed countries then existing studies might understate the relationship between respect for the rule of law and development.

Even if the ICRG's rule of law variable were properly characterised as a legal variable it would still be of limited utility. This is because as a measure of 'strength and impartiality' it does not refer to specific features of the legal system that can be modified to promote development. In addition, on account of biases and limits on the information available to the ICRG's experts, the ICRG variable probably does not provide a holistic assessment of any country's legal system. For example, the selection of illegal strikes as opposed violations of health and safety legislation to illustrate the concept of routine non-compliance with law is telling. The significance of this point—and this general mode of criticism—should not be overstated though. A study that suggests that further work is warranted on methods of enhancing the strength and impartiality of a legal system deserves to be regarded as a contribution to knowledge about the relationship between law and development; at a minimum any such study contradicts, claims that weak and biased legal systems are either irrelevant or even conducive to development.

It is worth noting briefly that although the ICRG appears to be the most popular source of rule of law data, there are other sources. The variables constructed by some of these other sources give rise to the same kinds of concerns about inclusion of non-legal information and aggregation as the ICRG data. For instance, researchers at the World Bank have constructed a rule of law index that combines variables drawn from a number of different sources, including the ICRG.[29] That index clearly captures subjective non-legal information embedded in crime data because in addition to the ICRG's law and order variable, it includes variables such as 'losses and costs of crime', 'kidnapping of foreigners', 'corruption in banking', 'crime',

---

28. This possibility is not completely far-fetched. As Carothers points out, as part of a more general trend towards democratisation, many developing societies have recently become more open and have begun to demonstrate greater tolerance for freedom of the press. See Carothers, *supra* note 7.

29. Kaufmann *et al.*, *supra* note 12.

'theft and crime', 'crime and theft as obstacles to business', 'extent of tax evasion', and 'costs of organized crime for business'.

B. Property Rights

There are a number of different sources of cross-national data on the protection of property rights. In fact, the term property rights is used so loosely by non-lawyers (as well as by some lawyers) that it often seems to refer to virtually every possible type of legal norm and it is not uncommon to see variables such as the ICRG's rule of law variable described as measures of the security of property rights.[30] However, among the variables explicitly defined as measures of the strength of property rights, the best known is probably the one contained in the Heritage Foundation/*Wall Street Journal* Index of Economic Freedom.[31] The property rights component of the Index of Economic Freedom is based upon information derived from publications by the Economist Intelligence Unit and the State Department (which tend to use locally based analysts). The calculation of countries' grades for property rights is in the following terms:

This factor scores the degree to which a country's laws protect private property rights and the degree to which its government enforces those laws. It also accounts for the possibility that private property will be expropriated. In addition, it analyses the independence of the judiciary, the existence of corruption within the judiciary, and the ability of individuals and businesses to enforce contracts. The less legal protection of property, the higher a country's score; similarly, the greater the chances of government expropriation of property, the higher a country's score.[32]

---

30. Stijn Claessens and Luc Laeven (2003). "Financial Development, Property Rights, and Growth", *58 J. Fin. 2401* (2003). For a similar complaint, see Clarke, Donald C. (2003). "Economic Development and the Rights Hypothesis: The China Problem", *51 Am J. Comp. L. 90*, 99.

31. The Heritage Foundation describes itself as a think tank "whose mission is to formulate and promote conservative public policies based on the principles of free enterprise, limited government, individual freedom, traditional American values, and a strong national defense." *The Wall Street Journal* is a well-known daily newspaper. The World Bank describes the use in published studies of the Heritage Foundation's property rights variable as "Low" but no other variables described as measures of property rights are described as being used more frequently. See *Indicators of Governance and Institutional Quality, supra* note 26.

32. Beach William W. and Marc A. Miles (2004). "Explaining the Factors of the Index of Economic Freedom", in *Index of Economic Freedom* (Marc A. Miles *et al.* eds.).

The actual grading scale used is as follows:

Score	*Protection of Private Property*	*Criteria*
1	Very High	Private property guaranteed by the government; court system efficiently enforces contracts; justice system punishes those who unlawfully confiscate private property; corruption nearly non-existent and expropriation unlikely.
2	High	Private property guaranteed by the government; court system suffers delays and is lax in enforcing contracts; corruption possible but rare; expropriation unlikely.
3	Moderate	Court system inefficient and subject to delays; corruption may be present; judiciary may be in fluenced by other branches of government; expropriation possible but rare.
4	Low	Property ownership weakly protected; court system inefficient; corruption present; judiciary in fluenced by other branches of government; expropriation possible.
5	Very Low	Private property outlawed or not protected; almost all property belongs to the state; country in such chaos (for example, because of ongoing war) that property protection is nonexistent; judiciary so corrupt that property is not effectively protected; expropriation frequent.

In addition to reporting numerical grades for property rights (and other variables), the Heritage Foundation provides brief discussions of the factors influencing the assigned grades. For example, here is the discussion of the property rights grade assigned to Jamaica in 2004:

Property Rights-Score: 3.0

The likelihood of expropriation is remote, and private property is protected. The US Department of State reports that, "Jamaica's legal system is based on English common law principles and the rules in relation to the enforceability of contracts are therefore based on the English common law. The Jamaican judicial system therefore recognises and upholds the sanctity of contracts." However, the judiciary lacks adequate resources, and this creates delays. In some cases, according to the US Department of State, "trials . . . are delayed for years, and other cases are dismissed because files cannot be located." An inadequate police force further weakens the security of property rights; the same source reports that "crime poses a greater threat to foreign investment than do politically motivated activities".

Similarly, here is the discussion of the grade assigned to India in 2004:

Property Rights-Score: 3.0

Protection of property rights is applied unevenly in India. The Economist Intelligence Unit reports that "large backlogs create delays—sometimes years long—in reaching decisions. Consequently, foreign corporations often include clauses for international arbitration in their contracts." According to the US Department of State, "Critics say that liquidating a bankrupt company may take as long as 20 years." Protection of property for local investors, particularly the smallest ones, is weak.

For present purposes, there are a number of striking features of the Heritage Foundation's property rights variable. The first is the fact that, like the ICRG's rule of law variable, it seems to be picking up both legal and non-legal information. For instance, the discussion of the Jamaican grade suggests that in some countries at least the Heritage Foundation uses crime rates as a factor in calculating the property rights grade. As outlined above there are a number of potential non-legal determinants of crime rates.

A similar concern arises to the extent that the property rights variable captures information about the likelihood of expropriation.[33] At first glance, this variable seems to be inherently legal in nature because it is simply designed to capture information about the behaviour of governmental actors. The complicating factor, however, is that the behaviour of those governmental actors is often influenced by non-legal factors.[34] For instance, officials' willingness to expropriate property is likely to be determined by levels of popular support for their actions which may in turn be shaped by non-legal factors such as whether ownership of property is concentrated in the hands of foreigners or particular ethnic groups.[35]

---

33. It is unclear from the Heritage Foundation's documentation whether they are concerned with measuring the risk of expropriation or the risk of expropriation without compensation.

34. cf. Glaeser *et al.*, *supra* note 24.

35. Amy L. Chua, (1995). "The Privatization-Nationalization Cycle: The Link Between Markets and Ethnicity in Developing Countries", *95 Colum. L. Rev. 223.*

There is yet another sense in which the utility of the Heritage Foundation's property rights variable is arguably compromised by the inclusion of information pertaining to non-legal factors. The discussions accompanying the grades for India and Jamaica reveal that the property rights variable takes into account whether the capacities of legal organisations such as the police or the civil courts are adequate in light of the demand for their services. It seems incorrect to presume that the demand for the services of legal organisations is wholly dependent on legal factors. For example, the demand for policing depends in part on the volume of crime. Similarly, the demand for civil trials depends in part on the volume of disputes in a society, which in turn depends, among other things, on culturally determined attitudes towards resolving disputes formally as opposed to informally.

The upshot of the preceding three points is that, along a number of dimensions, the Heritage Foundation variable seems to capture information about the interaction between legal and non-legal aspects of society, rather than purely legal variables. Generally speaking, it is not clear that this kind of information is useful because it makes it difficult to analyse the merits of legal reforms. To illustrate, consider the fact that by taking into account whether the courts are given enough resources to avoid delays, the Heritage Foundation variable appears, at least in part, to provide information on the extent to which legal institutions respond satisfactorily to local demand for protection of property rights. On the one hand, this kind of data can be used to justify claims that investments in hiring and training additional judges will be conducive to development. On the other hand, this information will be misleading if it turns out to be most cost-effective to invest in altering the non-legal rather than the legal side of the equation. For example, the easiest way of easing undercapacity in the civil courts might be to encourage non-legal forms of dispute resolution.

Another striking feature of the Heritage Foundation's property rights variable is the range of purely legal information that it appears to capture. In terms of legal categories, the country-specific discussions reproduced above suggest that the property rights variable encompasses virtually every aspect of the legal system, ranging from criminal law, to bankruptcy law, to contract law, to civil procedure. The aggregation of information about the protection of property rights from incursions by both the government and private individuals may be particularly problematic. At a purely doctrinal level, in some legal systems the question of whether there is an inviolable right to protection from expropriation without compensation is regarded as a matter of constitutional law, while the right to compensation for and protection from private actors' infringements of property rights is governed by norms that do not originate from the constitution. From a functional perspective this difference in sources of law will be significant if, as is frequently the case, it is more difficult to reform constitutional norms than it is to reform other types of norms. Consequently, even if the property rights variable only captures legal information, because it aggregates information about a number of aspects of the legal system which cannot necessarily be manipulated through the same mechanisms or with equal ease, the variable may be of limited use as a guide to legal reform.

Other variables purporting to measure the extent of protection of property rights suffer from some or all of the defects of the Heritage Foundation data. For instance, in connection with the preparation of the 1997 *World Development Report*, the World Bank conducted a survey of approximately 3000 enterprises in 69 countries. The purpose of the survey was to understand private firms' perceptions of the constraints that government action places on them. The two questions described by the survey's authors as having to do with "security of property rights" were as follows:

"Theft and crime are serious problems that can substantially increase the costs of doing business." To what degree do you agree with this statement?

"I am not confident that the state authorities protect my person and my property from criminal actions." To what degree do you agree with this statement?[36]

Both these questions seem to invite responses that describe existing levels of crime and the state's capacity to deal with them. Again, it is not clear to what extent crime levels are influenced by either the content of legal norms or the manner in which they are enforced. Consequently, it is not clear to what extent data derived from these survey questions can be used to test claims about the independent role that legal reforms might play in development.

---

36. *World Development Report* (1997). Private Sector Survey, *http://www.world bank.org/wbi/governance/wdr97data.html.*

Another popular source of cross-country data on property rights is the ICRG's measure of the risk of government expropriation.[37] This variable is much more narrowly focused than the Heritage Foundation's property rights variable. However, as discussed above, it is not clear that the risk of governmental expropriation is properly regarded as a purely legal variable.

C. *Contract Enforcement*

Aside from protection of property rights, enforcement of contracts is generally considered to be one of the most crucial economic functions that a legal system can perform.[38] Unfortunately, much of the cross-national data that purports to measure the enforceability of contracts is as unsatisfactory as the data on protection of property rights.

1. Contract Intensive Money

One prominent cross-country measure of the enforceability of contracts is Clague's 'contract-intensive money'.[39] CIM is defined as the ratio of non-currency money to the total money supply. The logic behind this definition is that the more effective legal methods of enforcing contracts and securing property rights are, the more willing actors in a society should be to hold money in a form other than currency. This is because the value of non-currency money depends upon both depositors' ability to enforce claims against banks and banks' ability to enforce claims against borrowers. Furthermore, because of its traceability, non-currency money is not likely to be an attractive medium of exchange in societies where the government not only declines to enforce but actively prohibits a large number of transactions. Thus, its creators suggest that CIM is a good measure of the quality of a society's legal institutions and, as we have seen, recommend that societies with relatively low amounts of CIM strive to improve the quality of their legal institutions.

However, one of the first things to notice about CIM is that it does not purport to be a highly specific measure of the enforceability of contracts. In fact, its creators describe CIM as a measure of both the enforceability of contracts and the security of property rights. This

---

37. World Bank, *Indicators of Governance and Institutional Quality, supra* note 26.

38. See Christopher Clague *et al., supra* note 15.

39. *ibid.*

aggregation across legal doctrines naturally limits CIM's potential utility for legal reformers.

More fundamentally, CIM seems to be a measure of the combined strength of both legal and non-legal factors that influence people's willingness to hold non-currency money. There is simply no way to determine whether societies with high CIM are societies in which actors have faith in legal methods of recovering the value embodied in non-currency forms of money, or are societies in which they have faith that some combination of moral norms and social sanctions will discourage other actors from reneging on their obligations.

2. ICRG

Another widely used measure of the enforceability of contracts is the ICRG's measure of the risk that government will repudiate a contract. This is defined as an assessment of "the risk of a modification in a contract taking the form of repudiation, postponement, or scaling down," due to, "budget cutbacks, indigenisation pressure, a change in government or a change in government economic and social priorities."[40] This variable is narrowly focused but, like the ICRG's measure of the risk of expropriation, it is not clear that it captures useful legal information since many of the factors that determine whether the government decides to repudiate a contract may be non-legal in nature.

3. World Business Environment Survey

A broader and perhaps more useful cross-country measure of the enforceability of contracts can be found in the World Business Environment Survey, which is administered to representatives of various types of private enterprises by the World Bank in 80 countries and one territory. One of the questions on that survey is as follows:

"I am confident that the legal system will uphold my contract and property rights in business disputes."

To what degree do you agree with this statement?

---

40. Rafael La Porta *et al.* (1998). "Law and Finance", *106 J. Pol. Econ. 1113.*

Now/3 years ago

(1) fully agree,

(2) agree in most cases,

(3) tend to agree,

(4) tend to disagree

(5) disagree in most cases, and

(6) fully disagree.[41]

This question requests data on a broad range of business disputes as opposed to just contractual disputes. Also, since it does not ask respondents to elaborate upon the grounds for their assessments, further research will be required to determine how various characteristics of the legal system influence those assessments. For example, one might be interested in whether confidence in the legal system is most greatly influenced by concerns about judicial integrity, or the time it takes a case to get to trial, or the social distance between judges and litigants. Nevertheless, the data provided by this survey question seems capable of providing more guidance to prospective legal reformers than do the ICRG or CIM variables.

4. The Lex Mundi Project

An even more useful source of data on the enforceability of contracts is a chapter entitled "Courts" derived from a study known as the Lex Mundi project.[42] The authors of that study collected data on the procedural steps required to enforce two simple types of contracts in 109 countries. Among other things they asked law firms in those countries to describe all of the steps required to evict a tenant and collect on a bad cheque in their country's largest city as well as the estimated time required to complete each step. They then demonstrate that the survey responses can be coded in such a way as to enable statistical analyses of the relationship between the norms and practices described by the respondents and various

41. *World Business Environment Survey, Measuring Conditions for Business Operation and Growth,* Private Enterprise Questionnaire, *http://info.worldbank.org/governance/wbes/wbes_questions.asp.*

42. Djankov Simeon *et al.* (2003). "Courts", *118 Q.J. Econ. 453.*

indicators of the overall quality of the legal system. Since the surveys poses highly specific questions and the norms and practices described by the respondents may be readily modified, these data ought to be eminently useful to would-be legal reformers.

It is worth noting, however, that despite claims to the contrary by the designers of the Lex Mundi study and others who have subsequently used the study for the purposes of testing the relationship between law and development, it is misleading to characterise data derived from this study as an overall measure of the enforceability of contracts in any given jurisdiction. At most, the data can be described as measures of the enforceability of particular types of contracts in each jurisdiction as there is no reason to presume that any given legal system treats all contractual claims similarly. For example, in many jurisdictions residential tenants are granted significant levels of protection from eviction for ideological reasons that have no application in cases involving commercial contracts. As for cases involving bounced cheques, in some societies cheques are rarely used as methods of payment and so it may not be reasonable to assume that proceedings based upon non-payment of a cheque will be routine and thus straightforward. This general concern seems to be inherent in the methodology used in this study because in order to obtain data that is comparable across countries from a survey of professionals it is important to question them about a specific scenario and there will inevitably be limits on the extent to which it is possible to solicit information about variants of that scenario, even in contexts where those variants are more relevant than the baseline scenario.[43]

D. Legal Heritage

It is now well established that there is a correlation between a country's legal heritage and its levels of economic growth.[44] Even if one accepts the notion that these studies succeed in demonstrating

43. For other examples of such surveys of legal professionals see also World Bank, *Doing Business in 2004: Understanding Regulation*, *supra* note 20.

44. See generally Mahoney, *supra* note 14.

a connection between legal heritage and development,[45] the studies are of little direct use to prospective legal reformers, simply because a society's legal heritage cannot be changed. From a reformer's perspective, the principal lesson to be taken from these studies is that an effort ought to be made to identify the distinctive contemporary characteristics of legal systems associated with each legal heritage so that the connections between those characteristics and indicia of development can be investigated directly. This is the approach taken by Lee, who posits that the essential structural differences between common law and civil law systems can be captured by variables measuring the length of judges' tenure, whether precedent is regarded as a source of law, and whether the ordinary courts have the ultimate authority to control administrative action.[46] Unlike legal heritage these variables represent specific features of a society's legal system that ought to be amenable to reform. Consequently, from the perspective of prospective legal reformers, Lee's variables seem to capture more useful information than the legal heritage variables.

Conclusion

Cross-country empirical analysis that purport to establish the existence of a causal relationship between legal reforms and development are premised on the assumption that the legal variables that they use reasonably capture characteristics of legal systems that are amenable to reform. As we have seen, that assumption is not necessarily valid. Many of the variables that are most commonly used

---

45. In a well-known series of articles, a group of scholars whose core consists of Simeon Djankov, Rafael La Porta, Florencio Lopez-De Silanes, Andrei Shleifer and Robert Vishny has uncovered relationships between countries' legal heritages—common law, French civil law, German civil law, etc.—and the extent to which their legal systems protect shareholders' and creditors' rights, regulate entry of new firms, regulate labour markets, and adopt formalistic judicial procedures. See Rafael La Porta *et al.*, "Legal Determinants of External Finance", *52 J. Fin.* 1131 (1997); La Porta *et al.*, *supra* note 39; Rafael La Porta *et al.*, "Agency Problems and Dividend Policies Around the World", *55 J. Fin. 1* (2000); Simeon Djankov *et al.*, "The Regulation of Entry", *117 Q. J. Econ. 1* (2002); Djankov *et al.*, *supra* note 41; Juan Botero *et al.*, *The Regulation of Labour* (May 2003) (unpublished manuscript). My understanding of these studies is that they are not designed to investigate the connection between legal heritage and development. If this interpretation is correct then these studies are beyond the scope of the present discussion.

46. Lee, Injae (2003). "Essays on Legal System and Economic Performance", Ph.D. dissertation, New York University, Department of Economics.

to measure respect for the rule of law, the protection of property rights and the enforceability of contracts, fail this test since they do not necessarily describe purely legal information. Meanwhile, the legal heritage variables do not seem to capture information about aspects of contemporary legal systems that are amenable to reform. Under the circumstances, the cross-country studies that use this data provide little basis for favouring an optimistic rather than a sceptical attitude towards the role of law in development. This suggests that additional empirical research employing more useful legal variables will be required in order to resolve this crucially important debate.[47] Fortunately, the state of the art in collection of this sort of data continues to improve—witness, for instance, the advances reflected in the data from the relatively recent World Business Environment Survey and the Lex Mundi project (as compared to the ICRG or CIM data)—and so eventually empirical research in this field may come to fulfill its promise.

47. For a similar methodological discussion with greater emphasis on concerns about the reliability of cross-country legal variables see Amanda Perry-Kessaris(2003). "Finding and Facing Facts about Legal Systems and Foreign Direct Investment in South Asia," 23 *Legal Studies* 649. For methodological critiques of studies relying upon other cross-country data on institutional performance see Kurt Weyland, "Good Governance" and Development: A Skeptical View", unpublished manuscript, and Michael Johnston (2002). "Measuring the New Corruption Rankings: Implications for Analysis and Reform", in A. J. Heidenheimer and M. Johnston (eds.), *Political Corruption* (3rd ed.) 865.

3

Legal Structure and Economic Freedom of States in India

BIBEK DEBROY AND LAVEESH BHANDARI

Introduction

A democratic system is composed of public institutional mechanisms serving the purpose of translating social preferences into public policies. These public policies are embodied in laws and regulations. Although these laws and regulations must be subject to interpretation and enforcement by the judicial system, but it is also true that economic freedom is furthered when the government does not interfere with personal choice, voluntary exchange, freedom to enter and compete in labour and product markets and entry into occupations and business activities.

Thus on one hand attempts should be made to reform the judiciary in order to enhance the country's political and social efforts to strengthen democracy, to enhance the protections of human rights and to foster private investment. Again on the other hand, the involvement of the government needs to be minimal, largely aimed at protecting property and life and facilitating smooth transactions.

The term economic freedom has many connotations. Different studies and measures of economic freedom use different definitions of economic freedom. According to Milton Friedman economic freedom is one part of the concept of 'human freedom'—which is a mix of economic, social and political freedom. The Index of Economic Freedom (Heritage Foundation, 2002) defines economic freedom as "the absence of government coercion or constraint on the production, distribution, or consumption of goods and services beyond the extent necessary for citizens to protect and maintain liberty itself". This work accepts this definition of freedom, but carries it a little further. While identifying that the government should not interfere in the working of the market, it further requires that the government should fulfil its duty of protecting life and property, and enforcing legal contracts and law. This study is more on the lines of the Economic Freedom of the World conducted by the Liberales Institut and the Fraser Institute for various years. (Liberales Institut, *Economic Freedom of the World*: Annual Report, various years; The Fraser Institute, Vancouver, Canada.)

India and its States

There are 29 large and small states and 6 union territories that make up the federation of India. The administrations are divided as those of 'States' and 'Union Territories'. Geographical sizes differ highly across states and UTs. The latter tend to be smaller than the former. All of these have independently elected governments. The administrative divisions are based on distinct language (West Bengal, Kerala, etc.), distinct cultural roots (Tamil Nadu, Rajasthan), colonial past (Goa, Pondicherry), and geographical characteristics (Himachal, etc.). These divisions largely aim at administrative efficiency.

States have elected legislatures with greater control over state level policy, own tax and revenue collection, and self determined expenditure allocations. Union territories have less freedom since they are centrally governed. Governance is mainly of a multi-tier form with intervention at the central, state, and local level. Each tier has its own elected representatives.

Some functions are exclusive to the State or Central Governments while they share others. The Constitution assigns functions through the state list, union (central) list, and concurrent list.

Under State Control	*Under Central Control*
Law, Order, Justice and local governance	Administrative functions such as defence, foreign affairs
Public health and environment	Labour, quality standards
Land and water	Railways, shipping, ports, airports, post & telegraph
Some types of taxes	Income tax, customs and excise
Infrastructure except national highways	Deals with the RBI, pubic debt
Some aspects related to Commerce and Industry	Natural resources

The Concurrent List

Both the State and the Central Governments have control over these areas. While it is mainly the states that decide, in case of disagreement, the decision of the central government prevails.

Under Common Control

Inter state interactions
Labour issues
Education
Environment
Power
Shipping and inland waterways

It is because of this division of control that certain indicators that are meaningful in terms of economic freedom at the national level are not valid indicators at the subnational or state level. This study considers only 20 out of the 35 states and union territories. Further, it considers areas that are predominantly affected by state-level efforts and not central/local government efforts.

The Legal Structure and Economic Freedom

This study aims to minimise subjectivity by not using any qualitative measures. Instead it creates an index value for each measure on the lines of EFW, calculates a mean index for each major area and then takes the arithmetic mean of the different category indices to arrive at the composite economic freedom index at the subnational level.

Data used for representing the level of economic freedom is defined in this section. Data have been taken from various government and private and a detailed list of the sources is presented in the appendix (Appendix A-3.1). Each of the different measures can broadly be categorised on the following lines:

- Size of government: expenditures, taxes and enterprises (Area 1)
- Legal structure and security of property rights (Area 2)
- Regulation of credit, labour, and business (Area 3)

The economic freedom index however is calculated for each of those categories, and also in the aggregate. Each category is important for indicating a specific aspect of economic freedom.

Area 1: Size of Government: Expenditures, Taxes and Enterprises

Economic freedom exists when the government plays the role only of providing protection to the citizens from physical harm and protects property rights. Interference of the government in the functioning of the economy or the role of the government as a producer and provider of services and goods or of redistribution of resources reduces the level of economic freedom. Government revenue expenditure, administrative GDP, and a large employment in the public sector are therefore indicators of size of the government. Power subsidy to domestic consumers, taxes on income, commodities and services, property and capital transactions, and other duties are indicative of the extensive role played by the government in the economy. Recently there has been a move towards privatisation of the public sector in India. This has also been captured in the economic freedom index through this category.

1) Government revenue expenditure as a share of gross state domestic product (GSDP): Higher revenue expenditure by the Government is indicative of a large size of the government. Inverse of this ratio is considered.
2) Administrative gross state domestic product as a ratio of total GSDP: Administrative GDP is the contribution of government services to the national product. This is not an addition to the production in the country. The lower this ratio, the better is the level of economic freedom as the government's role is lower.
3) Per capita subsidy on power for domestic consumers: This is the ratio of the amount of power subsidy extended to State Electricity Boards (SEBs) for domestic consumers to total population of the state. Inverse of this ratio is considered, as higher subsidy implies higher government intervention and lower level of economic freedom.
4) Share of government in organised employment: This is the ratio of employment with the government and quasi government institutions to total organised sector employment. This ratio is a direct indicator of the size of the government.

Inverse of the ratio is considered. A high value indicates higher economic freedom.

5) State taxes on income as a ratio of GDP: This is the ratio of income tax collected by the state to the GDP. Lower the state taxes on income, higher will be the economic freedom. Therefore, the inverse of this ratio has been incorporated.
6) Ratio of taxes on property and capital transactions to state GDP: This is the ratio of taxes on property and capital transactions to state GDP. High transaction costs and taxes tend to restrict the trade activities. Therefore, inverse of the variable is used and economic freedom is considered to be inversely related to level of taxation.
7) Taxes on commodities and services to GDP: This is the ratio of taxes collected on commodities and services i.e. sales tax, service tax, excise, etc. to the GDP. Lower taxes on commodities would result in a higher freedom index.
8) Stamp duty rate: Stamp duty is defined as tax collected by the state by requiring a stamp to be purchased and attached on the commodity. Higher duties impose higher constraints on trade and economic activities and curb the economic freedom of agents. Inverse of this variable is taken to ensure higher level of economic freedom is reflected by a higher ratio.
9) Disinvestment rate of public enterprises: This is the ratio of state level public enterprises that have been disinvested or that have been initiated for disinvestments to the total number of state level public enterprises. Disinvestment paves the way for privatisation of public enterprises and therefore the higher the ratio, the higher is the level of economic freedom.

Area 2: Legal Structure and Security of Property Rights

The efficiency of the government in protecting human life and property is measured by this category. Quality of the legal infrastructure is measured by the availability of judges, by the completion rate of cases by courts and the police. The level of safety in the region is measured by the recovery rate of stolen property, and by rate of violent and economic crimes.

10) Ratio of total value of property recovered to total value of property stolen: One of the key ingredients of economic

freedom is protection of property. This is the ratio of total value of property recovered to the total value of property stolen. Higher value of this variable would mean efficiency of law enforcing agencies in protecting property rights and would therefore signify greater economic freedom.

11) Violent crimes as a share of total crimes: This is the ratio of violent crimes, including murder, attempt to murder, culpable homicide not amounting to murder, rape, kidnapping and abduction, robbery, riots, arson and dowry deaths, to total crimes under the Indian Penal Code. Inverse of this ratio is considered, relating higher economic freedom to lower incidence of violent crimes.

12) Cases under economic offences as a share of total cases registered: This is the ratio of economic offences (criminal breach of trust and cheating) to the total crimes reported under the Indian Penal Code. Inverse of this ratio is considered. Lower incidence of economic offenses is indicative of better protection of property rights and therefore higher economic freedom.

13) Vacant posts in judiciary as a ratio of total posts sanctioned: This is the ratio of total vacant posts of judicial officers in district/subordinate courts to total posts sanctioned. A high value of the ratio indicates that adequate infrastructure for getting justice is not in place. Inverse of this ratio is considered.

14) Percentage cases where investigations completed by the police: This is the ratio of total cases where investigations were completed by the police as a ratio of total cases reported to them. Higher value of this ratio indicates higher economic freedom.

15) Percentage cases where trials were completed by courts: This is the ratio of total trials completed by the courts as a ratio of total cases tried. Higher value indicates higher economic freedom.

Area 3: Regulation of Credit, Labour, and Business

An entrepreneur needs to take many decisions that cannot cater to the sentiments of all the workers and management that his firm employs. Decisions such as retrenchments, etc. at the time of a slump are an essential part of maximising profits. Constraints on exiting seriously hamper an entrepreneur's freedom. Labour laws for many decades have unduly favoured the 'rights' of the workers in the country. The number of strikes and industrial disputes that take place in the economy portray the amount of economic freedom in terms of the control that an entrepreneur has over his own business. Other areas where an entrepreneur may lack control over his own business is in terms of unavailability of adequate infrastructure and raw material. Such limitations severely constrain the entrepreneur's ability to enforce decisions that may be beneficial for his business. High transaction costs are well known deterrents of trade and economic activity. They also contribute to 'black' market transactions. Higher the costs, in terms of licences, the more constraints they impose on carrying out trade and economic activity and therefore serve as restraints on economic freedom of agents. Corruption also translates into higher transactions costs.

16) Ratio of average wage of unskilled workers (males) to minimum wages: Yearly average of daily wages for harvesting for males is considered as a ratio of minimum wages in the state. A higher ratio indicates that wages received by workers is higher than the specified minimum.

17) Average wage of unskilled workers (females) to minimum wages: Yearly average of daily wages for harvesting for females is considered as a ratio of minimum wages in the state. A higher ratio indicates that wages received by workers is higher than the specified minimum.

18) Man-days lost in strikes and lockouts/total number of industrial workers: This is the ratio of man-days lost due to disputes (strikes and lockouts) resulting in stoppages to the total number of workers. A large number of man-days lost indicates the inability of arbitration and other consensus mechanisms. Lower the man-days lost, the better the economic freedom. Therefore, inverse of the variable it is considered.

19) Unorganised labour force as a ratio of organised labour force in the manufacturing sector: Economic freedom would ensure that the entrepreneur is able to hire and fire in order to maximise efficiency of workforce and profits. A higher value of this ratio implies higher economic freedom.

20) Number of special economic zones (SEZs): No subsidies are given to units in SEZs, but tax breaks are given, regulations are also fewer and less intrusive in SEZs. SEZs offer a free-market atmosphere to traders, implying a higher level of economic freedom.

21) Inverse of minimum licence fee for traders: Traders are required to pay a minimum amount of fees for obtaining a licence from the government to indulge in market activities. Therefore, the higher the licence fees, the more restricted traders get in trading in the market. Inverse of the variable is taken for higher levels of economic freedom.

22) Market fees charged by government run/regulated market boards on all commodities as a percentage of estimated value of commodities.

23) Implementation rate of Industrial Entrepreneurs Memorandum (IEM): IEM denotes the intention to invest. However, when there are bureaucratic or other delays, the rate of implementation is low. This indicator is the ratio of total amount invested as a ratio of total amount proposed for investment through IEMs.

24) Inverse of power shortage as a percentage of total demand (power shortage exists either due to low investment on the part of the government or due to low levels of private sector generation). This is the ratio of power shortage to the total power demand. Higher power shortage will tend to slow down the production process and thus would relate directly to inability of an entrepreneur to control his business. Again, inverse of the ratio is taken.

25) Pendency rate of cases registered under prevention of corruption and related Acts: This is the ratio of cases pending investigation from the previous year of cases registered under Prevention of Corruption and related Acts as a share of total cases registered under the same Acts. Economic freedom is higher when justice is served promptly.

26) Persons arrested as a share of total cases being investigated under Prevention of Corruption and related Acts: This is the ratio of persons arrested under prevention of corruption and related Acts as a share of total cases registered under the same Acts. The higher the ratio, the higher is the level of economic freedom.

Measuring Economic Freedom

The Economic Freedom Index has been calculated for 20 states of India. Ideally, all 35 states and union territories should have been included; however, data unavailability prevented this. (Efforts are currently on to expand the number of states, the next year's ratings are expected to include all the states of India.) As a result only those states and union territories are included, for which data were available for most of the variables that are used to construct the index. No imputations were made.

Further, many variables that would have found a suitable place in this index could not be included, as data were not available for many states. Eventually 26 variables covering diverse aspects of economic freedom from different areas were utilised to arrive at the composite freedom index. There were a few variables where in data were not available for some of the 20 states. However, since the indicator was essential for the credibility of the index, such indicators were retained.

There are many different ways for constructing a composite index. One way to do this is to assign subjective weights to different variables. However, in order to ensure objectivity, this ranking refrains from such an exercise. No subjective weights have been used and as a result each variable is considered to be equally important.

The following steps were followed in constructing the economic index:

- Identifying the appropriate variables: The variables in the freedom index were chosen such that a comprehensive view of economic freedom could be obtained while working within constraints of data availability.
- Normalising the variables: The size and composition of the states are not uniform. Indian states vary in their

geographical area, topography, social and economic milieu. Depending on the variable and what it aspires to measure, each variable has been appropriately 'normalised'.

- Comparability of data: Since data is collected at the state level, care has to be taken to ensure that the data are defined in the same way for different states and also that they are for the same time point. Further, since the ranking exercise implies that higher values reflect better performance, appropriate ratios have been developed. Often this implied taking an inverse of a particular indicator or subtracting a percentage from 100.
- Creating an index of each variable: While the composite index gives an overall view of freedom, it may be that while a state performs extremely well in certain indicators, its performance may not be as satisfactory in others. An index of each variable or indicator is also constructed, so that a ranking of the states is available for a detailed understanding of the situation of freedom. Details of the construction of individual indices are presented ahead.
- Creating a composite index for each category: Simple arithmetic mean was used to calculate the category indices.
- Calculating a composite/overall index: This final step required all 3 category indices to be put together to come up with a composite indicator of relative economic freedom for 20 states.

The last three steps in constructing the economic freedom index are now explained in detail.

Creating an index of each variable: An index is obtained for each of the 26 ratios as mentioned earlier. The following formula was used to obtain each of the 26 indices:

$$I_{ij} = \frac{S_{ij}\ Min\ (S_{1j},\ S_{2j},\ldots,S_{20j})}{(Max\ (S_{1j},\ S_{2j},\ldots,S_{20j})\ Min\ (S_{1j},\ S_{2j},\ldots,S_{20j})}$$

Where S_{ij} represents the value of ratio j for state i. The index is constructed for 20 states of India and therefore i ranges from 1 to 20. There are ratios for which the indices have been constructed, j=1,2,...,26. Iij is the index value that is derived for state i over ratio j. The index value lies between 0 to 1 for each ratio. The state corresponding to index value 0 can be interpreted as having the lowest level of economic freedom and the state with index value of 1 can be said to have the highest level of economic freedom relative to other states.

Creating a composite index for each category: Arithmetic mean was used to calculate the category index as follows:

$$C_{ik} = \frac{\sum_{j}^{n} I_{ijk}}{n}$$

Where C_{ik} is the category index of the ith state for the kth category over n indices within the category.

Calculating a composite/overall index: Once all the indices for the ratios were obtained, a composite index was obtained using all these indices. An arithmetic mean of all the indices helped to arrive at the additive index. The formula used to calculate the composite index is as follows:

$$M_i = \frac{\sum_{k=1}^{N} C_{ik}}{N}$$

Where M_i is the additive index value for the ith state over the N category indices of freedom. Here N is 3.

Figure 3.1

Composite Economic Freedom Index for India-Ranks

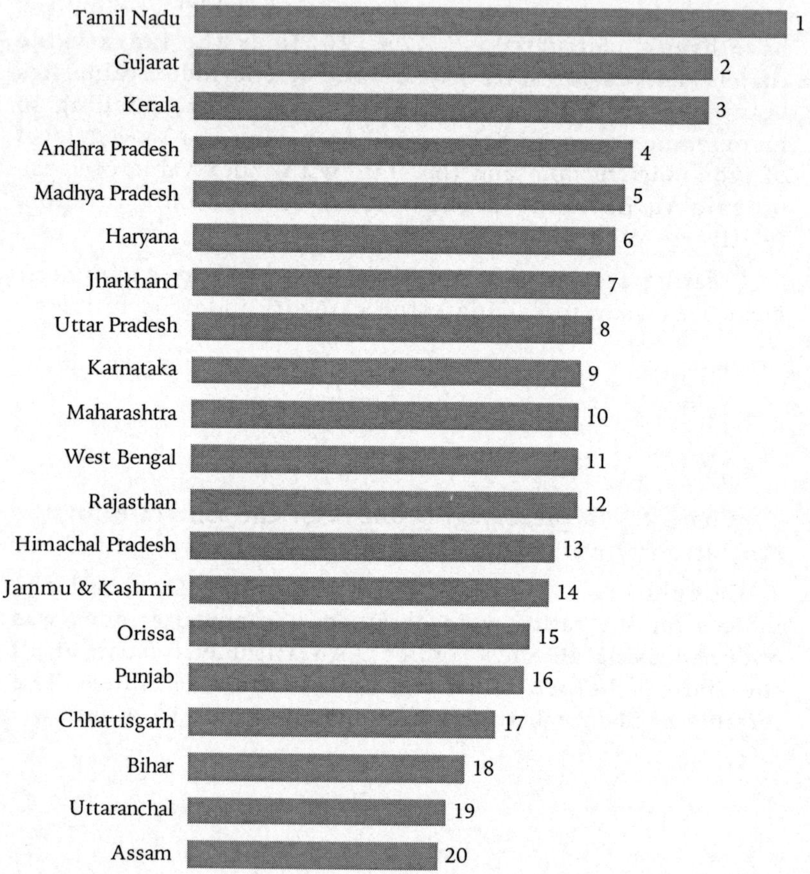

Table 3.1

Composite Ranks and Economic Freedom Index

State	*Rank 2005*	*Rank 2004*	*Economic Freedom Index 2005*	*Economic Freedom Index 2004*
Tamil Nadu	1	5	0.515	0.371
Gujarat	2	1	0.450	0.404
Kerala	3	3	0.447	0.374
Andhra Pradesh	4	2	0.381	0.377
Madhya Pradesh	5	9	0.374	0.332
Haryana	6	8	0.366	0.348
Jharkhand	7	16	0.354	0.294
Uttar Pradesh	8	13	0.347	0.303
Karnataka	9	12	0.337	0.309
Maharashtra	10	6	0.335	0.365
West Bengal	11	14	0.335	0.299
Rajasthan	12	7	0.335	0.348
Himachal Pradesh	13	15	0.317	0.296
Jammu & Kashmir	14	10	0.311	0.328
Orissa	15	11	0.295	0.316
Punjab	16	17	0.290	0.292
Chhattisgarh	17	4	0.266	0.373
Bihar	18	19	0.240	0.265
Uttaranchal	19	18	0.224	0.276
Assam	20	20	0.218	0.222

Summary of States

This section broadly introduces the major changes in the rankings of the states. Details on why certain states have improved or deteriorated in their ratings are provided in the following sections where each area is discussed separately.

In 2005, the top 3 states in the composite economic freedom index are Tamil Nadu, Gujarat and Kerala. Tamil Nadu has moved up four places from the previous year on the strength of better performance in areas 2 and 5. That is, legal structure (area 2) and regulation (area 3) have both shown significant improvements. Gujarat has moved down from the first place to second in 2005, a major part of the fall being accounted for by area 2, which deals with the legal structure. Other areas regulation (area 3) and government size (area 1) have shown improvements compared to the previous year. Kerala maintains *status quo* at number 3. The overall rating for Kerala however shows a rise, the fall in area 2 being made up by an improved performance in area 3.

Like the previous year, Bihar, Assam and Uttaranchal share the bottom 3 places in the index for 2005. While Assam remains at number 20, Bihar and Uttaranchal have exchanged positions. Uttaranchal has shown an improvement in legal structure, but it is not enough to offset the poor performance on account of a large government size. Bihar shows a decline in the overall rating although its rank in the index has improved due to a marginal betterment in the regulatory environment in the state.

States that have registered major changes in their positions from the previous year are Chhattisgarh, Jharkhand and Rajasthan. Chhattisgarh moves down 13 places to number 17 in 2005 due to poor performance in all 3 areas, *viz.*, government size, legal structure and regulation. On the other hand, Jharkhand has shown a great improvement in respect of the size of the government (area 1) and legal structure (area 2) due to which its rank shoots up to 7 from 16 the previous year. Rajasthan has fallen five places to number 12 owing to a decline in the performance in government size (area 2) and regulation (area 3).

States and Size of Government: Expenditures, Taxes and Enterprises

The top five states in the overall economic freedom index do fairly well in terms of size of the government. Tamil Nadu, Gujarat, Andhra Pradesh and Madhya Pradesh all have relatively small sizes of the government, but Kerala is the worst of the top five states with a large government size relative to its economy. Among the lowest five states as per the overall index, Uttaranchal and Chhattisgarh show poor results while Punjab, Assam and Bihar are placed in the middle range of the index for this particular area.

Size of the government can be measured by many indicators, one of them being government revenue expenditure as a share of

Table 3.2

Area 1: Size of Government: Expenditures, Taxes and Enterprises

State	*Rating 2005*	*Rating 2004*
Andhra Pradesh	0.413	0.419
Assam	0.276	0.280
Bihar	0.314	0.359
Chhattisgarh	0.231	0.472
Gujarat	0.522	0.457
Haryana	0.324	0.289
Himachal Pradesh	0.287	0.300
Jammu & Kashmir	0.209	0.210
Jharkhand	0.522	0.356
Karnataka	0.374	0.355
Kerala	0.273	0.287
Madhya Pradesh	0.326	0.319
Maharashtra	0.386	0.342
Orissa	0.184	0.173
Punjab	0.312	0.301
Rajasthan	0.248	0.265
Tamil Nadu	0.330	0.344
Uttar Pradesh	0.280	0.282
Uttaranchal	0.144	0.334
West Bengal	0.370	0.358

the state's GDP. West Bengal, Maharashtra and Gujarat show the lowest values for this ratio, while Himachal Pradesh, Jammu & Kashmir and Assam have the highest values.

The contribution of government services to GSDP is also considered to gauge the size of the government. In Gujarat, Haryana, Karnataka and Jharkhand, only a small share of the GSDP is accounted for by government services. The poor performers under this indicator of economic freedom are Jammu & Kashmir, Bihar, Uttaranchal and Himachal Pradesh.

The government should play a very minimal role as a subsidiser of non-essentials. Power subsidies to domestic users as a ratio of population of the state are lowest for Jharkhand, Bihar, Karnataka and Gujarat, signifying greater economic freedom. On the other hand, the same ratio is quite high for Kerala, Himachal Pradesh and Andhra Pradesh.

Income tax and other taxes, act as constraints on economic freedom. In an economically free state individuals have the right to receive fully the returns from their efforts, whether manual or intellectual. In Assam, Chhattisgarh, Andhra Pradesh, Madhya Pradesh and Maharashtra, income tax revenues as a ratio of GSDP are quite high whereas tax revenues account for a small share of the GSDP in Haryana, Kerala, Tamil Nadu and Uttar Pradesh.

Total revenues from taxes on property and capital transactions as a ratio of GSDP are much higher in Haryana, Karnataka, Kerala, Maharashtra and Uttar Pradesh as compared to the states of Jammu & Kashmir, Jharkhand and Himachal Pradesh.

Most states ranking high on the composite economic freedom index show high ratios of taxes on commodities and services to GSDP. These essentially include Tamil Nadu, Gujarat, Haryana, Andhra Pradesh and Kerala. West Bengal, Jharkhand, Bihar and Assam do not generate a large proportion of their revenues from this head of taxation.

Likewise, high stamp duty rates as observed in Orissa, Haryana, Bihar, Jharkhand, Karnataka, Uttar Pradesh and Uttaranchal signify lower economic freedom. On the other hand, considerably lower stamp duty rates are seen in Andhra Pradesh, Punjab, West Bengal and Maharashtra.

Larger the proportion of government and quasi-government employees in the organised labour force, lower is the economic freedom in a state. Assam, Gujarat, Kerala, Karnataka and Maharashtra perform quite well in this indicator, while the poor performers include Bihar, Chhattisgarh, Jammu & Kashmir, Orissa and Uttaranchal.

The number of state-owned enterprises also indicates the size of the government. The rate of disinvestments in state level public sector enterprises is quite high in Uttar Pradesh, Madhya Pradesh,

Himachal Pradesh, Andhra Pradesh and Gujarat as compared to the states of Bihar, Haryana, Jammu & Kashmir, Maharashtra and West Bengal.

Table 3.3

Area 2: Legal Structure and Security of Property Rights

State	*Rating 2005*	*Rating 2004*
Andhra Pradesh	0.431	0.451
Assam	0.129	0.140
Bihar	0.099	0.136
Chhattisgarh	0.430	0.467
Gujarat	0.311	0.389
Haryana	0.554	0.476
Himachal Pradesh	0.429	0.368
Jammu & Kashmir	0.313	0.277
Jharkhand	0.178	0.127
Karnataka	0.399	0.344
Kerala	0.462	0.486
Madhya Pradesh	0.611	0.543
Maharashtra	0.221	0.257
Orissa	0.346	0.354
Punjab	0.373	0.374
Rajasthan	0.472	0.454
Tamil Nadu	0.755	0.545
Uttar Pradesh	0.401	0.274
Uttaranchal	0.279	0.269
West Bengal	0.175	0.169

States and Legal Structure and Security of Property Rights

Crime rates and the police and legal machinery are the chief components of this area of economic freedom. The top five states in the composite economic freedom index perform quite well in this indicator but for Gujarat. Among the lowest five states in the index, most perform quite dismally with the exception of Punjab and Chhattisgarh, which are moderate performers.

Protection of property rights is an essential ingredient of economic freedom. A high rate of protection would be indicated by a high recovery rate of property stolen, which is the case in Tamil Nadu, Haryana, Uttar Pradesh, Punjab and Rajasthan. As against this, Gujarat, Bihar, Maharashtra, Kerala and West Bengal show very low recovery rates for stolen property.

The share of total crimes under the Indian Penal Code being accounted for by economic offences is quite low in Chhattisgarh, Himachal Pradesh, Madhya Pradesh and Tamil Nadu. On the other hand, the high proportion of economic offences in Punjab, Uttaranchal, Uttar Pradesh and Andhra Pradesh indicate lower economic freedom.

Safety of life is also an important component of economic freedom. Uttaranchal, Uttar Pradesh, Jharkhand, Jammu & Kashmir, Bihar and Assam have a high proportion of violent crimes to total IPC crimes, while these crimes are much less rampant in the states of Tamil Nadu, Gujarat, Andhra Pradesh and Madhya Pradesh.

A higher level of economic freedom is indicated if justice is served more efficiently and effectively. In Chhattisgarh, Gujarat, Haryana, Madhya Pradesh and Rajasthan, a larger share of the cases taken up by the police are seen through to their completion, unlike in Jharkhand, West Bengal, Punjab, Assam and Bihar. Also, the completion rate of trials by courts is high in the southern states of Tamil Nadu, Andhra Pradesh and Karnataka as compared to West Bengal, Maharashtra, Gujarat, Chhattisgarh, Bihar and Orissa.

The ratio of vacant posts to posts sanctioned for the judiciary is high in Assam, Jharkhand, Bihar, Madhya Pradesh, Uttar Pradesh and Uttaranchal. The same ratio is low for Kerala, Punjab, Karnataka, Himachal Pradesh, and Chhattisgarh.

Table 3.4

Area 3: Regulation of Credit, Labour and Business

State	*Rating 2005*	*Rating 2004*
Andhra Pradesh	0.301	0.262
Assam	0.249	0.245
Bihar	0.308	0.299
Chhattisgarh	0.139	0.181

Contd. ...

Contd. ...

State	*Rating 2005*	*Rating 2004*
Gujarat	0.517	0.367
Haryana	0.221	0.279
Himachal Pradesh	0.235	0.221
Jammu & Kashmir	0.411	0.496
Jharkhand	0.360	0.398
Karnataka	0.238	0.228
Kerala	0.607	0.348
Madhya Pradesh	0.186	0.134
Maharashtra	0.399	0.498
Orissa	0.355	0.420
Punjab	0.186	0.200
Rajasthan	0.284	0.326
Tamil Nadu	0.458	0.223
Uttar Pradesh	0.360	0.353
Uttaranchal	0.248	0.224
West Bengal	0.461	0.371

States and Regulation of Credit, Labour, and Business

Regulation of credit, labour and business serves as a direct constraint to the free market mechanism, adversely affecting the level of economic freedom in the region.

The top five economically free states perform from moderate to well, except for Madhya Pradesh, which shows very poor performance under this indicator. As for the bottom 5 states in the composite index, with the exception of Bihar and Assam, which are average performers, the other three perform quite poorly on this front.

Lower wages to workers may indicate lower levels of economic freedom for the workers. Bihar, Gujarat, Haryana, Jammu & Kashmir, Tamil Nadu and Rajasthan exhibit much higher average wage rate than the specified minimum for males. As for females, Bihar, Gujarat and Haryana are the best performers in this ratio. Andhra Pradesh, Madhya Pradesh and West Bengal perform poorly when it comes to average male wages while in case of female wages, West Bengal, Andhra Pradesh, Karnataka, Kerala, Orissa and Madhya Pradesh exhibit poor ratios.

Industrial disputes are major constraints for an entrepreneur and his business, and hence, are considered harmful for economic freedom. In Assam, Madhya Pradesh, Orissa, Gujarat and Uttaranchal the least number of man-days were lost due to strikes or lockouts as a ratio of total industrial workers in the state. The disruption rate in West Bengal, Rajasthan, Karnataka and Kerala was much higher.

An unorganised labour force contributes to a higher likelihood of availability of cheap labor. Ability to employ contract and casual labour ensures flexibility to the entrepreneur to hire and lay off as per market ups and downs. The ratio of unorganised to organised labour force is among the highest in Bihar, Jammu & Kashmir and Orissa while the lowest ratio is observed in Haryana, Gujarat and Punjab, signifying lower economic freedom on this count.

Constraints on trade imposed by market and licence fees have also been included in this area of economic freedom. A high rate of market and licence fees would indicate lower economic freedom. Gujarat and Maharashtra exhibited low minimum licence fee for traders, while Chhattisgarh, Madhya Pradesh, Uttar Pradesh and Uttaranchal charge a very high licence fee. The market fee charged by Gujarat, West Bengal, Maharashtra, Karnataka, Assam and Andhra Pradesh is low compared to Uttar Pradesh, Uttaranchal, Madhya Pradesh, Haryana and Chhattisgarh.

In recent times, many Special Economic Zones have been set up or approved to be set up in the country. Although no subsidies are given to units in SEZs, tax breaks are provided and regulations governing them are fewer and also less intrusive. This promotes trade and production. Gujarat, Uttar Pradesh, Tamil Nadu, West Bengal and Kerala have a large number of such zones.

After reforms in the 90s, most of the licensing were abolished. However industries not requiring compulsory licensing have to file an Industrial Entrepreneurs' Memorandum (IEM) to the Secretariat for Industrial Assistance (SIA). This is however similar to licensing and therefore implementation rates of IEMs are considered as indicators of economic freedom. Assam, Haryana, Rajasthan and West Bengal are among the top performers here, while in Uttaranchal, Orissa, Bihar and Chhattisgarh a large number of IEMs do not get implemented.

A severe constraint on business can be a power shortage at peak production hours and hence this variable is taken as an indicator of economic freedom. Himachal Pradesh, Rajasthan, Bihar, Tamil Nadu and Andhra Pradesh are among those with least power shortage, but

Gujarat, Punjab, Uttar Pradesh and Maharashtra count among the poor performers.

Corruption is measured in terms of cases pending investigation from the previous year as a ratio of total cases for investigation in the current year under Prevention of Corruption and related Acts and is included in the freedom index. In Tamil Nadu, Gujarat, Maharashtra, Andhra Pradesh and Orissa a smaller proportion of the total cases are pending investigation from the previous year, as opposed to the poor situation in Chhattisgarh, West Bengal, Bihar, Uttaranchal and Jammu & Kashmir.

We also considered persons arrested as a share of total cases being investigated under the Prevention of Corruption and related Acts. Tamil Nadu, Maharashtra, Haryana, Gujarat, Madhya Pradesh and Andhra Pradesh have a high value for this ratio, while Kerala, West Bengal and Uttaranchal show a lower ratio, indicating greater economic freedom.

States that perform well in the overall economic freedom index do not necessarily perform well in all individual indicators of economic freedom. Similarly, states that rank low in the overall index do exceedingly well in certain individual indicators. The point to be noted is that all states have scope for improvement in providing an economically free environment for their citizens; however, the individual areas requiring attention differ from one state to the other.

Bibliography

Byars, J., R. McCormick and B. Yandle (1999). *Economic Freedom in America's 50 States*, Clemson University, Clemson, USA.

Debroy, Bibek and Laveesh Bhandari (2003). *How are the States Doing?*, Confederation of Indian Industry, New Delhi, India.

Dexter Samida, Glenn Mitchell and Chris Schlegel (2002). *Economic Freedom of North America*, Fraser Institute, December.

Gwartney, James D. and Robert A. Lawson (2003). *Economic Freedom of the World: 2003 Annual Report*, Liberales Institute, The Fraser Institute, Vancouver, Canada.

O'Driscoll Jr., G P., K. R. Holmes and M. A. O'Grady (2002). *The Index of Economic Freedom, 2002*, Heritage Foundation.

Appendix A-3.1

Data Sources

Normalised Variables	*Variables*	*Year*	*Units*	*Source*
GSDP/Revenue expenditure	GSDP (1993-94 prices)	2002-03	Rs. Crore	CSO & estimates
	Revenue expenditure	2002-03	Rs. Crore	RBI, State Budgets
Percentage of GSDP accounted for by public administration	Percentage of GSDP accounted for by public administration	2002-03	Per Cent	CSO
Population/Subsidy on power for domestic consumers	Population	2001	Number	Census 2001
	Subsidy on power for domestic consumers	2000	Rs. Crore	Rajya Sabha Unstarred Question No. 1957, dated 9.8.2000
Total organised employment/ Government employment	Total employment in organised sector	31st March 2002	in '000	Directorate General of Employment & Training, Ministry of Labour
	Total employment in government and quasi government institutions	31st March 2002	in '000	Directorate General of Employment & Training, Ministry of Labour
GSDP constant prices/State taxes on income	GSDP (1993-94 prices)	2002-03	Rs. Crore	CSO & estimates
	State revenues from income tax	2002-03	Rs. Lakh	*State Finances*, RBI
GSDP constant prices/State taxes on property and capital transactions	GSDP (1993-94 prices)	2002-03	Rs. Crore	CSO & estimates

Contd. ...

Contd. ...

Normalised Variables	*Variables*	*Year*	*Units*	*Source*
	State revenues from taxes on property and capital transactions	2002-03	Rs. Lakh	*State Finances*, RBI
GSDP constant prices/Taxes on commodities and services	GSDP (1993-94 prices)	2002-03	Rs. Crore	CSO & estimates
	State revenues from taxes on commodities and services	2002-03	Rs. Lakh	*State Finances*, RBI
Stamp Duty Rate	Stamp Duty Rate	2005	Per Cent	*www.indiaproperties.com*
SLPEs in which disinvestment process initiated or completed /Total SLPEs	Number of state level public sector enterprises (SLPs) where disinvestment process initiated or completed	2002-03	Number	Deptt. of Disinvestment, Ministry of Finance
	Total number of SLPEs	2002-03	Number	Deptt. of Disinvestment, Ministry of Finance
Total value of property recovered Value of property reported stolen	Total value of property recovered	2003	Rs. Lakh	Crime in/ India, 2003
	Total value of property reported stolen	2003	Rs. Lakh	
Total number of posts in judiciary/Vacant posts	Total judiciary posts sanctioned in district/subordinate courts	1998-2002	Number	Rajya Sabha Starred Question No. 101, dated 22.07.2002.
	Vacant posts of judicial officers in districts/ subordinate courts	1998-2002	Number	

Contd. ...

Contd. ...

Normalised Variables	*Variables*	*Year*	*Units*	*Source*
Total cases/Economic offences	Total incidence of crimes under Indian Penal Code (IPC)	2003	Number	*Crime in India,* 2003
	Economic offences (criminal breach of trust, cheating and counterfeiting)	2003	Number	
Cases completed by police/ Total cases registered with police	Cases where investigation completed by police	2003	Number	*Crime in India,* 2003
	Total cases registered for investigation by police	2003	Number	
Trials completed by courts/ Total cases for trial by courts	Total number of trials completed by courts	2003	Number	*Crime in India,* 2003
	Total number of cases awaiting or undergoing trial by courts	2003	Number	
Total cases/Violent crimes	Total incidence of crimes under Indian Penal Code	2003	Number	*Crime in India,* 2003
	Cases of murder, attempt to murder, CH not amounting to murder, rape, kidnapping and abduction, preparation and assembly for dacoity, robbery, riots, arson and dowry deaths	2003	Number	
Yearly average of daily wages for harvesting (Males)/Minimum notified wages	Yearly average of daily wages for harvesting (Males)	2003	Rs.	Labour Bureau, Ministry of Labour, Govt. of India

Contd. ...

Contd. ...

Normalised Variables	*Variables*	*Year*	*Units*	*Source*
	Minimum notified wages	As on 30.06.2003	Rs. per day	Wage Cell, Ministry of Labour, Govt. of India
Yearly average of daily wages for harvesting (Females)/Minimum notified wages	Yearly average of daily wages for harvesing (Females)	2003	Rs.	Labour Bureau, Ministry of Labour, Govt. of India
	Minimum notified wages	As on 30.06.2003	Rs. per day	Wages Cell, Ministry of Labour, Govt. of India
Total number of industrial workers/Man-days lost in strikes and lockouts	Total number of industrial workers	2001	Number	ASI Data, CSO
	Man-days lost in strikes and lockouts	2001	Number	Industrial Disputes in India, 2001, Ministry of Labour
Unorganised labour force/Organised labour force	Unorganised labour force in manufacturing sector	2000-01	'00	NSSO, 56th round`
	Organised labour force in manufacturing sector	2000-01	Number	ASI Data, CSO
Number of SEZs	Number of Special Economic Zones	2005		*sezindia.nic.in*
Minimum lincence fee for traders	Minimum licence fee for traders (Rs. per Annum)	2002	Rs. per annum	Task Force on Agricultural Marketing Reform (2002)

Contd. ...

Contd. ...

Normalised Variables	*Variables*	*Year*	*Units*	*Source*
Market fee charged on all commodities as percentage of estimated value of commodities	Market fee charged by government run regulated market boards on all commodities as percentage of estimated value of commodities	2002	Rs. per	Task Force on Agricultural Marketing Reform (2002)
Actual IEMs/Value of Proposed IEMs	Actual value of industrial Entrepreneurs Memorandums that were implemented	1991-2005	Rs. Crore	Secretariat for Industrial Assistance, Govt. of India
	Total value of proposed Industrial Entrepreneurs Memorandums	1991-2005	Rs. Crore	Secretariat for Industrial Assistance, Govt. of India
Met peak demand/Peak demand	Met peak demand for electricity	Apr.-Nov. 2004	MW	*Source:* Rajya Sabha, Unstarred Question No. 645, dated 08.12.2004
	Peak demand for electricity	Apr.-Nov. 2004	MW	
Total cases registered for corruption/Cases pending investigation	Total cases for investigation under prevention of corruption and related Acts	2003	Number	*Crime in India,* 2003
	Cases pending investigation from previous year	2003	Number	
Total cases registered for corruption/Persons arrested for corruption	Total cases for investigation under prevention of corruption and related Acts	2002	Number	*Crime in India,* 2003
	Persons arrested under prevention of corruption and related Acts	2003	Number	

4

Justice and the Poor: Does the Poverty of Law Explain Elusive Justice to Poor?

VIDEH UPADHYAY

Introduction

A point from legal history: There are people who have written texts on legal history in modern India, but the treatment begins and ends with the description of constitutive laws passed by the imperial legislature in the colonial era. There are people who have written volumes on history, with only a fleeting glance at some critical laws, but missing the contradictions and complexities of the colonial legality. Even the relatively recent tradition of subaltern studies, providing an alternative perspective of study of history and society has been "comfortable with disregard of law."[1] The problems in these approaches are perhaps the reason why an understanding of law from the standpoint of poor people remains an unexplored area of analysis and understanding.

A point on understanding of 'justice': At another level 'justice' under the Constitution has been neatly seen as having social, political and economic facets.[2] In a country where more than a quarter of the population is steeped in poverty and a third of the citizens lack basic reading and writing skills, it will be reasonable to expect that substantive justice to them could be mere slight improvement in their lives. What exactly do law and justice mean to the poor and the disadvantaged? What obstacles do they face in living a dignified life and does law have a role in mitigating some of them? What are the strategies they have adopted to fight injustices in their lives and for

1. Baxi, Upendra, (1992). "The State's Emissary: The Place of Law in Subaltern Studies", in *Subaltern Studies VII*, Oxford University Press, Delhi.

2. Preamble to the Constitution of India.

sheer survival in many cases? How effective or ineffective has the 'developed legal system' been in their efforts? Far from getting the answers, these are all questions that have never been closely understood by the best of legal luminaries and generally, the intellectual fraternity.

This present chapter will be conscious of these realities while exploring the linkages between public law, poor people and their elusive quest for 'Justice' in the country. The chapter is in two parts. The first part raises some critical questions on the foundations of our judicial system itself to explore whether the poverty of law is one of the reasons behind persistence of poverty and lack of substantive justice to the most desperate clients of the legal system. To ensure that the narrative would not remain autonomous to the various social and political contexts within which the interpretation of law relevant to the poor people is carried out, the second part would hope to strengthen and illustrate some of the concerns in jurisprudence identified in the first part, with examples from the lives of tribal poor, urban poor, and the forest dependent communities from various parts of the country.

I

THE POVERTY OF THE JUDICIAL SYSTEM EXPLAINED

The Constitution, Rule of Law, and the Marginalised Community

The Constitution of India empathetically declares India to be a "sovereign, socialist, secular and democratic" nation.[3] The Preamble affirms a determination to secure economic, political, and social justice for all citizens of India. It also speaks of equality of status and opportunity so as to ensure the dignity of people. The rights of the people and the obligations of the State in this regard were ensured by the Constitution framers by incorporating detailed and comprehensive chapters on the fundamental rights of the citizens of India and Directive Principles of State Policy.[4]

3. *ibid.*
4. Part III and IV of the Constitution.

The object of Directive Principles is to embody the concept of a welfare state. There is a definite obligation on the State to enforce these basic directives, so that justice in its true sense can be secured to the people, especially to the disadvantaged groups, and inequalities of every form can be rooted out from society.[5] The Constitution guarantees to all people of India equality before the law[6] and equality of opportunity and employment in public offices.[7] These are enforceable rights of Indian citizens that can be invoked before courts of law. Especially over the last two and a half decades, the progressive provisions of the Indian Constitution have received the widest possible interpretation by the judiciary. The courts have always adopted an activist approach while interpreting these provisions, so that the fundamental needs of a human being can be read into them and be protected. For example, the right to live with human dignity,[8] the right to livelihood,[9] health,[10] shelter,[11] etc. have been established as fundamental rights of citizens.

But the formulation of rights and their implementation are two different things. The lack of enforcement of these rights can convert a rights regime into a right without remedies regime. As a recent study points out "Different sections of the citizenry may be differentially protected by the State, the rule of law may apply to some but not to all, an autonomous face of power may emerge that inflicts injustices on the weaker groups of society, and so on. Examples of all these abound in India...."[12] It is thus not surprising that despite progressive legislation, 'Justice' still eludes the marginalised community.

Despite the Constitution's promise of achieving liberty, equality and justice for all, the poor remain largely voiceless and deprived of their entitlements in society. Even though the government's business is conducted in the dominant local language in the states, its mystical

---

5. For details, refer to Art. 38 and 39.
6. For details, refer to Art. 14.
7. For details, refer to Art .16.
8. *Francis Coralie Mullin vs. Administrator, Union Territory of India (AIR 1981 SC 746).*
9. *Narendra Kumar vs. The State of Haryana (JT (1994) 2 SC 94).*
10. *State of Punjab vs. Mohinder Singh Chawla (AIR 1997 SC 1225).*
11. *UP Avas Vikas Parishad vs. Friends Cooperative Housing Society Ltd. (AIR 1996 SC 114).*
12. Jayal, Gopal Niraja (2001). *Democracy and the State: Welfare, Secularism and Development in Contemporary India*, OUP.

procedures, obscure rules, lack of transparency and the uncaring attitude of many a functionary have resulted in distancing the disadvantaged and the poor from the mainstream.

The Absence of 'Law from Below' Tradition

When the formal system for delivering justice does not meet the needs of the disadvantaged, they take recourse to informal and alternative mechanisms to have their grievances redressed. With the backdrop of this understanding the present author was involved in a UNDP study where the focus was firmly on what the poor and the disadvantaged people themselves think about justice, the nature and extent of their awareness about their rights, including their perceptions about the legal system. Using participatory techniques to gather data, three questions specified by the UNDP formed the backbone and the common thread among the specific case studies. These were: (a) How do disadvantaged people define 'access to justice'? (b) What obstacles do they face which prevent them from seeking justice when they have grievances? and (c) What strategies have they developed to overcome such obstacles?[13]

That one study apart, the author is not aware of any research study on the views of the poor, on how they can access justice, their understanding of the legal system and the efficacy of the judicial process and the justice delivery mechanism from their standpoint. It is good to learn that UNDP intends to carry out more such studies in near future. But there is no escaping from the larger fact—this is one of the blind spots when it comes to research and studies on access to justice in the country. In fact, most of the legal texts on social and economic rights of the marginalised and on legal aspects of development, begin and end with the description of constitutive laws passed by the legislature, along with interpretations of its provisions by the Supreme Court and the High Courts. As pointed out at the outset, the more recent tradition of subaltern studies has also contributed little to understanding the 'judicial' needs of the poor.

---

13. See *Access to Justice for the Poor and the Disadvantaged People in India: Lessons from Specific Case Studies*, UNDP, 2004. The disadvantaged groups in India included in this study were the tribals of the Scheduled Areas in southern Rajasthan, the de-notified tribes of the rag-picking Pardhi community in Bhopal, the pavement-dwellers in Mumbai, Maharashtra, the *Dalits* in Sabarkantha, Gujarat, people with HIV-AIDS in Delhi, and the differently-abled people in Betul, Madhya Pradesh. All the studies were discussed in the specific formal legal context that exists in each of the states.

There is a reason behind this blind spot in our 'learnings of the law'. There are really two ways to understand the legal system. The first one is from above with a clear focus on formal law sources, including codified legislation and judicial opinions. The other way is from below, when the focus is on 'the lived experience of the ordinary people'. While the law from the above genre is dominant, indeed all-pervasive and the obvious favourite of the Bar and the Bench, the need to develop and understand law from below is non-existent and that explains the scarce socio-legal research around the lives of the poor and the disadvantaged in India. There are people who believe that unless popular resistance is written into the very text of law, realising rights and accessing justice will remain little more a pipedream.[14] It is difficult to see how that can happen in the Indian context in the foreseeable future, given the reality of the dominant legal culture in this country.

The Diminishing Role of Customary Law and Legal Pluralism

In the context of the fact that the legal culture needs to be more 'people-oriented' to augment the capacity of the legal system to deliver substantive justice, an area that deserves a close evaluation is the customary law of the people or the 'non-state legal formations', beginning with what happened to these in the colonial times. This aspect has direct linkages with the question of justice to the poor, because any restrictions on traditional access to resources were bound to impact the village poor adversely. The understanding that the British swept away all traditional and customary norms, replacing it by a state–sanctioned, statute-driven regime might be true at a general level, but for many areas, would sound too simplistic. The interface between the customary or 'informal' systems and the 'formal' laws deserves to be better understood. Here the process of codification of laws—mostly beginning with the second half of the 19th century—and seeking to assimilate custom in the formal legal framework deserves critical examination. Lawyers need to know more about documents like the *Wajib-ul-arz* and *Nistar Patrak* for specific village

---

14. Balakrishnan, Rajgopal (2005). *International Law from Below: Developmen Social Movements and Third World Resistance*, Cambridge University Press and Foundation Books. Quoting another author, Rajagopal points out that the substance of democratic agitations of mass movements "is not taken seriously as constituting alternative conceptions of territory, autonomy, rights or identity".

areas (and surviving in present day Madhya Pradesh, for example) as a case study of recorded rights.[15] Specifically, understanding the three processes of (a) recording of rights under revenue settlements, (b) specific statutes mandating these settlements and giving legal basis to the recorded rights, and further (c) conflicts arising out of these in the courts, would all need careful study and frankly, they are overdue for some time now.[16] As a nation, we are still waiting to understand how the entire process affected the rights of the people—some of which were at best converted into privileges in independent India—including its implications for economic empowerment of the rural poor.

The fact that understanding of these processes was not very clear in those times (and they continue to be not clear today!) could be part of the reason why efforts at crystallising Constitutional values by national leaders were thin on economic justice issues, even while having strong references on civil liberties and social justice issues.[17] That may also suggest why B.R. Ambedkar, the Chairman of the Drafting Committee of the Constitution "could not persuade the Constituent Assembly to incorporate his preferred principles of 'State Socialism' and 'Economic Democracy'."[18]

All of the above issues should suggest that they may have contributed to a poverty of law in modern India. The fact that laws themselves are poor, is partly evidenced by the fact that increasingly we are moving towards a regime of state-centric and statute-driven laws. The 'non state legal formations' are generally being dubbed as 'informal' and thus falling out of the formal legal framework with the

---

15. *Wajib-ul-arz*, also called the village administration paper, has statutory recognition. It records the customs "in each village... in any land or water not belonging to or controlled or managed by the state government or a local authority". On the other hand, the *Nistar Patraks* incorporate the rights of the village people on public lands.

16. This should be supplemented by a comprehensive reading of the statutes codifying customs and in particular, the Privy Council decisions interpreting some of these provisions.

17. These include the Constitution of India Bill 1895 or the 'Tilak Constitution'; The Bombay Resolution of the Congress 1918, The Common Wealth of India Bill 1925, The Nehru Committee Report 1929, although it had references to right to Property and public employment and access to public facilities. It was only in 1931 that the All India Conference of the Congress resolved in clear terms that in order to end the exploitation of the masses, political freedom must include real economic freedom of the starving millions.

18. Sudershan, R. (2002). "'Stateness' and Democracy in India's Constitution", in *India's Living Constitution*, Permanent Black, Delhi.

latter, for all practical purposes, being seen as the operative part of the law. Decisions of the court since Independence, including some recent ones, show that the customary rights would need to be recorded as state-sanctioned formal rights to be relevant. 'Law' in society (including customary laws) has to somehow be seen as part of today's law 'for' society (formal laws laid down by statutes and courts) for them to find ready acceptance from policy and law makers.[19] Having said that, the norms of natural law, customary and traditional practices, have continued to hold their appeal not only with the intelligentsia, but also critically with law-framers. This has most notably been visible in the design of policy and laws for the tribals. However, here also, while the point is accepted, in principle, little has been done to give operative content to these principles. Thus, while there is some literature on customary practices and norms, there continues to be very little understanding of what are the existing customary laws in various parts of the country. This has also led to virtual vanishing of the tool and the conceptual framework of legal pluralism for understanding, interpreting and arguing of basic issues in law and justice relevant to the poor.[20]

The Non-existent Interface of Suffering and Rights

The poverty of law in modern India is also traceable to the fact that, but for a short period of initial burst of Public Interest Litigation, the legal systems exposure to 'direct experience of pain and suffering' has been minimal. The point has been convincingly argued by Upendra Baxi as he says that "the status human rights discourse in its enunciations of human rights does not relate to languages of human pain and social suffering. In contrast, people's struggle against regimes practising the politics of cruelty stand rooted in the direct experience of pain and suffering".[21]

Take one example to illustrate the point further. The last year's drought, like the year before, and like many such years before that,

---

19. Upadhyay, Videh (2003). "Customary Rights over Tanks—Some Plain Talking on Limits of Customs", *Economic and Political Weekly*, November 1.
20. A legal pluralism perspective, instead of focusing only on State law, emphasises that multiple legal and normative frameworks exist, including religious and customary laws, government and autonomous entities rules and regulations and unwritten local norms.
21. Baxi, Upendra (2002). *The Future of Human Rights*, OUP.

brought to the fore (with good help from the seasonal eye of the media) the extent of human suffering due to severe drought conditions in various parts of the country. There were water riots, deaths, special water trains, death of cattle where they are the sole source of livelihoods, and even people not getting married, only due to lack of water. Yet like in the many summers of the past, the last year too, the judiciary and the legal system's exposure to 'direct experience of pains and suffering' were minimal to non-existent. Else, the suffering in drought when seen together with existence of a fundamental right to water of every person would have hurt the judicial psyche hard. The fact that this does not happen enough in the country is a major reason behind the existence of a huge body of 'justifiable human suffering'. Its existence is a painful testimony to the fact that the fundamental right to water intended to alleviate suffering, has failed miserably to meet its intentions. If you feel the lives of those who suffer and see it with the way law in this area operates, and then bear the pain, you will know that it hurts more.[22] This is a process that happens little in India today and is partly explained by the aforesaid fact that we do not have law from below tradition. The fact that role of customary laws is progressively diminishing and the tradition of legal pluralism is in a moribund stage is also not helping the situation.

Living with the Paradox: Poor Man with a Rich Assortment of Rights

All the above factors help explain why there is a paradox that exists in the country—the paradox of a poor man living with a rich assortment of rights. The paradox exists because through an activist interpretation of the Constitution, the fundamental rights of a poor man have been growing in recent years, even while not making any significant impact on his/her life. This has led to a regime of substantial rights with slow remedies, with obvious implications on limiting access to justice.

While throughout history, poor people have been suffering the wrongs, they have also failed to enforce even the most basic of the rights that have come their way, especially following Indian Independence. Even where the court has responded to the concerns

---

22. For a very brief version of this argument in the context of right to water, see Upadhyay, Videh (2003). "I Claim 40 Litres", *Down to Earth*, August 15.

of the needy and the marginalised, the compliance of its directions has remained a problem. There has been very little follow up of judicial decisions from the perspective of how those decisions impact the community for which the decision was meant in the first place. The fact that there is very little literature on the aftermath of the judicial verdicts, especially from the standpoint of those poor and the disadvantaged directly affected by these verdicts, have also limited our understanding of how the judicial systems can respond better to those that need them the most.

In a rare exception, a recent well-known work highlights, in around 50 printed pages, how a famous public interest litigation, with a landmark verdict on abolition of the practice of bonded labour all over the country, has been blatantly and consistently violated, with the Supreme Court failing to arrest the repeated flouting of its own orders! [23] This points to central problem that, even where rights exist, remedies stay elusive due to the some inherent structural limitations of the judiciary. In High Courts, like in Delhi, normal adjournments are for 4 to 6 months, the trial dates are not available before 2 years and settlement of the suit takes place over 15 years.[24] Apart from this making a daily mockery of the fundamental right to speedy trial, it constitutes a denial of justice. Besides, as the judicial system is structured in such a way that the poor have to reach out to the courts, this has meant that a very small percentage of issues that are legal in nature actual end up in courts. These are pointers to the essential link between a weak judicial system and its direct implications for the poor.

II

SEARCHING FOR JUSTICE IN LOCAL CONTEXTS

The first part of the chapter hopefully has thrown some light towards understanding how the poor as a citizen and as part of historically deprived groups can struggle with a legal system which is

23. Shourie, Arun (2001). *Courts and their Judgments,* Rupa and Co. New Delhi.

24. Around two years back, when, in a reply to a Parliamentary Question, the High Court at Delhi was asked to provide information on how much time it takes to deliver a judgment after the arguments have been heard, the High Court chose not to respond on the ground that it would compromise judicial independence. Nariman, Point, (2004). "Let's make Judiciary Accountable", *The Indian Express* , July 26.

prone to working to his/her little advantage and many disadvantages. In this part we explore the linkages between the judicial system and the poor with three specific examples, with peculiar emerging issues in the Scheduled Areas (predominantly tribal areas scheduled under the Constitution), urban areas and protected areas, while examining the interplay of legal dynamics with the poor in these areas. Varying themes, from exclusion of the poor people from law-making processes to securing engagement of the State for accessing justice in the lives of the disadvantaged people and successful and failed attempts at their empowerment, are suggested through these examples from various parts of the country.

Tribal Poor Search for Justice: 'Gaon Ganrajya' Movement in Rajasthan

The Constitution of India, through its 73rd Amendment, paved the way for a separate and progressive legal and administrative regime for tribal areas to usher in genuine tribal self-rule. The framework was laid down by Provisions on Panchayat (Extension to Scheduled Areas) Act (hereinafter PESA), a law enacted in pursuance of the Constitutional mandate in 1996. All 10 states with tribal areas were to adopt this law within one year. Perhaps the most progressive law passed since Independence, PESA was to enable the *Gram Sabha*, i.e, the collectivity of village adults, and the *Gram Panchayat*s to take control of their destinies. It empowered villages to protect community resources, control social sector functionaries, own minor forest produce, manage water bodies, give recommendations for mining leases, be consulted for land acquisition, enforce prohibition, identify beneficiaries for poverty alleviation and other government programmes and have a decisive say in all development projects in villages.

Here's what Rajasthan did with the law. It adopted the law, but took three years in doing so, after PESA came into being in 1996. It then affirmed all provisions of the law in principle, but made their applicability subject to framing of rules or "as may be prescribed". Those rules then refused to come and only in last two years some feeble perceptions began to surface, primarily through revocable official circulars. The operative provisions not being in place, a promising radical law has been redefined as a sterile chapter law.[25]

---

25. See Upadhyay, Videh (2003). "For Tribals only Paper Pledges", *The Indian Express*, May 8.

It is precisely the failure to take PESA out from the books and on to the ground that has prompted over 200 villages in Rajasthan to declare themselves as 'Gaon Ganrajya' (village republic), doing for themselves what the state couldn't do. The *ganrajya* movement in Rajasthan is a reminder that time might be running out for formal law and policy framers to redeem themselves. Having said that, one needs to understand the nuances of how the law is working or more precisely not working—for the tribals in southern Rajasthan. The two voluntary organisations which are playing a key role in spreading of the *Gaon Ganrajya* movement in Rajasthan first sought to build pressure on the state government to develop a state law, adopting the central PESA, and later decided to establish *Gaon Ganarajya,* beginning with the laying down of *shilalekhs* (rock edicts).[26] This laying of *shilalekhs* was part of a well thought out strategy to help people relate to the law. The *Gaon Ganrajya* initiative seems to be driven by the motto of "*apna gaon apna rajya*" (our village, our rule), which is regarded as central to the tribals' pursuit of justice. However lack of recognition of the *Gaon Ganrajya* by the state machinery and the *Panchayat* functionaries is perceived to be one of the biggest barriers in taking the spirit of the self-rule movement further. The lack of law from below tradition, the reducing relevance of customary laws in the larger state and national context, the absence of a legal pluralism perspective and the little interface of sufferings of tribal people in two of the poorest districts of Rajasthan, i.e Bansawara and Dungurpur, where the *Gaon Ganrajya* movement has been most active, has all made the barriers more difficult to overcome. Nevertheless, the logic of the movement seems to coincide with the popular arguments today that decentralisation and local empowerment will lead to improvement in the quality of service delivery at the village level. Before concluding this section, two specific but critical points directly relevant to those concerned with improving access to justice may also be noted:

- An integral part of the strategy of the *Gaon Ganrajya* initiative is to formalise the perceived 'informal' practices being carried out at the village level. There is a growing sentiment that even though PESA is a top down law, the elements in it can be gainfully utilised to formalise the *Gaon Ganrajya* initiative and thereby strengthen the movement and the attainment of its goals.

26. These two organisations are the Astha Sansthan and Vagad Mazdoor Kisan Sangathan (VMKS).

- The *Gaon Ganrajya* initiative also shows that the traditional/customary modes of dispute resolution need to be seen in the larger national context. The absence of any authoritative study on the customary modes and their efficacy in relation to the modern social ethos and the Constitution, even where formal law provides it legitimacy (as in PESA), means that such traditional and customary modes of dispute resolution cannot be operationalised on a wider scale. There are some nascent attempts in some villages of southern Rajasthan—as for example the *Nyaya Samiti* experiment in Dungurpur—but a close assessment needs to be made about their relevance and impact.

Urban Poor Search for Justice: Questions from Delhi and Mumbai

From the tribal poor in the Scheduled Areas, let us briefly understand the plight of slum and pavement dwellers, constituting the bulk of the urban poor, especially in mega cities of the country. Their problems should be better appreciated in the legal context of the fact that the image of the urban poor before the higher judiciary has taken a beating over the years. This is clearly seen in how the language of the court has changed *vis-à-vis* them over the last two decades. In the early and mid-eighties, when right to livelihood was being seen as a fundamental right, slums were seen by the Supreme Court as a reflection of structural social inequality in the country and the principle that 'humbler the dwelling, greater the suffering and more intense the loss' animated the judgments. However, 15 years following such verdicts, the Supreme Court in early 2000 had a completely different view on 'encroachment' by slum dwellers. Bemoaning the fact that instead of 'slum clearance' there is 'slum creation' in Delhi and simplistically dubbing slum dwellers as encroachers, it said that "rewarding an encroacher on public land with free alternate sites is like giving a reward to a pickpocket".

In this context, take the case of slum dwellers in Delhi. It is worth noting here that all the major cases with implications for urban governance, decided and pending in the Supreme Court and the Delhi High Court—for a clean Yamuna, for removal of slums and unauthorised colonies, and even for providing basic amenities to slum dwellers—had only one overall effect: pushing the urban poor further to the margins. In this scenario, organisations representing slums and resettlement colonies in Delhi have been making repeated attempts to intervene in the policymaking processes, but seem to be failing in eliciting any positive response so far. The officials have evaded queries in this regard on the ground that there is no legal requirement of public debate on formulation of policy, although even the existing laws dictate otherwise, although one still hopes that this would change in the new legal context mandate flowing from Right to Information. This pinpoints the core of the problem, that the government needs to be conscious that the process of formulation of any policy is as important as the policy itself and to the extent this process is fully transparent and participatory, the policy gives itself the best chance of being accepted and implemented. The case of slum dwellers in Delhi deserves to be seen in this regard and their uneasy attempts to knock at court doors, with little success and large failures, is also worth an intensive exploration.

At another level, notice the problems of thousands of pavement dwellers in the city of Mumbai. It is notable that, while in the first three decades since Independence, the Municipal Corporation in Mumbai had a so called 'law and order approach'—and not necessarily a legal approach—to slum dwellers, from the 1970s, slums began to be viewed as housing solutions with legislation and policy seeking to provide civil amenities, including *in situ* upgradation of slums. However, unlike the slum dwellers, the pavement dwellers did not get any protection from law and policy till the mid-90s. It was after the intervention of 'Urban Alliance', including SPARC founded by a group of middle class professionals, which then led to form *Mahila Milan* (literally women together), a collective of women pavement and slum dwellers, together with National Slum Dwellers Federation (NSDF), that things began to change for the pavement dwellers. Through their publications and efforts, the Alliance worked towards demolishing the myths that 'pavement dwellers were itinerant beings, here today and gone tomorrow' without any fixed address. In fact, as most pavement families had lived in the same location for more than two decades, it required an approach in law and policy akin to those of slum dwellers. The small success stories here of the interventions of the Muslim pavement-dwelling women have served to emphasise the potential that women's groups can have in improving the lives of the poor family. The strategic and selective use of courts in Mumbai in their quest for justice has also been a lesson here. The strategies of engaging the state, like by providing systematic data collected by the federation of these pavement dwellers themselves, in the absence of official data, has apart from being a source of power, also fed into devising of plans and policies. All these aspects need to be learnt more closely to develop some larger lessons that could be of use to such communities in other cities too.

The author discovered some of the above silver linings in an otherwise long and protracted struggle of the pavement and slum dwellers in Mumbai on a personal visit to these areas a couple of years ago. The massive demolitions, earlier this year, have served to underline that you tend to see silver linings only when you are amidst dark clouds! This has suggested to him that politics and the politics of law are more important and decisive than the law itself. The experience both in Delhi and Mumbai can make it obvious that substantive social, political, and economic justice to the urban poor can be achieved not by tinkering with nut and bolts of legal provisions, but by introducing paradigm shifts in legal approaches towards them. That explains the larger significance of the need to address the foundations of the judicial system, including the need to address the biases and prejudices that still haunts it.

Forest Communities Search for Justice: Customary Rights in Protected Areas

Let us take an altogether different context of forest-dependent communities who live in and around the forest and the protected areas in the country. The officially designated Protected Areas (PAs) include over 500 national parks and sanctuaries, covering close to 5 per cent of the landmass of the country. If the other forest areas are added to this, they cover one-fifth of the country's territorial area. A very large number of people living near the forests and dependent on them are among the poorest, with forest produces forming their life support systems. Whether the legal regime governing forest preservation and use reflect this understanding would be a question that we need to explore in all its details. One major source of concern is whether traditional rights of access, and customary rights of villages, in the vicinity of the Protected Areas, has been duly recognised by law or not. In Madhya Pradesh, for example, certain customary rights in respect of grazing of cattle, obtaining fuel wood, non-timber forest produce, etc., called 'Nistar Rights', have been made subject to the satisfaction of the Divisional Forest Officer through critical law and policy changes. In Nagarhole National Park in Tamil Nadu, a dominant perception that participation in new government initiatives could cause people to lose their customary rights upon the forest had an adverse impact on trust building between the forest department and the people. Also note in this context the position in the Great Himalayan National Park (GHNP) in Himachal Pradesh, where on the basis of the forest settlement report in 1886, the names of forests and of the people allowed to use them, were recorded, along with recording of rights of the local people in the forest. Astonishingly, this 1886 report has been the basis for settlement of rights of the local people in GHNP, that was completed in May 1999, and which led ultimately to only 349 families being entitled to compensation. This sparked off widespread local protests from other households, which had traditionally been entering the Park for resource use and extraction. Whether they had the legal right to do so and how much of their traditional and customary practices can qualify as customary rights today, are critical questions that need answering, if legal minds can put these questions in their agenda.

One can however prejudge some of the answers to the questions raised in the various local contexts above if one understands the biases of our judicial system outlined in the first part above.

Concluding Remarks

To the question in the sub-title of the present chapter, "Does the poverty of law explain elusive justice to the poor?" the short answer has to be yes. The chapter provides an elaboration of that answer in two parts. The first part has sought to identify some cross cutting factors that has led to a poverty of the judicial system itself. The second part of the chapter has then attempted to underline these limiting factors by seeing how they influence search for justice in various local contexts.

One last point: Any mapping of search for justice in local contexts can throw some obvious larger lessons. Justice—often more a feeling for poor people than a value laden concept—is understood differently by different segments of the disadvantaged groups. The emphasis of people on the various facets of justice—social, political or economic—is a function of the nature of their struggle and of the context in which their struggle is located. A direct implication of this is that strategies to overcome barriers to achieve justice will be most effective when they are devised for, and are located in, the specific local contexts. Thus, we need to know more about local realities to tailor localised interventions for improving the prospects of justice to the poor. The trouble however is that this is too messy an approach for even our well-intentioned lawyers and judges for whom better understanding of phrases like 'non-state legal formations', 'customary norms and practices', 'legal pluralism perspective', and 'interface of suffering with rights' amounts to a leap into the unknown.

This is also because the role of law and of rights in combating large-scale deprivation is little understood, although the public law jurisprudence hinges on the paradigm of deprivation. Even where it is appreciated, the consciousness of limits of these rights—as opposed to their reach—has been all pervasive.

5

Contemporary Views on Access to Justice in India

JUSTICE G.C. BHARUKA

'Access to Justice' is one of the constitutionally recognised human and fundamental rights. The need for a pragmatic and scientific approach to reforms aimed at making this right a reality, in conditions typical to India, has become gradually critical in the recent years.

Broadly, the constitutional scheme is of distribution of powers between the three main wings of governance—the Legislature, Executive and the Judiciary. To the judiciary is assigned the role of imparting justice to the people and to ensure that each wing remains within the limits delineated for it. It is generally felt that all the three organs are under strain. Faith of the people, particularly in the quality and integrity of the executive wing, stands eroded. At such times, the judiciary remains the only hope. As an institution, the Indian judiciary commands the respect of the people of India. Because of his/her conviction of living in a just and fair society, a common man continues to pose faith and confidence in the system. It is because of this perception that the superior courts occupy a position of pre-eminence among the three organs of the State in the eyes of the public.

Briefly stated, a judicial system is a dispute resolution system and it must be recognised as a 'service', which provides consumers expeditious and effective resolution of these disputes. It offers a mechanism for the enforcement of rights and obligations of individuals, a function which is essential in a functioning polity or economy. Therefore, an effective and efficient judiciary is an essential foundation of good governance.

However, of late, one can witness disturbing and serious lacunas in the functioning of the judicial system as well. The common man's perception about access to justice has been very eloquently expressed by Sri A.P.J.Abdul Kalam:[1]

> I would like to share with you a point that has direct relevance to common man's access to justice. Equality before Law and equality of access to courts is only a theory. Even for literates, it is not easy to file a case which is the first basic step to law. The process is so complex. What will be the fate of others? Can they be freed from the web of complexities? The channel of communication between the courts of law and the common man is now complicatedly phrased in un-understandable legalese whether it is summons or any other format. This forces the common man to rush to practitioners of law which of course, as you all know entails expenditure and makes access to justice that much more difficult. Therefore, there is need to make all these formats and procedures user-friendly so that access to justice is easy, meaningful, cost-effective and productive. And let me say, that would be justice.

In the present context, the concerns expressed by our present Prime Minister, Dr. Manmohan Singh, are also of great contemporary relevance:[2]

> There are concerns that are being voiced in some quarters about the delays in disposal of cases and the consequent backlog that has built up over the years. The concern about the cost of litigation and the cost of obtaining justice; about the number of undertrials in our prisons; about the conviction rate in criminal cases; and last but not the least, occasional noises about probity—or the lack of it—in some sections of the judiciary. While there is enough cause for pride in the quality and effectiveness of our judicial system, it is incumbent upon any healthy institution to continue to reflect from time to time on its role, on the expectations from it and on its deficiencies in the larger scheme of governance so that steps can be initiated to improve its performance to meet the fast changing needs of the times that we live in.

The Report of the National Commission to Review the Working of the Constitution[3] has raised certain pertinent questions and issues:

> About half a century of the Constitution at work has tossed up many issues of the working of the judiciary: from the difficult problems of appointments to the superior judiciary to the problems of court clog-

---

1. "Judiciary: The Guardian of Civilised Society", Inaugural Address at All India Seminar on *Access to Justice*, A.P.J. Abdul Kalam, President of India, 26 April 2003, New Delhi., *http://presidentofindia.nic.in.*
2. Singh, Manmohan (2004). Conference of the Chief Ministers and Chief Justices, 18 Sept, New Delhi, *http://pmindia.nic.in/speeches.htm.*
3. National Commission, (2002). *Report of the National Commission*, para 2.22.5, Volume1, Universal Law Publishing.

> ging and judicial delays. A wide variety of issues have arisen. Who should appoint the judges? Should they be 'judges' judges' or 'peoples' judges'? Should the composition of the judiciary reflect the pluralism of the society? Particularly disturbing has been the chronic and recurrent theme of the near collapse of the judicial trial system, its delays and the mounting costs. The glorious uncertainties of the law have frustrated the aspirations for an equal, predictable and affordable justice.

One may remind oneself that the Indian judiciary is held in high esteem in many of the developing and developed countries of the world. The judgments delivered by our courts, particularly the Supreme Court, are oft-quoted by jurists and judges around the world, who are appreciative of the quality of the judgments. But these are all about the content and quality of justice. The concerns are more about delays, costs, transparency, probity and accountability.

According to Justice R.C. Lahoti, former Chief Justice of India, criticism is often from uninformed or misinformed quarters that the Indian judiciary is unable to clear the backlogs of the cases. According to him, at times, question marks have been placed on the credibility of the judiciary on account of some aberrations which are not the product of system, but are individual in nature and are isolated cases. These actors have a tendency of bringing a bad name to the entire system. He, after setting out the figures and statistics showing satisfactory disposals by the Supreme Court, High Court and subordinate courts, posed a pertinent question, "Whether the judiciary is solely responsible for the backlogs?"

The Indian Judiciary—History and Hierarchy

India, given its size and population, is unable to have a centralised administration of justice such as that in England. It is also very different from that found in the United States. With the exception of the federal Supreme Court sitting in New Delhi composed of the Chief Justice and 25 judges, the development of the judicial system during the British regime, like that of the laws, took place in three presidencies of Mumbai, Chennai and Kolkata separately. In course of time, with formation of common Central Government and a Central Legislative Council, a uniform and well-organised judicial system came to be established for the whole country, which the country inherited on its becoming independent on 15th August, 1947.

Administration of justice and organisation of courts was a provincial subject under the Government of India Act, 1935. The Constitution of India, which came into force on 26th January, 1950, adopted the scheme set out in the Government of India Act, 1935. Creation of the Supreme Court and the High Courts are under the mandate of the Constitution. They are, courts of records and have the power to punish for contempt of itself. But so far as the district and the courts subordinate thereto are concerned, these are created and established under State enactments.

The High Court is not a court 'subordinate' to the Supreme Court. The High Court exercises power of superintendence under Article 227 of the Constitution over all subordinate courts and tribunals; the Supreme Court has not been conferred with any power of superintendence. If the Supreme Court and the High Courts both were to be thought of as brothers in the administration of justice, the High Court has larger jurisdiction, but the Supreme Court still remains the elder brother. There are a few provisions which give an edge, and assign a superior place in the hierarchy, to the Supreme Court over High Courts.[4]

As far as the appellate jurisdiction is concerned, in all civil and criminal matters, the Supreme Court is the highest and the ultimate court of appeal. It is the final interpreter of the law. Under Article 139-A, the Supreme Court may transfer any case pending before any High Court to another High Court or may withdraw the case to itself. Under Article 141, the law declared by the Supreme Court shall be binding on all courts, including High Courts, within the territory of India. Under Article 144, all authorities, civil and judicial, in the territory of India—and that would include the High Courts as well—shall act in aid of the Supreme Court.

Judges in India

The Judges of the Supreme Court and the High Court are appointed by the President of India by following the procedure laid down under the Constitution and as interpreted by the Supreme Court.[5] Their conditions of service are determined by an Act of Parliament. According to Articles 124(4) and 217, the judges of the Supreme Court and High Court cannot be removed from their office

---

4. *Tripati Balaji Developers Private Limited vs. State of Bihar,* (2004) 5 SCC 1.
5. *Supreme Court Advocates on Record Association vs. Union of India,* (1993) 4 SCC 441.

except by an order of the President, based on a resolution passed by the Parliament, supported by a majority of not less than two-thirds of the members present in the House on the ground of 'proved misbehaviour or incapacity'. But so far as the members of the subordinate judiciary are concerned, they are subject to similar disciplinary proceedings as are available for the other government servants.

Independence of Judiciary: Need, Reality and Dangers

Independence of the judiciary occupies slots of pristine glory everywhere—it is there in the United Nations Universal Declaration in the International Covenant, the European Convention, the American Convention and in diverse array of international law generating documents. Most significantly, it is the subject of the specific United Nations sponsored studies on the Independence of Justice[6] leading to vital declarations on the independence of justice at Montreal and the formulation of draft principles on independence of justice.[7]

During the British rule, the District Officer acted both as the Administrative Officer and the Magistrate, the Executive, the Legislature and the Judiciary in his/her area; he/she made the regulations and then sat as the Magistrate to interpret and enforce the same. The history of the judicial system in India, if traced from 1912, would show that strong demands were raised for separation of the judiciary from the executive.[8] The Joint Parliamentary Committee[9] had stressed the necessity of securing the independence of subordinate judiciary.[10] It opined that it is the subordinate

6. Singhvi, L.M. (1985). Special Rapporteur, UN Study on the *Independence and Impartiality of the Judiciary, Judges and Assessors and the Independence of Lawyers* (31.7.85; E/CN 4/Sub2/1985/18).
7. Singhvi, Abhishek (1999). "Independence of Judiciary and Judging the Judges", in *Judging the Judges*, p. 121, Gyan Publishing House,
8. *State of West Bengal vs. Nripendra Nath*, AIR 1966 SC 447, pr. 8; See also *Chandra Mohan vs. State of U.P.*, AIR 1996 SC 1987, pr.14 at p.1993.
9. (1933-34) JPC Rep, Vol. I, p. 201, pr. 337.
10. *ibid.* "This subject is not mentioned in the White Paper, but there are aspects of it which seem to us of such importance that we think it right to state our opinion upon them. The Federal and High Court Judges will be appointed by the Crown and their independence is secure; but appointments to the Subordinate Judiciary, must necessarily be made by authorities in India who will also exercise a certain measure of control over the Judges after appointment, specially in the matter of promotion and posting. We have been greatly impressed by the mischiefs, which have resulted elsewhere from a system under which promotion from grade to grade in a judicial hierarchy is in the hands of a Minister exposed to pressure from members of a popularly elected Legislature. Nothing is more likely to sap the independence of a magistrate than the knowledge that his career depends upon the favour of a Minister...."

judiciary in India which is brought most closely into contact with the people, and it is no less important, perhaps indeed even more important, that their independence should be placed beyond question than in the case of the superior judges. The Constituent Assembly, while drafting the Constitution of independent India, took notice of this foundational requirement and included Article 50 in the Chapter on Directive Principles of State Policy that the State shall take steps to separate the judiciary from the executive in the public services of the State. This provision has been described by Granville Austin[11] as "the conscience of the Constitution." It embodies the social philosophy of the Constitution and its basic underpinnings and values. It plainly reveals without any scope for doubt or debate, the intent of the constitution makers to immunise the judiciary from any form of executive control or interference.[12]

The judiciary stands between the citizen and the State as a bulwark against executive excesses and misuse and abuse of power by the executive. It is, therefore, absolutely essential that the judiciary must be free from executive pressure or influence, which has been secured by making elaborate provisions in the Constitution with details. The independence of judiciary is not limited only to independence from executive pressure or influence; it is a wider concept, which takes within its sweep independence from any other pressure and prejudices.[13]

In India, we have instances when the executive had tried to endanger the independence of the judiciary. The judicial history will always recall with certain amount of dismay, the way three senior-most judges of the Supreme Court were superseded in appointment of the Chief Justice of India in 1973. In another instance, which happened towards the end of the Emergency, in the case of State of Rajasthan Union of India,[14] wherein the scope of judicial review of an executive act of dissolution of state assemblies arose for decision. During that period, the independence of the judiciary was threatened by the executive in ways which are well known. Justice P.K. Goswami was a member of the Bench which decided the Rajasthan case. The

---

11. Austin, Granville (1966). *The Indian Constitution: Cornerstone of a Nation.*
12. *Union of India vs. Sankalchand,* AIR 1977 SC 2328, pr. 52, p. 2356.
13. *C. Ravichandran Iyer Justice A. M. Bhattacharjee,* (1995) 5 SCC 457, pr. 10, p. 469.
14. AIR 1977 SC 1361, (1977) 3 SCC 592.

concluding remarks made by him in a separate opinion warned of a different kind of threat from within, with the potential of eroding the independence of the judiciary. Justice Goswami did not hesitate to frankly record his opinion thus:

> "I part with the records with a cold shoulder. The Chief Justice was good enough to tell us that the acting President saw him during the time we were considering judgment after having already announced the order that there was mention of this pending matter during the conversation. I have given this revelation the most anxious thought and even the strongest judicial restraint which a Judge would prefer to exercise, leave me no option but to place this on record hoping that the majesty of the high office of the President, who should be beyond the high watermark of any controversy, suffers not in future."

The above remarks of Justice Goswami were made undoubtedly to caution the future judges and to warn the executive of the potential threat to the independence of the judiciary from seemingly innocuous acts over the years, with vast erosion in moral values and unwarranted transgressions. On an earlier occasion, the judiciary witnessed a major threat to its independence when the decisive role and primacy of the executive in the appointment and transfer of judges was judicially recognised in *The First Judges'* case.[15] This uncontrolled power in favour of the executive was, however, subsequently curbed by the Supreme Court to some extent in *The Second Judges'* case.[16]

The growth of judicial review is the inevitable reaction to ensure proper check on the exercise of executive power. This is undoubtedly a recent global phenomenon, but more so in India. The growth of this phenomenon with its ready acceptance is not only by the people, but also by the other wings. The logical corollary of this ready acceptance of the expanded role of the judiciary is that the exercise of power of judicial review must be only for the achievement of public interest. The discharge of the duty and obligation towards the people of India requires that it should have no semblance of assertion of the judicial power over the other wings, except when it becomes necessary for upholding the majesty of law and for granting relief to the have-nots against injustice.[17]

It is self-restraint, with constant awareness of the inherent limitations of the judiciary, which alone can act as an effective check

---

15. *S.P. Gupta vs. Union of India*, AIR 1982 SC 149, 1981 Supp SCC 87, (1982) 2 SCC 365.
16. *Supreme Court Advocates-on-Record Association vs. Union of India*, AIR 1994 SC 268, (1993) 4 SCC 441.
17. Verma, J.S. (1995). *Independence of Justice—Some Latent Dangers*, Justice P.K. Goswami First Memorial Lecture, 18 Nov. Guwahati.

on a strong judiciary in the role of the final arbiter. The caution needed is even greater when the judicial activism is in a matter of self-interest to the judiciary, resulting in grant of a benefit to itself. In all such matters, if the circumstances permit, the option of leaving the matter to any other competent branch must always be kept in view, and examined first.

This realisation for self-restraint led to the note of caution in the *Second Judges'* case, which upheld the primacy of the judiciary in the matters of appointments and transfers of Judges. It was observed:

"O! it is excellent

To have a giant's strength;

But it is tyrannous

To use it like a giant."

(Shakespeare in *Measure for Measure*).

There are aspects of our judicial system which have come under increasing public scrutiny. There are concerns that are being voiced in some quarters about the delays in disposal of cases and consequent backlog that has built up over the years.

Accountability of the Indian Judiciary as an Institution

The principal object of the judiciary is to provide quick, affordable and incorruptible justice to the people. The Indian judiciary would thus be accountable as an institution to the Indian citizenry at large, in case it fails to achieve this principal object. Justice Krishna Iyer, way back in the 1980s, in his book *Justice at Crossroads,* said, "Today the court system is ossified to the point, priced to the level, and slow to the degree where they cannot flexibly assist disputants in solving their everyday disputes."

In 2001, the Supreme Court[18] said, "The time is running out for doing something to solve the problem which has already grown into monstrous form. If a citizen is told that once you resort to legal procedure for realisation of your urgent needs, you have to wait and wait for 23 to 30 years, what else is it if not to inevitably encourage and force him to resort to extra-legal measures for realising the required relief. A Republic governed by the rule of law cannot afford

18. *Gaya Prasad vs. Pradeep Shrivastava,* (2001) 2 SCC 604.

to compel its citizens to resort to such extra-legal means which are very often contra-legal means with counter productive results on the maintenance of law and order."

We have to find a solution. But the judiciary by itself cannot do anything. It is trite that the judges neither control the purse nor the sword. They neither have the army at their disposal nor access to the state treasury. In a showdown with other branches of Government, the judge is bound to be outdone, a calamity against which he/she can be immunised only by the confidence and faith of the people who can be expected to back him. The people alone can neutralise the arrogance of the political power and the venality of the bureaucrat. The judiciary, under the Indian polity, has to depend on the executive for its infrastructure and resources, both human and material. Unless this is provided on a need based analysis and planned endeavour, the ailments cannot be cured.

Judicial Accountability of a Judge as an Individual

The Greek philosopher, Socrates, 470-399 B.C. described four qualifications of a judge: (a) he should be able to hear courteously; (b) answer wisely; (c) consider soberly; and (d) decide impartially. Through the ages, it has been assumed that judges, by and large, live up to these qualifications. The belief has persisted despite some evidence of serious deficiencies and deviations in individual cases.

It is expected that a judge should work like a horse and live like a hermit. Lord Roskill, recounting his experience, said, "Work load is intolerable, seven days a week, fourteen hours a day." If someone knows about the Indian Judges and the pressure under which they have to work, they will agree that they are equally subjected to a similar work load.

The notion of accountability filters through public life. It is probably fair to say that at the present time, it is an expectation of the citizen that all aspects of government ought to be accountable. It is probably also fair that the same citizen would expect the judiciary to be accountable. Yet the reality is that the judicial branch of government has probably been historically and in actuality, one of the most accountable areas of government. Judicial accountability is manifested in the following ways—the business of all courts is, except in extraordinary circumstances, conducted in public. Judges resolve disputes under the obligation to publish full reasons for their decisions. Each decision, other than those of the ultimate court of appeal, is subject to being appealed. Appeal court criticism may be published without limitation. Academic lawyers are free to criticise judicial reasoning. Media attend hearings and, in some circumstances, may have a legal right to be heard in relation to closure of the court. Despite these structural guarantees of exposure of the business of the courts to the scrutiny of legal examination and the glare of public scrutiny, it is sometimes considered that the judicial branch needs to become more accountable.

Such demand for more accountability, on a logical analysis, seems to rest primarily on the need for reducing delays and arrears. The Indian judiciary as an institution and an Indian judge, as an individual, now need to utilise their energy towards achieving that goal to be able to effectively respond to the need of more judicial accountability.

In the context of accountability, it is worth noticing the causes attributed by Sri A.P.J. Abdul Kalam for judicial delays, namely: (i) inadequate number of courts; (ii) inadequate number of judicial officers; (iii) judicial officers not fully equipped to tackle cases involving specialised knowledge; (iv) dilatory tactics by the litigants and their lawyers who seek frequent adjournments and delay in filing documents; and (v) role of administrative staff of the Court.[19]

Information and Communication Technology (ICT) in Indian Judiciary

Domestic and international expert studies conclusively reflect that use of information and communication technology (ICT) in the judiciary, implemented with vision and well-devised plans, can enhance the quality of justice, reduce the court congestions and ensure timely disposal of cases. This has also been established through clinical researches[20] conducted in India.

Use of ICT is not something new to Indian courts, which had been using the technology since 1990, in varying degrees. But it also remains a fact that in most of the courts, use of ICT has not been

---

19. Kalam, A.P.J.Abdul (2005). President of India, Address at the inauguration of the all India seminar on Judicial Reforms with special reference to arrears of court cases, New Delhi, *http:// presidentofindia.nic.in/.*

20. Bharuka, G.C. (2003). *Rejuvenating Judicial System through e-Governance & Attitudinal Change*, Wadhwa & Co., First Edition.

explored to the fullest extent to facilitate the judicial process and decision making, so as to render relief to the litigants. One of the primary reasons for non-use of ICT to the desired extent was that the courts, as an institution, function on the basis of the legal system. Any change in the system has its immediate impact on the functioning of judges, lawyers and the subordinate staff, as also the litigants. The system is composed of its codified rules, the traditions and practices regularly followed in the court and the procedures judicially recognised. All these governing rules of procedure and court management are not always uniform for all the jurisdictions. Therefore, no handy software providing whole solutions to the legal system is commercially available. It is required to be developed under the day-to-day guidance and supervision of persons well-versed with ICT and the particular justice delivery system.

With a view to implement ICT in the Indian judiciary, on a proposal mooted by Shri R.C. Lahoti, former Chief Justice of India, the Government of India sanctioned[21] establishment of E-Committee in the Supreme Court to assist the Chief Justice of India in formulating a National Policy on Computerisation of Indian judiciary and advise on the technological, communication and management related changes. The E-Committee submitted its initial Report in May 2005 and prepared a targeted National Policy and Action Plan in August 2005. The Action Plan provides for diverse initiatives: providing of computers with broadband internet access in all 2,500 court complexes across the country; laptops for around 15,000 district and subordinate court judges; extensive ICT training to the judges and court staff; extension of computer facilities from filing counters to the judges' chambers and home offices; gradual extension of these facilities to all branches and sections of the court registry; facilities for video conferencing between undertrials and the courts; digital archiving, use of advanced ICT tools, including biometric facilities; and gateway interface with governmental agencies.

Case Management

It is well known that case management methods could do with improvement at subordinate levels. Keeping this in view, the

21. Vide notification dated 28th December, 2004, issued through the Ministry of Law and Justice.

Supreme Court in the case of *Salem Advocates Bar Association vs Union of India*[22] had *inter alia* constituted a Committee headed by a former judge of the Supreme Court and Chairman, Law Commission of India, Shri M. Jaganaddha Rao, to devise model caseflow management formulae, as well as rules and regulations. The Committee, in its Report, framed and suggested adoption of Model Caseflow Management Rules. A three-Judges bench of the Supreme Court presided by my esteemed brother, Justice Y.K. Sabharwal, after considering the Model Rules, has required the respective High Courts to examine the same and after due deliberations, take steps for its adoption, with or without modification to provide fair, speedy and inexpensive justice.

The Action Plan framed by the E-Committee has also provided for supporting caseflow management by providing for creation of database of pending cases for generating live statistics and tracking of flow of cases in order to foster professional management of the justice delivery system in court administration. It has also provided for court management support systems and knowledge management by proposing to make online availability of statute law, case laws and law literature to all the stakeholders through web technology. The online availability of legal resources will help in increasing efficiency and capacity building of the judges and the lawyers alike.

Additional Courts

It is a well recognised fact that there is a physical limitation to the quantum of cases any judge can handle. The requirement of requisite number of courts based on judge-case ratio cannot be postponed any further. Despite provision of technology and other resources, unless the Government takes effective measures for providing requisite number of judges with associated infrastructural facilities, possibly, the delay reduction programmes may not succeed. The Supreme Court, taking a lead from the 120th *Report of the Law Commission of India* (1987) on Judicial Manpower Planning, had issued directions to increase the judge strength from existing ratio of 10.5-13 judges per million (10 lakh) persons to 50 judges. The direction is still awaiting compliance. In the meantime, in the Chief Justices' Conference, 2004,[23] it was

22. (2003) 1 SCC 49.

23. Held on Sept. 4-5, 2004.

resolved to constitute a Committee comprising of Chief Justices of 3 High Courts[24] to find out the norms for governing judge-case ratio. The Committee, on the basis of empirical data received from the High Courts, submitted its Report on 15th September, 2004 that the judge-case ratio should be between 500 to 600 for district and subordinate courts. Presently, the total numbers of courts in the country are about 12,148. As per the case population ratio, we need an additional 38,741 courts. The pendency, as on 1st October, 2005, is 31.2 million. Taking pendency as a basis for creation of additional courts, we may require 34,222 courts. Therefore, the number of additional courts required for the disposal of cases within a targeted period of one year or so, by any standard, would be about 35,000.

Change Management

Management science tells us that any organisation will perform only if it has clear shared goals and specific time bound plans to achieve them. The plan prepared by the E-Committee seeks to achieve the objectives by effective use of ICT through its implementation in a phased manner over a period of five years. One has to be prepared to face enormous challenges in implementation of the plan, particularly because of its geographical and horizontal dimensions. No doubt hardware deployment in the courts can be made within 2 to 3 years and some of the judicial processes can be automated, but in order to avail the best of the technology to answer the basic needs and avowed objectives, there has to be a sustainable change in the attitude, work culture and transformation of processes, which are time consuming. It requires continuous overviewing, training and fine tuning to make the change management happen, till it becomes an integral component of organisational behaviour.

The implementation of ICT in the judicial sector will embark upon a challenging journey of change. The implementation of e-governance has the potential of an impact in all areas—systems, processes and most importantly, institutional human resources. It has been established by recent research[25] that 41 per cent of ICT-led change projects fail and of the 59 per cent that succeed, only half

24. Justice B.C. Patel, Chief Justice, High Court of Delhi; Justice Devendar Gupta, Chief Justice, Andhra Pradesh High Court; Justice Markandya Kartzu, Acting Chief Justice, Allahabad High Court.

25. S.C. Index/AMA Survey.

meet the expectation of top management. A global survey of 500 organisations has shown that 9 out of the 10 top barriers to change are people-related. For example, limited change management skills, poor communications and internal resistance from interest groups. The judiciary, as an institution, cannot be an exception to these challenges.

Alternative Dispute Resolution (ADR)

Alternative dispute resolution refers to resolving of disputes other than by way of litigation or adjudication by the state courts. Among the popular alternative dispute resolution systems available are negotiation, mediation, conciliation and arbitration. It has been noticed in recent times that disputants prefer these methods to solve their disputes than by way of litigation.

However, there are two distinct concepts which should be clearly borne in mind as far as use of alternative dispute resolution systems is concerned.

One is that unless the adjudicatory system at any place is strong, the success of the use of alternative dispute resolution cannot be ascertained. The main criticism of alternative dispute resolution methods, voluntary or otherwise, is that such mechanisms generally work better when the courts are efficient. In other words, parties to a dispute have incentives to settle when they know what court judgments they will get; courts complement ADR systems. However, this is clearly not the case in many developing countries, where ADR systems function as substitutes. But to function in this matter, they need to effectively represent the community for whom they adjudicate. The *Lok Adalats* in India, for example, are not very popular since they do not offer adequate compensation for victims, who face high costs in the courts to enforce their rights. These are more likely to be for the poor people.[26]

Secondly, it is worthwhile noticing that an overemphasis on the use and implementation of alternative dispute resolution, and thereby according a back-seat to courts, would actually result in hampering and weakening of the judicial system itself. The more time and efforts and money we spend over establishment of alternative dispute resolution systems, the less are we attending to the task of

---

26. *World Bank Development Report(2002)*. Chapter 6, "Judicial System", p.127.

strengthening our judicial system. The discounting of everyday civil justice in the state courts, the official pessimism about reform, the 'load shedding', into the *Lok Adalats*, and the flourishing of alternative forums reflect a 'hollowing out', of the Indian State.[27]

A cumulative analysis of the above two propositions would lead us to ponder over the excessive use and stress on alternative dispute resolution. Until and unless our foundations are strong, the structure above it cannot stand the test of time. Our courts are the foundation. We need to make that strong with regular study and necessary reforms. Only then will alternative dispute resolution, in whatever form, be a success.

Financial Autonomy

Policy makers, especially from within the judiciary of late, have started feeling that the blame for huge backlog of cases cannot be attributed only to the judiciary. According to them, to a great extent, the failure of the system has arisen because of the fact that during the last 50 years after the Independence, little attention has been paid by the Government for improvement of the infrastructure of the judiciary. There is dearth of courts and judges and buildings, both for courts and judges and officers and staff. In several cases, even minimum facilities have not been given. The reason is that there is no planning and proper budgeting for the court's requirements in consultation with the judiciary, as is done in other countries, nor is there a long range plan or at least a Five Year Plan for the purpose. The result is that most courts are burdened with cases on civil and criminal sides, delay results in a serious infraction to speedy trials and violation of human rights in various cases. A stage has reached where the parties are thinking of taking the law into their own hands.[28]

Former Chief Justice of India Mr.A.S.Anand[29] opined that some of the ills with which India's administration of justice is presently afflicted are capable of being cured if financial autonomy is granted to the judiciary. The edifice of the administration of justice rests on the shoulders of the subordinate judiciary, as the majority of the litigants

---

27. Galanter, Marc (2002). *Debased Informalism: Lok Adalats and Legal Rights in Modern India*, p. 61.

28. "Consultation Paper on Financial Autonomy of Indian Judiciary", circulated by the National Commission to Review the Working of the Constitution, Ch. 1.

29. Presently, Chairman, Human Rights Commission.

go only up to the district level. The High Courts have power of superintendence over the state judiciary, but they do not have any financial power to create even one post of a subordinate judge or subordinate staff, acquire or purchase any land or building for courts, decide and implement any plan for modernisation of court working. Chief Justices and their companion judges of the High Court are best suited to know the requirements of the judiciary in their respective states. Their assessment and demand should receive proper consideration and should not be 'rejected' on account of merely financial constraints. The Chief Justices of the High Courts who are high constitutional functionaries, know the needs of the judiciary of the state. They need to be given financial powers *vis-à-vis* the state judiciary, by transfer of financial powers from the executive to enable them to function effectively. One of the essential elements of rule of law is judicial independence and every society has seen the need for it. Financial dependence on the executive, to an extent, impinges upon the independence of the judiciary when it is required to 'negotiate' every time with the largest litigant—the State.[30]

After due deliberations upon the issue of financial autonomy of the judiciary, the National Commission to Review the Working of the Constitution concluded[31] that judicial administration in the country suffers from deficiencies due to lack of proper planning and adequate financial support for establishing more courts and providing them with adequate infrastructure. It further opined that neither has any provision for any funds for the judiciary been made under the Five Year Plans for several decades, nor has the Finance Commission made any separate provision to serve the financial needs of courts. In view of these observations, the Commission recommended the setting up of a 'Judicial Council' at the Apex level and Judicial Councils at each state at the level of the High Court. There should be an Administrative Officer to assist the National Judicial Council and separate Administrative Officers attached to Judicial Councils in states. These bodies must be created under a statute made by the Parliament. The Judicial Councils will be in charge of the preparation

---

30. Anand, A.S. (2002). "Approaching the Twenty-First Century: The State of the Indian Judiciary and the Future Challenges", in *Justice for Women: Concerns and Expressions*, p. 58.

31. *Report of the National Commission to Review the Working of the Constitution* (2002). p. 142, pr. 7.6.

of plans, both short-term and long-term, and for preparing proposals for annual budgets.[32] With regard to a streamlined financial planning for the judiciary, the Commission was of the view that the budget proposals in each state must emanate from the State Judicial Council in regard to the needs to the subordinate judiciary in that state, and will have to be submitted to the State Executive. Once the budget is finalised between the State Judicial Council and the State Executive, it should be presented to the State Legislature.[33]

However, the eminent jurist, Dr. Madhav Menon, is of the opinion that though financial autonomy is necessary for improving efficiency and productivity in the judiciary, financial autonomy in the present state of the system may not be a wise step in the public interest. If administrative autonomy is not able to arrest the deterioration, giving financial autonomy also, without revamping the administration can be potentially counter-productive. No one will dispute the need for more resources, for modernisation of infrastructure and court control of administration. But the onus is on the judiciary to demonstrate that judges are determined to put the system back on rails and ensure optimum use of scarce resources diverted to them from equally pressing demands on public funds.[34]

32. *ibid.* pr. 7.7.

33. *ibid.* pr. 7.8.1.

34. Menon, N.R. Madhava (2001). *State of Justice: An Agenda for Change*, p.8-9.

6

Delays in the Administration of Justice

CARL BAAR

Introduction

Court delay continues to be an enormous challenge for courts throughout the world. This chapter focuses on how delay has developed, particularly in the British Commonwealth; the consequences of the extreme delays that afflict many of our courts; and the steps that can and should be taken to reduce case backlogs and establish prompt, fair and accessible trial court practices. It will argue first that delay is a particularly difficult problem for commonwealth courts precisely because of the British heritage they share. For in fact what they share, is not a heritage of the British justice and a British legal system, but the heritage of the British colonial justice and a British colonial legal system. And it is the characteristics of this British colonial legal system that have created roadblocks to reform in general and to the reduction of court delay in particular.

It will argue secondly that the consequences of extreme delay go beyond the maxim that 'justice delayed is justice denied', because that maxim assumes that litigants go to court on behalf of just causes. Extreme delay may in fact turn the common understanding about litigation on its head.

It will argue thirdly that court delay not only should be reduced, but can be reduced—in both common law and civil law systems and in both rich and poor economies. The achievement of delay-free courts, however, is not a guarantee that courts will act justly or help achieve a just society.

The chapter will then discuss some of the steps that can be taken to reduce delay. It will remind us that for most courts, reducing delay is a two-step process, beginning with backlog reduction (dealing with old cases), but moving on to delay reduction itself, which focuses on the best practices for dealing with cases from the time they are commenced. It will highlight selected control processes and administrative supports necessary for successful backlog and delay reduction.

The Development of Delay

Most presentations on court delay begin by reminding their audience that delay has always been with us. There are verses 13-27 of Chapter 18 of the *Book of Exodus*, where Moses, having brought the Ten Commandments to the people of Israel, finds his people exhausted after spending all day waiting to bring their cases before him. It is Moses' father-in-law Jethro who recommends that others be trained in the law so that they can handle the simple cases and reserve only the difficult ones for Moses.

This story can act as a reminder to court administrators that their field did not spring fresh from the mind of American law professor Roscoe Pound in 1906. Court delay not only has a long history, but also a long history of successful efforts to reduce such delays. Moreover in Jethro's words, it can be seen that even as Moses was applying the Ten Commandments, Jethro told him that he was not doing justice if the effort was exhausting the very people it was supposed to benefit.

If court delay is neither inevitable nor universal, its existence is a result of human action—and in particular over the past 200 years, the result of policy decisions made by public authorities. In the context of the commonwealth, these were policy decisions of British colonial authorities who, historical legend tells us, bequeathed to their colonies the blessings of the English common law.

These authorities also created a colonial court system and legal process that combined elements of home-country legal practice with elements of colonial administration. Thus High Courts of justice were established in far-flung outposts of empire, emulating the cathedral of justice in the metropolis. But the bulk of the everyday work of the courts would be done by a sprawling network of so-called subordinate courts, staffed not by the lay volunteers found back home, but by a new generation of law-trained civil servants. Supervision of subordinate judges would be made the responsibility of the High Courts themselves. This step did reflect an awareness that the principle of judicial independence requires that supervision of individual judges be done within the judiciary and not by government. However, it also built into commonwealth court systems some of the characteristics that still plague today's postcolonial courts.

First, the judicial hierarchy has become an administrative hierarchy, so too few subordinate courts have developed the managerial skills, personnel, processes and institutions to govern their own affairs.

Second, the subordinate judiciary remains too much in a civil service mold and mindset. Thus, a predominantly youthful corps of judges is constantly mindful of not offending their superiors in hopes of receiving favourable assignments and future promotions. And reporting and record keeping has transformed court statistics gathering into a form of balance sheets, work weighting and managerial accounting, rather than a way of improving performance and expediting justice.

Third, the elaborate 19th century adversary process still visible in postcolonial trial courts—but often removed from the discipline of lay decision making provided by temporary bodies of citizens assembled into juries—has fragmented the trial process to the point where trials have become a deconstructed sequence of discrete events that continue for years. Twentieth-century innovations in court procedure (e.g. pre-trial disclosure of evidence and pre-trial examination for discovery) are often missing, so judges find themselves playing a continuing role in a discontinuous and lengthy process.

Fourth, the principle of party control of litigation, seen by the English as the central characteristic of common law procedure, places the bar in a position of strength and discourages reform initiatives from the judiciary. While the English closed out the 20th century by abandoning the principle of party control in favour of Lord Woolf's approach to civil procedure, the bar in many commonwealth countries has reached levels of power unknown in the mother country, retarding needed change.

Fifth, the desire to establish what the British understood as the rule of law meant that the excesses of law enforcement were accepted as long as they took place within the 'ordinary courts' of the colonial civil establishment. Thus, long periods of pre-trial incarceration existed in colonial times despite principles of the presumption of innocence, because judicial review however open-ended and generous to government—was in theory still available.

Taken together, these characteristics of the British colonial legal system produced results substantially different from what occurred back in England. They have left too many post-colonial countries with a procedurally elaborate system that relies too much on hierarchical and bureaucratic control mechanisms and finds change very difficult. As a result, systems that should have transformed themselves in the years after Independence now operate in a manner that combines an abandoned colonial regime with an abandoned model of the British justice.[1] Court delay is one symptom of the malaise.

Given the mixed motives of many post-Independence regimes, it is perhaps fortunate that the courts survived with as much of their dignity and independence intact as they have. But even so, the time for reform and improvement is well overdue in too many commonwealth countries. Fortunately, the current generation of court reform, buoyed by rule-of-law initiatives in the development community, provides a basis for thoughtful and sustainable reform. But is it worth the effort? The next section argues that it is.

The Consequences of Extreme Delay

What happens when court delay and related defects in case processing become so serious that trial courts can no longer perform many of their basic functions? While reformers everywhere lament that justice delayed is justice denied, the time for taking cases to trial or other disposition is typically within parameters sufficiently manageable that courts can still effectively assess evidence and apply principles of law. However, court systems today often struggle with such extreme delay and large backlogs that their best efforts to maintain judicial independence and the rule of law have gone hand

1. Latin American countries provide an interesting historical parallel. They achieved Independence from Spain from 1810 to 1825, so their civil law systems missed the major changes in continental European procedure in the 19th century, and remain excessively paper based. A major exception is Cuba, which remained a colony until 1898. As a result, the current Cuban regime is pressing its Latin American neighbours to add more oral proceedings—the same recommendations that come from the US consultants funded by USAID and the World Bank, and have been attacked by bar associations claiming that American reformers do not adequately understand civil law traditions.

in hand with criminal processes that punish the innocent and acquit the guilty, and civil processes mobilised by those without valid claims in order to pressure adversaries to abandon legitimate claims.

On the criminal side, extreme delay has undermined the operation of what is now termed "the criminal justice system" to the point that it cannot achieve either of its fundamental objectives. Some 40 years ago, American legal scholar, Herbert Packer, laid out what he saw as two competing purposes of the criminal process: crime control and due process.[2] Rather than tilting the system in one direction or another, extreme delay in criminal courts has undermined both of these objectives. Accused persons' rights are jeopardised because they often spend long periods of time in pre-trial detention. In turn, crime control objectives are jeopardised because by the time these accused are brought to trial, witnesses are unavailable and acquittals are routinely entered.

While it is difficult to obtain court case statistics that can be validly compared across jurisdictions, especially from one national legal system to another, it appears on the basis of available data that conviction rates are much lower in countries with longer periods of pre-trial delay. The author has seen figures of 25 per cent and 30 per cent conviction rates at trial in Pakistani courts in which, cases average as many as 100 appearances before a disposition is entered. Where there is less delay, conviction rates may fall below 50 per cent but generally rise to 60 per cent or more following trial. Obviously, conviction rates are higher when prosecutors are more diligent in screening cases, and when guilty plea dispositions are added to trial dispositions. But even with these factors taken into account (and some of them actually make the differences in trial dispositions appear smaller than they are), it is clear that extreme delay makes it less probable that an accused will be found guilty at trial.

Because extreme delay undermines both due process rights of the accused and crime control objectives of law enforcement, it is not surprising that the greater the delay in criminal cases, the higher the percentage of those in custody who have not been convicted.[3] Thus it would not be unfair to characterise the resulting process as 'punishment before trial'.

---

2. Herbert, L. Packer (1968). *The Limits of the Criminal Sanction*, Stanford University Press, Stanford.
3. The highest estimate I am aware of is 80 per cent, provided by a senior corrections official in Ethiopia (which has an inquisitorial system based on the Indian Penal Code of 1908).

On the civil side, extreme delays provide an incentive for individuals to bring invalid claims. Those without valid claims can prevent individuals with valid claims from securing a court order vindicating those claims. As the litigation drags on, pressure builds for the parties to settle. If the litigation involves members of the same family, someone with a valid claim may be pressured to abandon his/her claim or (more commonly) his/her defence in order to reestablish peace within the family. Settlement, perhaps facilitated by a mediator (a process that should be welcome in a well-functioning legal system), becomes yet another tool for continuing dominance of the stronger party regardless of what the law provides.

Extreme delays not only encourage litigants with invalid claims, but also discourage litigants with valid claims. Redress of wrongs is then sought through extra-legal means, and private enterprises emerge to serve individuals who seek 'justice' outside the legal system. Some of these means may involve peaceful processes, such as the settlement of auto accident claims through an agreement in which the injured party's car is repaired by an agent of the party who takes responsibility for the damages. But other means may be more coercive and neither consensual nor legal.

As a result, civil litigation becomes largely a symbolic exercise for those litigants who truly believe they are pursuing valid claims. As all parties go on with their lives several years after the conflict from which litigation arose, the case drags on until the claimant can tell his story to the judge and obtain satisfaction knowing that however matters turned out in reality, the judge agreed that his claim was valid. Courts with extreme delay often suffer more from their past sins and omissions than from their present level of activity. They are often—even typically—able to keep up with their heavy caseloads. But the elapsed time for cases to move from initiation to disposition is excessively long, because delays in past years result in current pendencies so high that the judges are constantly focusing on matters from previous years before new litigants can expect attention to be given to their matters.

Too often, these backlogs increase more quickly than courts can respond to them. This may be a function of increased demand, as large numbers of new cases overwhelm the current complement of judges, and by the time help arrives, a new higher level of pendencies has been established. Or it may be a function of decreased resources, as individual judges are shifted and promoted, and their court workload is temporarily redistributed to colleagues who are often in a position to do little more than maintain the *status quo* until the next recruitment cycle brings some relief.

In some respects, backlog reflects well on the judges themselves. In Pakistan, for example, subordinate judges serve as elections officials, a credit to the respect in which they are held by the public. Every time the national regime decides to hold an election (even one challenged as unconstitutional by bar associations throughout the country), numerous judges are called away for training and for election duties as returning officers. Courts adjourn early and courtrooms stand empty for the day. By the time the courts return to normal, newly-instituted cases further outnumber case dispositions, and the ability of the courts to do justice in future cases is further undermined.

The Merits and Feasibility of Reducing Backlog and Delay

This brief discussion of the consequences and characteristics of extreme delay underscores the need to address court delay as an essential step in ensuring that courts can do justice for litigants and the public.

Before recommending the steps in a strategy to reduce delay, it is necessary to address a prior question: Is there any evidence that delay can be reduced? An expert's prescriptions can sound reasonable and even persuasive, but have they ever worked? Are there any court systems without delay, especially among former British colonies? If so, what conditions have facilitated expeditious justice? And finally, at what cost? Can we ensure that a fair and just legal system emerges from a delay-free court?

The best-known success story in the post-colonial court world is the Republic of Singapore. Its subordinate courts have been recognised internationally for their innovations in management and legal processes, and the courts have extended their leadership across the Asia-Pacific region.

The key to their success is that the subordinate courts have taken responsibility for managing the pace and quality of their adjudication. Judicial leaders constantly monitor what is happening within and around the courts, so they can respond before problems become visible to the public. As a result, these courts have a manageable inventory of cases that can be (and typically is) dealt with so expeditiously that backlog rarely if ever develops.

However, to the extent that the Singapore courts are used to bolster an argument that delay can be reduced, a counter argument could be made that their success is a reflection of that country's wealth, and particularly the human, material and technological resources that have been secured by the subordinate courts.

There are two responses to this counter argument. The first is that while resources are a key element of the Singapore success story, resources alone do not reduce delay. If they did, courts in the United States and Canada would be delay-free; instead, some of the most prosperous metropolitan areas struggle with accumulated backlogs. While courts in prosperous countries are rarely subject to the ills arising from extreme delays, they often have difficulty keeping up with incoming cases, because they fail to anticipate changes in their immediate environment. In contrast, the Singapore courts have the ability to scan their environment, identify their resource needs, build a case for these needs, and effectively mobilise their new resources. The combination of managerial skill and judicial leadership that makes this possible, is what sets them apart and produces a court system committed to establishing and maintaining high standards of performance.

The second response would consider whether in fact backlogs and delays can be reduced in countries with a less prosperous and even impoverished public sector. Available evidence suggests a surprisingly strong positive answer. On the backlog reduction side, courts in three countries with resource constraints and extreme delays have all reported examples of successful backlog reduction: Pakistan, India, and Ethiopia. Over several months in Pakistan in 2001-02, subordinate courts in Karachi (especially in District Central, after the District Judge returned from a study tour to Singapore) showed an impressive reduction in pendencies during an Asian Development Bank pilot project. While pilot courts in Lahore were less successful, a number of district judges in other centres in Punjab province had strong records of effectively managing their caseloads. In Bangalore, India, a thoughtfully-organised local initiative was able to eliminate over 100,000 pending cases in the subordinate courts. In Ethiopia, the poorest of the three countries, a pilot project in the populous Amhara Region could by 2005, report continuing annual reductions in pending cases.

There are other examples of court systems with limited resources but strong traditions of expeditious case processing. Courts in Russia and former Soviet republic typically take cases from initiation to disposition in a matter of weeks or at most months—not years. Even in Moldova, reputedly the poorest country in Europe, trial courts have little backlog, with no more than 10-15 per cent of civil and criminal cases carried over from one year to the next. Courts in Cuba report prompt disposition of cases as well.

While cross-national data on the pace of litigation are not available in a form that allows systematic comparison and ranking of court systems on that dimension, the accumulating evidence shows widespread variation among courts in how fast cases move from initiation to disposition. At the same time, however, it appears that some of the most expeditious systems are ones that critics would identify as having powerful governments less constrained by an active and independent judiciary. Is fast-paced and delay-free adjudication therefore associated with regimes that are less rights-based and democratic?

In fact, this is not the case. Two of the countries mentioned above with extreme delay, Pakistan and Ethiopia, have had military regimes and less well-established democratic traditions. The successes that have been achieved with backlog reduction in those two countries are associated not with particular regimes or ideologies but with the commitment of judicial leaders and their understanding of how they can effectively monitor and control the movement of cases in the face of complex local community and professional pressures.

Still, given the countries that have successfully reduced court delay and maintained a more expeditious pace of litigation, does court delay reduction represent the triumph of justice values, or the successful mobilisation by strong governments of the coercive power of judiciaries? Have we moved from the maxim of 'justice delayed is justice denied' to a new principle that 'justice rushed is justice crushed'?

Observation of the subordinate courts in Singapore, several years ago, suggests that a well-managed court accommodates the competing values of due process and crime control. While the absence of judicial review authority in Singapore limits the ability of the Singapore judiciary to use constitutional standards to nullify legislative action,[4]

4. For example, in cases raising issues of human rights and fundamental freedoms, or the constitutionality of limits on judicial sentencing discretion.

and the courts' swift processing of large numbers of civil and criminal matters reinforces the government's crime control and social control agenda, the pace of litigation can be and has been modulated to ensure fairness. Thus, for example, capital offences do not proceed to disposition as expeditiously as non-capital offences of similar complexity. Additional time is given for persons accused of capital offences to obtain counsel, and for their counsel to discuss charges with the Director of Public Prosecutions (DPP) (an appointed official serving on good-behaviour tenure). Given the lack of judicial discretion in sentencing for capital offences, these built-in delays allow the DPP to consider reducing capital charges to non-capital ones. Thus, it is the administrative apparatus and practices of the Singapore subordinate courts that allow expeditious justice to proceed under strong judicial leadership across a wide range of cases, while slowing the pace when the interests of justice suggest doing so.

Strategies for Reducing Backlog and Delay

The previous section, in examining how it has been possible to reduce backlog and delay, has already referred to some of the key principles, usually associated with the concepts of case management and caseflow management, that are prerequisites for successful use of particular strategies and techniques.

Thus, for example, the courts' responsibility for the pace of litigation was emphasised, along with the need for judicial leadership to reduce backlog and delay. These are well-known axioms, but they are still overshadowed by a tendency to blame lawyers and litigants for court delay. Obviously, if every witness appeared in court ready to testify, and every litigant was ready to proceed without asking for an adjournment, some critical defects in the current process would be alleviated. But what courts would be ready to respond effectively if this happened next Monday? What accommodations could be made so that those witnesses and litigants would not be sent away after they complied with the standards of responsible behaviour that have been asked of them in the past?

The most effective response to this imaginary scenario would require a degree of flexibility unknown in far too many commonwealth courts. Overcoming this inflexibility requires a degree of planning, coordination, concerted action and even cultural change uncharacteristic of those institutions today. Judges acting together can reach these new levels of achievement as long as they have the support and encouragement of their colleagues in positions of court leadership, whatever their titles—District Judge, Senior District Judge, Senior Resident Magistrate, Administrative Judge, Court President, and Vice-President.

However, if we return to reality, and witnesses do not appear as scheduled, and litigants routinely seek adjournments because they are not ready to proceed to the next step in the process, what happens then? Are judges simply there to respond when the parties and their lawyers are ready, or does the judiciary have a responsibility to make the system work? Given the widespread deterioration of court systems under the assumption of party control, the alternative of court control is no longer optional—it is mandatory. The debate over court control *versus* party control has little meaning today when the adjudication process is out of control.

This does not mean that the concept of control requires draconian or unilateral action. The term 'control' should not be used in the coercive sense associated with authoritarian institutions or dictatorial individuals (what my friends back home would label "control freaks"). The term is most effectively used in the tradition and meaning of Mary Parker Follett, from her 1930s essay, "The Process of Control". Follett, whose writings on conflict resolution became the intellectual basis for Fisher and Ury's book, *Getting to Yes*, saw control not as a superior directing a subordinate, but as the product of the interaction of all elements in an organisation or a social setting. According to Follett, control emerges from the reciprocal relationship of all the elements in a situation. As a result, it follows that control is a continuing process, and is more effective when it occurs in the early stages.

Follett's essay reads like a handbook for case and caseflow management. We know that effective case management normally requires a common understanding of how litigation will proceed right from the initiation of a case. In a complex case, control in the early stages is reflected in a case conference or directions hearing to establish ground rules and expectations so that later difficulties can be anticipated and addressed. Control must be continuous in the sense that there is always a date set for future action.[5] All

5. In the Toronto Superior Court, civil cases dealt with under the Simplified Procedure that have no future date are referred to colloquially as "black hole cases".

participants, including parties and counsel, need to be aware of these expectations as well.

Conversely, judicial attempts to exercise control from the bench in a traditional more coercive manner, but without the understanding of control as a process or the development of a caseflow control system, are doomed to failure. As my Canadian co-author, Judge Perry Millar, used to say years ago, "I only give an adjournment when it is necessary, but the problem is that adjournments are always necessary by the time I'm on the bench, and I can't do anything about them." In the same way, I have seen resolute, determined and independent judges in Asia and Africa issue orders suspending the pay of police officers who do not appear as witnesses in court—a step unheard of in Canada or the United States. It usually results in the particular witness appearing, but does not address the continuing administrative difficulties that lead to this happening again and again in the future.

Once we move beyond general concepts of responsibility, leadership and control, we need to consider how to develop a management strategy for a court and a court system. This requires first that we distinguish between backlog reduction and delay reduction. They are not the same. If the cases pending in a court are too numerous for them to be disposed of within a prompt and appropriate period of time, those cases make up that part of the court's inventory that is termed the backlog. Before a court can set up a case management system that moves cases from their initiation, a court must reduce its backlog so that new cases can be dealt with when they are in fact still new.

Most of the so-called delay reduction efforts applying caseflow management principles in development projects have in fact focused on backlog reduction. These have been worthwhile and even essential initiatives but fail to spell out in detail how to approach and measure backlog reduction and they do not focus on delay reduction itself.[6] That is why it is ironic that a valuable backlog reduction initiative undertaken by the Government of India in recent years has been

---

6. Baar, Carl and Robert G. Hann, (2005). "The Reduction of Case Backlog in the Courts: A Framework and Strategy", paper prepared for the Third Biennial Meeting, Commonwealth Judicial Education Institute, hosted by the National Judicial Academy, Bhopal, India, March 14-18.

labelled 'Fast Track Courts' even though these courts only work on resolving old cases that went off any fast track months or years before. Unless we move from backlog reduction to delay reduction, we are simply clearing the dockets of stale cases so that we can apply the same all-too-stale approach to the fresh cases. What is needed is a fresh approach as well.

What I propose is that as case backlog is brought under control, an individual pilot court or courts should be set up and given an inventory of cases but no backlog. In other words, rather than establishing a new court and then dividing the existing caseload (for example) six ways instead of five, the new court should have only enough cases to fill its time but not so many that it is unable to hear new matters according to a set of optimal time standards and adjournment policies. Lawyers and litigants would need to understand that this court is operating under a new set of assumptions and policies, and has been designed so that it can put those assumptions and policies into practice. It is therefore what could be termed a Best Practices Court.[7]

Implementing a Best Practices Court is a major challenge, but its benefits could be substantial. It would mean that new cases going to this court would be dealt with while issues were still fresh. Adjournments would be held to a minimum under new expectations spelled out to all participants. As a result, dispositions would occur earlier in the process with fewer appearances, reducing the average amount of judge and staff time spent per case.

Administrative Supports for Backlog and Delay Reduction

Neither backlog reduction nor delay reduction occurs without substantial effort and organisation. That is why the strategy chapter cited above is put forward as a checklist so that those developing a programme miss a key component needed to ensure that a new and effective control system emerges.

For example, in keeping with Follett's concept of control and with the practical experience of backlog and delay reduction initiatives around the world, a committee or committees should be struck with

7. This was the term used in a similar proposal made by a technical assistance team in Delhi in 2004. It echoes a proposal made in a caseflow management study report for Addis Ababa, Ethiopia, in 2003, and is analogous to the proposal of a Zero Tolerance Court made by former District Judge, Singh, in Delhi prior to 2004.

membership representing all participants in the litigation process. On the criminal side, this is likely to include sessions judges and magistrates (or their counterparts), court administration, prosecution, defence, legal aid, police and corrections. On the civil side, representation is likely to reflect the judiciary, court administration, the private bar and major litigant groups.

The committees should be used to mobilise the knowledge and build the commitment of participants. The plan that emerges from committee discussions may not be the ideal solution envisioned at the outset, but it is likely to be a more feasible and sustainable one. I recall when one of the Karachi district judges assembled such a committee to explore problems in handling criminal cases, no comprehensive plan had yet evolved to address backlog, but the problems that interfered with case processing were well known. So for example, police officials were asked why undertrial prisoners did not appear in court as scheduled. In response, the police complained that sufficient vehicles were not available, but then suggested that if appearances of accused held in custody could be scheduled in both the morning and the afternoon—and not only in the morning as had been the practice for many years—transportation of more prisoners could be arranged even with the existing vehicles. It is these simple operational solutions that can only arise when knowledgeable participants are part of a continuous problem-solving process.

In the same way, lawyer participation is essential to ensure that the practicing bar can adjust to the demands of a new system. While some lawyers may resist change, most simply need to voice their concerns and make suggestions that facilitate effective implementation of proposed changes. Too often, we treat the local legal culture as if it represents centuries of art and wisdom, rather than decades of ingrained habits. Part of the necessary adjustments may reflect something potentially more onerous—the impact of backlog and delay reduction on legal fees and lawyers' incomes. But while backlog and delay reduction may reduce the income of lawyers who rely on billing for multiple appearances in protracted cases, it may increase the income of lawyers whose clients can obtain more expeditious resolution of their cases. "Don't call it caseflow management," said a successful Canadian plaintiff's lawyer 15 years ago, "call it cash flow management."

One of the key technical supports for backlog and delay reduction is the statistical information necessary to monitor and evaluate the effectiveness of reform efforts. Analysis of statistical data in fact serves multiple purposes. It allows court leadership to monitor current progress and identify potential problems. For example, a backlog reduction programme may be successfully reducing the number of older cases, but new cases may be entering the courts in larger numbers than before, obscuring or even jeopardising real progress. By having the data to make valid assessments of the courts' progress, court leaders can also identify and inspire those who are successful. Finally, these statistical assessments provide the kind of evidence that funding authorities, both within the country and internationally, have come to expect when they evaluate performance in the public sector.

A wide range of data is necessary to avoid misinterpretation of results. For example, changes in performance may be a result of changes in the mix of cases: dispositions might increase sharply on the criminal side but decline on the civil side, or serious criminal cases might fall further behind while judges build up their numbers by increasing dispositions of minor matters.

At the same time, it will be useful to identify some fairly simple and readily understandable measures of success, both for backlog reduction and delay reduction.

For backlog reduction, it is possible to use the balance sheets traditionally found and still maintained in many trial courts, showing pendencies at the beginning of a month, new institutions, disposals, and pendencies at the month's end. I have found it effective to compare the performance of individual courts against their performance one year before. In that way, there is an incentive not only to reduce pendencies but also to maintain or increase dispositions in comparison with the previous year. Furthermore, judges are not competing against each other's records, but can focus on the continuous improvement of their own performance. These figures can be aggregated to cover a number of criminal courts in a district, or a number of civil courts.

For delay reduction, I recommend a new but simple statistic that, Bob Hann, has labelled the "time-specific disposition rate". It is simply the percentage of cases disposed of within a particular period of time. For example, what percentage of the cases commenced within a specific period of time has been disposed of within 3 months of initiation? Within 6 months? Within 12 months? How does this compare with the percentages for the same periods 1 year or 2 years ago?

There are a number of advantages to using these time-specific disposition rates. Ordinarily, it is very difficult to obtain valid measures of the pace of litigation. When the pioneering research was conducted in the United States, the pace of litigation was measured by sampling from all dispositions in a particular period of time (usually a 12-month period).[8] However, doing this penalises a court that is effectively reducing its backlog, because that court will be targeting and often dismissing its oldest cases. The result would be an increase in dispositions, but also what appears to be a slower pace of litigation.[9] Furthermore, sampling only from dispositions ignores cases that may be sitting indefinitely among the court's pending cases perhaps because an accused has left the jurisdiction, or because a plaintiff has lost interest in or even settled its claim.

One way to avoid this difficulty is to measure the pace of litigation by sampling from all newly-initiated cases in a given year. However, while this sampling method is more valid in theory, it is relatively useless for assessing the current work of a court. For example, how far back would one need to go until arriving at a year when enough cases had been completed? Furthermore, if one compares the average time to disposition for cases initiated in 2004 with cases initiated in 2003, the result will invariably be that the 2003 dispositions take longer—because a larger number of them will have been completed over a longer period of time. Similarly, if we analyse the 2004 cases as of July 2005, and then analyse them a year later (in July 2006), we will inevitably find that they have taken longer to complete, because once again a longer time has elapsed during which more cases can be completed.

The proposed 'time-specific disposition rates' provide a measure of case progress that is not only more accurate, but is also more immediate and timely. If a new case management process is put in

8. Church, Thomas W. *et al.* (1978). "Justice Delayed: The Pace of Litigation in Urban Trial Courts", National Center for State Courts, Williamsburg, Virginia.
9. For example, I was asked late in 2002 by the World Bank to examine some statistics that appeared to be anomalous. After a major backlog reduction effort in the Philippines Court of Appeal, it still took 10 years to dispose of 90 per cent of the cases. A quick examination of the data suggested that if the backlog reduction initiative properly targeted the oldest cases, it would not be surprising that its success would lead to over 10 per cent of the cases being extremely old. The important question to ask was whether the court was handling its new appeals more expeditiously than the appeals it had received the year before (or two years before).

place on January 1, 2006, one can calculate a 6-month disposition rate (that is, the percentage of cases disposed of within 6 months of initiation) by December 31, 2006, that will cover half of the total cases for 2006 (that is, all cases initiated from January 1 until June 30). In the meantime, one can sample a comparable group of cases (that is, the same case types) initiated in the first half of 2005, and calculate what percentage of those cases were disposed of within 6 months. It is therefore possible for example to evaluate the impact of a Best Practices Court very early in its development.[10]

10. Time-specific disposition rates were used to evaluate the impact of early mandatory mediation in civil cases in Toronto and Ottawa during a pilot project in 1999-00. Not only could earlier case disposition be documented, but variations could be identified in the impact of mediation on several different case types.

7

The Problem of Court Congestion: Evidence from Indian Lower Courts

ARNAB KUMAR HAZRA and MAJA B. MICEVSKA

I

Introduction

Court congestion, legal costs, and delays are the problems most often complained about by the public in most countries, and thus often perceived as the most pressing (Buscaglia and Dakolias, 1996; Brookings Institution, 1990). India is not an exception. The popular press and court administrators from year to year described the condition of the Indian judiciary as "beyond redemption", "distressing", or "a huge problem". In 2001 the Union Minister of Law commented, "If there is one sector which has kept away from the reforms process, it is the administration of justice."[1]

In India congestion and delays are pervasive in administration of both civil and criminal justice. There are about 20 million cases pending in lower courts and another 3.2 million cases in High Courts.[2] According to Nagaraj (1995), a termination dispute that is contested all the way can take up to 20 years for disposal.[3] In the Principal Labour Court in Bangalore, for instance, 90 per cent of termination disputes are not disposed of within a year. Writ petitions in High Courts take about 8-10 years and in some courts nearly 20 years for disposal. The dockets of civil cases have been overcrowded and it may take years to get a trial on merit.

1. R. N. Malhotra Memorial Lecture on *India's Judicial Reforms*, at India International Centre, New Delhi, February 14, 2001.
2. There are also pending cases in various tribunals. However, the precise number of pending cases in the tribunals is not known.
3. If land is involved, it may take even longer time for disposal; a particular land-related case took more than 600 years to be resolved (Debroy, 2000).

Large backlogs of cases and delays may affect both the fairness and efficiency of the judicial system, which in turn weakens democracy, the rule of law, and the ability to enforce human rights. To solve the problem, the Indian government has launched a number of judicial reforms. In addition, economists and judicial scholars have paid increasing attention to the problem of court congestion (e.g., Dhawan, 1978; Khan *et al.*, 1997; Rao, 2001). The problem has been, however, the lack of systematic data on court congestion, performance and efficiency. Data of relatively good quality have been available only for the Supreme Court and High Courts, while data for lower courts were only presented in a highly aggregated form (e.g., at the country level). The lack of relevant data and solid empirical analysis has hampered policy prescriptions, which then invariably tended to lose focus. As a result, the attempts to solve the problem of court congestion have produced half-hearted results. Except for the Supreme Court, where arrears have decreased significantly, the other tiers of justice have been strained further.

This chapter aims to describe, analyse and explain the problem of court congestion in Indian lower courts and to provide data and advice to those designing, undertaking or evaluating legal and judicial reforms. In so doing, it focuses on a distinct set of indicators of judicial performance, including pending cases, clearance rates, and incoming cases. In particular, we have assembled a data set of congestion and performance indicators covering 27 states and union territories (UTs) over the period 1995-1999. An important advantage of our data set is that it allows us to abstract from an international platform and focus on internal differences of a decentralised judiciary. This guarantees a common institutional framework in which the judicial quality is measured and not different systems.[4]

In India, lack of judges has been historically cited as the main reason for court congestion and delays.[5] Indeed, the number of judges per capita has been low compared to other countries. For instance, data for 30 selected countries from the World Bank *Justice Sector at a Glance* database indicate that in 2000 the average number

4. Cross-country studies on judicial performance are often subject to criticism, as each country has its own legal framework and legal culture. The main problem is related to comparability of institutions: the jurisdiction of courts might not be the same in different countries; what is a commercial case in one country might be classified as criminal in another, etc.

5. See Literature Overview (this chapter), for more on this issue.

of judges per 100,000 inhabitants was 6.38.[6] The corresponding number for India is about 2.7 judges.[7] Without a closer analysis, however, one cannot draw the conclusion that the court system is to blame for the backlogs because it is under-staffed or under-funded. As our analysis shows, while the number of judges may still be important, this factor is hardly ever the only cause for the deficiencies.[8]

Our approach consists of the following steps. First, we construct several measures of court congestion. This allows us to identify the nature and level of court congestion across the Indian states, and to perform a number of checks on our results. Second, we ascertain structural and procedural problems of the court system by examining empirically the relative importance of both supply-and demand-side factors affecting court congestion. This helps to identify the reasons why some state judiciaries face larger caseloads or higher congestion rates than others. Third, having identified the most important determinants of court congestion, we attempt to pinpoint judicial areas in need of decongestion reform and the substantive nature of reforms that may be useful.

The rest of this chapter is organised as follows. Section II presents an overview of the Indian judicial system and reviews the literature on the congestion problem in Indian courts. A discussion of the data, the variables used in the study, conceptual issues related to variables introduced to measure court congestion, and the econometric analysis is given in Section III. Section IV concludes by summarising the main findings of our analysis and outlining strategies for further research.

II

Institutional Framework

A. Context

In terms of structure and procedure, India's legal system is based on English common law, codified laws, and non-codified religious and

6. The number of judges per 100,000 inhabitants ranged from 0.13 in Canada to 23.21 in the Slovak Republic, not showing significant correlation with GDP per capita. It should be noted, however, that for some of the countries the statistics covered only the federal court system (excluding the state or provincial court systems).
7. The actual number of judges is even lower, since the calculation is based on sanctioned judge strength, not accounting for vacancies. This is a point we will return to later in this chapter.
8. This is in line with Hammergren's (2002) conclusion that in Latin America the traditional, institutionalised remedies have not worked any miracles and occasionally have even made things worse.

customary laws. The judiciary is vertically structured with the Supreme Court at the top. The Supreme Court exercises appellate jurisdiction for final appeals in civil, criminal and administrative matters, as well as original jurisdiction in constitutional matters.[9] The state judiciary consists of a High Court and lower courts. The High Courts have the appellate jurisdiction for the lower courts in the respective state or assigned union territory.[10] They establish the administrative procedures for the lower courts and, through precedent, outline standards the interpretation of the Code of Civil Procedure and the Indian Evidence Act for civil and administrative cases and the Code of Criminal Procedure for criminal cases.

The lower judiciary consists of district, subordinate, sessions, and magisterial courts. The first two cater to civil cases and the latter two deal with criminal cases. In addition, there are other types of courts such as specialised tribunals (e.g., labour land, and tax tribunals), consumer courts, family courts, etc. The tribunals were created because they were thought to be faster than the court system, being free of cumbersome procedures. However, decisions taken in tribunals are not final, as there is always scope for appeal to the High Courts and the Supreme Court.

The system of alternative dispute resolution is in its nascent stage. In this regard, the system of *Lok Adalat*s is an interesting experiment. The *Lok Adalat*s were initiated in the late 1970s as a system of voluntary organistions for informal dispute resolution to provide cheap legal services to the poor.[11] There is also an additional layer of informal rural judiciary. *Panchayat*s are traditional institutions for individual dispute resolution, administrative issues, and allocation of common goods in rural areas. Unfortunately, there is no comprehensive statistical data on the use of *Lok Adalat*s or *Panchayat*s.[12]

9. The original jurisdiction of the Supreme Court also extends to any dispute between the Union and the states or between the states.

10. Only six of the High Courts (the High Courts of Chennai, Delhi, Himachal Pradesh, Jammu and Kashmir, Kolkata, and Mumbai) exercise original jurisdiction, i.e. civil suits can be directly filed in these courts, provided the monetary value of the suit is above a certain amount.

11. The Legal Services Authorities Act of 1987 regulates the *Lok Adalat*s as voluntary agencies utilisng arbitration and conciliation.

12. Examining court congestion in conjunction with alternative ways to settle disputes could provide valuable insights. However, what happens outside the courts system is hard to measure and is outside the scope of this study. We will just mention here that conciliation, mediation, and arbitration have never taken off in India. One of the problems with conciliation and mediation has been a lack of credible conciliators and mediators. Arbitration, on the other hand, has not been freed from the apron strings of courts. For a more extensive discussion on the alternative dispute resolution mechanisms in India, see Debroy (2000).

B. Literature Overview

Among academic attempts, only Dhawan (1978, 1986) studied extensively the problem of judicial delays in India. However, his work was confined to the Supreme Court and was conducted in the late 1970s and the early 1980s, a period when a considerable backlog of cases existed in the Supreme Court. Recently the Supreme Court has managed to drastically reduce its arrears and now the backlog there is trivial.

Apart from the work of Dhawan, the literature on court congestion is official, i.e., it is compiled in various reports by the Law Commission of India (LCI) and special committees appointed by the Government of India (GoI) of these reports tend to expound in detail various procedural aspects that the High Courts as well as the cases are subject to. In the process, the reports usually get caught in the quagmire of myriad procedural laws. This deters any policy maker who does not have a legal background. Therefore, our primary attempt has been to delineate the legal predicament from the problem of court congestion and present the enormity of the impasse in simple terms.

One of the first government efforts to study the efficient functioning of the judicial system was undertaken by the Civil Justice Committee in 1924, also known as the *Rankin Committee Report*. The report contained a "note on causes of delay in civil courts" and listed the insufficient judge strength in some of the High Courts as the main cause for delays. The High Court Arrears Committee, set up in 1949 under Justice S. R. Das, recommended that inordinate delays in filling up vacancies in the High Court bench should be avoided as much as possible. The Committee also advocated an immediate increase in the judge strength of High Courts, which had not been commensurate with the existing volume of work.

The LCI was constituted in 1955 to undertake the task of reviewing the system of judicial administration in all its aspects. The 14th Report of the LCI chided bureaucratic obstacles posed by the Ministry of Home Affairs in increasing the judge strength, which in its view had led to accumulation of arrears. It advocated a limited role of the state executive in the matter of appointment of judges and also mentioned the delays in filling up vacancies as well as unsatisfactory appointments in High Courts. The High Court Arrears Committee, appointed in 1972 under Justice J. C. Shah, expressed the same views (GoI, 1972). It recommended an increase of the permanent judgeships in High Courts and appointment of additional and *ad hoc* judges for clearing the arrears. These observations were reiterated in the 79th Report of the LCI (LCI, 1979) and in the 31st Report of the Estimates Committee (GoI, 1986a).

The 121st Report of the LCI (LCI, 1987) and the 124th Report of the LCI reiterated the earlier views on filling up vacancies expeditiously, augmenting the judge strength and appointing ad hoc judges to tackle the problem of arrears. The Report of the Arrears Committee (GoI, 1990), known as the *Malimath Committee Report*, also agreed with these views. It concluded that various reports "in one voice" highlighted the same factors, but "nothing worthwhile appears to have been done, resulting in worsening of the problem of arrears".

We can conclude that the main focus of the government reports has been on the supply-side solutions to the problem of court congestion. However, since recently, increasing attention has been paid to the need to tackle the problem from the demand side by looking at the areas wherein litigation is at the maximum, and then devising methods to curtail frivolous litigation. The Report of Justice Satish Chandra Committee (GoI, 1986b) and *The Malimath Committee Report* are dealing extensively with reforms that can lead to a decline in the litigation rates. Both reports have identified a host of demand-related reasons for the congestion problem in Indian courts, including the original civil jurisdiction of some High Courts, accumulation of first appeals, extensive use of second appeals, granting of unnecessary adjournments, etc.

In summary, the government reports have mainly pointed out the infrastructure bottlenecks associated with dispute resolution, as the main culprit. However, the reports have not tried to estimate the extent of infrastructure requirements. We next turn to an empirical estimation of the relative importance of both supply-and demand-side factors identified in the government reports as the most important causes of court congestion.

III

Data and Empirical Results

A. Data and Variables

The analysis that follows is mostly based on raw data provided by the Department of Justice of the Government of India. Data was available for 27 states and UTs during the period 1995-1999. We could collect a comprehensive data set of various judicial indicators, including civil and criminal caseloads, civil and criminal litigation, disposed cases, number of judges, vacancies, etc.[13] We were also able to compute indicators of judicial performance, such as clearance rates. Finally, we were able to differentiate among cases based on their duration. In the interest of brevity, only the results of the analysis using the data on civil and total cases are presented.[14]

Table 7.1 presents definitions and summary statistics of the variables used in this study. The first problem is how to normalise the variables in order to account for significant variations in population and judicial infrastructure across the Indian states and UTs. In the absence of data on the total number of transactions or disputes, or even the number of legal entities that may be eligible to file these cases, we use both the per capita and per judge numbers as the normalisation.[15]

We first focus on the dependent variable, i.e., on the court congestion. Of the 20 million pending cases in Indian lower courts, criminal cases constitute around two-thirds, while civil cases make up one-third of the total caseload.[16] About 63 per cent of civil cases are more than a year old (31 per cent are more than 3 years old), while 59 per cent of criminal cases are more than a year old (25 per cent are more than 3 years old). This implies that civil cases tend to be dragged on for longer periods. Since most civil cases are commercial disputes, this hampers the settlement of economic disputes, leading to higher transaction costs and general inefficiency in commercial activity.

---

13. In India the civil law cases include personal contract and property disputes, rather than just the narrower group of commercial cases.

14. The analysis based on criminal cases produces qualitatively similar results. These results are available from the authors upon request.

15. On the problem of normalisation for comparative purposes, see Ietswaart (1990).

16. For criminal cases, the magisterial courts account for about 90 per cent of the caseload.

Table 7.1

Variable Definitions, Sample Means and Standard Deviations

Variable	*Definition*	*Mean*	ó
LDT_pc	Total caseload per capita	0.020	0.017
1YT_pc	Number of cases older than a year per capita	0.011	0.010
LDCI_pc	Civil caseload per capita 0.007		0.006
1YCI_pc	Number of civil cases older than a year per capita	0.004	0.004
LDT_pj	Total caseload per judge (in '000)	1.625	1.354
1YT_pj	Number of cases older than a year per judge (in '000)	0.889	0.869
LDCI_pj	Civil caseload per judge (in '000)	0.590	0.421
1YCI_pj	Number of civil cases older than a year per judge (in '000)	0.353	0.285
CNRT	Total congestion rate (the ratio of total cases older than a year to total cases disposed)	0.762	0.567
CNRCI	Civil congestion rate (the ratio of civil cases older than a year to civil cases disposed)	1.244	0.987
JUD	Actual number of judges (the sanctioned judge strength minus vacancies) per 1,000 inhabitants	0.026	0.053
VAC	Vacancy (the ratio of unfilled judicial posts to sanctioned judge strength)	0.080	0.091
CLRT	Total clearance rate (the ratio of total cases disposed to total cases filed)	1.044	0.198
CLRCI	Civil clearance rate (the ratio of civil cases disposed to civil cases filed)	0.993	0.157
LTGT_pc	Total litigation (the number of total cases filed) per capita	0.017	0.018
LTGCI_pc	Civil litigation (the number of civil cases filed) per capita	0.004	0.004

contd. ...

contd. ...

Variable	*Definition*	*Mean*	σ
LTGT_pj	Total litigation (the number of total cases filed) per judge (in '000)	1.342	1.228
LTGCI_pj	Civil litigation (the number of civil cases filed) per judge(in '000)	0.354	0.313
Log(GDP)	Logarithm of real net state domestic product per capita	4.595	0.466

Note: The means and standard deviations are calculated for the pooled data set, i.e. across all the Indian states and UTs over the period 1995-99.

In our analysis we use several measures of court congestion. This allows us to identify the nature and level of court congestion across the Indian states and to perform robustness checks on our findings regarding the effect of different factors. Standard indicators of court congestion include caseload per capita (LDT_pc, LDCI_pc) and caseload per judge (LDT_pj, LDCI_pj). Although the caseload does not provide information on the delays within the system, this indicator usually reflects the situation perceived by the population. Namely, the more cases are pending in the system, the less a quick decision can be expected. Among the Indian states and UTs used in the study, Gujarat has the highest average backlog of 70 cases per 1,000 inhabitants, followed by Chandigarh and Delhi with pendency figures of 66 and 36 cases, respectively. With the number of cases per judge varying from about 7 in Arunachal Pradesh to 6,240 in Gujarat, the mean across the sample is 1,625; in the US state courts the mean is 1,164 (Dakolias, 1999).

The measures based on caseload per capita or per judge do not take into account that most cases require a certain minimum timeframe to be disposed. An operational definition of backlog would consider only cases still pending after a certain period of time. We assume that only cases older than a year constitute the 'real' backlog and construct two additional measures: the number of cases older than a year per capita (1YT_pc, 1YCI_pc) and per judge (1YT_pj, 1YCI_pj).[17] According to these measures, the problem of congestion is mainly concentrated in Goa, Gujarat, Chandigarh, Maharashtra, and West Bengal.

17. Additional research is needed to determine what time periods are reasonable for case resolution in the context of Indian judiciary.

Table 7.2

Correlation Matrix for Various Indicators of Court Congestion

Variable	LDT_{-pc}	$1YT_{-pc}$	LDT_{-pj}	$1YT_{-pj}$	CNRT	$LDC1_{-pc}$	$1YCI_{-pc}$	$LDCI_{-pj}$	$IYCI_{-pj}$	CNRCI
LDT_{-pc}	1.00	0.89**	0.93**	0.81**	0.18**	0.78**	0.77**	0.73**	0.78**	0.37**
$1YT_{-pc}$		1.00	0.87**	0.93**	0.40**	0.69**	0.80**	0.66**	0.82**	0.48**
LDT_{-pj}			1.00	0.92**	0.24**	0.65**	0.64**	0.78**	0.82**	0.38**
$1YT_{-pj}$				1.00	0.42**	0.54**	0.63**	0.67**	0.82**	0.51**
CNRT					1.00	0.08	0.25**	0.10	0.28**	0.81**
$LDCI_{-pc}$						1.00	0.95**	0.86**	0.84**	0.14
$1YCI_{-pc}$							1.00	0.78**	0.87**	0.30**
$LDCI_{-pj}$								1.00	0.93**	0.18*
$IYCI_{-pj}$									1.00	0.37**
CNRCI										1.00

Note: The correlation coefficients are calculated for the pooled data set, i.e. across all Indian states and UTs over the period 1995-1999.

** Correlation is significant at the .01 level.

* Correlation is significant at the .05 level.

The last measure we use is the congestion rate (CNRT, CNRCI) calculated as the ratio of backlog of cases older than a year to cases disposed. This measure reflects the time it would take a court to dispose of the cases older than a year given its current efficiency and clearance rates.[18] For instance, given the current productivity of courts in Bihar, it would take more than two years to dispose of their 'real' backlogs, while courts in Mizoram would need less than a month. For civil cases, the expected time for disposition of the 'real' backlog ranges from about a month in Mizoram to more than four years in Bihar.

Table 7.2 shows the correlation coefficients of the various measures of court congestion defined above. While the measures based on caseloads and the numbers of cases older than a year are strongly correlated among each other, their correlation with the congestion rates is much weaker. That is, the states with highest caseloads do not necessarily have the highest congestion rates. This anticipates the findings of our econometric analysis: the nature and level of court congestion differs across the states and, therefore, the set of judicial reforms to be considered in each state might also differ.

Our set of independent variables consists of indicators measuring various aspects of judicial performance. The first independent variable of interest is the number of judges per 1,000 inhabitants (JUD). In particular, we look into the effect of the actual judge strength defined as the difference between the sanctioned judge strength (the number of allowable or 'desirable' judgeships in the respective courts) and the number of vacancies. Assam, Uttar Pradesh and West Bengal have the lowest number of judges per capita.[19]

According to the Constitution, the power to appoint judges and determine the judge strength of High Courts is vested in the President. As for the lower courts, the Chief Justice of the respective High Court determines the number of judges and this figure is supposed to be calculated based on caseload, case content, case delay and other factors.[20] This implies that JUD could be endogenous with our

---

18. The ratio has no units and multiplying it by 12 gives the figures in months.

19. Unfortunately, it is not possible to break up the number of judges into judges that deal only with civil cases or only with criminal cases.

20. The Supreme Court authorises expansions in lower court judgeships suggested by the Chief Justice. As in other countries, politics plays a role in both the calculation of the number of judgeships by the Chief Justice and the court expansion decisions of the Supreme Court. See de Figueiredo *et al.*, (2000) for interesting findings on how much politics matters in comparison with caseload pressure when it comes to court expansion decisions of the Congress in the USA.

measures of court congestion. However, the Hausman test could not confirm any endogeneity and we did not instrument this variable.[21] This is understandably so since quantitative data on judicial backlogs and performance were, at least until recently, very poor. Thus, in reality the number of judges could not have been determined based on congestion data.

The second independent variable of interest is the percentage of vacancies (VAC). This is an important variable in the Indian context, since most Indian courts have vacancies and are very seldom at full strength. The problem is most severe in Delhi, where almost 40 per cent of the judicial posts are unfilled. One of the reasons for vacancies is that a large number of judges are appointed for chairmen of various commissions, committees, etc. Another, probably more important, reason is the delay in appointment of judges.[22] The Chief Justice should be in a position to determine when a vacancy is coming up and initiate the proposal well in advance. However, such advance planning is seldom done. Furthermore, district court appointments are made by the governor of the state, who consults with the Chief Justice. The governor has to check the integrity of the candidate and this also takes a long time. Indeed, there is a stipulated time of one month by which the governors have to give their opinion, but this deadline is seldom obeyed, nor is there any effort to strictly enforce it.[23]

The third independent variable is the clearance rate (CLRT, CLRCI), measured as the ratio of cases disposed to cases filed. This indicator is a measure of court productivity in dispute resolution and a determining factor in the growth of pending cases. Only when the clearance rate is greater than 100 per cent are the courts able to catch up on case backlogs. The total clearance rate (CLRT) varied significantly across the Indian states and UTs with some of the lowest values calculated for Andaman and Nicobar (70 per cent) and some of the highest in Manipur (242 per cent). However, for most states the

21. The Hausman test could not reject the null hypothesis regardless of whether we used the actual or the sanctioned judge strength in our specification.

22. *The Malimath Committee Report* deals extensively with various causes of vacancies.

23. Frequently, the governor recommends his own candidate and a new proposal has to be drawn up, delaying further the appointment process.

CLRT remained between 90 and 105 per cent. This is similar to the United States, which has a median clearance rate of 97 per cent in its state courts, and stands in sharp contrast to many developing countries that have much lower clearance rates and are not able to meet the demand for judicial services.[24]

The fourth independent variable is litigation (LTGT, LTGCI), which measures the number of new cases filed each year. The number of cases filed per capita or per judge is usually used to determine the demand on the court system, the expected caseload, and the ability of the court system to manage the national docket.[25] In India the situation is somewhat special, given the fact that courts are slow and overburdened, but nevertheless heavily used. The average number of filed cases per judge during the 1995-1999 period was about 1,300 which is again comparable to the US average.[26] The courts in Chandigarh have the highest workload, reporting on average 6,000 filed cases per judge.

Since the large backlogs and delays might be an additional incentive for litigants to misuse the court system by fraudulent litigation, the litigation variables could be endogenous.[27] Alternatively, as noted by Priest (1989), the extent of congestion could have an important influence on the motivations of the parties to settle or litigate a dispute. Indeed, the endogeneity of the litigation variables was confirmed by the Hausman test and they were instrumented for use in our regressions. We used the following instruments: cases disposed per capita (or per judge), population density, percentage of urban population, literacy rates, and *Panchayat*s per capita.

Finally, since the level of economic development might be an important explanatory variable, we control for per capita income, i.e., the logarithm of per capita net state domestic product in constant 1980 rupees.

---

24. Clearance rates in the US state courts vary from 35-266 per cent (Dakolias, 1999).
25. The number of cases filed per year may not reflect the full demand on the judiciary, however, as it does not account for those disputes not filed because of resource constraints of the parties, lack of confidence in the judicial system or other reasons.
26. In contrast, German judges receive only 176 cases per year (Dakolias, 1999).
27. Indeed, the early and very influential study by Zeisel *et al.*, (1959) has been largely criticised for its failure to account for endogeneity of litigation. That is, the authors presumed that the rate that disputes were brought to litigation was exogenous with respect to court congestion.

B. Econometric Analysis

Our data set combining time series and cross sections calls for a panel analysis. Although data are available only from 1995-1999, the data set includes the Indian states and UTs that display considerable variation, thus reducing the risk of spurious results and weak inferences. Tables 7.3 and 7.4 report the results of fixed effects regressions.[28] The state fixed effects account for unmeasured factors determining court congestion, such as a jurisdiction's local legal culture and its informal rules of litigation behaviour. The standard errors are listed in parentheses below the variables. All significance tests are two-sided asymptotic *t*-tests that are consistent in the presence of heteroskedasticity. Since autocorrelation was detected for the pending cases older than a year, the FGLS procedure was used (Greene, 2003) and AR(1) consistent standard errors are listed for regressions (2), (4), (8), and (10).

We first run a set of regressions to examine the effects of independent variables on total caseloads (Table 7.3). As shown by our estimates, the number of judges per capita appears to offer little in the way of explaining the total caseloads. The coefficient on JUD has a significantly (though only marginally) negative effect only on the congestion rates, while its effect on the other measures of court congestion is insignificant. This allows us to conclude that increasing the number of judges may not always solve the problem. Similarly, the coefficient on vacancies is mostly insignificant. However, eliminating the vacancies seems to be particularly important in jurisdictions with a large number of pending cases per judge.

The clearance rates have a significant and negative effect on caseloads per capita and per judge, as well as on the congestion rates. That is, court productivity is a very important factor in reducing court backlogs and congestion. The effect of CRLT on the backlog of cases older than a year is insignificant, indicating that the courts are focusing mainly on the new cases filed each year and are not addressing their pending cases. Indeed, during the period 1995-99, the courts tended to adjust their productivity only to the number of cases filed, not to their full caseloads. Such measures make it difficult to reduce the 'real'

28. The Hausman test for the fixed and random effects regressions confirmed that the fixed effects model is the better choice.

backlogs.[29] Other studies (Goerdt *et al.*, 1989; Dakolias, 1999) have also found that an increase in filed cases may cause courts to internally adapt to the change to maintain their rates of case resolution.[30]

As expected, the litigation has a positive and significant effect on the caseloads. This is consistent with the argument often raised by litigation economics that there are factors offsetting the effect of delay reduction programmes. The negative effect of litigation on the congestion

Table 7.3

Fixed Effects Estimates for Total Cases

	(1)	(2)	(3)	(4)	(5)	(6)
Dep. Var.	LDT_{-PC}	$1YT_{-PC}$	LDT_{-PJ}	$1YT_{-PJ}$	CNRT	CNRT
JUD	.0042	.0281	-.5144	-1.650	-6262*	-7.344*
	(.0639)	(.0634)	(5.647)	(5.640)	(3.882)	(3.899)
VAC	.0011	.0003	1.392**	.9367***	-.2212	.0487
	(.0072)	(.0037)	(.6326)	(.3494)	(.4354)	(.4368)
CLRT	-.0034**	-.0011	-2900**	-.1030	-.5315**	-.5039***
	(.0015)	(.0007)	(.1365)	(.0674)	(.0921)	(0.942)
$LTGT_{-pc.}$ [1)]	.4013***	.3782***	-	-	-11.70**	-
	(.0750)	(.0611)			(4.551)	
$LTGT_{-pj}$ [1)]	-	-	.4687***	.1532***	-	-.1969**
			(.1015)	(.0557)		(.0700)
Log(GDP)	-.0166***	-.0039	-1.210***	-.4619**	-.7906***	-.7919***
	(.0028)	(.0024)	(.2452)	(.2283)	(.1709)	(.1693)
No. obs.	132	105	132	105	132	132
Adj. R^2	.9748	.9778	.9698	.9672	.9156	.9166
	.0027	.0013	.2353	.1185	.1634	.1625

Note: In regressions 1, 3, 5 and 6, White heteroskedasticity-consistent standard errors are given in parentheses. Regressions 2 and 4 are estimated by FGLS procedure correcting for autocorrelation and AR(1) consistent standard errors are given in parentheses.

*** indicate significance at the 1 per cent level, ** at the 5 per cent and * at the 10 per cent level.

1) In regressions 1, 3, 5 and 6, the variable have been instrumented to correct for possible endogeneity bias. The instruments used were: cases disposed per capita (or per judge), population density, percentage of urban population, literacy rate, and *Panchayats* per capita.

---

29. The 1924 *Rankin Committee Report* was the first one to mention this problem: "So long as such arrears exist, there is temptation to which many presiding officers succumb, to hold back the heavier contested suits and devote attention to the lighter ones. The turnout of decisions in contested suits is thus maintained somewhere near the figure of institution, while the really difficult work is pushed back into the ground."

30. On the other hand, Priest (1989) argues that there is a reverse causality. According to him, there is some equilibrium level of court congestion. When reforms are implemented and delays decrease, more cases are filed in the courts thereby bringing congestion back toward an equilibrium level.

rate again confirms that the courts are adjusting their productivity merely to the number of filings.[31]

The negative coefficient on income can be explained by the fact that higher amount of available resources contributes to a higher clearance rate.[32] Alternatively, the size of the government increases

Table 7.4

Fixed Effects Estimates for Civil Cases

	(7)	(8)	(9)	(10)	(11)	(12)
Dep. Var.	$LDCI_{-PC}$	$1YCI_{-PC}$	$LDCI_{-PJ}$	$1YCI_{-PJ}$	CNRCI	CNRCI
JUD	-.0135	-.0286	-1.903	-3.787	-7.173	-8.239
	(.0159)	(.0305)	(1.733)	(2.760)	(6.333)	(7.151)
VAC	-.0017	-.0016	.2110	.1663	.2468	.5126
	(.0018)	(.0016)	(.1920)	(.1502)	(.7027)	(.7922)
CLRCI	-.0012**	.0002	-.1199**	.0116	-.3107*	-.3762
	(0005)	(.0005)	(.0500)	(.0459)	(.1843)	(.2063)
$LTGCI_{-PJ.}$ 1)	.2621***	.1219*	-	-	-183.3***	-
	(.0716)	(.0707)			(28.46)	
$LTGCI_{-PJ}$ .1)	-	-	.5985***	.0954*	-	-.9229***
			(.0634)	(.0557)		(.2617)
Log(GDP)	-.0018***	-.0021**	-.1769**	-.2162**	.1126	.2194
	(.0007)	(.0011)	(.7361)	(.1053)	(.2716)	(.3038)
No. obs.	132	105	132	105	132	132
Adj. R^2	9863	.9770	.9706	.9437	.9284	.9099
	.0007	.0005	.0720	.0509	.2650	.2973

Note: In regressions 7,9,11 and 12, White heteroskedasticity consistent standard errors are given in parentheses. Regressions 8 and 10 are estimated by FGLS procedure correcting for autocorrelation and AR (1) consistent standard errors are given in parentheses

*** indicate significance at the 1 per cent level, ** at the 5 per cent, at the 10 per cent level.

1) In regressions 7,9, 11 and 12, the variable have been instrumented to correct for possible endogeneity bias. The instruments used were: cases disposed per capita (or per judge), population density, percentage of urban population, literacy rate, and *Panchayats* per capita.

31. In a separate set of regression, the number of cases filed displayed a robustly positive effect on the disposal of cases. This effect is stronger than the positive effect of the filings on the backlog of cases older than a year, resulting in a negative effect of the filings on the congestion rate.

32. Indeed, regressions using clearance rates as a dependent variable revealed a significantly positive effect of the per capita income.

with the per capita income (Mueller, 2003). Thus, a higher per capita income can explain more judges per capita, higher clearance rates, and lower caseloads.

Table 7.4 presents yet a further effort to explain civil court congestion. The coefficients on JUD and VAC are insignificant, regardless of the measure of congestion used.[33] The clearance rates and volume of litigation have similar effects as in the case of total cases. The coefficient on income remains mainly negative and significant.

The results of our empirical analysis imply that the effect of any single reform measure will differ across state jurisdictions as the values of the various measures of court congestion across jurisdictions differ. Thus, for example, a doubling of judges within one jurisdiction may have a substantially different effect from a doubling of judges in another jurisdiction if there are differences between the jurisdictions in their congestion rates. Similarly, even within a single jurisdiction, a reform such as a doubling of judges in one year may have a substantially different effect than a doubling in a different year since the congestion rate changes over the years.

In summary, our estimates help us move away from the general 'one-size-fits-all' remedies for observed deficiencies in the court system and develop more focused approach tailored to the needs of individual states and UTs. Thus, while increasing the number of judges might lead to reduction in congestion rates, this solution is not likely to contribute to an improvement of the situation in the court systems facing large caseloads. On the other hand, elimination of vacancies seems particularly relevant for judiciaries with large caseloads per judge. The clearance rates have a well-defined, negative effect on both caseloads and congestion rates. This suggests that improvements in court productivity are crucial for reducing the congestion in all state judiciaries. Finally, reduction in litigation rates, coupled with an increased emphasis on resolving cases that are pending for a long time, is also likely to assist lower courts in every state to address their backlogs.

---

33. Note, however, that the coefficients on JUD and VAC have mostly the expected negative signs but have large standard errors. One reason for these insignificant results may be the measurement of the variables. We were not able to obtain data on the number of judges dealing exclusively (or mainly) with civil cases, or to measure the time the judges spend on resolving civil cases.

IV

Conclusion

Long delays in processing cases are common in the Indian judicial system. This is despite the fact that for more than 50 years judges, lawyers, and policy makers in India have experimented with ways to speed the processing of civil and criminal cases. Solutions have been usually sought in such structural reforms as increases in the number of judges and changes in procedures. Most of the delay reduction programmes, however, have ended in failure. We argue here that a possible explanation for the failure of these programmes is that they tended to give general prescriptions regardless of the nature and level of court congestion facing individual states and UTs.

In this chapter, we conduct an empirical analysis of the congestion in Indian lower courts. Econometric analysis of institutions, such as the judiciary, has faced serious criticism since institutions tend to reflect the norms of the society they exist in. However, our data set covering 27 Indian states and UTs over the period 1995-1999 guarantees a common institutional framework in which the judicial quality is measured and not different systems.

We use several measures to capture court congestion. These include caseloads per capita and per judge, the number of cases older than a year per capita and per judge, and congestion rates calculated as the ratio of cases older than a year to cases disposed. We can conclude that the Indian state judiciaries differ with respect to the nature and level of congestion they face. We can also identify the reasons why some judiciaries are more congested than others. The results show that large number of judges per capita is negatively related to congestion rates, while vacancies have significantly positive effect on caseloads per judge. Court productivity captured by the clearance rates has a significant and negative effect on both caseloads and congestion rates and seems to be crucial for the effectiveness of congestion-reduction programmes. Finally, judiciaries with lower litigation rates display relatively better performance with respect to current caseloads, but are not efficient in addressing the 'real' backlogs of cases pending for more than a year.

Based on our findings, we discuss remedial measures, which can essentially be in two directions. The first involves improvements in infrastructure and court productivity, while the second involves adoption of procedurally and substantively efficient rules. Besides these remedies, a well-defined programmes for judicial reform needs to include a host of considerations that we have not attempted to canvass, but that would merit additional research. These include: the redefinition and/or expansion of legal education programmes and training for students, lawyers, and judges; increasing the availability and efficiency of ADR mechanisms; the existence of judicial independence (i.e., budget autonomy, transparency of the appointment process, and job security) coupled with a transparent disciplinary system for court officers; etc.

In addition, future research could look into whether the findings of this study are relevant across national legal systems. As emphasised by Posner (1998), legal reform is an important part of the modernisation process of poor countries. Probably the most important lesson emerging from our study is that a well-conceived legal reform programme should be based on solid empirical evidence. Empirical analysis is also crucial for evaluating progress in court performance, planning for future needs, and strategising for new reform efforts. Although every court system is unique, reformers in other countries can look for appropriate data to identify the nature of congestion, highlight potential pitfalls of justice systems, or even suggest new approaches for delay reduction that are suitable for their unique local legal culture.

Finally, future study of courts as agents of legal government could move away from broad macro analysis of congestion, proceed to the micro level and actually examine the types of cases that are being over-litigated and where the accumulation of arrears has taken place. Analysing court cases, category by category, and exploring the costs and benefits of different types of cases that are litigated, are the subject of a next stage of our research.

Bibliography

Brookings Institution (1990). *Justice for All: Reducing Costs and Delay in Civil Litigation*, Brookings Institution, Washington, DC.

Buscaglia, Edgardo and Maria Dakolias (1996). "Judicial Reform in Latin American Courts: The Experience in Argentina and Ecuador", *World Bank, Technical Paper No. 350*, World Bank, Washington, DC.

Clark, David S. (1990). "Civil Litigation Trends in Europe and Latin America since 1945: The Advantage of Intracountry Comparisons", *Law and Society Review* 24, pp. 549-569.

Dakolias, Maria (1999). "Court Performance Around the World: A Comparative Perspective", *World Bank Technical Paper* No. 430, World Bank, Washington, DC.

Debroy, Bibek (2000). "Some Issues in Law Reform in India", in Jean-Jacques Dethier (ed.), *Governance, Decentralization and Reform in China, India and Russia.* Dordrecht, Kluwer Academic Publishers, The Netherlands.

Dhawan, Rajeev (1978). *The Supreme Court Under Strain: The Challenge of Arrears,* M. N. Tripathi Pvt. Ltd, Bombay.

———. (1986). *Litigation Explosion in India,* Bombay: M. N. Tripathi Pvt. Ltd.

de Figueiredo, M. John, Gerald S. Gryski, Emerson H. Tiller and Gary Zuk, (2000). "Congress and the Political Expansion of the U.S. District Courts", *American Law and Economics Review* 2(1), pp. 107-25.

Goerdt, John, Chris Lomvardias, Geoff Gallas, and Barry Mahoney (1989). *Examining Court Delay: The Pace of Litigation in 26 Urban Trial Courts, 1987,* National Center for State Courts, Williamsburg.

Government of India (1972). *High Court Arrears Committee,* Supreme Court of India, New Delhi.

———. (1986a). *The Thirty First Report of the Estimates Committee to the Parliament,* Ministry of Law, Justice and Company Affairs, New Delhi:

———. (1986b), *Report of Justice Satish Chandra Committee,* Ministry of Law, Justice and Company Affairs, New Delhi.

———. (1990). *Report of the Arrears Committee.* Supreme Court of India, New Delhi.

———. (1989-90 to 1999-2000). *Annual Report of the Ministry of Law, Justice and Company Affairs,* Ministry of Law, Justice and Company Affairs, New Delhi.

Greene, William (2003). *Econometric Analysis,* Prentice-Hall Inc., New Jersey.

Hammergren, Linn (2002). "Fifteen Years of Judicial Reform in Latin America: Where We Are and Why We Haven't Made Any Progress", unpublished manuscript.

Ietswaart, Hellen F.P. (1990). "The International Comparison of Court Caseloads: The Experience of the European Working Group", *Law and Society Review* 24 (2), pp. 571.

Khan, Amir Ullah, Pushpa Sharma and Aparna Rajagopal (1997). *Identification of Bottlenecks in Judicial Procedure,* Allied Publishers, New Delhi.

Law Commission of India (1958). *The Fourteenth Report on Reform of Judicial Administration,* Ministry of Law, Justice and Company Affairs, New Delhi.

———.(1979). *The Seventy Ninth Report on Delays and Arrears in High Courts and Other Appellate Courts.* Ministry of Law, Justice and Company Affairs. New Delhi.

———.(1987). *The One Hundred and Twenty First Report on a New Forum for Judicial Appointments.* Ministry of Law, Justice and Company Affairs. New Delhi.

———. (1988). *The One Hundred and Twenty Fourth Report on High Court Arrears: A Fresh Look.* Ministry of Law, Justice and Company Affairs, New Delhi.

Milgrom, Paul R., Douglass C. North, and Barry W. Weingast (1990). "The Role of Institutions in the Revival of Trade: The Law Merchant, Private Judges, and the Champagne Fairs", *Economics and Politics* 2(1), pp.1.23.

Mueller, Dennis C. (2003). *Public Choice III,* Cambridge University Press. Cambridge, NU.

Nagaraj, V. (1995), "Labour Laws", in N.R. Madhava Menon and Bibek Debroy (eds.), *Legal Dimensions of Economic Reforms,* Allied Publishers, pp. 31-80, New Delhi.

Posner, Richard A. (1998). "Creating a Legal Framework for Economic Development", *The World Bank Research Observer* 13 (1), pp. 1-11.

Priest, George L. (1989). "Private Litigants and the Court Congestion Problem", *Boston University Law Review* 69(2), pp. 527-59.

Rao, Bathula V. (2001). *Crisis in Indian Judiciary,* Legal Aid Centre, Hyderabad.

Zeisel Hans, Hans Kalven, and Bernard Buchholz (1959). *Delay in the Court,* Greenwood Press Publishers.

8

Legal Reform and Economic Development in India: Case of Alternative Dispute Resolution

NANDAN NAWN

"The course of justice is like the alternation of the seasons. There is the hope and inspiration of spring and the achievement and reward of summer, and there is the descent and sacrifice of autumn and the moral and intellectual destitution of winter, and the changes in our jurisprudence will come accordingly in spite of us, however much we may be the appointed instruments in their consummation" (Gane, 2005).

"Market economies tend to rely on firm support from appropriate legal rules, and these rules can, often enough, greatly aid market-based economic development" (Sen, 2003).

Introduction

Conflicts have been inevitable to human life since time immemorial. Likewise, techniques for conflict resolution have been developed, as can be seen from ancient historical records and religious scriptures. One may question the authenticity of the latter, but the very fact of inclusion of the process of dispute resolution confirms the existence of the same in the earlier societies. Be it negotiation between Eve and the snake over the apple in the *Bible*, or between Muhammad and God on the number of times that followers ought to pray, or mediation by God between Abraham and Sara when she wanted Abraham to expel Hagar and her son, resolution of disputes with or without the assistance of a third party was part and parcel of human existence.[1]

1. Information obtained from UNESCO, interpretation is of the author.

In a celebrated text on statecraft written roughly 2000 years ago, Kautilya, the master tactician, pronounced four methods for dealing with conflicts along with the difficulties in the adoption of each. The methods are *sama* (adopting a conciliatory attitude), *dana* (placating with rewards and gifts), *bheda* (sowing dissention among enemies) and *danda* (using force). Further he stated, that *dana* is twice as difficult as *sama, bheda* is thrice difficult and *danda* four times (Kautilya, 1987: 113-4). Kautilya was of the opinion that disputes involving immovable property "shall be decided by the elders of the neighbourhood. If there is no unanimity, the decision shall be made either by majority or by adopting the opinion of those honest people who are acceptable to both parties.... Where the claims of all the disputants fail, the property shall revert to the Crown" (p. 432-33).

With the passage of time, this simplistic juridical system gave way to a more complex, elaborate, ritualistic, expensive and time-consuming one. Rise in population and increase in economic activity gave birth to conflicts that were qualitatively different and quantitatively huge, which led to a system where access to justice, especially for the poor, has become a constraint in the path of development. Moreover, with almost every developing country following a process of economic reform, with increasing number of 'economic transactions towards the market domain and shifting away from public administrative spheres of the state', (Buscaglia, 2000) need for court services has been unprecedented.

Beginning in early 1970s in the United States,[2] alternative forms of justice delivery systems are being suggested, formulated and implemented. They are arbitration, negotiation, mediation, conciliation and mix of two or more of these processes. In India, while at least one of these processes existed as per law, since the end of 19th century, widespread use of these techniques can be seen only towards the end of 20th century, almost 100 years later. Whatever be

---

2. In 1976, then Chief Justice Burger, convened The National Conference on the Causes of Popular Dissatisfaction with the Administration of Justice. The papers presented at the conference were published in a bound volume entitled *The Pound Conference: Perspectives on Justice in the Future.* Prof. Frank Sander in his speech at the conference suggested that dispute resolution required flexible and diverse processes to meet the systematic requirements of entire categories of certain types of cases and also the unique circumstances presented in particular cases. His remarks are often credited with the birth of ADR movement.

the form of the justice delivery system, involvement of the state is common. Be it providing incentives to the potential disputants for choosing the appropriate system, binding the 'verdict' or award, developing the human resource, creating newer and better institutions, it is necessary for the state to take the initiative in the correct direction. All these take time, and any wrongly designed system will not only result in unnecessary conflicts of interests in the short run, but will also develop suspicion and undermine the credibility among the stakeholders that will defeat the very purpose of the 'alternate' system.

While Section I will provide an introduction to the alternative approaches, Section II will shed light on the appropriateness of a system using the economic approach. Section III of the chapter will provide a broad overview on the developments in India.

I

Disputes that are culmination of an unresolved conflict can be resolved through three approaches, as the literature suggests: power-based, rights-based and interest-based. Costs and benefits associated with these approaches vary greatly. Costs can be measured by using four broad based criteria: transaction costs (such as the time, money, and emotional energy expended in disputing), satisfaction with procedures and outcomes, long-term effect of the procedures and outcomes on the parties' relationship, and recurrence of disputes.[3] In terms of cost, interest-based ones are more cost effective than the rights-based ones, while the latter is more cost effective than power-based ones. Examples of power-based approaches are war, strikes, lockouts, ignoring the minority, etc. while that of right-based ones are courts, binding arbitration and of interest-based ones are negotiation, mediation, etc. All societies have experience in dealing with all the three approaches, beginning with power, followed by rights and then interest based. While the transformation from one to other took a much longer time in oriental societies, the rapid

3. Ury, W.L., J.M. Brett and S.B. Goldberg (1993). *Getting Disputes Resolved: Designing Systems to Cut the Costs of Conflict*, Program on Negotiation, Harvard Law School and Murray, J.S. (1990). "Dispute Systems Design, Power, and Prevention", *Negotiation Journal* 105, as quoted in IoG, p. 13.

change could be seen in the western societies more prominently in the last one hundred years.

The shift in focus from power-based approaches to rights-based ones is obvious in a democratic society, and thus a reproduction is avoided here. What is more interesting is the reasons related to cost,[4] quality of decision,[5] satisfaction of disputants, etc. behind the choice of interest-based approaches over others. One may note however that not all categories of disputes are suitable for every type of resolution approaches due to reasons to be stated later. An efficient dispute resolution system may use all the three approaches with use of power-based ones in the least proportion, right-based ones higher than the previous and interest-based approaches being used in the highest number of disputes.[6]

While a society is better off in having largest number of disputes being resolved through mediation and conciliation it is important to create conditions for them. It cannot happen that one fine day all the litigants will choose a particular system of dispute resolution. Present euphoria over the various forms of ADR misses that point precisely. Before proceeding further however, it is important to classify the various forms of ADR. One way is to classify them on the nature of the processes themselves, that is to segregate ADRs as Preventive, Negotiated, Facilitated, Fact-finding, Advisory, Non-binding and Imposed ones.[7] One can classify the entire spectrum, as can be seen in the figure below.[8]

---

4. "The modern ADR movement originated in the United States in the 1970s, spurred by a desire to avoid the cost, delay, and adversarial nature of litigation" (World Bank, *Legal Institutions of the Market Economy, http://www1.worldbank.org/publicsector/legal/adr.htm)*.
5. Research suggests 90 per cent satisfaction in Mediation type approaches, IoG, *op. cit.*
6. IoG, *op. cit.*, p. 7.
7. IoG, *op. cit.*, p. 4.
8. Figure 2, IoG, *op. cit.* p. 9 which is taken from Costantino and Merchant (1996). "Designing Conflict Management Systems: A Guide to Creating Productive and Healthy Organisations", (San Francisco: Jossey-Bass).

Figure 8.1

Spectrum of ADR Techniques

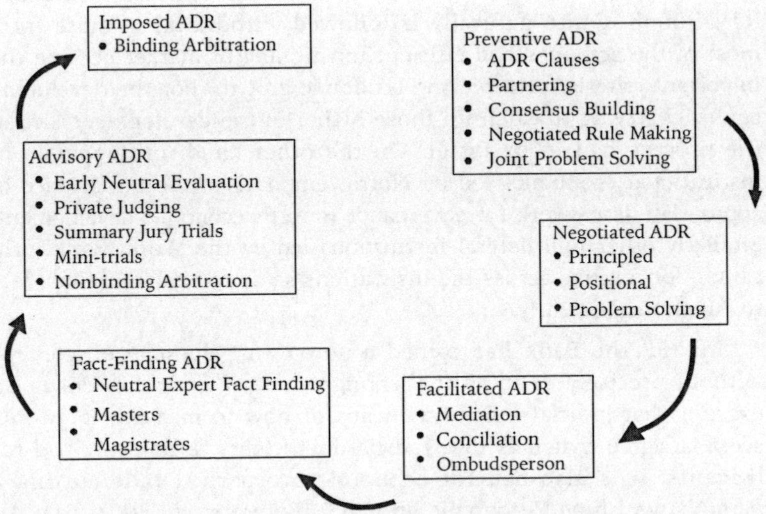

One may note that adversial process of litigation and its alternative *avatar*s are not suitable for each and every type of dispute. Be it through enactment of new laws, or using the market mechanism of increasing the transaction cost, the litigants will opt for a particular mode depending on certain characteristics. It is important to identify the same for any feasible and practical judicial reform.

Today ADR is not confined to the commercial or labour cases but can be seen in all areas of civil jurisdiction. In USA, it is found in Antitrust, entertainment, health care, construction, natural resources, intellectual property, telecommunication, technology industries, etc (Main, 2005: 11, fn. 39). In India, *Lok Adalat*s are taking up "cases involving mutation of lands, land *patta*s, forest lands, bonded labour, land acquisition cases, matrimonial and family disputes, bank loan cases, etc." (Ramaswamy, 1997: 97). Moreover, pre-decided arbitration in commercial cases are well known, and is adopted in many countries including India.

II

Since the late eighties and early nineties in general, and more specifically with the end of the Cold War, capitalism has established its triumph. Quite naturally it followed withdrawal of state from most of the activities and efficient functioning of market became the important criteria for achieving economic growth. For the developing countries, trying to catch up those higher in the development ladder, the process had to be faster. On the other hand, protagonists of institutional economics led by North, emphasised the importance of appropriate framework for governance towards economic development. Similarly other multilateral institutions led by the World Bank were calling for reforms across the institutions so as to enable the markets to function efficiently.

Indeed, the Bank has coined a new term, "judicial efficiency" without precisely defining it. "Though there is little consensus on exactly what judicial efficiency means or how to measure it, people seem to agree that it is low. Judicial inefficiency is not only bad for litigants, it is also bad for economic prosperity, undercutting a nation's wealth and economic growth." (Botero *et al.*, 2003: 61). An efficient judicial system shall provide speedy redress and less expensive court services to the parties involved. In an efficient judicial system, basic elements include: relatively predictable outcomes within the courts; accessibility to the courts by the population regardless of income level; reasonable time to disposition; and adequate court-provided remedies.

It was also held that there exist strong connections between efficient judiciaries and economic development. One, according to this view, efficient courts will reduce the possibilities of abuse by the government and uphold the rule of law, and second, by creating an atmosphere conducive to transactions between parties which is important for a market-based economy. For judicial reform there are plenty of schools of thought, (Botero *et al.*, 2003) ranging from adequate funding to simplifying procedures. Common elements of different schools for enhancing the efficiency of the judiciary are reduction of the delay,[9] decrease in the backlog, removing the hurdle

9. Way back in 1982, one District Chief Judge of California, USA, found the following sources of pre-trial cost and delay: (1) complex and unclear pleading practice, (2) client's feelings of alienation from the legal process, (3) poor and indirect communication between the parties, etc. (Rosenberg and Folberg, 1994).

for the poor to access justice and so on. Alternative forums for dispute resolution are expected to improve the competition and enhance the choice among the litigants, which will increase the judicial efficiency. Further, these forums along with small claims courts and specialised courts, are expected to reduce the workload of the formal courts. However, one may note that, not all types of disputes are suitable for ADR mechanisms, and more specifically and correctly one can identify the areas, higher will be the efficiency of the justice delivery system.

For the purposes of identifying types of disputes suitable for alternative means it is useful to distinguish *ex-ante* (before the disputes arise) and *ex-post* agreements (after the disputed arise) between conflicting parties and identifying possible source of benefits to both the parties. Shavell (1995) has argued for incentives provided by state in order to induce potential disputants to opt for alternative mechanisms to formal court proceedings. Commercial arbitration is an example of *ex-ante* agreement, and their role of state in increasing efficiency is minimum except developing the human resource. Potential litigants for their own private benefit will opt for the alternative saving the formal court from the trouble of settling the dispute. On the other hand, role of the state for motivating litigants for *ex-post* agreements is tremendous.

Further, one can also distinguish two types of cases in terms of suggesting alternatives as a choice in contrast to the conventional justice delivery systems. That is, whether the ADR would facilitate the existing court procedure or provide a completely separated alternative. Secondly, for disputes involving substantial public rights and duties, whether the ADR mechanism will be suitable at all (Edwards, 1986: 671). One may conclude this section with a cautionary note. That is, though this mechanism, which was intended to be flexible, but "is now becoming as complex, law-laden, and law-ridden as the traditional practice of law" (Menkel-Meadow, 2001).

III

"Don't stand by the water and long for fish; go home and weave a net."

— Chinese Proverb.

Various alternative mechanisms tasted success in varying degrees in western countries, where the system had been in place for some time. But blindly following any one country might not result in achieving the objective, as happened in the Law and Development movement. For fostering development through law, a programme was started in 1960s involving academicians from leading law schools of the North America, sponsored by number of United States based donor agencies and private donors. The idea was to reform the judicial systems and substantive laws of countries in Asia, Africa, and Latin America by exporting the US legal system wholesale to them. The movement had an early death—within a decade or so. Though there existed differences over the details, the dominant view of flag-bearers, which included practitioners and theorists was that law reform could lead social change—that law itself was an engine of change. The assumption was that law is central to the development process and that law was an instrument that could be used to reform society and that lawyers and judges could serve as social engineers. The protagonists failed to acknowledge that such reforms, even if successfully implemented, would have minimal effect at best, and that too at a superficial level; that cannot assume the proportions of a 'movement'. Post-mortem of this failed endeavour provides interesting insights for any aspects of future judicial reforms, including the one under discussion.[10] Indeed it is important to learn from the mistakes of the other countries in implementing ADRs.

Experience in other countries further suggests that apart from benefits,[11] there exist several limitations to alternative dispute resolutions that are applicable to all the types.[12] First, the awards in ADR processes are not published and even otherwise cannot be used as precedent. Second, similar disputes may be resolved in different manners depending on the local norm or custom; consistency may be the casualty. Third, ADR depends heavily on the established legal

---

10. The interested reader may see Messick (1999).
11. See Appendix A-8.1 for a comparison between Arbitration and Litigation.
12. USAID, 1998.

standards; in the absence there exists possibility of award reflecting the power imbalance, and thus it is completely unsuitable for addressing discrimination, human rights, etc. which are part of the existing social construct.[13] Fourth, in cases of extreme power imbalances ADR programmes do not work well; similarly, for protecting group or class rights, formal judicial procedure will produce better result. Fifth, as the awards are not public, there is no deterrent, educational or even motivational effect of the ADR programmes. In sum, ADR can at best be used for clearing the backlog of dockets, and can in no way substitute or even supplement the formal court procedures.

For any successful mechanism, alternative or conventional alike, a number of steps are required to be taken by the state. The present euphoria over *Lok Adalat*s is exclusive to selected areas, namely those related to family and motor accident cases *ex post* and commercial cases where parties themselves bind them for resolving disputes through arbitration. There are number of limitations faced by *Lok Adalats* (Chodosh *et al.*, 1998). First, in contrast to other countries like the United States, there is no obligatory mediation and any conciliation requires consent of both parties or the decision by the court. In other words, the advantages of early neutral evaluation in terms of saving time cannot be obtained. Second, any form of mediation is absent at present; arbitration and conciliation are the two forms which are available. Further conciliation process involves lawyers normally, and the parties are somewhat insulated from the process. Third, the procedures for ADR mechanisms are complex enough to keep the parties themselves approaching the forums for resolution of dispute. Fourth, already number of *Lok Adalat*s are facing backlog, and there is no mechanism to prevent either side from buying time in conciliation. Even "arbitration, once considered an alternative to litigation, is now afflicted by the same problems of cost, delay, complexity, and dependence on legal representation."[14]

---

13. Women did not like the *Lok Adalat*s for family disputes. Resolution of disputes were based on local norms and customs, and not on rights *per se*. So were those from lower castes for similar reasoning. Whitson, Sarah Leah, Spring 1992, 'Neither Fish, Nor Flesh, Nor Good Red Herring' Lok Adalats: "An Experiment in Informal Dispute Resolution in India", *Hastings International and Comparative Law Review*, 15 (3), pp. 391-445, as cited in USAID 1998, p. 22.

14. World Bank, "Alternative Dispute Resolution", *http://www1.worldbank.org /publicsector/ legal/adr.htm.*

In order to make it more inclusive, the government in India needs to develop human resources first, and then provide adequate financial resources for infrastructure and the like. Most importantly, the process of development of neutrals requires greatest attention, and institutionalisation of the same would be a welcome move.

Bibliography

Anderson, James H., David S. Bernstein, and Cheryl W. Gray (2005). *Judicial Systems in Transition Economies: Assessing the Past, Looking to the Future*, The World Bank, Washington DC.

Botero, Juan Carlos, Rafael La Porta, Florencio Lopez-de-Silanes, Andrei Shleifer, and Alexander Volokh (2003). "Judicial Reform", *World Bank Research Observer*, 18(1), Spring, pp. 61-88.

Buscaglia, Edgardo (2000). "Law and Economic Development", *Encylopedia of Law and Economics*, Edward Elgar.

Chodosh, Hiram E., Stephen A. Mayo, A.M. Ahmadi and Abhishek M. Singhvi (1998). "Reform of the Indian Civil Justice System: Limitation and Preservation of the Adversarial Process", *http://www.isdls.org/ law_review_article_india.html.*

Gane, Douglas M. (2005). "The Birth of a New Equity," *The Solicitors' Journal & Weekly Reporter*, 67, p. 572, (May 26, 1923), quoted in Main.

Kaufman, Daniel (2002). "Transparency, Incentives and Prevention (TIP) for Corruption Control and Good Governance: Empirical Findings, Practical Lessons and Strategies for Action based on International Experience", Background Chapter for Qinghua University-Carnegie Conference on Economic Reform and Good Governance: Fighting Corruption in Transition Economies, Beijing, 11-12 April, *http://www.worldbank.org/ wbi/governance/pdf/quinghua_chapter.pdf.*

Edwards, Harry T. (1986). "Alternative Dispute Resolution: Panacea or Anathema?", *Harvard Law Review*, 99 (3), January, pp. 668-684.

IOG (1999). "Dispute Resolution Systems: Lessons from other Jurisdictions", The Institute on Governance, Ottawa, Canada, *http://www.iog.ca/publications/dispute_res.pdf.*

Kautilya (1987). *The Arthashastra*, Edited, rearranged, translated and introduced by L N Rangarajan, Peguin Books.

Main, Thomas O. (2005). "ADR: The New Equity", Chapter 479, ExpressO Preprint Series, Berkeley Electronic Press, *http://law.bepress.com/expresso/eps/479.*

Medaglia, M. Elizabeth (2004). "Alternative Dispute Resolution: An Overview", Prepared for and presented to the Minority Corporate Counsel Association, 3rd Annual CLE Expo, April 2, Chicago, Illinois, US, *www.jackscamp.com/publications/ Alternative_Dispute_Resolution_An_Overview.pdf.*

Menkel-Meadow, Carrie (2001). "Ethics in ADR: The Many "Cs" of Professional Responsibility and Dispute Resolution", Georgetown University Law Center 2001 Working Chapter Series in Public Law and Legal Theory, *Working Chapter No. 288805*, and subsequently published in *Fordham Urban Law Journal*, Volume 28, April 2001, *www.ssrn.com* (chapter ID 288805).

Menon, N.R. Madhava (2004). "Taking power to the people", *The Telegraph*, August 23, Kolkata Edition.

Messick, Richard E. (1999). "Judicial Reform and Economic Development: A Survey of the Issues", *The World Bank Research Observer*, 14 (1), February, pp. 117-136.

Ramaswamy K. (1997). "Settlement of disputes through *Lok Adalat* is one of the effective alternative dispute resolution (ADR) on statutory basis", in P. C. Rao and William Sheffield, eds., *Alternative Dispute Resolution: What it is and how it works*, The International Centre for Alternative Dispute Resolution and Universal Law Publishing, Delhi.

Rosenberg, Joshua D. and H. Fay Folberg (1994). "Alternative Dispute Resolution: An Empirical Analysis", *Stanford Law Review*, 46(6), pp. 1487-1551.

Sen, Amartya (2003). "Law, Economics and Social Change," Inaugural Keshab Chandra Basu Memorial Lecture, the West Bengal National University of Juridical Sciences, Kolkata, 20th December.

Shamir, Yona (2003). *Alternative Dispute Resolution and their Application*, Technical Documents in Hydrology, UNESCO, IHP and World Water Assessment Programme, PC+CP Series, No. 7, *www.unesco.org/water/wwap*.

Shavell, Steven (1995). "Alternative Dispute Resolution: An Economic Analysis", *The Journal of Legal Studies*, 24 (1), January, pp. 1-28.

Tsuru, Kotaro (2003). "Toward Enhancing Judicial Efficiency - Role of ADR as Engine of Judicial Reform", *Economics Review*, 16, *http://www.rieti.go.jp/en/special/economics-review/016.html*.

USAID (1998). "Alternative Dispute Resolution Practitioners' Guide", Technical Publication Series, Center for Democracy and Governance, Bureau for Global Programs, Field Support, and Research, U.S. Agency for International Development, Washington DC

Wolski, Bobette (1998). "The Model of Dispute Resolution Procedure for Australian Workplace Agreements: A Dispute Systems Design Perspective", *Bond law* Review, 10, pp. 7-41, *http://www.bond.edu.au/law/blr/vol10-1/2-Wolski.pdf*

Appendix A-8.1

Comparison Between Arbitration and Litigation

Litigation	Arbitration
1. Public process.	1. Private process.
2. Any party can institute a litigation.	2. Initiation of arbitration under an agreement.
3. Adversarial procedure.	3. May be less adversarial.
4. Formal and inflexible.	4. Less formal and more flexible
5. Rules and procedures strictly followed.	5. Simpler procedures, no formal rules of evidence.
6. Broad discovery.	6. Discovery limited to some documents, no interrogatories or depositions.
7. Parties have no voice in selection of adjudicators (judge or jury).	7. Generally adjudicators are selected by parties.
8. Adjudicators are generalists.	8. Adjudicators are selected on the basis of their qualification and expertise.
9. Adjudicators apply the law; decisions to set precedents.	9. Adjudicators pay less attention to law. Their decisions do not formally set precedents.
10. Appeal against decisions	10. No appeal. Vacation of award generally limited to arbitrator's misconduct and bias.
11. Remedies may include compensatory and punitive damages injunctive relief.	11. Arbitrators normally are empowered to grant compensatory damages, including provisional relief.
12. High costs.	12. Usually reduced costs.
13. Delayed justice.	13. Quick justice.

Source: International Council for Alternative Dispute Resolution, *http://www.icadr.org/services2.html.*

9

Pursuing Best Practice Levels of Judicial Productivity—An International Perspective on Case Backlog and Delay Reduction in India

BARRY WALSH

Introduction

Unlike some British imperial legacies, such as English literature and the sport of cricket, judicial and court administration in India bears important dissimilarities to its British progenitor. These differences are substantial. Some of them, however, are subtle and seem to gain scant recognition, even to many who practice in India as judges, advocates or commentators on the Indian court system. The direction for improving the Indian court system is to be found by recognising those differences and the lessons they may offer.

The essential thesis of this chapter is that the practices and associated expectations of participants in the Indian court system are significantly different from most other countries who have inherited their legal systems from the British; and that those differences will help to identify the strategies which may be pursued in overcoming the case backlog and delay problem in India. Most of the literature on the performance of Indian courts tends to rely on Indian experience and aspirations rather than on international comparisons. The conclusion this chapter offers, however, is that comparisons with courts in other jurisdictions are not only useful and appropriate, but demonstrate new opportunities for reforming the Indian court system that may hitherto have been overlooked. If the reader agrees with the author's arguments and conclusions then this chapter offers a novel range of areas in which reforms may be advanced. If, on the other hand, the effect of this chapter is to provoke a contradictory response from Indian commentators by reference to practices in other countries, then it will have achieved its purpose in seeking to gain recognition of the value of international comparisons as a means of identifying court system reform strategies in India.

Differences in Practices and Expectations

The constitutional and legislative features of the Indian court system suggest that it is very much modelled on the English adversarial common law system. With notable qualifications, such as the abolition of the jury system in 1956, Indian trial and appellate courts follow the English model. The application of that system in India, however, has resulted in practices which are significantly divergent from those of England and other English speaking former British dominions that adopted English law—such as the USA, Canada, Australia and New Zealand. Unlike India, these other systems have been generally successful over the last 20 years or so in overcoming endemically large backlogs and delays in case disposals. Through trial and error, and bitter experience in some cases, those other systems have identified the causes of backlog and delay and successfully applied usually similar methods to overcome them.

Judicial Productivity

A view widely shared among judges and commentators on the Indian judicial system is that there are not enough judges for the workload they have to bear. Three arguments are commonly offered in support of this. The first is that high rates of case pendencies[1] across India is a reflection of there being not enough judges to dispose of the cases before them. There is a logical and proper numerical relationship between a society's population and the number of judges needed to service that population. The proportion of judges relative to the population in India is very low by world standards. Moreover, in those societies which are particularly litigious, and possibly India is one, the proportion of judges relative to population should be even higher compared with less litigious systems. The evidence that might support these arguments is readily at hand. Pendency figures and population statistics are quite accessible. However, one necessary assumption which seems to be implicit in this argument is that Indian judges are efficient in disposing of their caseloads. If, for example, there were good reasons why Indian judges can be expected to be less

1. Pendencies mean the number of pending cases. The terms 'pending caseload' and 'backlog' are also used to describe such cases.

productive than judges in other countries, then presumably there would be an argument for having more of them relative to population. Similarly, if for no good reasons Indian judges are less productive than other systems, then there might be an argument for not increasing their numbers until their productivity is improved by other means. But evidence about the productivity of Indian judges, as distinct from their workloads, is seldom if ever raised as a factor in support of a case for increased judicial numbers. More commonly it seems to be assumed that judges are sufficiently productive, perhaps as productive as they will ever be.

It is difficult to evaluate judicial productivity without identifying an objective benchmark to indicate just how productive a judge could be. If judges across India share common managerial problems, such as low numbers and poor resources, as many believe to be the case, then it is unlikely that an objective benchmark of judicial productivity can be found within India. International comparisons are more likely to be illuminating. The problem in looking to other systems, however, is in finding a system that is sufficiently similar so as to permit reasonable comparison. This is difficult. Civil law systems, for example, are especially unlikely to offer useful comparisons because most civil law trial court benches comprise at least three judges, whereas most trial court benches in common law systems, such as India, are of judges sitting alone. Common law systems, on the other hand, can also offer unhelpful dissimilarities by reason of geographic spread, size of populations and economic and cultural differences. These differences can be compensated for when data relevant to productivity is available. Often systems which might bear comparison with Indian experience do not necessarily offer accessible data that would permit useful comparison. Data that has been readily accessible to the author, however, has been data about court practices in Australia and the Delhi court system. As it turns out, comparing the court system of the National Capital Territory of Delhi with all of the courts of Australia does offer some useful insights into the question of judicial productivity in India. Delhi, for instance, has 13.8 million people whereas Australia's population is not much greater than 20 million. Both are common law systems that rank their courts into generally three levels. Both operate under codified constitutional federal systems and each has jurisdictional ranges that are generally comparable for criminal, civil and appellate jurisdictions. Here are some figures about each system that can be related to judicial productivity.

Judge to Population Ratios: Allowing for High Court judges in Delhi, but excluding the Supreme Court judges, there are 30.8 judges in Delhi per million of population.[2] The comparable Australian figure is 44 judges per million of population.[3] This indicates that Australia has half as many judges again than Delhi when compared proportionately to population. This comparison strongly supports the argument for increasing judge numbers in Delhi to match the ratios achieved in Australia—assuming, of course, that the ratios in Australia represent an appropriate benchmark for India.[4]

Disposals per Judge: A useful indicator of judicial productivity is the ratio of judges to disposals per year. It is better to consider disposals, rather than pendencies, because disposals represent actual productivity, whereas pendencies represent productivity that is yet to happen. Looking at disposals is useful because it gives an insight into judicial productivity in terms of what they do, rather than in terms of the population they serve. It also offers an indicator that can be related individually to each judge. In Delhi courts this ratio was 701 disposals per judge per year.[5] The comparable figure for Australian courts was 1,511 disposals per judge or around double the level of Delhi disposals.[6] This suggests that Delhi judges have to work twice as hard to dispose of as many cases as Australian judges.

Judges per Lakh[7] of Disposals: Another indicator of judicial productivity is to measure the number of judges needed to dispose of 100,000 cases in a year. This is useful for the purpose of justifying

---

2. Sanctioned rather than working numbers of judges are used to ensure comparability with Australia. The working number of judges in Delhi is closer to 21.5 judges per million of population. The sanctioned numbers used are 33 High Court and 392 district courts judges in Delhi as against a population of 13,782,976 as determined in the 2001 census.
3. Australian judge numbers were 881 as at January 2005–Source: website of the Australian Institute of Judicial Administration *http://www.aija.org.au/JudgesMagistrates.htm.* Australian court disposal figures in 2003/04 were 587,900 civil cases and 742,900 criminal cases. Source: Productivity Commission of Australia, *Report on Government Services 2005*, Chapter 6.
4. For example, Australia's judges are distributed over a landmass 2.5 times the size of India, whereas Delhi is effectively a city state, a factor which implies that Australia might need more judges than Delhi to cover a more widely dispersed population.
5. Based on disposals of 79,297 civil and 95,898 criminal in district courts and 32,346 disposals in the High Court in 2004. Judge to disposal ratios are based on working, rather than sanctioned numbers of judges which is taken to be 296 in Delhi in early 2005.
6. Productivity Commission of Australia, *Report on Government Services 2005*, Chapter 6.
7. In India a lakh means 100,000 and is more commonly used as a numerical measure than 'thousands' or 'millions'.

additional judge appointments in tandem as a consequence of increases in caseloads. In Delhi district courts 153 judges are needed to dispose of 100,000 cases. The comparable figure for Australian courts, however, is 66 judges; which verifies the point already made that Australian judges have double the disposal capacity of Delhi judges.

Disposals per Lakh of Population: A further variation is to look at the number of case disposals per year per lakh of population. In Delhi the number of cases disposed per 100,000 of population is 1,506. The comparable Australian figure, however, is 6,651 or almost four and a half times greater. This suggests that the population of Delhi is, at most, one quarter as litigious as the Australian population. It would seem that level of litigation is not necessarily a factor affecting the ability of Delhi judges to dispose of cases.

These different ways of examining judicial productivity in India reveal an extraordinary but logical conclusion: If litigation rates in Delhi rose to levels equivalent to Australia, then the average productive capacity of the Delhi courts would need to increase at least eight fold to cater for the additional work. If the working number of judges in Delhi were to be doubled so as to match the ratio of judges to population in Australia, it would only account for around half of the required increase in productive capacity. Thus, it could be said that no increase in judicial numbers would overcome the reality that Delhi judges are only half as productive as Australian judges in terms of case disposal capacity. One might question the precision of these figures, being based on the latest available yearly figures rather than figures compiled over time. However, the degree of difference between judicial productivity of Delhi and Australia is so great that numerical errors are unlikely to affect the basic conclusions.

Why are judges in Delhi, and presumably across India, so much less productive than Australian judges? The answer is that, despite the similarities of each system, Indian courts administer cases in ways that are significantly different from the ways of Australian courts. It is unlikely that Australian judges work harder than Indian judges; nor are they necessarily more learned or experienced. What is different is that they generally use case management and court management methods and practices which Indian courts generally do not use or are less effective in using. These methods and practices are referred to in this chapter as 'best practice'. Many courts in England, USA, Canada, Australia and New Zealand use best practice methods, but not all of them. And those that do use best practice methods are not without their problems from time to time. But the judicial leadership of each would vouch for the fact that when those practices are consistently used, they work. So how is it that Indian practices differ from best practice?

Low Civil settlement Rates

A key reason why Australian judges dispose off more cases per judge than Indian judges is because they conduct fewer trials. Overwhelmingly, the dominant means by which cases are disposed of in Australia is by voluntary settlement by the parties, rather than by a judge-adjudicated verdict. In best practice systems 70 per cent or more of civil disposals can be expected to settle before a trial begins.[8] In Indian trial courts the settlement of a case by voluntary agreement between the parties is a rarity. In civil matters the typical proportion of cases that settle is around 5 per cent and most of those settlements reportedly occur after a trial begins.[9] The causes of these low rates in India are not well researched. The main cause may be that the incentives for parties to settle disputes in best practice jurisdictions are either absent in India or are rendered less compelling by other factors.

In systems that apply best practice, and probably in all common law systems, there are two types of cases which are prone to settle. The first kind, which we may call early settlement cases, are either cases where all parties are in an ongoing relationship of some kind and want to resolve their dispute quickly, or cases where the cost of settling for both parties is not high and where settlement would allow them to pursue other, more worthy things. In early settlement cases there is a prospect that the parties will settle early in litigation, often without the direct involvement of a judge, by using methods like private arbitration, mediation, court-supervised settlement conferences or old fashioned advocate-to-advocate bargaining.

---

8. The proportion of instituted cases that went to trial in the trial courts in the Canadian province of Ontario was consistently below 10 per cent in the period 1978 to 2000. This, of course, is a practical settlement rate of 90 per cent. (*Ontario Courts Annual Report 2002-2003*).

9. This figure is based on the results of a listing survey conducted in early 2005 which, among other things, measured the means by which cases were disposed in 21 trial courts over a three week period—of all the disposals recorded in that period only 5 per cent were by way of settlement (*Listing Survey Report, May 2004*, ADB/GoI India Administration of Justice Technical Assistance Project TA4437-IND).

The second kind of case that is prone to settle, which we can call late settlement cases, are cases in which the parties are in sharp dispute but who reach a point in time where one of them starts to believe three things, i.e. (i) unless they settle, they will lose the case at significant cost to themselves; (ii) the time of loss is imminent or is not far off; and (iii) when they lose, they will quickly be forced to pay a higher price than if they decided not to settle. In Australia, a high proportion of settlements are both early settlement and late settlement cases. In well managed courts that encourage case settlement, early settlement cases are filtered out of court lists relatively early, sometimes before the case is listed before a judge. But late settlement cases usually remain in court lists until case preparation is completed and a date for trial is set. When a trial date is set in most Australian courts the psychological pressures on parties to consider compromise begin to coalesce, with the common result that settlements occur, as is often said, "at the door of the court"; meaning that a high proportion of cases settle on the morning of the first day of a trial. The psychology of late settlement cases is so reliably predictable that many civil courts in Australia and other systems confidently list more trials than there are available judges in the expectation that a proportion of them will settle before their trial begins.

Undoubtedly there are early settlement and late settlement cases in Indian trial courts. But few of them appear to settle. Why would this be so? In answer, two reasons can be offered. One reason is that voluntary settlement is not the custom in India, the English adversarial system being well ingrained since the British era. It might also be said that concern about corruption in the legal profession and the judiciary make Indian litigants wary of settlement processes. Customary inhibitions, however, even concerns about transparency of settlement processes, can be overcome by managerial initiatives in courts, such as the development of formalised court annexed mediation schemes.

The second reason for low settlement rates, which is considerably more compelling, is that Indian courts do not offer the essential preconditions of late settlement—they do not offer a party in a case the opportunity to reach the point of realising that they will lose the case; that they will lose soon; and that they will soon have to pay for it. Why would those preconditions be absent from Indian courts when they are evidently present in Australian courts and other systems? The answer to this question is much simpler: Because most

Indian trial courts cannot offer litigants what may be called outcome date certainty—i.e. they cannot indicate or direct with reasonable certainty when a particular trial will be completed and when a readily enforceable and final verdict will given in favour of one party. The absence of outcome date certainty in Indian courts is the quintessential difference between most Indian courts and most courts of Australia and other systems which apply best practice methods. Before elaborating on the reasons for the absence of outcome date certainty, however, it is useful to point out an important difference that affects settlement in criminal cases in India.

Low Criminal Plea Rates

Plea rates are the proportion of criminal cases in which the accused person pleads guilty and thereby avoids a trial. Sentencing a person who pleads guilty requires fewer resources for a court and the prosecution; and avoids the uncertainty of putting the accused to trial. It also enables the decision on sentencing to take into account factors that may mitigate a sentence, such as contrition of the accused. Accused persons are motivated to plead guilty when they believe that a finding of guilt by trial is likely and when they believe they will get a lighter sentence by pleading guilty. Best practice criminal justice systems endeavour to give accused persons ample incentive and opportunity to plead guilty and they do this by usually offering efficient prosecutions that have a high probability of a finding of guilt, they provide outcome date certainty and they assure consistency in sentencing. In Australian magistrates courts over three quarters of criminal cases are disposed by plea or by comparable processes that do not involve a defended hearing.[10] In contrast, rates of guilty pleas are not measured or reported by Delhi sessions courts or magistrates courts. Presumably the same applies to most other Indian criminal courts. However, anecdotal feedback from Indian judges and advocates suggest that plea rates are uncommon if not rare, except possibly in non-custodial matters. The sad reason for this is likely to be that there is no incentive to plead guilty when there is a high probability in Indian criminal courts that the accused will be acquitted, either at trial or on appeal. Conviction rates indeed appear to be low. The 2003

10. Magistrates Courts in the Australian state of New South Wales disposed of 133,105 criminal cases in 2003. Eighty-six per cent of those cases were disposed of other than by defended hearing. Source: Website of the NSW Bureau of Crime Statistics and Researchat *http://www.lawlink.nsw.gov.au/lawlink/bocsar/ll_bocsar.nsf/pages/bocsar_lc_stats9903*.

annual report of the Delhi district courts, for example, reported that only 31 per cent of criminal sessions cases and 55 per cent of magistrates cases resulted in a conviction. To date little information is available on plea rates, let alone research on the causes. What is clear is that in most Australian and other criminal court systems that apply best practice methods the rates of guilty pleas account for sizable proportions of criminal lists, allowing judges of criminal courts much higher disposal rates than are achieved in Indian criminal courts.

A Predominance of Contested Hearings

Settlement and plea rates in civil and criminal are influenced purely by subjective assessments of self interest. If a defendant sees advantage in settling a civil case rather than wait for a judge to enter a verdict, the defendant will settle. Similarly, if an accused person believes that he or she will be convicted and may suffer a worse penalty on a plea of not guilty, then the accused will consider a plea of guilty. These are truisms of human behaviour that apply irrespective of culture or jurisprudential traditions. Settlement and plea rates in India are usually low because there is uncertainty about the likely outcome; about when that outcome will occur, and because defendants thereby perceive advantage in delay or indecision. To reverse this trend it is necessary to offer more certainty of outcome and to deny advantage to litigants who procrastinate. For courts this means being able to ensure that trials are finished within a certain period known to the parties and that the prosecution in a criminal case is well prepared to secure a conviction. Furthermore, civil defendants who go to trial without settling and who then lose should expect to pay more than they would have been required to pay, had they settled. Similarly, accused persons who plead not guilty and are found guilty should expect that their penalty will be worse. Courts have little direct control over the quality of the prosecution. However, they can have control over the timing of a criminal trial, as they do in civil cases. This is what is called the concept of trial (outcome) date certainty[11] in Australia and other systems that endeavour to apply best practice. In India, however, the idea that trials can be given near certain completion dates is peculiar and quite rare.

---

11. Whilst the expression 'trial date certainty' applies in Australia and elsewhere, this chapter uses the term outcome date certainty' in recognition of the fact that setting a date for the commencement of a trial in India does not really indicate when that trial is likely to finish.

A Propensity to Adjourn

Outcome date certainty is difficult to achieve in Indian courts because most cases are adjourned multiple times and in unpredictable ways, even after a trial begins. In Australian courts the reduction of the average number of case adjournments has been a major managerial priority in backlog and delay reduction for at least the last 20 years. Criminal case attendance rates[12] for most courts in Australian states range from 0.3 to 6.3 adjournments per disposed case.[13] Civil attendance rates are in the range of 1 to 5. In India attendance rates appear not to be counted by any court. Estimates offered by individual Indian judges and advocates, however, put the rate of adjournments in Indian trial courts as typically between 20 and 40 times over the life of a case. Some cases are adjourned many more times. An ADB study revealed that on a single randomly selected day in March 2004 the High Court of Delhi had listed before it an average of 100 cases per judge of which 80 per cent were adjourned to another day.[14] Another ADB study conducted in Delhi district courts over a three week period in early 2005 showed that 80 per cent of a much larger sampling of listed cases were adjourned. These figures suggest that whilst Australian courts devote a lot of effort to minimise case adjournments, Delhi courts depend upon high rates of adjournment to get through their daily cause lists. With almost no exceptions every Delhi judge's cause list contains at least a dozen cases daily (often several dozen) and each case will typically be called and given some attention, if only for a few minutes, before being adjourned again. It appears that the trends in Delhi are reasonably typical of most Indian courts.

---

12. The term 'attendance' is used in Australia in lieu of 'adjournments' when counting to total number of courtroom events—thereby ensuring the first court event is counted. The American term 'appearances' has not been adopted in this chapter as it can mean something else in other jurisdictions i.e. in Australia. 'appearance' usually refers to whether or not a particular party or legal representative actually attended a scheduled hearing.
13. Average attendance rates can be less than one because many cases are disposed before being listed before a judge.
14. *Final Report of the ADB/GOI Administration of Justice Technical Assistance Project* –TA4153 IND 26 May 2004, page 44.

Absence of Continuous Trials

The propensity of Indian courts to adjourn cases compared to Australian courts can be explained by a fundamental difference of view about how cases should be managed by courts. Australian courts share with many courts in England, the USA, Canada and New Zealand a convention that a trial should as far as possible be conducted continuously, i.e. ordinarily a judge should conduct a trial in a particular case, and normally no other, from start to closing submissions with minimal interruptions. This convention probably stems from the jury system which demands that evidence be, presented to jurors as quickly as possible so that they can deliberate on their verdict and then be discharged. Even in those jurisdictions in which juries are no longer used, the commitment to pursuing continuous trials remains because of the recognised efficiencies they provide. For reasons unclear, however, continuous trials in India have become largely extinct. Whilst Indian jurists and advocates would agree that continuous trials are desirable, it almost never happens.[15]

High adjournment rates in India appear to have two distinct causes. The first is what appears to be a well established practice that there be a separate hearing for each of the main stages of a prosecution or a civil action. It is an undisputed practice, for example, that once the plaintiff's evidence in a civil case has been given and cross examination is complete, then the case should normally be adjourned to another day for the purpose of hearing the defendant's evidence. Australia does not have this convention—there is normally an expectation that evidence for all sides and submissions will occur within a continuous, mostly unbroken, trial. Indian courts on the other hand work on the assumption that a trial ought to occur in no less than five stages, each separated by an adjournment, i.e.

- issues and charges,
- plaintiff's or petitioner's evidence,
- defendant's or respondent's evidence,

---

15. The practice exists under legislative authority that a higher court in India can exceptionally direct a lower court to try a particular case 'from day to day'. But even in these circumstances such a direction is taken to mean no more than a requirement to hear one case at least for part of the day, each consecutive day, whilst other cases are also heard.

- final argument, and
- order and judgment.

A second evident cause of high adjournment rates is the effect of rising backlogs and case delays. Given that courts already routinely fragment trials into separate formal stages, the response to rising caseloads has been to subdivide them even further. Generally, as case lists have grown, individual cases have been listed for hearing no less frequently; but less time is available for them at each hearing by reason of there being more cases in each cause list. There is a commonly held view among judges and advocates alike, for example, that it is better to take the evidence of one available witness and then adjourn, rather than risk that witness not being available on the next occasion. Australian courts, however, would resist this practice. Instead, Australian courts would seek to deal with rising caseloads by maintaining a commitment to continuous trials and by applying other measures to deal with rising caseloads.[16]

So why is it better to preserve continuous trials rather than to fragment trials into shorter but regular hearings? The answer is that continuous trials offer outcome date certainty whilst fragmented trials do not. Once a trial starts under a continuous trial system, the date of the outcome becomes readily predictable and permits the parties to consider settling their case. But when trials are fragmented into multiple adjournments there is no predictability about the time of a final outcome, thereby reinforcing the reluctance of parties to settle. So it would seem that if Indian courts aimed at more continuous trials then they could induce more case settlements with consequential reduction in their trial volumes and pendencies.

Fragmented Hearings

The advantages of continuous hearings are not limited to encouraging more case settlements. They also reduce the duration of trials overall. Not all Australian court trials are continuous. Many non-jury trials are adjourned 'part heard' for various practical reasons. Part heard adjournments, however, are resisted by Australian judges because they are inconvenient and costly. A trial adjournment

16. In an environment of large trial backlogs, Australian courts will ordinarily list a case for trial whenever there was available time for a continuous trial—effectively resulting in longer waiting lists for a trial date.

before evidence is closed usually represents an unscheduled disturbance in a system that assumes that all essential evidence will be available at the scheduled time. Thus, if an adjournment is sought then an Australian court will usually penalise the party who seeks it, if that is a practical option. And the prospect of a penalty being imposed is usually an effective deterrent against such things as failing to prepare for a hearing. Regrettably there appears to be little research available on the efficiency of trials in India. So it is not possible to offer certain conclusions about it. However, one might confidently infer that a system which usually fragments the taking of evidence into numerous instalments will be less efficient and more time consuming than a system which seeks to assure an unbroken presentation of evidence and submissions by contesting parties.

Deterring Misbehaviour

There is a widespread view among Indian judges and advocates that the Indian justice system offers ample opportunity for a litigant to evade court decisions, or to intimidate opposing parties by appealing or by lodging an interlocutory application. A high proportion of pendencies comprise such applications with the result that delays in disposing of them afford ready opportunities for litigants to evade court decisions. Similarly it is said that there is a remarkable degree of court tolerance of incompetence in the legal profession and of litigants in general. The ADB survey of court adjournments conducted in early 2005, for example, indicated that 43 per cent of cases listed were adjourned due to the fact that either a litigant or legal representative failed to attend or was not sufficiently prepared for the hearing. High levels of case adjournments also offer opportunities to evade court decisions, often for many years, and also defeat the incentive of either party to settle. Whilst Australian courts also need to deal with unmeritorious appeals, incompetent advocates and ruthless litigants, they are generally effective in discouraging them. The primary way they achieve this, is by ensuring that adjournments are minimised and by offering early decisions on interlocutory applications and appeals. But what underlies the success of these methods is the presence of an effective means of punishing those who misuse court processes. Courts achieve this by enforcing cost penalties against misbehaving litigants and by using an effective disciplinary system against misbehaving advocates. India has both a system of party/party cost sanctions and a system for disciplining misbehaving advocates. However, it seems to be common knowledge that neither system is consistently effective in offering a deterrent to misbehaviour. The reasons for this and the likely remedies are necessarily speculative, as little formal research into these problems appears to have been done. Whatever the reasons, it may be said that it is recognised in Australia that effectively deterring behaviour which defies or seeks to evade judicial policy and court orders is a key to assuring judicial productivity. Arguably this connection is yet to be recognised in India.

Slow Evidence

Oral evidence in most Indian courts is generally typed in real time by the presiding judge's stenographer using a word processor. In some cases manual typewriters are also used and sometimes the judges themselves record evidence by hand. In most cases the words typed by a stenographer are dictated by the judge after the judge hears the questions asked by advocates and the answers given by witnesses. Much court time is often spent supervising the typing of testimony in this way including dealing with arguments from advocates about the accuracy of the words dictated. Consequently, oral evidence in Indian courts tends to be taken slowly and incompletely. This is often made more onerous if the language of the witness is not English, whereupon the judge must also act as interpreter when dictating in English. No court in Australia uses this method. Instead they use shorthand writers, stenotype machine operators or electronic sound recording with associated verbatim transcript production. Voice recognition technology is still unreliable in a court environment. Consequently, the preferred technology in courts that apply best practice is sound recording of court proceedings and full or partial text transcription from the recordings by typists (transcribers) working outside the courtroom. The introduction of sound recording to Indian courts, however, would not be a simple matter of installing new courtroom hardware. It would presage enormous change in the dynamics of courtroom usage. It would require, for example, that courtrooms become relatively noiseless; something that most Indian judges and advocates are not used to and would have trouble adapting to. It is probably unlikely that any studies have examined the efficiency of present Indian methods of court recording. However, one can speculate fairly confidently that unlike current Indian methods, which necessarily impede the pace at which oral evidence can be taken, sound recorded courts would enable evidence to be taken much faster, possibly at twice the speed. Until that happens, of course, Indian courts will remain less efficient at taking evidence than courts which successfully use sound recording.

In this regard, it can be mentioned that the 188th *Law Commission Report* on proposal for constitution of hi-tech fast-track commercial divisions in High Courts has made various recommendations where Video Conferencing equipment is to be used for recording of evidence. Specifically, the report under "Functioning of VC" mentions, "In each E-Court, there will be a VC System with two cameras, one facing the Judges and the other facing the advocates. There will be two plasma screens in the Court, which can be viewed by the Judges and the Advocates. There will also be a Document camera for projecting paper documents on the Plasma screens, a good Public Addressing system with wireless microphones, two 29 inch TV sets, DVD recorder for recording the VC proceedings and a computer system with Internet connectivity. This VC System will be connected to a remote VC System installed either within or outside the country. These two locations can be connected using three pairs of ISDN lines, providing 384 kbps connectivity. With this capacity of connectivity, though the pictures will not be of the quality of usual TV pictures, but it will provide comfortable viewing of people on the screen. If the remote VC Unit with which the EC 135 Court's VC is connected is not in the same city, then STD rates of that city will be applicable as call charges, during the period of VC Conference. As the VC facility is easy to operate, with little training to the Court staff it can be operated by themselves without any difficulty."

Conclusions

Some key points of comparison explained above are now summarised.

Judicial Productivity: If the Australian court system is used as a hypothetical benchmark; (i) there are almost half as many more judges in Australia as a proportion of population than there are in Delhi; (ii) the average case disposal capacity of a Delhi judge is only half that of an Australian judge; and (iii) per lakh of population, the number of cases disposed by Australian judges is eight times greater than Delhi judges.

Settlement Pates: Delhi judges, and probably most Indian judges, appear to be less productive because they administer more trials as a proportion of overall disposals than Australian judges. Over 70 per cent of Australian disposals are settled voluntarily without a court verdict, whereas the comparable rate in India is probably around 5 per cent. Around three quarters of Australian criminal cases are disposed without a defended hearing, usually involving a plea of guilty, whereas most Indian criminal cases are defended. Only around half of criminal cases in India result in a conviction, whereas much higher rates of conviction are typically achieved in Australian courts.

Adjournment Rates: Typically a case in an Australian court will be adjourned up to half a dozen times. In India cases are typically adjourned 20 to 40 times before being disposed. The fragmentation of the taking of evidence by frequent adjournments results in reduced efficiency in trial management. This inefficiency is compounded by the method of court recording by dictation, which probably doubles the time taken to record oral evidence compared with sound recording methods used in Australian courts.

Continuous Trials: Most trials in Australia are run continuously, i.e. a judge conducts the trial in one case, and normally no other case, from start to closing submissions with minimal interruptions. In India continuous trials almost never happen, with most trials being adjourned at the conclusions of each of up to five stages of trial. Adherence to continuous trials and minimisation of adjournments are key reasons why Australian courts have high settlement rates for civil matters and high rates of undefended hearings in criminal cases with consequent benefits for judicial productivity. Continuous trials and low adjournments are achieved by having effective means of deterring misbehaviour by litigants or advocates.

Courts that apply best practice tend to be preoccupied with increasing judicial productivity, minimising adjournments and increasing certainty of trial listing and verdicts. The intended by-product of each of these strategies is to increase overall case settlements rates and to increase the proportion of case settlements that occur early. Discussions about case delay and backlog problems in India, however, seldom invoke these kinds of issues. Not only is the Indian court system different from other common law systems, but arguably contemporary public debate about the problems that beset Indian courts has not yet recognised those differences. Indian courts need to acknowledge those differences and to act upon them. If this happened then the following major changes in judicial policy might be contemplated:

- Shifting the debate about judicial numbers to a debate about judicial productivity.
- Adopting case settlement rather than case adjudication as their primary strategic goal of Indian courts.
- Substantially reducing case adjournment rates in India to levels achieved in other systems.
- Implementing continuous trials as the preferred trial method for cases that do not settle.

Each of these options, if applied with any vigour, would be regarded as radical in India. All of them, however, have already been successfully applied in other systems. The challenge for those that influence the policies and practices of Indian courts is to accept that the key to successfully reforming the Indian court system is to apply methods used in other systems that have been shown to be effective. Indian practice should emulate best court management practice and improve upon it just as Indians have done so well with English literature and the sport of cricket.

10

The Reduction of Case Backlog in the Courts: A Framework and Strategy

CARL BAAR and ROBERT G. HANN

I
THE IMPORTANCE OF BACKLOG REDUCTION

The maxim that justice delayed is justice denied has achieved the dubious status of a cliché. The reduction of court delay can purely be justified on the grounds of fairness and access to justice. The rise of judicial reform projects and 'rule of law' initiatives supported by national and international development agencies also suggests that improvements in the administration of justice in the courts have other benefits for governance and for society. In fact, comparative research has shown that judicial reform—of which delay reduction is a key component—is directly related to the enhancement of both economic development and democratic political institutions.

Court backlog is both a result of court delay and a cause of court delay. Past delays and deficiencies in the courts have led to the growth of pending cases in such great numbers that new cases can no longer be dealt with as promptly as they could and should be. Thus, even the best efforts of the judges to keep pace with incoming matters may fall short because of the volume of old cases they face day in and day out.

Backlogs therefore emerge as a major impediment to court reform, because they make it so difficult to improve court performance that the judiciary and the bar appear to resist reform, when in fact courts are capable of significant innovation—once key participants feel it is worthwhile to make the effort.

The Relationship between Caseflow Management and Backlog Reduction

The existence of court backlog makes it difficult to implement caseflow management. Courts cannot meet time standards effectively when large numbers of cases are waiting for appearance dates. And to the extent that principles of caseflow management are applied successfully, new cases will move more quickly to pre-trial and trial stages. As this takes place, however, the court will not be able to provide timely dates for hearing because too many existing cases will already be awaiting trial. Thus, unless a court's backlog is addressed, efforts to apply principles of caseflow management have less chance to succeed.

Backlog reduction is not merely a matter of increasing efficiency, but is essential for increasing effectiveness and enhancing justice. Litigants who must spend unnecessary time awaiting resolution of legal claims are not well served; nor is the public at large. The cost of justice increases with each additional month that elapses before a case is resolved.

Backlog reduction requires focused effort of the judiciary and support of the bar and government. But it is worth the effort, both in improving the adjudication process and in establishing effective working relations between the judiciary, bar and government.

Toward Statistics that have Value to Courts

Court statistics have value only if they provide information that improves court planning and management in a way that allows the court to better achieve its goals and objectives. Otherwise, the production and consideration of court statistics represents no more than an additional burden on an otherwise overburdened court system.

A chapter on the court statistics required to reduce backlogs and delays must therefore be firmly grounded in and derived from an understanding of the types of planning and management decisions that must be made by the court to reduce backlogs and delays, and the types of information needed to improve those decisions. The current chapter, thus, pays considerable attention to developing a framework for understanding the types of planning and management decision making that should be part of an effective backlog and delay reduction initiative. Then and only then do we make suggestions about the types of statistics needed.

Necessary and Unnecessary Court Delay

Court delay is a fundamental characteristic and endemic part of the administration of justice throughout the world. While the law's delay is often seen as inevitable, it is essential to distinguish three aspects of the judicial process that produce delay:

1. the time necessary for the parties to prepare their cases for consideration by the court;
2. the time necessary for the court to hear and reflect on the matters at issue; and
3. the time when neither (1) nor (2) occurs, but when participants must still wait for key events to occur and key activities to be completed.

It is the third type of delay, the unnecessary time that elapses from the initiation of a case until its disposition—whether that disposition is in the form of a judgment following trial, or a settlement following preliminary discussions, motions or other court appearances—that undermines the ability of the courts to do justice in individual cases.

Inventory *versus* Backlog

A court's backlog of cases must be distinguished from a court's inventory of cases. Put simply, the court's inventory is all of its pending cases. The court's backlog is that part of its inventory that has been pending too long. While this begs the question of "how long is too long?" it is also safe to say that both civil and criminal cases now typically take too long to move from initiation to disposition. Recently instituted actions may not yet be part of the court's backlog, but it is likely that a high proportion of the pending cases are.

Caseflow Management

The effort to identify and eliminate unnecessary delay has evolved into an approach or discipline that is now termed caseflow management. Its practitioners (whether they are judges, court staff or outside consultants) apply a set of basic principles to cases as they enter the court system and as they move through key stages of the litigation process. By establishing time standards for stages of litigation, the court can monitor the timeliness of court action and ensure that cases move expeditiously to disposition. And by managing the flow of cases from the early stages of litigation, it is possible to reduce the time and cost of resolving disputes, with benefits both to the courts and to the litigants.

II
OPTIONS FOR BACKLOG REDUCTION

Before identifying particular steps to reduce the number of pending cases in a single court, it is important first to consider the full range of options for reducing backlog. This way one can choose the option or group of options that will be the most cost-effective in achieving court objectives.

Two Aspects and Three Potential Options

In theory, backlog reduction has two aspects—Taking action on cases that are part of the existing backlog; and reducing the number of cases that are entering and will enter the backlog in the future. Three potential options can be identified within which specific steps can be identified to reduce backlog:

1. Reducing the demand for court resources.
2. Increasing the court resources available to meet demand.
3. Introducing more cost-effective ways to deliver court processes.

Option 1: Reducing Demand for Court Resources

The first option can be reducing the demand for court resources, and this can be achieved in two ways:

- decreasing the number of cases requiring the court's attention, and
- decreasing the demands made on court resources by cases that do require the attention of the court.

Decreasing the number of cases is an option that has come to be identified with 'ADR' or alternative dispute resolution mechanisms. But ADR covers a variety of different approaches, and obscures or ignores other ways of decreasing the number of cases in court.

ADR can take the form of pre-charge diversion in criminal cases, or contractual agreements for non-court resolution of civil cases, or the creation of administrative tribunals to handle high-volume specialised matters (e.g. traffic, industrial accidents). In all three of these instances, disputes that might have gone to court are handled by different processes or by different bodies. Contractual agreements for compulsory arbitration, for example, use non-judicial dispute resolution mechanisms to pre-empt any court involvement. In other words, private individuals and firms bind each other to an ADR process. Or, as in Shanghai, China, foreign companies are required by government to resolve disputes outside the public court system, and in fact use a set of private arbitrators whose qualifications in commercial law exceed those of the country's state judicial apparatus.

Beyond defining alternative ways to resolve disputes outside the courts, we also need to consider how to avoid disputes in the first place. The best way to remove cases from the courts is not to shift them elsewhere, since other venues may still require public funding, but to establish conditions that reduce the likelihood that disputes will arise in the first place. For example, debt collection cases were the largest proportion of civil matters in the 19th century American courts, but the emergence of debt consolidation and refinancing in the 20th century reduced those cases in absolute and proportional terms; in this sense, private organisations like the Household Finance Corporation may have removed more cases from American courts than any ADR mechanism. Are there new opportunities for dispute avoidance in countries and societies dominated by other types of disputes (e.g. over property or estates)? The lower litigation rate in auto accident cases in Japan may be a function of the additional effort to assess the cause of an accident at the time it occurs. Canadian lawyers who handle construction lien cases (disputes arising out of construction projects) have observed that some large and complex projects can be dispute-free if certain conditions exist.

ADR can also be used in cases that have already been initiated in the courts, if the courts make alternatives available, and judges encourage parties in litigation to use those alternatives. Thus, criminal cases can be decreased by post-charge diversion, for example by referral to treatment in a drug court. And civil cases may be referred to mediation, arbitration or some combination of both when a judge concludes that a case has dragged on in the court when it could be resolved by means short of an expensive trial. These alternatives may be court-annexed or free-standing, just as treatment options for criminal matters may be based within the court or in the outside community. Having these alternatives available is often useful in civil cases, but they may come too late to avoid many of the costs associated with complex protracted litigation.

The second broad approach to reducing demand for court resources is to decrease the demands made on court resources by cases that remain in the court. Many caseflow management practices are designed to reduce the amount of judge-time spent on a case. For example, reducing the number of adjournments by definition reduces the number of appearances in a given case. Thirty years ago, a comprehensive study of one of Canada's largest criminal courts concluded that the court had an appearance crisis, not a caseload crisis. So if (in that court), appearances per case could be reduced from 9 to 6—or better yet, 3 or 4—more judge time would be available to handle the entire caseload. A 2001 survey of closed cases in the two largest cities in Pakistan showed an average of over 100 appearances in cases that went to judgment following trial. While caseflow management requires the continuing supervision of the progress of pending cases, it does not require the frequent perfunctory court appearances that characterise those and many other trial courts, using valuable judicial time and increasing legal bills for the parties.

The demands on court resources can also be reduced if the worthwhile functions performed during court appearances can be done outside the courtroom. For example, if time standards can be incorporated in court rules, a typical or 'standard track' case need not go before a judge at a directions hearing. Events can be scheduled by a trial coordinator or a similar court official, even by telephone, rather than requiring an appearance by counsel and the time of a judge in a courtroom.

However, sometimes shifting activities out of court reduces the demand on court resources, but increases other costs. For example, the extensive written information required at the early stages of civil litigation under the English Woolf rules is likely to save court time but add to the hours spent by counsel on preparing cases.

Option 2: Increasing Court Resources Available

Option Two, increasing the court resources available to meet demand, can be achieved in three ways:

- Increasing the level of resources (e.g. the number of judges and court staff, and the volume of other resources).
- Increasing the amount and proportion of judicial and courtroom time available for adjudication.
- Increasing the effectiveness of judges and court staff, so their tasks are done better and hence are less likely to require redoing.

One of the first and most common requests from courts faced with large and/or growing backlogs is for the appointment of more judges. Obviously, an increase in the number of judges will enhance the amount of judge-hours available to schedule cases for trial or other hearings. But that benefit also requires that other resources be available, such as court facilities, courtroom staff, and prosecutors to prepare and present cases in a criminal court. Furthermore, the addition of more judges should be balanced against other court resource needs. Could a master relieve the judges of a variety of pretrial tasks? Could a court administrator improve court operations so that the existing judges' capacity is enhanced? Could information technology save time for court staff, and more expeditiously produce information needed by the judiciary? Could temporary resources be mobilised; for example, senior lawyers conducting early neutral evaluations or pretrial hearings on a *pro bono* basis?

While the need for more judges and court staff often seems self-evident to those working in a backlogged court, it is equally evident that the additional cost will encounter resistance from governments anxious to hold expenditures in check—especially when additional costs entail long-term commitments, such as paying the salary of a judge appointed for life. This reality has prompted proponents of caseflow management to search for ways of using existing resources more effectively.

Thus, for example, it is possible to increase resources by reducing the time judges spend in court on what is essentially administrative work: setting dates for trial, or hearing and approving requests for adjournment. Judges throughout the world, regardless of differences between legal systems or levels of economic development, spend a portion of their courtroom time on non-adjudicative matters that could be handled outside court and with the aid of qualified court staff. Saving half-an-hour per day of a judge's five hours of sitting time would increase capacity by 10 per cent. It is also possible to increase judicial resources by reducing courtroom 'downtime' through improvements in court scheduling. Appointing more judges only allows a court to schedule additional matters before the additional judges; it does not guarantee that matters scheduled in court will be heard, or that the judges' time will be well spent. The collapse of a scheduled trial is not necessarily a bad thing—for example, if a mutually agreed settlement has been reached between the parties. The problem occurs if the settlement is so late that no other matters can be scheduled. Avoiding downtime is primarily a function of effective trial coordination, but this can be enhanced by the way the judiciary is organised to hear cases (e.g. it is harder to overbook cases when scheduling for one judge than when scheduling for a group of two or more judges).

Finally, it is possible to increase judicial resources by increasing the effectiveness of judges and court staff, so that their tasks are performed more thoughtfully and carefully—and are therefore less likely to require redoing. Thus judicial education for trial judges should enhance the quality of trials and judgments and reduce the volume of appeals. Training in mediation would allow the judiciary to use alternative approaches when promptness and fairness suggest they would be beneficial. Programmes for training and retention of court staff can enhance their effectiveness and provide more timely and trusted support for the judiciary.

The development of trial management has been an important step in enhancing judicial resources. The philosophy of trial management is that a more active judge can guide and focus the trial so that it does not drift on for longer than necessary and undermine rather than enhance the quality of evidence and the clarity of legal argument. One way to manage the length of a more complex trial is through a trial management conference. Rather than focus on settlement, as often happens in pretrial conferences in many courts, the trial management conference judge asks counsel for the parties how much time they need to present evidence and arguments. Then it is possible for the trial judge to encourage counsel to respect those time estimates.

Chief judges and chief justices can also increase the effectiveness of the court by their allocation of cases among their judicial colleagues.

In courts that use a master calendar system, for example, work must be allocated between motions courts and trial courts. A proper allocation, regularly reviewed and adjusted, would smooth the flow of cases, avoiding long queues at one stage but not another. Similarly, an imbalance between judges allocated to civil cases and those allocated to criminal cases may result in more backlogs in one area than the other, and lead to more wasted time as cases collapse and adjournments increase.

Option 3: Increasing Effectiveness and Efficiency of Court Processes

Option Three, introducing more cost-effective ways to deliver court processes, could entail the court—and particularly Chief Judges and other judges with caseflow planning and management responsibilities—undertaking reforms in one or a combination of seven key areas associated with effective management and efficient operations within a court.

1. Clear Vision and Leadership

- Focusing on the disposition of pending cases rather than simply the processing of immediate tasks. Too often, for example, a court is asked to rule on a motion and does so without asking parties whether the motion is necessary, and whether the case could be resolved.
- Leadership by the judiciary. In backlog reduction, as in caseflow management, the court must take control of the movement of cases rather than assuming that counsel for the parties will do so.
- Clear and measurable objectives for backlog reduction, including short-term targets set jointly with individual judges and/or groups of judges.
- Detailed work plans with specific accountabilities and deadlines for tasks and final results.

2. More Effective Planning, Management and Coordination

- Analysis to develop better understanding of court workloads, resource usage, performance and challenges. The court needs to know what kinds of cases make up the backlog, and monitor what happens when action is taken on those cases.
- Improvement of the court's manual and automated information systems, so that data used by the court are valid

and are provided in usable form to those who need the information.

3. Removal of Unnecessary Steps in the Court Process

- Minimising the number of discrete steps that must be taken in processing each case. This involves both the reduction of unnecessary procedural requirements and the control of adjournments.
- Making simplified procedures available to parties who want a prompt and affordable disposition of their dispute.

4. Introduction of New Processes for Key Tasks in a more Cost-Effective Manner

- Early mediation built into court rules. In this approach, mediation could be used to resolve issues, discuss settlement, reduce need for subsequent use of pretrial discovery, and exercise some supervision over the movement of the case immediately after the pleadings stage.
- Early case conferences in complex cases. This is already done as part of Commercial Lists in many courts, and it is the use of processes for early control that make these commercial lists effective.
- Use of specialised tracks with time standards appropriate for those cases (e.g. a fast track or a standard track, or a track for cases involving particular subject matter).
- Automatic monitoring and generation of appropriate notices to ensure that cases that are outside time standards are identified and acted upon.
- For backlog reduction in particular, the removal of inactive cases by summary administrative means such as dismissal rules. In any court, some of the pending cases are likely to be inactive; for example, a settlement may not have been reported to the court. Typically, courts that have tried to reduce backlog by calling the cases on the trial list discover that most of those cases are not ready for trial once the list has grown unmanageably long. Internal rules that purge lists by dismissing inactive cases can remove the very matters that take up unproductive time and space in a court. On the civil side,

for example, the oldest cases should be identified to ensure that they are resolved if in fact they remain active, and dismissed if they are not. On the criminal side, does the court still list as pending those cases in which an accused has failed to appear and an arrest warrant has been issued? As long as the prosecution monitors these cases, they need not be on a court list and need not be scheduled for a periodic appearance.

- Electronic filing of court documents. E-filing fits in this category, but while the technology for electronic transfer of records is now well established, e-filing of court documents remains a process that many courts, even those with the financial resources, have been unable to implement.

5. Smoothing the Flow of Cases through Improvements in Core Court Processes

- Early intervention in the process, so that the number of additional steps or events necessary to resolve a case are reduced. At the same time, these early requirements should not increase the burden faced by litigants in normal cases (e.g. in contrast to the lengthy written submissions required by the English Woolf Rules).
- Differentiated case management, through the use of specialised tracks as noted above.
- A strict adjournment policy that encourages litigants and counsel to be prepared on the date set for them to appear.

6. Improving the Efficiency with which Specific Processes are Performed

- Use of disclosure instead of preliminary hearings in criminal cases.
- Use of video remand instead of transportation to court for hearing bail applications.
- Use of will-say statements instead of examinations for discovery in civil cases. This is an important example, since it illustrates an improvement in efficiency without the use of new technology.

7. More Efficient Organisation and Allocation of Responsibilities for Different Tasks

- Creation of specialised dockets so that cases similar in subject matter can be dealt with in the same courtroom (e.g. commercial cases, small claims, family matters, and cases involving young offenders). This is only an effective option when monitoring mechanisms and related caseflow management processes are in place. Otherwise, specialised dockets can drain resources without reducing delay. Many years ago, for example, when a large American city set up a 'speedy trial court' for criminal cases, so many cases were transferred there that they took longer to reach than cases in the regular criminal courts; an accused who wanted to delay his trial would then bring a motion to go on the speedy trial list.
- Reallocating appropriate judicial tasks to quasi-judicial personnel, including masters and registrars.
- Allocating administrative tasks to non-judicial personnel.

III
IMPLEMENTING BACKLOG REDUCTION

The foregoing detailed itemisation and organisation of available options provides a context within which an individual court can choose particular steps to reduce its case backlog. Courts normally focus on the use of a specific process or procedure, or make particular resource demands, without seeing those steps as part of a larger set of options.

While this section of the chapter talks in terms of stages or steps in implementation, it is assumed that different steps will often be taken at the same time rather than in sequence. Step two (identifying the backlog) seems logically to come before step three (devising a backlog reduction plan). But life is not logical, even the life of the judiciary. It is quite likely—and typical—that a court will begin devising a backlog reduction plan (or at least assembling the key participants needed to implement the plan) before it has a clear picture of the magnitude or nature of the backlog problem.

Frequently, a court will implement particular backlog reduction techniques, but without an overall plan and adequate measures of whether the plan has succeeded. These steps can all be worthwhile. But if more analysis is done in advance, the plan can be more fully developed, and backlog reduction has a better chance to be implemented effectively.

This part will discuss the following steps and strategies:

- Step One: Taking Leadership and Assuming Responsibility
- Step Two: Identifying and Differentiating the Backlog
- Step Three: Devising a Plan-Who should be involved? And what should be in the plan?
- Step Four: Fleshing out the Plan-Selecting Cases, Dismissing Inactive Cases, Screening and Moving the Active Cases, Monitoring the Results, Using Settlement Processes.
- Step Five: Toward Caseflow Management-Time Standards, Strict Adjournment Policy, and Control of Case Movement throughout the Process

Step One: Taking Leadership and Assuming Responsibility

The various options and strategies reviewed in the preceding part of this chapter share a common assumption: that the court and the judiciary have assumed responsibility for backlog reduction. Not all the means to reduce backlog are within the control of the judiciary; courts can neither create permanent judgeships nor adopt dispute avoidance strategies that require legislation. But there are an impressive range of initiatives that the court itself can take to reduce the demand for court resources, increase the court resources available to meet demand, and deliver court processes in more cost-effective ways.

While the judiciary requires the support and cooperation of court staff, the bar, and a variety of the court's clientele to be effective, the judiciary is in a unique position to mobilise that support and cooperation. The judiciary has the highest status of the key actors. A judge (either a chief judge or a judge designated by the chief judge) can take leadership and play the role (to use current management lingo) of a champion for change. In more prosaic terms, that judge can call a meeting of the key officials and individuals that must be brought together to ensure that changes are effectively implemented. That judge can follow up with these key people to ensure commitments made at a meeting are put in place. That judge can reconvene meetings of this team as necessary to ensure that worthwhile changes are sustained over time.

This general orientation—that the judiciary must take leadership and assume responsibility to ensure that backlog is reduced and caseflow management techniques are implemented—is a requirement for what is prescribed in this chapter. Other steps, strategies and ideas are merely suggestions. They are suggestions born of experience and observation, but all experience is rooted in particular courts and societies that may work quite differently from the courts and societies whose judges and lawyers are reading this chapter. Those who will play key roles in reducing backlog in their courts should adapt the ideas in this chapter to suit their situation, choose the strategies that will be most welcome and most effective, and use the ideas creatively to devise new ways to do their work.

Step Two: Identifying and Differentiating the Backlog

How particular court goes about assessing its backlog will depend upon how it already organises and classifies its cases, regardless of whether it does so manually (with chapter files and typewritten case lists) or with the help of computer technology.

Courts typically classify cases by subject matter, at least differentiating civil and criminal cases, and often using additional subdivisions by subject matter or seriousness of the case. Some courts then distribute these cases among individual benches, usually consisting of one judge, so it should be possible to determine the cases pending on each bench (or in each courtroom). Other courts maintain case files centrally, and distribute individual cases only when they have had a date set for hearing. Pendencies would be reported for the court as a whole, with a minority of those cases awaiting trial, on trial, or awaiting preparation of a written judgment.

No matter how the court is organised, participants need to know how many cases or matters are pending in the court as a whole. This total should be broken down into the major case categories used in the court (e.g. civil and criminal), and by the year the claim was instituted or the case initiated, so one table on one sheet of chapter lists the number of civil cases by year, criminal cases by year, and so forth. This not only provides a snapshot of the court's inventory, but also facilitates comparison with future snapshots so that progress can be assessed over time.

The other key information to have available is the status of individual cases. Where are the cases in the workflow? That is, what was the last key event noted in the court file or on a court list? What is the next scheduled event? (E.g., Are pleadings complete? Is the case awaiting trial? Awaiting reasons for judgment?) A list of the cases pending in the court of a particular judge, listed chronologically beginning with the oldest case, and indicating the current status of each case, can be useful not only for that individual but also for the judge responsible for overseeing the effectiveness of the larger programme. As this information is gathered, key participants will need to develop the backlog reduction plan.

Step Three: Devising a Plan

Who Should Be Involved?

Because we are conceptualising a backlog reduction effort that could affect a more substantial proportion of the court's inventory—hundreds and even thousands of pending cases, a planning process is essential. Even if the court is able to identify cases that are ripe for disposition, lawyers for the parties will need to be notified and will need to review their files and be in a position either to verify that a case is inactive (or has been settled) or to indicate that a case is still alive and requires attention by the court. Unless lawyers have an opportunity to respond effectively to an increased volume of requests from the court, backlog reduction will quickly stall.

The planning process begins by assembling a team or teams of key participants—the judges who will take the lead, court officials who will need to provide administrative support, lawyers who will have to respond (including both public prosecutors and defence counsel on the criminal side), and other key actors whose cooperation and effectiveness will be essential (these may include for example police, process servers, court reporters and those responsible for transporting prisoners).

What Should Be in the Plan?

A backlog reduction plan should include targets, activities and responsibilities, procedures, resources and support systems.

Targets: For example: how many case dispositions should occur in the next quarter (three-month period)? By what percentage should the number of pending cases be reduced? These numerical targets may be set for the court as a whole, for different case categories (e.g. civil and criminal), and for individual benches. Targets should also be set for disposal of the oldest cases pending in the court and before the individual benches (e.g. 20 of the oldest 25 civil cases); a particular focus on these cases will encourage the judge to deal with substantive issues in some of the court's more intractable cases, rather than dealing only with matters that can be disposed of with the shortest amount of courtroom time. The judge could also alert parties and counsel that theirs is a case with a high priority for disposition.

Activities and Responsibilities: For example: what tasks need to be done to reduce case backlogs? Which ones should the judiciary do? Which ones could be shared with administrative staff? Who should be accountable for ensuring that these tasks are carried out and completed on time? What support activities are needed to ensure that the judiciary's core tasks can be effective (e.g. getting notices to the bar, conducting education and training workshops)?

Procedures: For example: what sorts of pretrial procedures should be put in place? What changes should be made to existing pretrial processes? Should additional procedural requirements be placed on the parties? Should existing procedural requirements be modified or eliminated? Can the conduct of trials be simplified or expedited? Should settlement processes be identified—or put in place within the court?

Resources: For example: what additional resources should have the highest priority? What additional resources could be made available on a temporary basis to reduce backlog? (E.g., should private lawyers do dispute resolution or mediation on a *pro bono* basis?) How should additional resources be allocated? (E.g., if new judges are appointed, should pending cases be spread evenly among the new judges, or should a pilot court—with an inventory but no backlog—be set up to model effective caseflow management practices?) Who will be responsible for obtaining the resources and making sure they are in place as needed?

Support Systems: What has to be done to ensure that the plan can be effectively put into operation? The answer to this question becomes a check list of the various support functions that must be recognised and in place—communications systems (getting information out to the bar and the litigants, as well as to other judges and court staff); training (who needs to know what?), and information systems (generating, interpreting and clearly and simply presenting data on cases and caseloads).

Step Four: Fleshing out the Plan

Selecting Cases

With the information generated on the backlog cases in Step Two, it will be possible to identify some portion or segment of those cases to target for disposition. For example, priority could be given to:

- The oldest cases in each category. These could be assigned to a special court, or could be given priority by individual judges in their own courts, or both.
- Cases with no scheduled event pending. These could be subject to an administrative review by court staff, and particular staff personnel could be designated to clarify the status of individual cases.
- Cases with no recorded activity within a particular period of time (e.g. one year). The length of time would depend upon how many cases would be captured within the time period. If a court rule specifies that a case will be dismissed if there is no activity within a specified period of time, many inactive cases could be eliminated. However, depending upon local court practice, parties may appear in court on a regular basis and simply ask for an adjournment; in those cases, the judge will need to ensure that some steps are taken by the parties to resolve the matter.
- Cases from particular law firm(s). This way, rather than finding that a backlog reduction initiative stalls because the same lawyer or law firm finds it impossible to appear in different court rooms or court locations on the same day or at overlapping times, a number of cases can be considered at once.

Dismissing Inactive Cases

Reducing backlog requires that a court eliminate its inactive cases and move its active cases to disposition. With a large volume of pending cases, it may be difficult to differentiate active and inactive cases. Ideally, if that can be done administratively—by reviewing case files outside the courtroom—judicial time can be focused on moving the active cases to disposition.

Thus, a first step would be to identify a set of old cases that appear to be inactive, and notify each party that their case will be eliminated from the court's pending caseload (i.e. as appropriate given local terminology, it could be stricken from the list, purged, or dismissed)—unless a party appears in court on a specific date to inform the court that the case is still active. The use of notices or 'status letters' will help to separate the active pending cases from the inactive 'pending' cases. The use of a dismissal rule will allow the inactive cases to be stricken from the pendencies in the court, eliminating any requirements that files be kept in an active file area, that cases be called or kept on the court list, or that parties be asked to appear when their dispute is no longer alive.

If an old case has in fact been settled, the court may not previously have been notified of the settlement (this often happens in Canadian provinces). Thus, if a notice or status letter is sent by the court, the parties may then inform the court that their case has settled. At that point, provision should be made for the case to be dismissed by administrative action. If cases are handled administratively, all dismissals should be listed publicly so that these administrative actions have an appropriate degree of transparency. Then if any case has been dismissed when one or both parties believe it is still active, either party can have it returned to active pending status.

Screening and Moving the Active Cases

While these administrative procedures can often reduce a court's nominal backlog (especially if the court has not used similar procedures in the recent past), it may be less effective when a court's backlog is high. In that situation, parties may have been less inclined to settle, since: (1) the incentive caused by the pressure of an immediate trial date is often absent, and (2) the dispute may be so old that the parties have gone on with their lives and the dispute continues primarily so that the aggrieved party can argue before the judge on a matter of principle. As a result, the purging of the list of pending cases may not eliminate as many matters as the court would hope. To the extent that the administrative screening process still produces cases that are identified as active, those cases should be given a priority date for a pretrial hearing or for the trial itself (a complex case will require a pretrial, a case with less evidence might proceed directly to trial).

This same process would then be repeated for another batch of cases, and then another—depending upon the number of judges available for pre-trials and trials, and the number of active cases that emerge from each wave of notices.

What if the judiciary is not in a position to give administrative staff a major role in screening old cases and preparing lists of active cases for pretrial conferences or case conferences? In that situation, the judges may find themselves playing these administrative roles in their courtrooms—calling cases, setting dates for active cases and dismissing inactive cases. Clearly, the preferred option is to have non-judicial staff perform these tasks, and staff must be trained and must be committed to the effort. In too many countries, court staff personnel are so poorly paid and have such weak qualifications that judicial officers hesitate to entrust any responsibilities to them. However, a backlog reduction plan must address these limitations so that staff development over the short and medium-term can overcome the historical deficiencies. Otherwise, judicial time will inevitably be consumed by non-judicial tasks—time that judges could otherwise spend working with parties and counsel to resolve active cases.

Monitoring the Results

As this process of separating inactive and active cases—and moving active cases to disposition—continues, the court should be preparing the monthly status reports both a summary report on total cases initiated, disposed and pending, and special reports on pending cases by year by major category—e.g. civil and criminal. These reports would show whether there is a decline in pending cases, and particularly whether the oldest cases are proceeding toward disposition.

If a party and a lawyer assert that their case is still active even though court records show that no activity has occurred for a number of months or even for over a year, it is likely that the case is ripe for disposition, perhaps by settlement. So if the case is set for trial, a last-minute settlement might still occur in a substantial percentage of cases; or if the case is set for pretrial, either a settlement might occur or the pretrial judge might encourage the parties to reach a settlement or the pretrial judge might urge the parties to use mediation in an appropriate case where issues can be resolved through a more expeditious and affordable process.

Given this range of alternative outcomes, the court will also need to monitor the number of active cases that are set for hearing, to ensure both that those cases can go forward on the date scheduled for hearing, and that there are sufficient cases on the docket given the probability that a percentage of those cases are likely to settle on the eve of trial. As these old cases move to disposition, court staff (clerks and trial coordinators) will need to track the patterns of settlement *versus* trial to ensure both that court time is used efficiently and that parties do not come to court and find that their case is not reached. This is a problem of how much overbooking is appropriate; the precise number of cases set for hearing in a given day or week cannot be stated in advance, but must be determined by minimising both courtroom downtime and the unnecessary time spent in court by parties and their lawyers.

A key here is to avoid adjourning cases and finding matters returning to court once again. Ensuring that a matter will be reached by the court on the day set for hearing encourages parties and counsel to be prepared on that day. At the same time, parties and counsel who are not prepared cannot expect cases to be adjourned, especially for long periods of time. Judges universally agree that adjournments should only be given when they are necessary, but just as universally, judges find themselves facing conditions of necessity day in and day out. Breaking the adjournment cycle is a key to the ability to reduce backlog, and to use judicial resources efficiently and effectively. By following the steps outlined here (including taking responsibility, identifying the backlog, and monitoring the movement of active cases), courts can schedule matters with more certainty, and by so doing can demand more timely preparation of counsel and can alter the patterns of behaviour that often characterise the 'local legal culture' in trial courts throughout the world.

Using Settlement Processes

If a large number of old but active cases could benefit from third party intervention short of a full trial, the judge may be in a position to play a mediating role, using either of the two main approaches: (1) rights-based mediation, where the third party indicates what a judgment would be if the case went to trial; and (2) interest-based mediation, where the third party encourages the adversaries to consider how to settle the case without trial by understanding how a settlement could help each side realise its primary objectives. Note however that a judge who has been actively involved in settlement discussions for a particular case should normally not act as the trial judge in that case. To do so would not only compromise the appearance of impartiality, but would also create a coercive climate during the settlement conference, undermining its legitimacy.

At the same time, this third-party mediation role need not be played by a judge at all, but by outside third parties asked by the court to serve as mediators on a temporary voluntary basis. This strategy was used successfully some 20 years ago in Montreal, where the Superior Court had a five-year waiting list for civil trials. The court's Chief Justice asked senior counsel (including a retired justice of the Supreme Court of Canada) to assist in conducting case conferences or settlement conferences for active cases identified by the judiciary. Through this process, parties could summarise their positions and obtain the advice of senior counsel about how to settle or what was likely at trial. The obligation was seen as an honour by the invited counsel, and parties were provided with a forum to tell their story to a respected and experienced lawyer.

In Toronto, another of Canada's major cities, a different approach was traditionally used for backlog reduction—the 'blitz court'. There judges from outside the city would be assigned to assist the Toronto judges, so that a large number of cases could be dealt with during a short period of time. Experience over the years confirmed the need for administrative screening of inactive cases; on previous occasions, visiting judges called cases on the trial list only to find that they had settled, or that the parties were not ready for trial. While the blitz was effective in reducing backlog, observers noted that the backlog would gradually begin again. This was often attributed to inadequate resources, but should also have been linked to the absence of a caseflow management system for most civil cases until recent years.

A more effective approach was used in Toronto by a former senior judge. His court staff identified every pending case in which the same pair of law firms represented the opposing parties. The two firms were then told that if they reviewed all of those cases with a view toward settlement, the court would provide priority dates for trial of any cases that were unable to settle. Given the court's large caseload, it was possible to identify as many as 25 cases involving one set of contending law firms, and settle a large proportion of those cases. While the firms' participation was voluntary, all their paired cases were included. While the approach proved effective some years ago, newer automated information systems could not provide the necessary breakdown of cases by law firm.

Another approach to dealing with old but active cases is the use of 'settlement weeks' or 'settlement fairs' in which a number of judges, assisted by court staff and volunteers, focus on resolving pending cases. In some respects, a settlement week could function in a manner similar to the blitz court or the invited counsel system or the paired law firms described in the three preceding paragraphs. The main difference is that settlement fairs are typically voluntary: the parties in any pending case (whatever its age) can bring their dispute to a third party. Thus the metaphor of a 'fair' is used to encourage participation by a wider variety of litigants, and to build interest in and even enthusiasm for settling cases. This has both advantages and disadvantages. The advantage is that the parties may be predisposed to consider settling their dispute. The disadvantage is that the most intransigent litigants and their cases will not be affected until the court intervenes. In turn, however, if a court orders a case to a settlement week, it may not produce a settlement, and the matter would then be back in a case conference or pre-trial conference, where options other than settlement can be dealt with.

A settlement week open to all pending cases on a voluntary basis could be part of a backlog reduction programme, but would be most useful in conjunction with other initiatives. For example, if used in conjunction with administrative screening, active cases could be identified, and appropriate cases could be referred to the settlement week along with cases whose parties attend voluntarily. Furthermore, a backlog reduction programme would monitor the results of the settlement week. How many cases reached disposition? How many cases made progress? What procedure will be used to ensure that cases still pending are set for pretrial or trial?

Step Five: Toward Caseflow Management

Caseflow management works most effectively when new cases are automatically part of an overall plan for moving and completing all of the court's pending work. Thus, the court monitors the initial steps from initiation to the close of pleadings, from the close of pleadings to the next pre-trial event (e.g. a mandatory mediation or a case conference or a 'directions hearing'). The amount of time is monitored in terms of standards that state the normal period of time in days or months that should elapse within each stage. Cases that exceed the standard can be identified and called for an appropriate hearing to move the case forward or see whether it is now inactive.

Depending upon the timing of the initial case conference, it may be used to explore settlement options (both whether to use an alternative process, or to guide negotiations between the parties), rule on preliminary motions, or narrow the issues (and reduce the list of witnesses) at trial.

In a backlog reduction programme, active cases should be called either for trial or for a court hearing or case conference. However, case management time standards will not apply prior to the time of the hearing or conference, because the active cases will typically have been pending longer than any reasonable and allowable time period.

At the same time, other principles of caseflow management do still apply. For example:

1) Once a date has been set for a case conference or pretrial conference or directions hearing, that event should take place as scheduled, and not adjourned to a later date. Similarly, the trial should begin on the date set for trial. There may be legitimate reasons why an adjournment is necessary, and the adjournment must be given if it is in the interests of justice to do so. But unnecessary adjournments—even when they occur with the consent of both parties—are perhaps the single greatest source of court delay, and every caseflow management system and any backlog reduction plan must establish, communicate and enforce a strict adjournment policy. A strict adjournment policy could include the following:

- Cases are expected to be ready to proceed on dates assigned in advance.
- No matter will be adjourned without cause.
- If cause is established, adjournment will normally be to an hour or date within the briefest possible time period (e.g. the afternoon of the same day, the following day, or within one week).

- Witnesses that appear for hearing should always be heard on that day.

2) The court must exercise control over the movement of cases from initiation to disposition, and ensure that disposition takes place in a timely fashion through a fair process. Even if backlog has developed as a result of forces external to the court (growth of litigation, lack of sufficient resources from government, delaying tactics of parties and counsel), the judiciary has little choice but to assume responsibility for managing the flow of cases, and to exert leadership in reducing delay and promoting effective justice. The public and the litigants fault 'the courts' for delay, and blame the judges as the most visible and authoritative manifestation of the court as an institution. To the extent that backlogs impede effective control over the flow of cases, and constrain the ability of the courts to do justice and respond to public needs, backlog reduction is a priority.

The assumption of responsibility is a critical and important step—the first step in implementing backlog reduction—and once it has been taken, backlog reduction is no longer a question of whether, but of how.

11

Driving Transformation: The Elements in Achieving Transformation in Courts through Technology

MURALI SAGI

I
INTRODUCTION

Law, legal practice and dispute resolution depend upon information and the communication of information.[1] The information can be the law—legislation, case law and learned articles—or factual and expert information relevant to particular issues or disputes. Typical legal information includes legislation, cases, textbooks, journals, opinions, practice directions, codes of practice, precedent documents, seminars and training and educational materials.

Richard Susskind in his study *The Future of Law: Facing the Challenges of Information Technology* argues that all lawyers, whether judicial officers or legal practitioners engage in the following tasks associated with legal information

- Document drafting (e.g. drafting legislation, legal documents or judges writing their decisions).
- Sending and receiving information (e.g. meetings, hearings, postal correspondence, electronic communication).
- Document management (most lawyers have significant management of electronic and/or printed documents).

---

1. Australian Legal Reform Commission, (1998). "Technology What it Means for Federal Dispute resolution", *Issues Paper* 23, 1998.

- Information consultation which refers to the recurring task of consulting
- Information sources by perusal, browsing and annotating.
- Following procedures whether laid down by the law or by custom or personal habit.
- Analysis and problem solving which refers to analysing facts and law and drawing conclusions and which is dependent on information gathered and considered.[2]

Technology can facilitate communication, which is at the heart of legal practice and dispute resolution. It allows for efficient exchanges with witnesses, experts, lawyers or alternate dispute resolution (ADR) practitioners. Audio-visual aids permit evidence to be taken, or the hearing or ADR session to be conducted at some distance. Participants no longer need to be in the same physical location. The Internet allows information about law and ADR processes and advertisements concerning dispute resolution to be disseminated to a broader audience.

Commenting on court services, Professor Stephen Parker, in an address to the Annual AIJA Court Administrators' Conference in August 1997 stated that it appeared that many people are dissatisfied with court services which are not user friendly, are hard to 'navigate around or indifferent to particular client sensitivities or special needs.[3] Empirical studies conducted in Australia and overseas suggest that courts tended to orientate themselves to the needs of the judges, court staff and the legal profession rather than towards their public clientele. It can be argued that good communication between courts and their public would build up confidence and improve the practice and the perceptions of service that the courts offer.

Technology allows a fuller and more varied dialogue between the public, lawyers and courts and tribunals on dispute resolution services. It has precipitated a change in litigation practice from the spoken word to the written document. The emerging change is from a printed document to an electronic document. Information relevant to disputes is being stored and retrieved electronically. It provides

---

2. Susskind, R. (1996). *The Future of Law: Facing the Challenges of Information Technology*, Clarendon Press Oxford, pp. 81-3.
3. Parker, S. and C. Treloar (1997). "Courts and the Public", Address to the Annual AIJA Court Administrators Conference 21 August.

the capacity for an expansion of information to be stored and accessed and the means for it to be effectively collated, sorted and managed.

Within the courtroom, real time transcripts, images, charts and diagrams are being used to explain or enhance the explanation of complex facts. Similar technology can be utilised in ADR. Electronic databases and publishing are revolutionising legal information and research. The electronic research library is open 24 hours a day for research that can be done from the researcher's own desk.

II
BEST PRACTICE USE OF TECHNOLOGY IN COURTS

Successful and innovative technological change generally requires funding, effective planning and informed decision making. Planning for technologies requires identification of objectives and purposes, assessment of current systems and current and future demands, training and motivational needs, a structured implementation plan and regular reassessment.

A court technology committee in Los Angeles highlighted the need for effective planning and integrated technological development for courts.[4] It identified two major obstacles: the lack of methodology for objectively evaluating current court technology and developing a strategic plan and a shortage of the expertise required to apply the methodology.

The US National Center for State Courts identified eight major criteria for achieving effective statewide court automation:

- Selling the concept on a state-wide basis and not merely relying on individual courts to determine, in isolation, their own plans.
- Adequate long term funding commitments.
- Organising people who are not directly involved in the technical aspects (a multidisciplinary technology committee could include judges, court administrators and staff).

4. The Judicial Council Court Technology Advisory Committee 'Court technology', <*http://www.courtinf.ca.gov/courtnews/06960796/court.htm.*>

- Recognising local needs but integrating these into a single software system.
- Appropriate testing and piloting projects.
- Coordinated training of all staff, having regard to individual levels of knowledge, experience and needs.
- Appropriate speed of transition and change.
- Ongoing support and communication between IT staff and end-users.[5]

The Commission of the Future of the California Courts identified the following criteria for assisting courts in the use of information technology:

- Data should be entered once into a system.
- Delays between steps should be reduced by consolidating steps; performing steps in parallel; accelerating the process; and eliminating scheduling conflicts.
- Wherever possible, telecommunications should be used to facilitate access; to reduce the need for travel to court facilities; and to speed up the process.
- Courts should manage their time and resources zealously to achieve an active, efficient and effective case management process.[6]

Courts and tribunals have their own particular technological needs that may be influenced by the nature of their jurisdictions, workloads, cases and parties, practice and procedure and case management requirements. Further, electronic filing may not be an urgent priority for some courts. Nevertheless, it is possible to determine general priorities which may help to inform debate about court and tribunal information technology strategies. One suggestion is that a fundamental priority should be automating repetitive and critical court and tribunal processes particularly those which are the domain of judges and tribunal members and their support staff.[7] Another suggestion is that courts and tribunals should focus on case

5. Walker, J., "The Challenging Voyage to Statewide Court Automation",*<http://www.ncsc.dni.us/ncsc/bulletin/v07n02.htm>*.
6. Commission of the Future of the California Courts, *Justice in the Balance - 2020* quoted by A.Stanfield 'Cyber Courts' (1997) 17 *The Queensland Lawyer* 126, 127.
7. Court Technology Bulletin (1996). "Court Technology in the 21st Century", 8(1), *<www.nsc.dni.us/ncsc/bulletin/future/future.htm>*.

management, word processing, electronic research, electronic document technology and training needs.

Other priorities may be to ensure that case management is automated and integrated with other agency systems which provide and receive information relevant to litigation such as word processing and email systems. If the need to communicate with litigants, their representatives and the public, is set as a priority, electronic filing, the website and interactive kiosks may be target developments.

Notwithstanding their different and changing priorities for technology, all courts and tribunals need to be able to share information, the 'collective wisdom' of other courts and tribunals in relation to their use of technology and, where it is appropriate, to ensure that compatible formats and systems are implemented. There is scope for greater collaboration between different courts and tribunals on case management systems and information technology as they have similar systems collecting the same type of information. For example, many courts and tribunals in developing their plans conduct their own surveys of national and local developments. This can be expensive, cause significant delays and duplicate work. If information technology systems across different courts and tribunals could be integrated, this would allow for the sharing of information between the organisations. To achieve this outcome it would be beneficial to establish a means of seeking to align each court's strategic plan with a common direction in which all courts in a country agree to move. The courts might wish to consider the following strategies:

- The establishment of a forum for sharing court technology within the various courts.
- Establishing a central repository for court information technology strategic plans (i.e. a site on the Internet).
- Holding an annual judicial conference (involving a mix of judges involved in information technology management, managers responsible for information technology within a court and information technology managers).
- Establishing a 'newsgroup' for the exchange of information *via* the Internet.[8]

8. Fosse, T de la and B. Finlay (1997-98). "The Council of Chief Justices Electronic Appeals Book Project", *Paper,* First AustLII *Conference on Computerisation of Law via* the Internet, 1997 Sydney 25-27 June.

A. Data Collection and Case Management

Technology in courts and tribunals lags behind that in other service industries. In the advanced economies computers were introduced into the court system in the 1970s and 1980s to ' provide both the means of collecting the information necessary to decide what is to be done, and the mechanisms for putting those decisions into effect'.[9] Over time the expanding needs of court and tribunal case management systems in these countries have surpassed the ability of the current systems to provide the information required. Given such deficits, most jurisdictions are reviewing their current information technology plans to replace or re-develop their existing case management systems.

Current case management systems enable most courts to provide basic information on all cases filed. However, much of the data collected is incompatible and sometimes in non-comparable forms. The implementation of systems, and the collection and use of information is often *ad hoc*. Issues that need to be considered are the type of information to be collected, how that information should be used and whether the data collected should be comparable as between different courts and tribunals.

It is difficult for governments to make major and early resource commitments in the absence of reliable information about past trends and future projections of workload and about productivity relationships between increased resources and expected outputs, in terms of disposition rates and delay reduction.[10] Data collected should include annual information, and historical information giving trends and that to ensure its accuracy and completeness, the information should be subject to internal and, where appropriate, external audit.

It is impossible to make comparisons across courts if there is no standard data collection procedure and different definitions were used. Agencies should be established to devise a set of common definitions and record-keeping conventions, designed to provide useful statistics as a management and evaluation tool for each court and for the merits review system generally.[11]

---

9. Matruglio, T. and G. McAllister, "The status of data collection and evaluation research in the Federal Court, the Family Court and the Administrative Appeals Tribunal January 1998", <*http://www.alrc.gov.au/*>.

10. Coopers and Lybrand and W. D. Scott (1989). *Review of the New South Wales Court System*, Sydney, p. 62.

11 Administrative Review Council (1995). *Better Decisions: Review of Commonwealth Merits Review Tribunals*, AGPS Canberra, 110, recommendation 69.

As far as case-processing information is concerned, the case management system should provide at the minimum, data entry fields for all basic information that enables the tracking of a case through the system (for example: case type, duration, outcome, and presiding judge for all court appearances). Information about appeals should also be recorded including whether it is to be an appeal to a single judge or to the full court, whether a case is a leading or linked case, whether any exhibits are held for the case, and whether a cross claim has been filed. Explanatory information should always be recorded. For example, while the court records when an adjournment takes place, the reasons for the adjournment, details about orders given and compliance of the parties with orders. Case outcome information includes the date and method of finalisation, details of monetary awards, transfers and appeals. Inactive cases can be identified through caseload status reports that are regularly provided to the principal registry. A typical case management system generally includes a 'Remarks' field into which any information relevant or helpful to the case can be entered. Responsibility for the accuracy of the information that is produced by each registry lies with the court registrar. Data entry takes place in each registry commencing with the filing of the application, and continues each time a case comes before the court or documentation is filed. Ideally courts should have computer-integrated courtrooms, so that all information need not be recorded manually on forms and later transcribed. While responsibility for the recording of this information lies with the Judges' assistants, final responsibility for data entry lies with the listing clerk and clerical staff.

Statistical reports can be produced within each registry and by a central location to monitor the day-to-day operations and general court administration. The case management system can be used to produce information for internal operational functions (including reports such as judicial availability, listing of matters according to specific criteria, hearing listings for specific days and locations) and for court management purposes such as monthly statistics, judgment reports, statistics on number of filings (monthly and in each registry),'days elapsed' reports for matters sorted by year, state and category and reserved decisions.

Most current computerised case management systems are set up to manage the flow of cases from filing to disposition. As a result, all systems record essential but basic information that enables the tracking of cases through the court or tribunal, the identification of the stage that cases are at, the method of finalisation and how long cases take to be finalised. However, it is difficult to undertake a more systematic analysis of performance information and provide users with more information on trends (and their cause) in court operations and activities [12] as the case management systems currently in place were generally not set up to provide this level of management information and specific programmes often have to be written to produce the information required. In some cases, manual searching of case files may be necessary as the particular information required is either not recorded in the computerised system or is not retrievable electronically. To overcome these deficiencies what is required is a multi-jurisdictional case management system that covers the entire court process and allows a data administrator and not a programmer to be able to easily configure it for any new court, without the need for reprogramming and be able to generate reports as required.

B. Information Management and Exchange

One way to view the modern courtroom is as the centre of a 'complex system of information exchange and management'.[13] Technology is a vital tool for managing the complex information needs of the various participants in court processes, with the potential to make significant savings in costs and time, improve the accuracy of information collected and enhance access to justice. The barriers to the extensive, or full, use of technology in courts and tribunals for information management and exchange include:

- The skill base of staff required to work with technology. Many judges, lawyers and court administrators have limited computer skills and would require training in order to operate or feel comfortable operating such systems. A Certain number of them are reluctant or opposed to undertaking such training.
- The paperless court may not be a realistic ideal. For example, the Australian Federal Court's *Information Technology Strategic Plan* has been developed on the basis that, while the IT systems defined in the plan would replace many paper documents with electronic ones, there is, and will always be,

---

12. Reynolds, R. (1991). *FEDCAMS Post Implementation Review Report*, Attorney-General's Department Information Management Branch Canberra, 12.
13. Lederer, F. (1997). "The Courtroom,: As a Stop on the Information Superhighway", 71 *Reform* 4.

a need for paper documents in the court's processes. Indeed much of the detailed examination and perusal of documentation associated with litigation can only be made of printed documents.

- Several legal issues remain to be resolved before a court or tribunal could move to full, electronic operation; for example, the issues of what constitutes a signature, how fees will be paid upon application and how to overcome the difficulty of authenticating and dating electronic documents. These issues are currently being examined by a number of bodies.
- A full electronic court or tribunal system will not be accessible to people who do not have the technology. Courts and tribunals must remain accessible to those who have limited resources. Advances in information technology could create a class of people who are 'information poor' as opposed to 'information wealthy.'

Notwithstanding such limitations and challenges to the use of technology in dispute resolution, there are many appropriate adaptations of court and tribunal processes by technology presently being used or trialled in many jurisdictions. For example in some jurisdictions email is used to effect ordinary service of court documents or in discovery processes and for directions hearings.

C. Standards for Electronic Filing and Communication

The Judicial Electronic Document and Data Interchange (JEDDI), an electronic filing system, established in America in conjunction with the National Center for State Courts allows exchange of data between computers that run with different operating systems or software packages.[14] The software also creates an Electronic Data Interchange (EDI) file that is used to enter data automatically into the computer docket system of the court registry or law firm.[15] Each case is stored in an electronic file folder which can be accessed by judges and registry staff. The folder can be customised to prevent unauthorised

14. This therefore allows each group; courts, firms, law enforcement agencies, etc. to maintain their own systems. McMillan J "JEDDI for Beginners: A Conversation", <*http://www.ncsc.dni.us/jeddi/jedijumy.htm*> (2 February; 'The Need for National Standards for Judicial EDI' <*http://www.ncsc.dni.us/jeddi/edijust.htm*>.
15. McMillan, J. "Judicial Electronic Document and Data Interchange (JEDDI)" <*http://www.ncsc.dni.us/jeddi/overview.htm*>.

access to particular documents. Documents can contain cross-references to other sections of the document or statute or case law.

However in most other jurisdictions at present there are no specific standards for the electronic exchange of judicial documents.[16] One objection to the creation of standards is the problem of having diverse procedural rules across state and federal jurisdictions, although this problem may be alleviated if uniform criminal and civil laws and uniform court rules are available. JEDDI has suggested that three areas should be addressed when formulating standards for electronic filing:

- Court processes and work flow for handling the materials and information comprising case files.
- The needs of judges and chambers staff in dealing with case files, and
- The interface between the court and those outside the court: parties and their counsel, and the public.[17]

D. Litigation Support Systems

A litigation support system[18] is an information management tool that controls the organisation and storage of documents, retrieval and analysis of documents, repackaging and presentation of information and delivery and dissemination of information. It may have the following integrated components: a database, an imaging system, a full-text retrieval engine and electronic mail. Basic report formats provided by a litigation support system include: a report of all documents in chronological order, a report of all the names of people and organisations mentioned in the database, a report of all documents/events where a particular name is referred to and a list of documents which is generally used to comply with an order for discovery.

Typically four types of cases have been identified as cases that would benefit from litigation support technology. These include cases

---

16. "The Need for National Standards for Judicial EDI", *<http://www.ncsc.dni.us/jeddi/edijust.htm>*.

17. A Stanfield 'Cyber Courts' 17 *The Queensland Lawyer* 126, *<http://www.netrail.net/~jeddi/report.htm>*.

18. This description of litigation support systems is from M. Warren "Using technology to manage litigation", Paper Designing and implementing a litigation support system Government lawyers CLE seminar Sydney 31, July 1996.

with extensive documentation, cases that involve a complex web of interrelationships among many entities; cases with time constraints; and cases where lawyers handle the same type of cases that have similar document needs. Litigation support systems assist in storing, searching for and retrieving documents in less time than a manual system may take. One such case example is a coalmine inquiry[19] in New South Wales where more than 50 large plans and maps were tendered as exhibits. Some of the maps exceeded 2 metres in length by 1.5 metres in width. For these plans to be made available to the ten parties, the judge and the witness each time the exhibit was referred to in court would have taken considerable time and required expensive printed copies. In fact the maps were presented and could be easily imaged on the screen, including when there was a need to focus on a particular portion of the map or plan. The courts have inherent jurisdiction to control their own proceedings including controls on the use of technology within the court.[20] An Internet based litigation support system can enable parties to share a virtual space to conduct electronic discussions and facilitate the exchange of documents.

E. Document Management Systems

A document management system comprises software and computer network systems which store documents in a database.[21] Such a system is typically a component of a litigation support system. The database is accessible to the lawyers, the parties, the judge, and if applicable, the jury. When documents are filed or tendered in court they are put in a scanner to create an electronic image of the page.[22] The image is stored on a computer disk and indexed. It allows lawyers to use computers to display images on computer screens.

---

19. Inquiry by Acting Judge Staunton into the drowning of 4 coal miners at the Gretley Colliery, Newcastle, NSW commenced 3 March 1997. See S. Davidson and M. Warren, "Using Internet Technologies to Facilitate Court Processes", Paper Law on the Internet '97 Conference University of Technology Sydney 25-27 June 1997.

20. Mason, K. (1983). "The Inherent Jurisdiction of the Court", 57 *Australian Law Journal,* 449.

21. A database is the computer equivalent of a filing cabinet.

22. Imaging was first used by large American corporations and federal government agencies to managelarge volumes of documents such as credit card receipts. Imaging was first used in US courts in the 1980s: National Center for State Courts <*http://www.ncsc.dni.us/ncsc/briefing/image.htm*>.

F. Court Transcript

The transcription of court proceedings has evolved from written shorthand with transcripts being typed at a later date, to real-time transcripts.[23] Transcription and recording services can be enhanced by the addition of indexes, for example, the names of witnesses or key words. In addition, a transcript analyser can allow the user to search for references to words in the transcript. The types of current court transcripts include:

Real time transcript: Stenography machines can be electronically linked to computers in courtrooms, enabling the transcript to appear immediately on computer screens on the bench and bar tables. The judge and practitioners can refer to the transcript immediately, make electronic notes on their copy and make corrections where necessary.[24]

Audio transcript: Audio transcript is the audio recording of court proceedings using either analogue or digital audio equipment. It is the cheapest form of recording as staff costs are minimised. Equipment can be operated by court staff and transcription of the recording to paper or disk takes place where required.

Video Transcript: Another form of transcript is the video recording of proceedings. This offers a more extensive view of the hearing—recording what was said as well as the demeanour and appearance of the participants. This is the most expensive form of transcript because of the infrastructure costs involved. The court video transcript, if adopted, may have a significant impact on the appeal process. A video of the hearing could provide appellate courts with live information on which to base a decision to overturn a trial judge's findings on, for example the demeanour of a witness or questioning by lawyers and judges at trial.

Voice recognition transcript: There may be applications of voice recognition software to create a transcript when appropriate technology becomes available in the future.

---

23. O'Brien, E. (1997). "Court Reporting Methods and Alternatives", Paper AIJA Annual Conference, Sydney, August.
24. Document imaging technology means that all the documents, exhibits and transcripts associated with a case can be stored and retrieved electronically.

G. Technology in Court Proceedings

Technology may be able to reduce costs and delay in pre-trial procedures. Documents that are imaged and stored on a database can be retrieved easily for discovery. The party giving discovery is able to provide a list of documents which can be looked at by using text retrieval software. The benefits of using technology in trials to present evidence can include:

- improving the quality of evidence—for example, images on computers can be magnified improved understanding of the facts of the case—for example, the use of computerised 3D modelling assists to explain technical facts;
- providing multiple access to the same image;
- the use of charts or diagrams to explain expert evidence,
- the use of different technologies to present legal arguments; and
- exhibit evidence is not handled as much—such handling can damage the evidence.

However the use of technology in appellate proceedings is more difficult. The Queensland Law Foundation Technology Services Pvt. Ltd. in consultation with the Council of Chief Justices has initiated an electronic appeals project in an attempt to 're-engineer' the current appeal book model. Part of this project is to examine how everything the judge needs to hear and decide a case at hand[25] will be available electronically in an 'Electronic Appeal Book'.

The electronic appeal book's content includes registry filed documents, transcripts, legal submissions, exhibits and legal research material. The project recommended that courts maintain an internal database of decisions delivered from the jurisdiction and consider publishing their decisions on the Internet to allow easy access to judgments. It is also suggested that transcript of court proceedings be maintained in electronic form by the court in which the hearing has occurred. A cost benefit analysis needs to be undertaken to determine its economic viability.

---

25. Sherman, J. (1997). *Electronic Appeals Initiative: Project Plan,* Queensland Law Foundation Technology Services Pvt. Ltd, 3.

H. Video Conferencing

Video conferencing can allow lawyers to make submissions and witnesses to testify *via* a quality video link.[26] It is commonly used in most jurisdictions. Some examples of its use include:

- Video conferencing from prisons so that arraignments and bail hearings can be held without transporting prisoners to court.
- Links in hospitals to enable medical professionals to provide expert evidence using hospitals' in-house facilities.
- Taking evidence from overseas witnesses.

The Internet can also be used for video conferencing between witnesses and courts and tribunals. Parties can also correspond by using email which is accompanied by video technology. Such technology is likely to cost less than dedicated video conferencing, though the quality of imaging may not be as high.

I. Judges' Use of Computers

Technological support for judges can include a computerised database of legal and statistically relevant information. The purpose of such a database would be to provide judges with rapid and easy access to the collective wisdom of the courts in order to assist them with their decisions. In addition, e-mail and bulletin boards allow judges to communicate with each other about legal issues and recent decisions or developments in the law.

J. Coordinating the Use of Technology

The advantages of using technology usually require all parties and the judicial officer or tribunal member to agree on the use of technology.[27] Sometimes one party will have its documents imaged, but other parties will prefer to use printed documents. This can mean that when a document is mentioned in a hearing one team of practitioners will bring it up on screen while another sorts through paper documents. The technology can also be denied to the court or

---

26. Williams, D. (1987). "Use of Video Recordings and Video Links by Courts and Tribunals", 17 *Western Australian Law Review* 257.

27. Sherwood, S. (1988). "Pros and Cons of Inhouse Litigation Support", 18(1) *Proctor*, p. 18.

tribunal member. At a day-to-day level, one lawyer may have a problem of emailing documents to another lawyer whose system is not at a standard where he is able to open the email attachments.

The best time to coordinate the use of technology for a hearing is usually at the pre-hearing stage, with consultation between parties, their representatives and the court or tribunal. Court and tribunal practice notes may also facilitate the use of technology. It could become a requirement that an electronic copy of the documents should accompany all documents filed. This would enable judges and practitioners who want to use technology to do so where possible.

III
PUBLIC ACCESS TO LEGAL INFORMATION

Any major policy issue associated with new technologies concerns the level of public access to legal information and the costs, if any, imposed for such services. One view is that legislation and reports of court and tribunal decisions should be freely available and that public authorities should provide legal information to the public,

i in a completed form, including additional information that is best provided at source, for example, catchwords for judgments;

ii in an authoritative form, including acceptable citations and numbering in a form facilitating dissemination;

iii on a marginal cost-recovery basis for the reproduction and dissemination of material; and

iv with no restriction on reuse for any purpose and with no licence fees.[28]

Governments can also assist in public education in the use of technology by including information about court and tribunal services in information programmes provided about other government services.

The Center for National Courts has argued that there are four main reasons for putting a court online:

- **Serving the court's constituents:** Online services allow people to get the information they want without having to come to a courthouse and lose time from work or other important activities. Instead of listening to information

28. Stanfield, A. (1997). "Cyber Courts", 17 *The Queensland Lawyer,* 126, p. 137.

repeated over the telephone, people can save online information on their own computer or print out a copy. As barriers to computer access fall (e.g. costs and user inexperience) more of a court's constituency will be demanding electronic access.

- **Saving money:** Online information can be accessed repeatedly without the court incurring additional costs. An online document can be accessed thousands of times without extra cost. Automated processes free court personnel to do other work. Reducing physical visits to courthouses reduces courthouse traffic and its attendant costs.
- **Educating the community:** Courts need to educate the community about their work. Online services can provide greater amounts of information tailored to suit the needs of the particular individual.
- **Preparing for Online Future:** As online communications develop within the community, courts must also use them or risk being left behind or unable to participate.[29]

A. Information for Litigants and Public

Any member of the public who can access a computer connected to the Internet can receive information about court and tribunal processes, ADR services, law firms, lawyers, and the law. In circulating such information, technology has the capacity to directly and significantly improve legal practice. The ways in which different technologies might be used to provide information and other services to litigants and the general public include:

- the role and functions of a particular court or tribunal,
- the range of dispute resolution options,

29. T. Carlson "Information Superhighway Implementation Guidelines", State Justice Institute <*http://www.futurelawyer.com/link pages*>. The Hon Chief Justice of Singapore, Yong Pung How *Keynote address* Technology Renaissance Courts Conference, Westin Convention Centre, Singapore Tuesday 24 September 1996. The Chief Justice suggested that evaluation criteria for the application of information technology for courts should: increase access to the courts through consumer friendly technology; enhance the role of courts as service institutions; improve the quality of justice; improve efficiency in management; assist the exercise of skills and judgment; enhance productivity and cost effectiveness and reduce delay; improve the decision making process by providing complete and accurate information be acceptable and convenient to end users; and accommodate the need for data integrity, confidentiality and the protection of privacy have a useful lifespan.

- how to find an appropriate lawyer for a particular dispute, the scale and reasonableness of fees charged by legal or ADR practitioners,
- how to assess the quality of services provided by a lawyer or ADR practitioner,
- what the total monetary cost of the litigation or dispute resolution is likely to be,
- the time estimated to resolve particular disputes
- what people can do if they are dissatisfied with the services provided by their lawyer or ADR practitioner.

Such information can take a variety of forms including:

- Broad public distribution of appropriately designed, simply written and informative court forms, precedents and other explanatory material.
- Point-of-entry advice to members of the public from courts and tribunals on available sources of professional advice and on other dispute resolution options.

It is generally assumed that if people have sufficient information about litigation and alternatives to it, they will be able to make informed choices about dispute resolution. The public needs information about law, legal process, litigation and ADR. People who know that they will be informed about the basis of legal charging before incurring any obligations and about likely total costs at an early stage may be more likely to investigate legal avenues for resolving disputes or clarifying rights and obligations.[30]

Technology can assist to provide information about ADR services, for example, through computer programmes or the Internet. ADR providers are establishing home pages and sites to provide information and services. For example court's website could include information on its range of dispute resolution services including information sessions, counselling, conciliation and mediation.[31] It could discuss the advantages of counselling and mediation in resolving disputes.

30. *<http://www.familycourt.gov.au/.*

31. New York Family Courts *<http://ucs.ljx.com/famjtst.html>*.

B. Legal Kiosks

Legal kiosks are a modified form of applied artificial intelligence. They generally provide information about court and legal services and assistance in completing forms and procedures for certain basic legal actions such as small debts, tenancy disputes and non-contested divorces. The consumer uses touch screen graphics and an alphabetical keyboard and receives instructions, oral and graphic. The suggested advantages of kiosks are that they are cheaper and more accessible for clients with simple matters and can reduce court and tribunal resources spent on directly advising clients.

Legal kiosks have been established in a number of countries. There are about 150 kiosks in Arizona and the system has been taken up in other parts of the United States. Florida is using the Quick Court kiosk system to offer advice on wills and estates. The New York County Supreme Court has been using kiosks to reduce the confusion and delay associated with a litigant's visit to court. The Court's kiosks are programmed in English and Spanish and offer Braille for the visually impaired as well as a variable hearing level for the hearing impaired.[32]

It should be noted that the kiosk is not designed to remove the need for lawyers or expert decisions but is primarily designed to provide basic information and to assist self represented litigants to complete uncomplicated legal matters. The kiosks can provide only generic legal advice and cannot deal with the particular circumstances of the case. There are concerns that some people may place too great a reliance upon information provided by the kiosk, which may be erroneous or misleading in particular circumstances and the person may incur additional costs and delays and potential legal problems.

Lord Woolf in his interim report supported the potential of dedicated kiosk technology located in court buildings and other places to guide the public on court and legal matters. In his final report he changed his view and favoured the use of court web sites as a source for electronically generated information and guidance.[33]

---

32. New York Family Courts <*http://ucs.ljx.com/famjtst.html*>.

33. Lord Woolf (1996). Access to Justice: Final Report to the Lord Chancellor on the Civil Justice System in England and Wales HMSO London 287.

A project in Maryland called the Peoples' Library compared kiosks with the Internet for providing legal information.[34] The project established a website organised as a set of libraries with information in major substantive areas such as family law, consumer law and landlord/tenant law. Each of the libraries contained information similar to that available through a kiosk. The user could directly fill out the forms on the screen and print them out on a local printer. According to one of the project authors the costs of developing a website are significantly lower than those associated with legal kiosks because there is no video component in the website. A video component requires an extensive storage capacity. The project planners considered that text on the website augmented by graphic presentations and streamed audio (which allows a listener to hear the information without having to wait) could be as effective as multimedia presentations that incorporate a large amount of video. In addition, according to the project designers, an Internet approach has other advantages over a typical stand-alone kiosk because:

- upgrades and changes to the substantive materials and surveys for feedback can be made in one central location rather than in many locations,
- material can be read at leisure and in the privacy of one's home or office rather than in a public place and with the potential pressure of queues,
- demographics about users can be instantly collected from a central location,
- other interactive functions such as electronic conferencing and online chat can be easily implemented,
- the Internet approach can easily be expanded to accommodate higher demand, the Internet is a more open system in that many people can readily contribute to the materials and content of programmes.

34. Granat, R. (1998). "Creating a network of community-based pro se (self-help) legal information centres", <*http://www.digital-lawyer.com/kioskl.htm*>.

One approach is for courts and tribunals to have a public information strategy that uses kiosks and Internet programmes and which takes into account consumer needs and preferences and provides effective coverage.

C. Unrepresented Litigants

Legal and court information is particularly required by unrepresented litigants. Many courts and tribunals have identified as an important issue their response to the needs of unrepresented litigants.

Unrepresented litigants within the civil justice system require information and advice on the variety of ways of resolving problems, information and advice on how to make a claim and how to respond to a claim as a defendant and advice and assistance on preparing and presenting their case.[35] At trial, such litigants may need special help in understanding the procedure followed during the hearing, presenting and closing their case, presenting their own evidence, testing the evidence of an opponent and cross-examination and preparing for and presenting an appeal.

Certain groups in the community have particular difficulties in obtaining access to legal information and services and to courts and tribunals. Their difficulties arise from language and cultural differences, geographical distance or physical or intellectual disability. Such groups can be assisted by appropriately adapted information systems. There are also many people who are not computer literate or who have a disability which prevents them using certain technologies. Differences in individual resources and capacity, experience and preferences may require some additional measures such as

- Advisers or instructors to provide assistance in the use of technologies or to assist in giving more information when there is ambiguity.
- Direct personal assistance and brochures and kits with a commitment to ensuring that the quality of interpersonal information services and printed material is satisfactory.

---

35. Lord Woolf Access to Justice: Interim Report to the Lord Chancellor on the Civil Justice System in England and Wales Lord Chancellor's Department London 1995, 120.

- Use of plain language in instructions and guidelines and the avoidance of technological jargon.

It should not be assumed that the newest technological innovation is necessarily the most useful and effective in providing information and services. For example, 'take home' DVD or videotapes may continue to be very effective tools for giving instruction partly because they can be viewed privately and replayed and also because most people have access to the players and are familiar with their use.

D. Privacy and Security

Privacy and security are two major and interrelated concerns with the use of new technologies in courts and tribunals and in legal and ADR practice. Information collected and collated through technology is much more readily accessible. There is no need to visit the court or tribunal to check on records which are available online, and which can provide details of parties to disputes, current listings and decisions concerning disputes.

The use of the computer is not necessarily anathema to privacy. For example, the centralisation of data made possible thorough computerised collection may lead to greater anonymity rather than less.[36] However, computers do offer greater potential for invasion of privacy in a more sophisticated and widespread fashion through:

i the potential for matching data offered by centralised systems and,for example, building up profiles or information on individuals,

ii the potential for computers to collect and store more information than previously possible,

iii the immediacy of online systems which can allow surveillance of the parties to transactions because an operator can determine the precise location of those concerned and

iv the potential for unauthorised, remote access which is known as 'hacking'.

36. Tucker, G. (1992). *Information Privacy Law in Australia,* Longman Professional Melbourne 7.

Another major concern in considering new technologies is the security of the processes. Much information generated in a legal context is sensitive, privileged or confidential. Courts and tribunals create large amounts of electronic information. The data is stored in a variety of locations throughout geographically dispersed courts and tribunals. Draft judgments in particular must be protected from loss, damage, misuse, interference, destruction or unauthorised disclosure. Users of any system, and those providing information, must be confident that such information is circulated only to appropriate and authorised clientele. Courts and tribunals have special security concerns that criminal records may be affected or tampered with, confidential information affecting hearings or future hearings may be inappropriately revealed and inadequate security could undermine public confidence in the justice system.[37]

It is difficult to assess the extent to which new technologies increase the risk of unauthorised use of information. For example, printed copies of documents may be stolen or lost or given to people who had no authority to receive them. Conversations on mobile phones may be intercepted or conversations taped. Faxes may be sent to the wrong location or read without authority. There is no system or method of recording or communication that will not have some degree of security risk. Some security risks may derive from the particular technology. Others may be due to lax or insufficient security measures, human error or omission. There are a number of particular security threats to information technology systems. These activities include industrial espionage and hacking, which may be achieved from inside or outside the organisation. 'Hackers' may wish to destroy, modify or steal data. A further security difficulty derives from computer viruses which refer to unwanted programmes which can reproduce themselves and corrupt other programmes. These viruses may lay dormant for some period and then contaminate whole systems.

Some of the common security measures are the use of passwords which are not easily recognisable and are changed frequently, use of encryption to ensure that a message cannot be read by anyone but the authorised receiver and that the message was not modified while being transmitted[38] and firewalls to verify that the communication is

37. Carlson, T. 'Information Superhighway Implementation Guidelines' National Center for State Courts *<http://www.ncsc.dni.us/ncsc/ISIG/guide.htm>*.

38. Carlson, T. *<http://www futurelawyer. com>*.

from authorised source. The procedures governing the use of information technology within courts and tribunals are normally prescribed in an information technology security manual. Each court and tribunal needs mechanisms in place to ensure compliance with such measures. While a detailed description of the contents of such a policy document is outside the scope of this chapter some of the areas that need to be addressed include

- the completion of a risk assessment,
- the physical security of IT equipment (denial of physical access to unauthorised personnel),
- external hacking and risk assessment,
- the prescription of a layered password regime,
- virus protection, Internet access,
- connections to external databases,
- logical access control (network directory access rights),
- information backup policy,
- changes to network configuration,
- remote access to network resources,
- uninterrupted power supply requirements,
- server redundancy,
- disaster recovery,
- activity monitoring,
- transmission of classified information by electronic means , destruction of electronic information,
- use of private contractors, recoverable services,
- reporting and investigation of incidents, and
- disposal of IT equipment.

E. Electronic Publishing on the Internet by Courts and Tribunals

Publication by courts and tribunals of judgments, decisions, court rules and other practice and procedure information could significantly increase access to justice. Judgments and decisions can be published on the Internet after they are handed down, without the delay involved in paper reporting. Many courts and tribunals maintain homepages on the Internet which offer significantly more information than just access to court decisions. Since 1990 the Supreme Court of the United States has provided public access to federal court information.[39] The Court's Electronic Bulletin Board System provides online access to the Court's automated docket, daily lists, Court opinions and Court rules. The Internet site of the Supreme Court of Florida[40] provides an extensive array of information such as judgments, legislation, Court lists, press releases, a legal research page, information on each judge, Court opinions and rules, information on CyberCourt, the Judicial Training Institute and the Kid's Court. Court proceedings can be viewed on video. There is a 'Self-help Centre' that covers a diverse range of legal issues such as adoption, civil rights, criminal law, wills and taxes, offering several articles on each topic. All these demonstrate the potential for publishing on the Internet, particularly with the aim of disseminating information to litigants and the public.

One of the challenges to improving the functionality of court documents published in electronic form stems from the way page numbers are handled in most electronic files. Pagination cannot generally be fixed in an electronic file. As a result, page numbers will vary according to the software used to view and print the document. The problem is best illustrated when court decisions and transcripts are published to the Internet. Court decisions and transcripts published on the Internet do not contain page numbers and accordingly the decisions cannot be cited without subsequent reference to commercially printed law reports.

Unlike page numbers, paragraph numbers are embedded in the body of the document and remain visible regardless of the file format or software used to view the document. Paragraph numbers provide a medium neutral citation form that is applicable to paper or electronic publishing. The benefits in providing court decisions in a medium neutral citation form include:

- reductions in the time taken to publish a judgment after it has been handed down,
- increased public access to decisions,

---

39. A directory of electronic public access services to automated information in the United States is at <*http://www.uscourts.gov/PubAccess.html*>.

40. <*http://www.flcourts.org/courts/supct/index.html*>.

- the ability to electronically link' decisions with other documents,
- the ability to search text and copy and paste between documents without retyping the text,[41] and
- a citation system compatible with new technologies.

In the United States, the American Bar Association (ABA) Special Committee on Citation Issues recommended in 1996 that all US jurisdictions adopt a medium neutral citation system for paper and electronic court decisions.[42] In addition, the Committee recommended that courts number the paragraphs in their decisions. In August 1996, the ABA approved a resolution made by the Committee calling for all state and federal courts to develop a standard citation system and recommending a format that could be used by state and federal courts. That resolution called for courts to identify the citation on each decision at the time the decision is made available to the public.

The High Court of Australia has recently moved to incorporate paragraph numbers into the body of judgments and allow the citation of court decisions in a medium neutral way where the decision itself has not been formally published.[43] Cases are cited by the year, court designator, and case number, with paragraph numbering for pinpoint cites.

IV
LIMITATIONS TO THE USE OF TECHNOLOGY

One difficulty with the growth of information technology in law is the tension between the greater accuracy and detail of information offered and the problem of managing increasingly large amounts of data. Some commentators argue that information technology has *'lessened'* control over information, by allowing the proliferation of unmanageable data. In the past, judges and lawyers were generally restricted to a relatively small number of reported cases. With the increasing use of technology to aid data storage and retrieval,

---

41. This can be especially useful to legal practitioners and judges when they quote from judgments.

42. The report is at <*http://www.abanet.org/citation/home.html*>.

43. See 'The Introduction of Paragraph Numbers in Court Judgments and the use of a Medium NeutralCitation System' <*http://www.hcourt.gov.au/short.htm*>.

significant numbers of unreported cases, as well as secondary materials, are available to lawyers and judges, potentially adding to legal practice and court research time. Judges and lawyers attribute today's escalating costs and delays in the courtroom to the document analysis and management tasks which that technology seems to require of them.[44]

Susskind claims that the problem is due to what he terms the 'technology lag'—while we have ever-increasing capacity to access vast amounts of information, knowledge-based systems are not yet sophisticated enough to analyse or manage the bulk of data.

Other types of technology may create a similar problem. For example, the use of audio-visual testimony may increase the number of witnesses involved in a court or tribunal appearance, thereby increasing costs to the court or tribunal and parties. An important question to consider is whether the benefits of new technologies outweigh any problems they may create, and whether technology has the solutions to the problem of information control that it has contributed to.

Technological change in any institution requires significant planning and funding. It is crucial to assess whether the benefits of implementing technological change outweigh the costs. There are a number of examples of cost-benefit studies in the area of technological change. One such Australian study focussed on the costs and benefits of electronic publishing (the delivery of information by computers) suggested that there was a compelling case for a wholesale shift in public administration to electronic distribution of reference information.[45] This shift was justifiable because it would result in financial savings for individual agencies and across the whole of federal administration, dramatic reductions in paper usage and saving in staff resources.

Technology may automate existing practices or act as a tool for innovative legal practices. One concern is that if technological developments are implemented without broad consideration of current procedures or without accompanying substantive reform, the technology may simply automate and entrench bad practice. The use of technology should not be regarded as an end in itself but as a

---

44. Susskind, R. (1996). *op cit.*, 59.

45. Intelligent Business Technologies, Nanabelles and STAT Tech <*http://www. softlaw. com.au*>.

means to improve access to justice, efficiency and effectiveness in relation to courts and tribunals and dispute resolution. Technology is simply one aspect of a broader reform agenda.

There is also a concern that the expansion of new technologies will create social classes of'information rich' and 'information poor'. In relation to legal disputes this could mean that some people involved in litigation may not have ready access to computers and other new technologies or may not have the necessary skills and experience to use them or to pay for assistance. Parties to disputes may have significant inequalities in technological resources. Parties who can use electronic technologies in collecting and retrieving information and presenting it in courts and tribunals may derive advantages from the technology which are unrelated to the strength or merits of their cases. Some parties may use their technological advantages to intimidate other parties and to pressure them to settle.

Protection of privacy is a major concern associated with the use of new technologies, particularly with the increasing use of the Internet. The use of new technologies can raise novel and important questions about the security of information technology systems data and communications.

A. Difficulties with the Use of Technology in Litigation

Implementing technological reform will often necessitate associated change to legislation and to practice and procedure. For example, the court rules relating to filing and service of documents may require change to cover new uses of technology, such as email. Problems may arise where court rules refer to a signature and it is not clear that an electronic signature or other form of electronic identification would be permitted. Forms and pleadings may also require revision and simplification.

Justice Olsson and Ian Rohde[46] suggest that there is likely to be a need to consider appropriate enabling legislation and rules of court to respond to matters such as:

- The means of authentication of court processes of all types issued by the auto-print process.

---

46. Justice L.T. Olsson & I. Rohde (1997). "Coming Ready or Not: Courts and Information Technology", 71 *Reform* 10.

- The replacement of the traditional hard copy affidavit with some form of electronically authenticated declaration having the same legal effect.
- The formalisation of processes related to remote applications to the court, the mode of administering oaths or affirmations to witnesses (whether within or outside the jurisdiction) for the purposes of giving evidence by video link, and a definition of the manner and circumstances in which it is permissible to give remote evidence by video link in civil and criminal cases.
- The manner and circumstances in which evidence by electronic charts, summaries from databases and interactive graphics, or virtual reality reconstructions or demonstrations, may be resorted to.[47]
- The enabling of processes such as pretrial activities by video link, without the parties and/or counsel physically being in the presence of the presiding judicial officer
- The creation, maintenance and archiving of electronic files to replace hard copy documentation as the court record
- The authorisation of service and the giving of notice of court processes by e-mail, subject to appropriate safeguards
- A comprehensive revision of all statutory procedures related to the conduct of litigation (especially in the criminal jurisdiction) to enable electronic procedures to replace those currently associated with use of hard copy documents
- Facilitating the proof of the court record and process outcomes by appropriately authenticated computer output.

In addition, courts and tribunals may be required to vary rules and processes to take into account changing practices associated with the use of technology, for example:

- whether there should be mandatory rules for electronically filed court documents so that solicitors sign that each witness has seen and approved electronic versions of the documents;
- to ensure that software protects against alteration of electronically filed documents;

47. Some attention has already been given to this type of problem in countries such as Singapore.

- whether the ambit of discovery rules needs to accommodate the changing scope and form of disclosed documents;
- the discovery of back-up disks of electronic documents must have accompanying indexes of the files, allowing opposing parties to search for relevant documents;
- will the imaging of documents increase costs by causing unnecessary documents to be imaged and referred to at trial by parties?
- will courts be required to make rules to deal with the gross inequities in resources and potential unfairness to one party where one side has access to, and plans to utilise, a variety of technological resources?

B. Costs of Technological Litigation Support

The cost of setting up a litigation support system may be passed on to the client.[48] The factors that will affect the cost of technological litigation support include the number and size of documents, the need for photocopies, anticipated hardware and software requirements of the litigation support design, whether documents are able to be scanned optically and/or by OCR and the length of the hearing.

Lord Woolf concluded that specific decisions were required on whether the cost of IT should be included in general overheads and/ or whether, in specific cases, the costs of specially tailored systems should be recovered from the parties.[49]

C. Government Funding

Another limitation to the use of technology in courts is ongoing funding. While Governments have a central role in funding technology in courts and tribunals they do not usually provide a specific budget allocation to IT for courts and tribunals—courts and tribunals make their own allocations from their budgets. New equipment, its installation and maintenance and associated staff training can be expensive. Courts and tribunals need to demonstrate the benefits of technological innovation, including the potential to

---

48. Warren, M. (1996). "Using Technology to Manage: Litigation Designing and Implementing a Litigation Support System", Government Lawyers CLE seminar Sydney 31 July, 6.
49. Lord Woolf Access (1996). *op. cit.*, pp.285-6.

reduce public costs, to receive additional funding for their IT programmes.

One possible source of funding sometimes used in the United States is public/private partnerships.[50] In some cases a technology vendor may enter an agreement with a court or tribunal for a project funded out of future savings. Another funding arrangement is outsourcing or privatisation of the court or tribunal's IT programme with the potential for the high front-end costs of using new technology being amortised by the outsourcing company and spread over the lifetime of the contract. In some cases private firms may provide technology free on the basis that they can use the experience to test and refine products and to advertise their products. There is concern, however, that public/private partnerships can compromise the perception of the independence and impartiality of courts and tribunals and their function as public institutions. Cost sharing of technology among courts, tribunals and other agencies is a further response to the costs of technology. Such arrangements are possible where the information and court and tribunal processes are the same or similar.

V.
CONCLUSION

In conclusion, technology can transform the business of courts and tribunals and make justice more accessible, but to achieve that transformation careful consideration needs to be given to the elements which would contribute towards that transformation. Some of the key elements include case management, legal research and information collection, the conduct of litigation, drafting of documents and providing judgments and decisions, access to the court and Court and tribunal administration.

Technology can improve the way in which courts and tribunals supervise the conduct of cases that come before them. This can include designating cases to particular dispute resolution options or litigation tracks and/or to particular personnel, identifying issues and setting timetables and schedules for litigation. Computer software

50. Court Technology Bulletin (1996). "Court technology in the 21st Century", 8(1) <*www.ncsc.dni.us/ncsc^ulletin/future/future/future.htm*>.

can accelerate the processes of case management by automating tasks previously done manually and performing additional functions. Conduct of legislation can be transformed with technology by identifying, retrieving and analysing legislation and cases and gathering relevant factual information, recording and presenting evidence and transcripts and communicating with parties and/or their legal representatives before and during hearings.

Judges and tribunal members can also use computers to research and write decisions. Websites and kiosks can improve access for unrepresented litigants, those seeking advice or assistance and the general public. Court administration can benefit by improved file management and correspondence, personnel and financial matters, and security and maintenance.[51]

Finally, there appears to be few aspects of dispute resolution or the operation of the courts and tribunals that will not be affected by significant changes in technology. Law, in particular, can be seen as a service that can benefit greatly from new technologies because of the need in law for accurate, up to date information (and often also for 'snapshots' of the law at particular points in time) and because of law's frequent cross-referencing and reliance on precedent. It is an information-rich service which can be ably supported by technology.

---

51. Australian Legal Reform Commission (1998), *op cit.*

12

Technology and its Impact on Backlog and Delay Reduction

AMARJIT SINGH BEDI

"Technology Does Not Drive Change—It Enables Change."

— Anonymous

Introduction

The Indian Judiciary is slowly recognising the detailed role that information communication technology (ICT) can play. The Report on Strategic Plan for implementation of ICT in Indian Judiciary[1] justifies the need of introduction of technology in a systemic way in the courts by explicitly stating that, "It needs no emphasis that Indian Judicial System is facing an appalling state of affair. It is apprehended that court congestion and delays in adjudication may acquire a perennial nature. Its functional credibility, both in domestic and international world is at stake. There is an urgency to take immediate steps to enhance its quality, productivity, accountability and transparency." Use of technology can help facilitate the judiciary in bringing greater access, transparency, and ultimately help in reducing backlog and delays in the court. Information technology is a tool that can improve court and justice system performance through instant, integrated, and linked information.

1. Supreme Court of India (2005). *Report on Strategic Plan for Implementation of Information and Communication Technology in Indian Judiciary*, E-Committee, New Delhi. This report was prepared by the E-Committee under the Chairmanship of Justice G.C. Bharuka, former Judge, High Courts of Patna and Karnataka, Justice Bharuka was supported by Shri N.S. Kulkarni, Member-Judicial, (District Judge, Karnataka Judicial Service) and Shri Manas Patnaik Member-Technical, (Director, Software Technology Parks of India). The report was presented to the Hon'ble Chief Justice of India on 11th May 2005.

The First National Judicial Pay Commission Report or the Shetty Commission Report[2] formulated a specific question on application of Information Technology in Court System and commissioned IIM, Bangalore to enquire whether the introduction of computers had brought about any sea-change in the work and efficiency in various activities of the court. IIM, Bangalore, in its report[3] recommended that information technology was absolutely necessary for improvements in operational efficiency, coordination, accessibility and speed in the judicial administration. The Report concluded that with information technology support, judges can assume greater control over cases and responsibility for case management. The report further highlighted the various advantages of computer based management system.

With a rapid expansion in cases filed, the courts have began to creak, throughout the country, under the burden of hundreds of thousands of cases being filed everyday. By the end of 2004, nearly 3.4 million cases were pending before the High Courts and another 27.8 million in the Subordinate Judiciary comprising around 8.2 million civil cases and 19.6 million criminal cases. During the 2002-2004, on an average, the subordinate courts disposed 13 million cases every year while the High Courts had disposed of 1.5 million cases every year. Moreover, the judge to population ratio is fairly low in India. These figures, therefore reflect, the fact that the judges are indeed under pressure to perform better despite working beyond their optimum levels.

While the solution perhaps lies in a judicious mix of increased judicial strength and implementation of improved case management techniques along with introduction of new technology in the

---

2. *First National Judicial Pay Commission Report,* Information Technology in the Administration of Justice Section, Question No. 56. As per Resolution of Ministry of Law, Justice and Company Affairs (Department of Justice) the First National Judicial Pay Commission was constituted by the Government of India on 21st March 1996. It is headed by Justice Jagannatha Shetty, Former Judge, Supreme Court of India. The members of the Commission are Justice P.K. Bahri (Rtd.), Former Judge of the Delhi High Court, and Justice A.B. Murgod (Rtd.), Former Judge of the Karnataka High Court. The Commission submitted its Report regarding Pay Structure of the Judicial Officers of the Subordinate Judiciary of the country during November 1999. Presently, it is examining the grievances of the staff of the Subordinate Judiciary as per the direction of the Supreme Court. This Report is also known as the Shetty Commission Report.
3. Indian Institute of Management, *Report on Improving Work Methods and Work Environment in the Subordinate Courts in India,* Bangalore.

courtrooms, this chapter specifically addresses the role that technology can play in reducing backlog and delay in the courtrooms. Effectively supported judicial decisions require timely, complete, and accurate information. Information technology helps the court user assist the court in delivering better quality of justice with less delay. Today a judge in the court needs access to case material instantly in a simple and lucid manner. Police and prosecution, judges and advocates need to know 'right now' about case histories and the existence and status of orders. No matter how complicated a case history is, advancement in information technology systems can help courts organise and manage the documents that are filed and the hearings that are held each day. Cases and information about them can be accessed any time, from the bench, in chambers, in administrative offices, on the road, and at home.

Whither Technology

Technology gives with a click of a mouse solution, where users can move with ease through data and information that formerly was either buried under old paper records or required a tedious process to get the relevant data. Click of a mouse technology increases efficiency of the court and help in giving the courts a faster turn around time (TAT). But new technology alone will not improve inefficient work processes. The new system must be well designed. The information delivered to end users must be accurate. The end users must know both what they are trying to do and how to do it. When information technology is applied skilfully, communication and decisions, both judicial and managerial, can be improved. There are several fields where information technology plays a role in the court functioning from case management systems and electronic data interchange to video and audio conferencing.

There are various reasons for delay and backlog in the courts. Perhaps the most important reason is the sheer numbers of cases that are filed in the courts and which is increasing everyday making it difficult for the disposal rate of the courts to keep pace with the fresh filing or the institution rate. Moreover, there exist huge vacancies and they are consistently lying vacant. There is an urgent need to increase the judge-to-population ratio.[4] There are also huge procedural delays

4. *All India Judges' Association vs. Union of India*, (2002) 4 SCC 247.

caused by lack of case management as well as caseflow management. Technology can provide great deal of assistance at this level.

For instance one of the typical problems faced in the court is to bring witnesses/accused in the courtroom. Given the length and breadth of our country and the geographic location of the courtrooms it is not always very convenient for a witness to take his day off and attend to a case where there is no certainty whether he will be able to give disposition in the case at the end of the day. Sometimes the witnesses have to travel far and between to reach courts where they can present themselves for a case which has been pending for many years. Despite all the efforts on the part of the witness to attend a court hearing, the court may have its own reason for adjournment of the case. It may be due to the advocate for the party not appearing, to the judge being absent or the matter may not reach on that particular day due to heavy cause list of the judge. But in all these circumstances, the witness is the sufferer.

Technology does not have a solution to the problem when a judge is absent but it does have solution in the form of tools like video conferencing which can greatly reduce the hardship both financial and in terms of time for the witness; in particular for those who are from outside the jurisdiction.

Video conferencing is a medium by which two or more users can hold conference using audio video capability, though being physically located at two different geographic locations. E-Committee[5] and various other studies have given importance to the use of video conferencing especially in criminal cases.

In international experience video conferencing has been found to be successful when used for expert witnesses, vulnerable parties, remote hearings and prisoners. High-end video conferencing linked with courtroom recording has the added benefit of recording the evidence (live) which can be used later for the purpose of checking the demeanour of the witness or for verifying the exact statement made by a witness, etc.

Video conferencing tool, if used efficiently for recording evidence can save a lot of court's time and the cost on the exchequer for

5. E-Committee was setup by G.O. Order dated 28.12.2004 for assisting the Chief Justice of India in formulating a National Policy on Computerisation of Indian Judiciary and advice him on the technological, communication and management related changes.

bringing and taking the undertrials from the prison to the courtroom. Infact some of the subordinate courts in India have already started reaping benefits of such facility. The Delhi subordinate court is in the process of installing video conferencing facility in its premise.

National Informatics Centre (NIC) has more than 127 video conferencing studios across the country. Having such a large footprint, the courts all over the country can conveniently use the facility of video conferencing for trying criminal cases where an accused is located in a different jurisdiction or where the witness/party is located outside its jurisdiction. The Supreme Court is proposing to establish video conferencing facility in the Conference Hall of the Supreme Court to enable the Judges to interact with the Judges of the High Courts, Government Ministries, etc.

Court Case Management

Caseflow management is "The court supervision of the case progress of all cases filed in that court. It includes management of the time and events necessary to move a case from the point of initiation (filing, date of contest, or arrest) through disposition, regardless of the type of disposition. Caseflow management is an administrative process; therefore, it does not directly impact the adjudication of substantive legal or procedural issues."[6]

It further goes on to describe, "Caseflow management includes early court intervention, establishing meaningful events, establishing reasonable timeframes for events, establishing reasonable timeframes for disposition, and creating a judicial system that is predictable to all users of that system. In a predictable system, events occur on the first date scheduled by the court. This results in counsel being prepared, less need for adjournments, and enhanced ability to effectively allocate staff and judicial resources."

A typical case management system (CMS) collects, organises, processes, stores, retrieves information, etc. There is no limit on the number or types of court events which the CMS can record and track. The CMS can record events from payment of process fee to change of jurisdiction, execution of judgments, etc. Doing so many events manually is not only tedious but also susceptible to errors

---

6. State Court Administrative Office (2004). *Caseflow Management Guide*, Michigan, USA.

and inaccuracy. Introduction of Information technology can automate the process and help the courts in ways that helps in reducing redundant data entry, delays, improving hearings and trials, improving the quality of sentencing with providing better information to the judges.

The trend of the leading courts in the world is to develop a robust case management system which is multi-tiered, multi-platform and web-based. A fully developed IT enabled CMS will be able to reduce case delays through more accurate and timely reporting on case status. An automated CMS can improve upon system of manual files by way of offering real-time update into the status of cases, and it can generate data for the specialist known as Information Analysts (IA) to ascertain the exact bottlenecks in the courts and the various sources of delay. The reasons for delay in progress of case in courtroom may vary from transfer of cases between the courts/ jurisdiction to non-presence of lawyers. The causes of delay ascertained through use of an automated CMS may pinpoint trends and highlight some of the major causes of delay. It may be that the CMS is able to highlight that a particular defence lawyer uses delay tactics at a particular stage of the case, the CMS may highlight that a particular judge is inherently slow in disposing particular type of cases. The benefits of using an electronic CMS are unlimited.

Sub-components of Case Management System

Process Serving: A fully automated CMS usually is linked with the process serving branch of the court. Process Serving Module of a CMS has the ability to track the progress of each individual processes issued by the court in each case. The processes can be tracked not only by case but can also be tracked by process-server, area, jurisdiction type, etc. Some states in India have already achieved this enhanced functionality of the process serving. The District Courts in Karnataka have successfully implemented Process Serving module which is being used very effectively for issuing summons. In the City Civil Court, Karnataka the Process Serving Department is located in a 6’ X 6’ room. It contains one computer and one person is working on it. That one person single-handedly is generating the processes for the entire court. This computer is in turn connected with the central server. How the process serving module works in Karnataka is fairly simple. Once the court issues notice to a particular defendant, the plaintiff then has to deposit the process fee in the registry. Once the same is deposited in the registry, the same will show up on the computer screen of the Process Serving Department. The one person operating the computer would then simply would have to take a printout and mark it to process servers/bailiff for the area. The court has achieved the ability to automatically generate summons/notices and does not require actual physical file movement for preparing summons. This has greatly helped in reducing the delay caused at the process serving stage of a case.

Listing and Attendance: Technology can help the judges in better control of their calendars (cause list). It can help judges to process a case with more effective hearings and fewer adjournments and readers to list cases in the cause list which are less susceptible to adjournments. One of the major causes of adjournment in the courts is due to the poor level of attendance at court hearings by advocates, witnesses and/or parties. There are various reasons why the court users are not attending court. From the advocates point of view they feel that there is no certainty of time when the case will be taken up for hearing. However, advocates who are regularly appearing in courts have over a period of time honed their skills and learnt from experience when a case might come up for hearing in the day. This method of lawyers regulating their daily schedule is not scientific and does not inspire any confidence in the court work process. Technology can bridge this gap by introducing methods which helps in making the court hearing more predictable. With the advent of mobile phones and short messaging service (SMS), court can send alerts to lawyers/litigant on the expected time when the case will come up for hearing. Publishing the status of court hearing (live) on the Internet is another option. Such a facility has already been implemented in the Supreme Court. By making available entire case history online also makes the lawyer/litigant better prepared for the hearing. Daily cause list generation with historical data of each case again gives time and opportunity for lawyers to prepare themselves and have lesser reasons to avoid attendance on the day of hearing.

File Tracking: A typical case file in the court is taken out and kept back numerous times during its life time. Sometimes it also gets transferred to other courts or other jurisdiction. Keeping a track of these huge volume of case files have been an issue and a cause for concern amongst the court staff. For example there are more than 4,00,000 cases pending in the Delhi district court alone and there are roughly 3,000 staff who have to track these files apart from doing other tasks. To manage such volume of cases considerable time of the court staff is spent which could be better utilised in managing other court related functions.

RFID: Bar coding technology is one answer to tracking files but it is fraught with its own problem. With the emerging new technologies such as RFID (Radio Frequency Identification Device), it is now possible to have embedded chips on the file covers which will enable the RFID readers to track a file even without opening a file cabinet to know the inventory of the files inside. RFID is based on radio wireless technology and thus does not require line of sight as is required by other wireless devices like a remote control which are based on Infrared (IR) technology. Companies are now offering RFID file tracking systems for law firms, courts and government agencies. The principle for working of RFID system is based on automatic identification and tracking of items through use of an identification chip or 'tag' that sends data to readers through wireless data communication. It is useful to think of an RFID system as one in which these tags enable items to 'speak' about their identity, location, activity or history through readers and, ultimately, to application software that can process and utilise this information. RFID tags can be read automatically when a tagged file comes past or near a reader, reducing the labour required to scan product and allowing more proactive, real-time tracking. RFID tags are more durable than bar codes, which can become smudged and unreadable.

A RFID enabled court will have file cabinets, bookcases, and doorway portals that provide immediate real time inventory of all file folders contained therein. Great benefit may be provided in the file room where file folder sorting takes the greatest amount of time. Folders previously lost on shelves, bookcases or file cabinets may be more quickly located. RFID readers may be strategically placed to provide security zones. Further, RFID readers may be integrated with digital security cameras for date and time stamping of digital film taken on document and people movement. Transponders on file folders or other assets can trigger alarms or discretely notify a supervisor, if they are improperly removed.

Document Management System (DMS): Document management is the ability to produce and store documents associated with the file. DMS is tightly integrated with the Case Management System. It consists of a database server which is linked to the CMS. Whenever a document is filed or saved in electronic format, it goes to the DMS (Database server), which then can be used by the CMS for accessing the binary large objects (BLOB). DMS is based on restricted access based on different level of rights, given to the users. The BLOB can be image file like jpg or Tiff or it can be document file like PDF or Doc. An image file can be created whilst scanning a document. This is particularly in cases where the court feels the need to digitise or electronically store the documents, specially the evidence. In some cases that have been pending for years it was found that majority of the document evidence was not in a condition to be presented before the court. There may be various reasons for the record to deteriorate to such a stage, not blaming only the poor storage techniques. But the net effect of such event is that another adjournment has to be granted for the court to enable to reconstruct the file. There is also the problem of storing the huge number of files in the court premises and the cost of transportation and storing the files. The Supreme Court has taken steps of digitisation of old records stored in the record room godowns, so as to make space available for the fresh records. This process has prevented the Supreme Court from loss of records, helped in saving storage space, manage records, and find documents quickly. As the scanned documents kept in the DMS are available centrally on Intranet, it has also helped in eliminating the need for file cabinets.

Technology can assist the court in this field not only to speed the process in how documents are received in the courtrooms but also to protect and safeguard the files (specially the evidence). Internationally DMS are closely linked with Exhibit Management System (EMS). An EMS enables the court to generate receipt and record the acceptance of exhibit (document). The record contains detail of the document, from whom the document was received from, the case or cases they relate to. The system also is able to track the flow and location of the exhibit (document) and date of return of the exhibit to its owner.

In Karnataka District and Subordinate Courts, judgments/orders are stored in DMS. While designing and implementing the DMS, the designer[7] faced peculiar problem, that, the language predominantly used by the judges at the district and subordinate court level was not English but Kannada. To train all of them to learn English for

7. Justice, G.C. Bharuka, Retd. Chairman E-Committee and then Judge of High Court of Karnataka.

dictating judgments in English would not make sense. Instead an innovative solution was found where a software called 'Surubhi' was integrated with Microsoft Word which allowed typing of judgments/ order in the local language i.e. Kannada. Once judgment/order were typed and signed by the judicial officer, it would be uploaded on the server (DMS) and once the judgment/order was released on the server the same could not be corrected/edited by the judicial officer. It would require a fresh order to be passed to modify the same. The DMS would also record the number of times a document was opened/ closed/edited/ with a time-stamp on it.

The DMS can be further used in conjugation with digitally signed certified copies. One of the many tasks performed by a judge is signing of daily orders on order sheets; judges would sign digitally on electronic copies using digital signatures. Fewer persons are required to man the job for issuing certified copies. Lawyers and litigants can then download these digitally signed electronic copies of orders and judgments. Benefit of using digitally signed copies of order is that it does not need to be cross-checked with the physical file as the DMS takes care of the checking the authenticity of the document. This can substantially reduce the delay in issuing certified copies from the court which in turn will benefit the caseflow as there will be one less ground for adjournment.

DMS can be linked with e-filing capabilities which can further save time for the court and user. Electronic filing or e-filing is a method of filing court documents in an electronic format rather than a traditional paper format. Filing of documents can be in person over the counter or through e-mail or over the Internet through court web portal. One of the great advantages of introducing e-filing is that not only can it save considerable time but also reduce other ancillary costs involved for the lawyers and litigants like making multiple copies on the paper, photocopying, etc.

Workflow Management

Courts are like businesses. They have lots of business rules. The cases move from one stage to another, from one location to another. Huge staff is there to man the files and its movement. For instance, to make sure that the cases are listed on the date they are required to be listed, issue summons/notices are to be issued. Lots of such business rules are dependant on the efficiency of the staff and due to human frailties, the possibility of human error is also huge. Each time there is a human error, it results in delay. Technology can subtly but surely help the courts in removing the chances of human error.

Incorporating the workflow system in the court is the ability to trigger reminders and assign actions to other staff, etc. Such a system will be able to generate alerts automatically for the judge and/or court officials, especially for cases that require special attention or accelerated case management, etc. This added functionality will enable any case management system to do automatic workload assessment.

The CMS implemented in the Supreme Court of India allows for automatic deletion/shifting of excess matters and proposing next listing date automatically. This has not only brought efficiency in the court but also helped in creating a more appropriate calendar list.

An essential workflow management has capabilities to (i) trigger automated reminders and assignment of tasks to different persons in the court; (ii) link up with the business rules of the district courts and reducing human intervention as well as the ability to support the assignment of further work tasks including rescheduling a task and repeating the task at a later date, and the ability to change the status of work tasks from a list of values; (iii) automatically alert the judge and/or court officials of cases that require special attention or accelerated case management; (iv) enable the system to automatically put the cases in different tracks as suggested in Supreme Court judgement; (v) maintain various Work Task related information such as who, case details, task type, task details, resource details, task type, action date, date completed, task status, special features; (vi) assign tasks to the Work Task List using various rules such as a specific date or 'not before' time delay; (vii) schedule or trigger a single or multiple Work Task(s) such as by a case outcome, another Work Task, document filing; (viii) support the assignment of further Work Tasks including rescheduling a task and repeating the task at a later date; (ix) generate notification of assignment/directive to officers concerned such as notification about the assignment of a task, the status of a task, the flow history of a task, reminder flags of a task, the delay in completion of a task, and the actual completion of a task; (x) view the full schedule of Work Tasks pending by case, date or diary holder.

Online Payment Gateway: We have seen the benefits of the use of online payment gateway system in commercial transactions. Most of the banks in India have come out with their portals where you can make payments electronically, check your balance online, order for drafts, new cheque books, etc. Introducing a similar facility in the courts will have a considerable impact on the way we do business. An online payment gateway is closely linked with Fee Management System (manage and record payments into and out of court). Most of the courts at the district level have not reached a stage where the courts are managing their records and/or payments electronically.

Presently, lot of time is spent either by lawyers and/or litigants to stand in the queue for making payments or for purchasing the court fees. Lot of cases get delayed from listing as the court fees paid is not appropriate. Similar is the case in issuing processes also as sometimes the appropriate court fees is not affixed on the process. Introduction of online payment gateway and linking it with fee management system will further boost facilities like e-filing, e-services, e-transaction and substantially benefit the user in reducing his costs, time (working at convenient hours), bringing in transparency, and improving efficiency.

With accurate real-time financial reports, courts will be better able to meet their fiduciary responsibilities. Information technology enables better use of court resources, including judges, staff, equipment, and courtrooms. The system can be more accountable. But these and other equally significant benefits are not guaranteed. Skill is needed in the design of Information technology and its day-to-day management, maintenance, and upgrade.

Differentiated Case Management (DCM): is early screening of cases for complexity based on established criteria. Once screening is done then assignment of cases to unique processing tracks based on screening assessment best suited to each track takes place. Technology can help DCM in this process. A fully developed DCM system can assign different management tracks to different cases in accordance with the nature and complexity of each case based on set business rules.

For instance in a recent judgment of Supreme Court,[8] the Hon'ble Court held that:

"The judge may shift a case from one track to another, depending upon the complexity and other circumstances of the case... where

8. *Salem Advocate Bar Association,Tamil Nadu vs. UOI* in CWP No. 496/2002.

computerisation is available, the monthly data will be fed into the computer in such a manner that the judge referred to in clause (2) above, will be able to ascertain the position and the stage of every case in every track from the computer screen. Over a period, all cases pending in his Court will be covered."

It is possible to develop DCM system for the courts in India which will be able to incorporate the rules set by Hon'ble Supreme Court in the aforesaid judgment and mark each case automatically to a different track based on the business rules. DCM system can be designed further in such a way that it will enable to bring in more changes as and when required based on new business rules, etc.

Workload Balancing: The senior judges of each jurisdiction have to allocate cases amongst the judges of his jurisdiction. However, there is no scientific process involved in this except for looking at the pendency in each courtroom before allocating cases. The result is that sometimes even though judges who are dealing with lesser number of cases, although they are more complicated in nature have to deal with additional cases to keep a 'balance' with other colleagues in the same jurisdiction. This only increases the backlog and pendency in that particular courtroom as the so assigned judge is unable to dispose off other cases. However, with introduction of workload balancing functionality in a CMS, the senior judges get a tool to allocate cases in their jurisdiction based on a scientific analysis done by the system itself on various parameters including age of cases pending, complexity of cases, sub-type of case, performance of judge, etc.

Appointment of Judges: One of the measures for reducing backlog and delay in the courts is by increasing the number of judges in the courts. Law Commission of India[9] (July 1987) had recommended under the chapter "Technological Advances and its Use in the Context of Judicial Appointments" that a database should be maintained of lawyers and judges. It enumerates the process of selecting a candidate to be elevated to the High Court. In respect of a member of the district judiciary, every judgment that is delivered and which has been dealt with in appeal by the High Court should be scientifically analysed with regard to his ability, speed with which

---

9. Law Commission of India (1987). *The One Hundred and Twenty First Report on a New Forum for Judicial Appointments*, Ministry of Law, Government of India, Delhi.

the case is disposed off, intimate knowledge of law, diction, rationality of conclusion and whether it is in tune with philosophy of constitution.

While dealing with a member of the bar, every case in which he appears and argues, the nature of his arguments may be collected from the judgments delivered and analysed to the same extent possible and fed in the computer.

Computerisation programme is undertaken and a watch is being kept over up-coming members of the Bar as well as members of the judicial service. This will be an additional advantage over and above getting objective material for scientific assessment of the person concerned.

Analysing KPI's: The importance of collecting and analysing data cannot be stressed enough. In fact one of the key ways of targeting and hitting on backlog in the courtrooms is to collate and gather data to act upon the weaknesses. A good case monitoring system enables the court to plan and budget in real-time, improve performance of court, make events more predictable, improve processes for better control, help in administrative decision making, etc. A well developed performance monitoring system, on other hand is able to use the CMS to collate and gather reliable data for making considered and specific predictions based on the trends. A performance monitoring team consists of IA's running world-class software like Cognas, SAS, etc.

Online Analytical Processing (OLAP): Tools provide analysis of data stored in a database. OLAP tools enable users to analyse different dimensions of multidimensional data. NIC has been able to develop various reports that meet the High Court requirement. However, these reports are fixed and number in for every report otherwise sought, it requires programming and developing time and there is lack of flexibility. With incorporation of OLAP tools and data warehouse servers, CMS will be able to generate reports 'on the fly' based on the information sought by the Court.

A simple method of measuring the state of health of court is to determine whether filings are outpacing disposals. However, the IA's use various other measures to determine the state of health of the courts including case age, filings, disposals, adjournment rate, number of hearings per case, etc.

The E-Committee[10] has envisioned that there will be development of National Judicial Data Centre. This implementation will be based on implementation of Relational Database Management System (RDBMS) and with Wide Area Networking (WAN), to create a national grid of court information. The benefit of having National Judicial Data Centre will be that there will be availability of national data broken down to the smallest denominator. It will enable the Court to take strategic decision on measures for reducing backlog and delay based on the reports generated from the data so collected in the National Judicial Data Centre.

Organisational MIS development: One of the benefits of having an Organisational MIS in a company is that it is able to manage its workforce with efficiency. Till recently the courts did not think of themselves to be an organisation which needs to man its staff as a company. But in the recent past, the mindset has changed where the courts are considering implementing Organisational MIS for better and efficient management of its workforce. The district court in Delhi has a total staff of more than 4,000 employees including class IV employees; however there is a lack of properly implemented Organisational MIS. Setting up such a system will enable the court administrator to better manage its staff and will be able to deploy the staff for optimum utilisation. Many of the courts in India are considering the option of implementing Organisational MIS with attendance recording system to record and monitor the attendance of the court employees.

The Supreme Court already has been reaping the benefits of having an Organisational MIS implemented in the court. Information of interest for the employees of the Supreme Court including telephone directory is available on Intranet.

Online Law Library: is a domain where one can organise and access statutes, rules, court opinions, and other legal works including online legal research databases, CD-ROM legal collections, and Internet services. Online query system is helpful for precedents, citations, codes, statutes, etc. Introducing online libraries in the court will be beneficial for improving the quality of research as more and precise material will be accessible quickly, in a form which is more

10. Supreme Court of India (2005). *Report on Strategic Plan for Implementation of Information and Communication Technology in Indian Judiciary*, E-Committee, New Delhi.

acceptable to court methods. It will be beneficial to lawyers holding many briefs as they will be able to do research for multiple cases on specific issues and come better prepared in the courts. It is assessed that one of the reason for adjournments in the courts is that the lawyers are ill-prepared for the case. However, having better tools such as access to law library with up-to-date case law can be of great benefit to the stakeholders.

Wi-Fi Network: Communication within the court and between the courts is very important. Normal physical channels of communication are time consuming and slow. Technology gives option for the courts to exchange data and communicate electronically using Local Area Network (LAN) or Wide Area Network (WAN). LAN/WAN enables the court to exchange data from the different courtrooms and the various court-complexes in the jurisdiction. LAN and WAN connections can be made either using wires like CAT cables. There is also the option for court to connect wirelessly using new and emerging technologies such as Wi-Fi[11] for LAN and the Wi-FiMax for WAN.

Introducing Wi-Fi also gives the option of providing 'hotspots'. A hotspot is a zone within which when a Wi-Fi enabled computer is brought then the computer can access internet/intranet provided, the user has necessary permission to log on to that network. Introducing such a facility can be a great boon both for the court staff and the lawyers who will be able to log on to the court server or portal of the court and access information relating to the case. Today Supreme Court and other High Courts are providing lot of information on the Internet including list of filing defects. Users like lawyers and litigants can log on to the website and access such information if courts are Wi-Fi enabled without having to bother with messy wires.

Conclusion

> "It should be kept in mind that there is nothing more difficult to carry out nor more doubtful of success nor more dangerous to manage than to introduce a new system of things; for the introducer has as his enemies all those who benefit from the old system, and only lukewarm defenders in all those who would benefit from the new system."
> - Niccolò Machiavelli, The Prince (1513), Chapter VI

---

11. A set of standards that set forth the specifications for transmitting data over a wireless network.

> "The first rule of any technology used in a business is that automation applied to an efficient operation will magnify the efficiency. The second is that automation applied to an inefficient operation will magnify the inefficiency." – Bill Gates

Effective court leaders are realistic about what technology can do, what it will cost, how long it will take to implement, and what is involved in its maintenance and upgrade. The knowledge required managing technology and its rate of change is considerable. Court leaders must know the fundamentals and ensure that they, and their technical staff, keep current with how other organisations, including courts, are successfully using technology. To establish and to manage expectations about technology, court leaders must know what options exist, how they are being used in courts and other organisations, and how technology is evolving. Only then can they oversee staff and vendors to ensure that the most appropriate solutions are implemented. No one can manage what he or she does not adequately understand.

It is difficult and sometimes impractical to mirror the full complexity of justice system and court processes in information systems.

Although the same rules and procedures may govern courts within a state, the size of the court, the nature of the facility and local legal culture, among other factors, drive differences in specialisation and the division of labour among staff. One-size-fits-all solutions do not work.

Court leaders must take responsibility for Information Technology. If the court lacks strategic vision about technology and a multi-year plan, they work with others to create them. A court leader must be able to articulate this vision, convince others inside and outside of the judicial branch to cooperate, and lead the management of political, policy, fiscal, and technical issues related to technology. They work with others to acquire sufficient resources and to oversee the analysis and improvement of the *status quo*.

There should be a clear vision of how technology can be applied to improve courts and the justice system: information technology can solve the problem of increased workload on courts by addressing and increasing the court technology capacities; technology can enhance the quality and timeliness of justice; provide equal and open access to justice; increase the accountability of judges and other court officials; bring in transparency; and improve the business practices of the judicial branch and their justice partners.

Training is another major component for successful implementation of technology in the courts. For the success of office automation, court users have to learn the use of technologies including electronic mail, word processing, spreadsheets, Internet access, and database tools and their application in the court environment. Implementation of technology in the courts such as court recording, video conferencing, CMS system, etc. without adequate training can cause major problems for smooth and efficient running of courts. Therefore all efficient courts in the world spend sufficient resources in training and providing support of troubleshooters to solve technology related problems in the courts.

Technology, if applied efficiently in the courts will help the judiciary in making available case, including all of the data, documents, evidence, and legal reference materials more efficiently to the people and to whom it matters. Technology will help to improve the speed, consistency, and fairness of decisions. The future for judiciary looks very bright and optimistic. There are new and emerging technologies for the court and judiciary from digital audio and video recording to video teleconferencing, voice recognition, to Internet, laptops, imaging and animation, electronic mail and calendars, integrated software, automated CMS, electronic evidence presentation, etc. Integration of court technology with other justice organisations will enable to open, smooth, and timely information flow. However, if not applied properly it will only magnify the inefficiency in the courts and create more chaos and confusion.

13

Crime Deterrence and the Need for Reforms: An Analysis of Indian States

DEBASHIS CHAKRABORTY,
ARNAB KUMAR HAZRA and PAVEL CHAKRABORTY

Introduction

History and comparative analysis support the view that a good judicial system fosters economic growth and promotes law and order. Good governance is essential for economic growth and so is the importance of judicial systems for good governance. One of the major goals of any democratic government is to foster economic growth as well as to improve the level of governance in various spheres of life, including a control on the illegal activities and curbing crime rates. Tackling crimes, be it violent or economic, is important for ensuring the rule of law. A fair justice delivery system (which includes both the judiciary as well as the police) is also essential for the promotion of law and order. Again, the rule of law has a direct linkage with economic growth. Therefore, crime, deterrence, good governance, an efficient/fair justice delivery system and economic growth are all interdependent.

Deterrence essentially aims at modifying the price of crime for all offenders. Consequently, the two available options of the policy makers are either to make punishment more certain and/or to make it more severe, both of which act as a disincentive to the seasoned criminals as well as potential violators. In case of the former choice, the government needs to spend more money on broadening the size of the police force to ensure that investigations are completed properly and on time and at the same time the courts are sufficiently decongested so that trial takes place with a fair amount of time certainty. Ensuring speedy resolution of disputes is a major component for enhancing certainty of punishment, so as to penalise the offenders at the earliest. In the latter case it needs to be ensured that procedural as well as substantial laws are in tune with deterrence objectives. Again a consequent action for ensuring severity of punishment would be to spend more money on building prisons to effectively ensure longer sentences, apart from increasing the number of guards, etc. Broadly, crime and deterrence is intricately linked with judicial reforms. Again police and prison reforms are essential arms of reforms in the criminal justice system that would go into controlling crime, enhancing deterrence and promoting law and order.

The determinants of various types of crimes and identifying effective deterrence policies have been a much-researched area. Many economists have viewed the crime scenario in a principle-agent framework, where criminals as rational agents react to the incentives or disincentives (i.e. punishments) generated by government (i.e., the principal) policies, e.g. expenditures on law enforcement (Becker, 1968; Ehrlich, 1973; Oliver, 2002). The empirical evidence shows that the expected cost of crime, i.e. the risk of being caught and the severity of punishment have a negative effect on crime rates. The robustness of the result has been put to test at times. Levitt (1999), in an attempt to analyse whether the negative relationship between crime rates and arrest rates in US originate from deterrence effects or are simply measurement errors, concluded in favour of the former relationship. It is generally believed that lack of opportunity plays a major role behind upsurge in crimes (Becsi, 1999). However, the empirical findings also showed that income levels and distribution is a more robust determinant of crime in comparison with unemployment rates (Ehrlich, 1973). It has also been observed that crime rates are much higher in big cities than in either small cities or rural areas (Glaeser and Sacerdote, 1996).

In the recent period, the Indian national media has been reporting an increase in various types of crimes in several areas, although the overall crime rate is at a moderate level. For instance, Bihar, an economically backward state, has been struck by a kidnapping spree, where the targets are mainly school children from relatively well off households, and despite the continuance of this trend for a considerable period of time, a successful deterrence mechanism is yet to be formulated. On the other hand, in various urban centres including New Delhi, instances of growing crime against women has been reported. Furthermore, economic offences (e.g. cheating, money laundering) tend to occur in most states. Given this scenario, there is a need to closely look into the present law enforcement mechanism, both in case of economic as well as violent crimes.

The current analysis is organised along the following lines. First, a brief note on economics of crimes, in terms of severity and certainty of punishment as an effective instrument for ensuring deterrence, is provided, which is followed by a panel analysis on the determinants of economic and violent crime rank of Indian states. The effectiveness of the deterrence mechanism both from the angle of police network and the judiciary is attempted next. Third, we focus on the interrelation between the conviction rate of both economic and violent crimes and their growth rates. Finally, the reform areas and issues *vis-à-vis* the criminal justice system are discussed.

The Economics of Crime: Ensuring Deterrence

Given the fact that most of the crimes are committed intentionally and not on the spur of moment, it is extremely important to ensure deterrence in the society. The certainty and severity of punishment puts a psychological pressure on the offenders. The procedure can be summarised in the following manner, "Criminal Law should minimise the social cost of crime, which equals the sum of the harm it causes and the costs of preventing it... The state should encourage *ex post* observable precautions, the state need not encourage *ex ante* observable precautions" (Cooter and Ullen, 2003).

As mentioned before, certainty and severity of crimes are the two choices before any policy maker. In Figure 13.1 we focus on the theoretical perspective of these two options. The C frontier in the figure shows the expenditure of the government in the certainty-severity plane. The curve D, the deterrence isoquant, P on the other hand depicts the combinations of certainty and severity of punishments representing the same level of expected punishment. The point of intersection between curve D and P shows the efficient combination of severity and certainty. It can be observed from the shape of the contours and the equilibrium points in the figure (E) that there is a trade-off between the two options, and the government, at least in the short run, cannot enhance both.

Figure 13.1

Allocating Resources to Deterrence

Case A: When certainty of punishment is more relatively more expensive than severity of punishment.

Case B: When severity of punishment is relatively expensive than certainty of punishment.

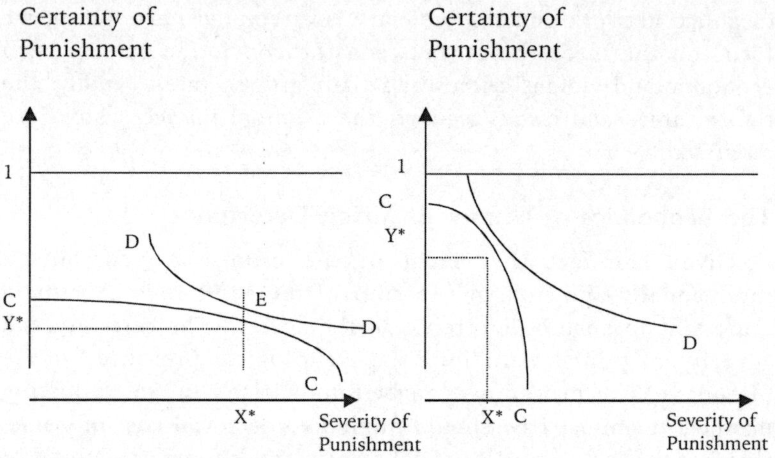

Apart from the direct policies to ensure deterrence, the indirect policies also play a major role in determining, i.e. to say controlling, the crime rate. It has been observed that increases in welfare expenditures are associated with reduced auto theft and murder rates (Becsi, 1999). However, uncertainty about the composition of the beneficiaries is a major component in these scenarios, since in an environment where it is impossible to distinguish between criminals and non-criminals as recipients of transfer payments, increasing government subsidies may increase the crime rate (Imrohoroglu *et al.* 1996). Therefore, it is difficult to arrive at a uniform conclusion on the behaviour of the determinants of crime, which portray a significant variation across countries.

The Analysis

In the following Figure 13.2, we present the three-year average growth rate in total cognizable crimes at all-India level over

1954-2002, on the basis of the data obtained from various issues of *Crime in India*. It is observed that the growth rate of crime was on the rise upto mid-seventies, but declined in the later half of the decade and even became negative in early eighties. However an increasing trend was noticed upto early nineties and the crime growth rate fluctuated in the following period. Nonetheless, during the last period noted (1999-2002), the growth rate was below 1 per cent. While this is a welcome trend in itself, there exists certain interesting regional dynamics in crimes, which we observe in the following. Furthermore, the existence of relatively lower crime rate sets the stage for systemic reform of the enforcement or deterrence mechanism, long overdue.

Figure 13.2

Average Growth Rate of Total Cognizable Crimes in India

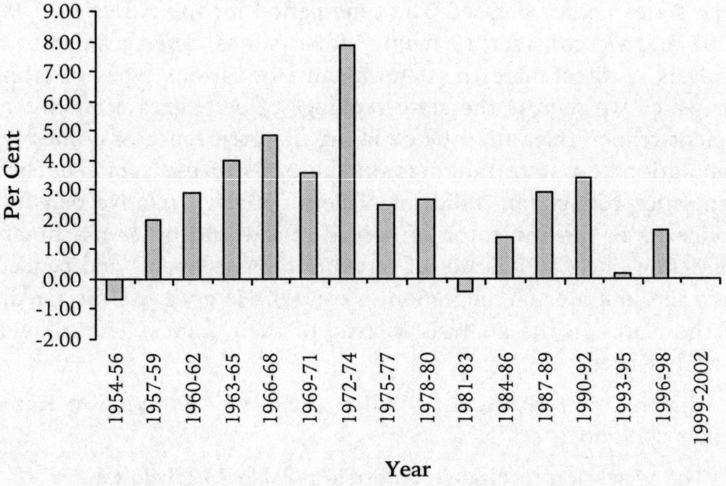

To effectively deal with the determinants of various crimes, we club them in two major categories, namely—violent crimes and economic offences. We consider only the select violent crimes reported under IPC (Indian Penal Code) category, which include murder, attempt to commit murder, culpable homicide not amounting to murder, rape, kidnapping and abduction, dacoity and robbery, preparation and assembly for dacoity, riots and arson. It should be borne in mind that our decision for not including SLL (special and local laws) crimes in the analysis in no way implies a decline in occurrence of crimes under that category in recent period, but simply reflects the nature of the crimes reported under it (e.g. Gambling Act, Indian Passport Act, etc.).[1] The economic offences considered for our analysis include cheatings, corruption charges, counterfeiting, etc. The data is taken from various issues of *Crime in India.*

A rank correlation analysis reveals that the economic crime ranking of the states is negatively related with the per capita state domestic product ranking (correlation coefficient -0.090). In other words, the occurrence of economic crimes is more prominent in relatively worse-off states. However, the violent crime ranking of the states is positively related with the per capita state domestic product (correlation coefficient 0.490), showing a positive correlation between development in the states and the selected crimes.

For the determinant analysis, we proceed with a cross-section time series pooled dataset. The time period for the analysis is 1994-2002 and we consider 19 major Indian states. The purpose of the analysis is to estimate the determinants of various types of crimes, for which we regress the state rankings of per capita economic and violent crimes (measured by deflating the occurrence of crimes with population) on state rankings on the basis of per capita net state domestic product (an indicator of development), relative density of police force (an indicator of spread of law and order machinery), conviction rate (an indicator of certainty of punishment) and pendency ratio (an indicator of congestion in courts). Here we use the rankings of the states in the analysis instead of their values. The following model is used:

$\text{Crime}_R = f(\text{PNSDP}_R, \text{Police Density}_R, \text{Conviction Rate}_R, \text{Pendency Ratio}_R, \varepsilon)$[2]

The regression results are reported in Table 13.1 below.

In case of economic crimes, the NSDP ranking is negatively related with crime ranking, but non-significant. The ranking bears a positive significant relationship with police density. However, there exists a

1. The authors are currently involved in an analysis of the state-level determinants of SLL crimes. The preliminary findings of the working paper show interesting results.
2. 'R' in subscript denotes the ranking of the states. The same model is used for both economic and violent crimes.ε stands for any omitted variable from the analysis.

Table 13.1

Regression Results of the Determinant Analysis

Dependent Variable	*Constant*	*Per Capita NSDP Rank*	*Police Density Rank*	*Conviction Rate Rank*	*Pendency Ratio Rank*
Economic Crime Rank	15.0747	-0.0295	0.1151	-0.3559	-0.2915
t-Statistic	15.50 (***)	-0.47	1.78 (*)	-5.48 (***)	-4.76 (***)
N = 171	Wald chi^2 = 121.77		Probability of Wald chi^2 = 0.0000		
Violent Crime Rank	5.2945	0.2322	0.5966	-0.3291	-0.0080
t-Statistic	9.48 (***)	5.47 (***)	14.01 (***)	-8.08 (***)	-0.22
N = 171	Wald chi^2 = 543.06		Probability of Wald chi^2 = 0.0000		

negative relationship with conviction rate and pendency ratio rank. In case of violent crimes, the NSDP and police density ranking are positively significant, while conviction rate rank is negatively significant. The positive sign of the coefficients for police density both in case of economic and violent crime rankings is slightly startling, and the possible explanation is that the causality is the other way round. In other words, the states characterised by higher crime employ more policemen, and more policemen in a state do not attract higher incidence of crime. The conviction rate rank is negatively significant as expected, i.e. higher conviction rate (certainty of punishment) discourages crime. However, the negative significant relationship between pendency ratio and economic crime is difficult to explain. Given the importance of good governance in ensuring lower crime rates, there is a need to focus on the functioning of the enforcement mechanism.

Looking through the Enforcement Mechanism in India

Owing to the resource constraint, a government in a developing country cannot maximise both certainty and severity at the same time. It has been highlighted on a number of occasions that the number of prisons is grossly inadequate,[3] i.e., the focus of the government action (from a theoretical perspective) is presumably not on the severity of punishment. In the following analysis, we

3. According to the PRO, Tihar Jail, the jail currently shelters 13,000 prisoners as against its capacity of 3,500. News Report in *Hindustan Times*, September 25, 2005. A similar scenario is observed in most of the prisons in India.

Table 13.2

An Analysis of the Deterrence Mechanism (Police Performance)

States	Growth Rate in Total Police Force		Number of Police Personnel per 1 Lakh Population		Number of Police Personnel per 100 Sq. Km		Charge-Sheeting Rate (IPC)		Charge-Sheeting Rate (Economic Offences)		Investigation Pending at the End of the Year (Economic Offences)	
	1995-98	1999-02	1994-98	1999-02	1994-98	1999-02	1994-98	1999-02	1994-98	1999-02	1994-98	1999-02
Andhra Pradesh	1.12	2.28	101.00	95.00	26.58	26.13	86.90	87.75	77.42	73.58	192	308
Assam	3.25	0.99	194.00	201.50	61.82	68.35	53.01	54.50	22.06	8.33	33	31
Bihar	1.04	3.87	85.40	78.50	46.74	55.05	71.08	78.35	10.34	5.30	173	215
Delhi	1.09	1.45	434.40	390.25	3403.10	3685.73	78.91	64.28	20.34	54.43	168	92
Goa	0.10	11.21	194.20	218.75	70.82	85.48	47.38	58.88	26.00	30.35	2	9
Gujarat	-0.61	-1.93	142.40	121.00	32.96	30.58	77.54	78.90	79.40	98.65	156	133
Haryana	7.86	0.73	160.60	146.75	67.24	68.20	81.47	77.35	54.68	49.90	118	150
Himachal Pradesh	-0.42	0.26	200.20	187.25	21.12	21.50	82.48	84.18	13.52	15.75	144	148
Jammu & Kashmir	8.13	10.30	413.80	499.25	32.96	49.70	63.23	71.90	37.90	34.30	288	339
Karnataka	1.58	-3.19	118.60	97.00	30.40	26.65	74.04	80.05	32.48	31.28	253	230
Kerala	1.16	3.43	122.00	130.00	98.08	107.33	90.21	91.73	20.40	14.93	282	457
Madhya Pradesh	2.89	-5.03	117.80	126.00	19.62	23.83	80.04	82.73	26.96	21.30	365	347
Maharashtra	-0.35	2.46	154.40	145.25	43.68	44.58	69.61	70.95	57.74	45.23	415	448
Orissa	1.10	0.87	100.64	96.25	37.78	22.55	84.79	83.73	27.90	29.73	419	343
Punjab	-0.28	0.18	268.40	286.50	112.80	136.53	79.56	79.45	76.28	87.03	323	357
Rajasthan	3.54	-0.84	155.60	114.75	40.78	18.58	80.83	82.53	18.52	13.95	431	1133
Tamil Nadu	4.10	-0.73	127.80	130.25	58.24	62.20	90.47	91.78	11.24	5.43	120	123
Uttar Pradesh	2.35	0.34	102.60	94.50	54.04	60.15	68.91	73.63	23.56	39.30	47	94
West Bengal	1.05	0.21	107.00	103.75	89.90	93.20	53.29	61.13	16.34	8.98	19	25
Total States	**1.73**	**-0.19**	**131.00**	**126.75**	**37.94**	**39.48**	**76.03**	**79.33**	**33.28**	**31.18**	**3809**	**4747**

Source: Constructed from various issues of *Crime in India*.

Note: (a) Total police force includes civil as well as armed policemen.

(b) Charge-sheeting rate depicts percentage of cases charge sheeted to total cases investigated.

(c) Figures on investigation pending at the end of the year have been rounded to the nearest integer.

attempt to form an idea about the Indian governments' policies over the last decade, ensuring the certainty of punishment. In Table 13.2 and 13.3, a number of certainty-related indicators of punishment (the performance of the police force and the judiciary) across states are analysed.

In Table 13.2, first we look at the growth rate of the total police force across states. In the aggregate level, i.e. for all the states taken together, the growth is actually negative in the recent period. The growth rate in police force is high only in case of the states with appreciable law and order problem, e.g. Andhra Pradesh and Bihar (naxalite violence), Jammu & Kashmir (militant threats), although states like Maharashtra and Kerala also registered the same trend. Although the number of police personnel per 100 sq. km has increased for most of the states, there is a growing concern that the growth rate has fallen short of the required level, as reflected from the decline in the number of police personnel per one lakh population. There is reason to believe that this decline leads to shortage of police personnel for investigation works as reflected through the column on charge-sheeting rates. Charge-sheeting rate is particularly important in ensuring deterrence as the document is prepared after verification of the evidences and is used by the judiciary later during the trial. While in case of IPC crimes, the charge-sheeting rate has improved in a number of states; the overall figure has gone down in case of economic crimes in the later period. Looking further on economic offences, we see the number of investigations pending at the end of a year has also increased considerably in a number of states. All these observations lead one to convince that there is enough scope to improve the deterrence to crime by enhancing certainty of punishment in India through suitable enhancement of the police machinery.

Table 13.3 shows the comparative performance of the judicial system during 1994-98 and 1999-2002. On the positive side, it is observed that the conviction rate has increased marginally both in cases of IPC crimes as well as economic offences, which might serve as a deterrence mechanism. However, conviction rate depicts per centage of cases convicted to total trials completed in a particular year. Therefore, there is a need to focus on the non-completed or pending cases as well. Pendency ratio as reported in the table is obtained by dividing the number of pending trials at the end of the year to the total cases brought for trial in that year. While pendency ratio has slightly declined for economic offences, it has increased

Table 13.3

An Analysis of the Deterrence Mechanism (Judiciary)

State	*Conviction Rate (IPC)*		*Conviction Rate (Economic Offences)*		*Pendency Ratio (IPC)*		*Pendency Ratio (Economic Offences)*	
	1994-98	1999-2002	1994-98	1999-2002	1994-98	1999-2002	1994-98	1999-2002
Andhra Pradesh	36.77	35.98	43.48	41.93	64.98	65.50	71.07	87.51
Assam	22.91	22.65	0.00	0.00	76.82	81.18	80.00	98.03
Bihar	24.04	21.05	74.28	69.13	82.38	86.50	98.41	93.28
Delhi	40.50	42.35	15.22	13.33	84.18	78.53	82.93	88.01
Goa	26.03	20.13	0.00	0.00	85.28	73.43	96.36	94.81
Gujarat	36.54	26.95	19.54	22.28	87.16	89.98	92.63	91.12
Haryana	41.72	33.45	27.82	19.90	78.64	82.05	87.22	86.06
Himachal Pradesh	27.73	26.13	3.92	18.28	83.40	83.48	84.82	79.07
Jammu & Kashmir	39.59	40.00	14.88	10.25	83.44	81.55	83.80	92.22
Karnataka	21.83	29.65	22.80	18.58	72.92	69.33	84.13	90.42
Kerala	30.17	46.58	49.66	72.30	73.30	77.75	72.90	83.03
Madhya Pradesh	51.35	50.23	35.48	42.58	83.42	81.03	83.05	78.36
Maharashtra	24.24	13.50	41.58	29.28	89.14	91.03	97.04	90.20
Orissa	13.66	15.10	29.44	18.65	85.80	84.58	94.80	96.45
Punjab	38.72	41.68	20.86	29.38	72.52	78.10	88.55	62.88
Rajasthan	50.16	52.03	23.74	31.75	80.80	78.03	91.52	77.88
Tamil Nadu	64.96	62.88	68.90	63.33	59.46	59.60	94.49	90.12
Uttar Pradesh	50.93	53.45	32.86	3.13	78.14	81.03	88.46	90.43
West Bengal	21.40	18.70	0.00	0.00	92.10	93.30	100.00	99.00
Total States	**39.59**	**40.45**	**30.10**	**30.20**	**81.06**	**81.95**	**89.77**	**88.67**

Source: Constructed from various issues of *Crime in India.*

Note: (a) Conviction rate depicts percentage of cases convicted to total trials completed.

(b) Pendency ratio is determined by dividing the number of the pendency trials at the end of the year to the total cases for trial in any particular year.

Figure 13.3

Police Infrastructure and Charge-Sheeting Performance (Economic)

A

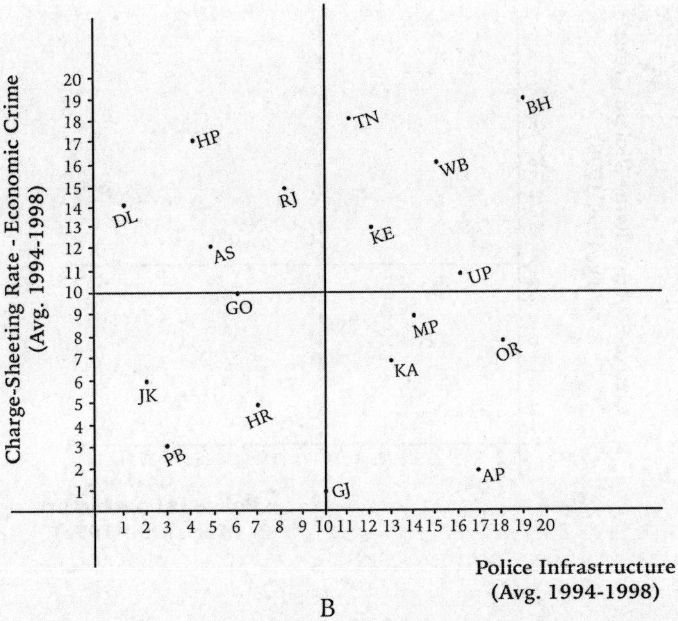

B

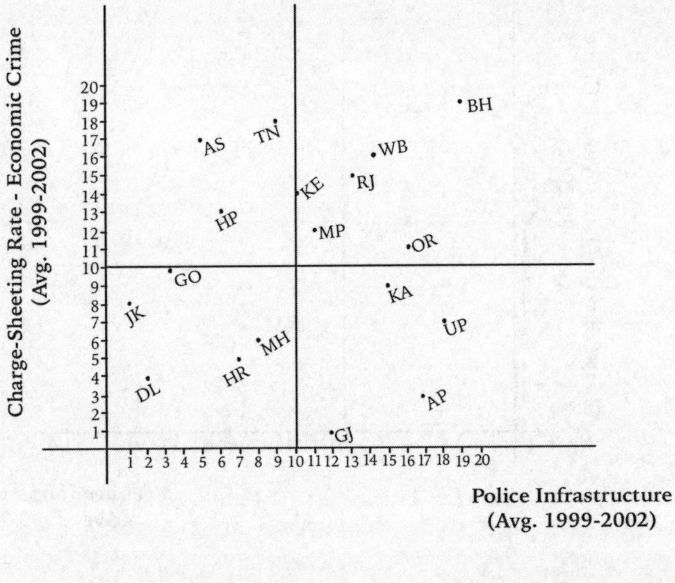

Figure 13.4

Police Infrastructure and Charge-Sheeting Performance (Violent)

A

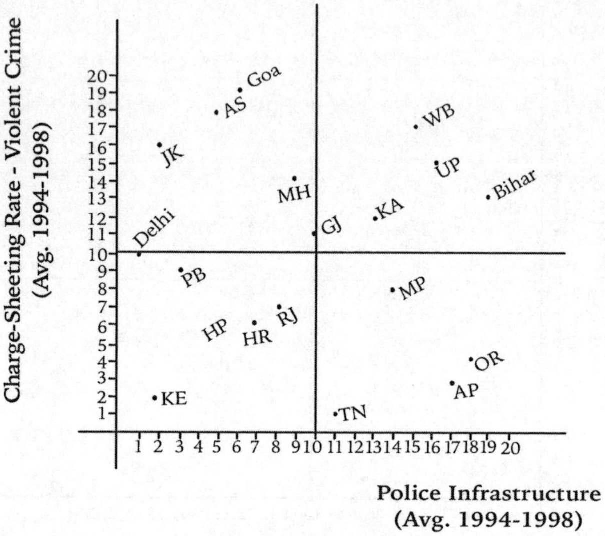

B

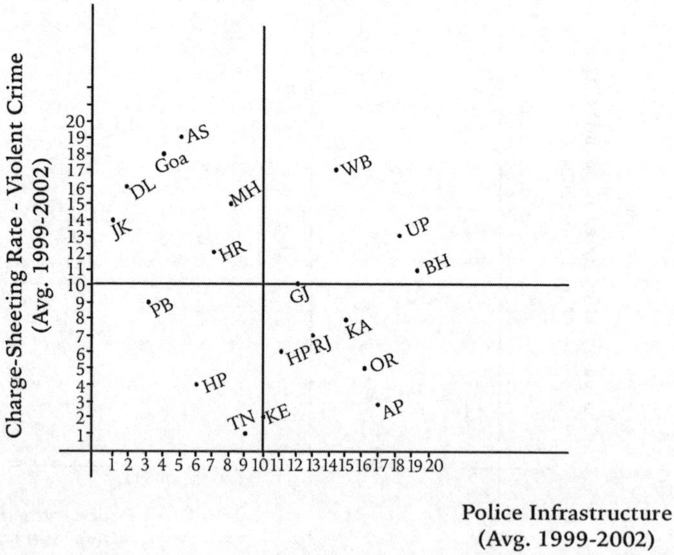

marginally for violent crimes. In a number of states like Bihar, Gujarat, Maharashtra, Orissa and West Bengal, the pendency ratio has consistently remained as high as 90 per cent over the years. In short, the certainty of punishment does not seem to be acting as a major determinant in ensuring deterrence.

An analysis of the states on the basis of their development pattern in the light of Tables 13.2 and 13.3 will not be irrelevant here. In terms of net state GDP, Delhi, Punjab and Maharashtra are the top performers, while Assam, Bihar, Orissa, Rajasthan and Uttar Pradesh come at the bottom. The top states share a mixed experience in terms of presence of police network and charge-sheeting performance. However, in case of Maharashtra, the conviction rate has declined appreciably. A mixed trend is noticed in case of pendency ratios as well. In case of the laggards, e.g., Bihar, UP and West Bengal, however, it is seen that there is enough scope for improvement, both in terms of police network as well as the performance of the judiciary

In the Figure 13.3 and 13.4, we attempt to focus on the relative position of the states in the two time periods on the police network and their efficiency. In Figure 13.3, it is seen that Bihar, UP and West Bengal is consistently showing a dismal performance in case of charge-sheeting of economic crimes. These states are placed in the fourth quadrant in both periods, i.e., are at the bottom on both counts.

Looking at Figure 13.4, it is observed that Bihar and West Bengal are consistently showing a dismal performance in case of charge-sheeting on violent crimes, while the rankings of the other states have undergone changes.

Conviction and Crime Rates: Effective Deterrence?

The literature on Law and Economics of Crime has highlighted the negative relationship between severity of punishment and the occurrence of crime at times (Ehrlich, 1973; Wolpin, 1978). Increases in probability of arrest, conviction and punishment are also supposed to affect crime rate (Cooter and Ullen, 2003). We attempt to estimate whether there is any relationship between the conviction rate in the past periods and growth rate in crime in recent periods. Stated alternatively, we want to test whether the deterrence mechanism, with a lag, is efficient. Like the earlier case, a panel analysis is performed over 1993-2002 for the 19 major Indian states.

Crime growth rate $_t$ = f (Conviction rate $_{t-n}$, ϵ) *ceteris paribus.*

where ^{a} stands for any other determinants of the crime growth rate

The regression results are reported in the following Table 13.4. One should rationally expect a negative relationship here. It is however observed that the relationship is positive in case of the first two lags, but negative for the next two both in case of economic as well as violent crimes. The relationship is however significant only for the first lag in case of economic offences, while it is significant up to two lags for violent crimes. While the coefficients in case of the third and fourth lags are negative, they are not significant.

Table 13.4

Working of the Deterrence Mechanism

Nature of Crime	*t – 1*	*t - 2*	*t – 3*	*t - 4*
Economic Crimes	0.725 (**)	0.534	- 0.035	- 0.013
Violent Crimes	1.391 (**)	1.412 (**)	- 0.089	- 0.027

Through an exploratory analysis, it is observed that the growth rate in crimes, economic as well as violent, does not depend on the police network (growth in police force, number of police personnel per one lakh population and number of police personnel per 100 sq. km), as the relationship is not significant. However, this result should hardly be interpreted as a rationale for not spending money on broadening police force in future. It "should rather" be argued as an indicator of the ineffectiveness of the current machinery.

Furthermore, while the obtained result sounds counter-intuitive, it needs to be analysed keeping the data problems in mind. First, there are a lot of anecdotal references to the fact that considerable degree of under reporting of the crime cases is a regular feature in a number of states (at the local level), which is however, more serious for the laggards. This invariably brings in a downward bias in the reported crime rate and is a data limitation. Furthermore, migration in India is currently on the rise (Srivastava and Sasikumar, 2003) and the entry of a part of the migrant population in urban illegal activities renders the relationship between conviction rate of the past population and the present growth rate of crimes in a particular state reasonably weak. Unfortunately, a long time-series data on migration and break-up of migration-adjusted crime rate is not available for the analysis. The obtained results look tenable in this light. Also the inherent problems of the criminal justice system produced a weak link between crime growth and its timely remedy through corrective steps. The remaining part of the chapter attempts to look into these problem areas.

Looking at the Systemic problems

Both severity and certainty of punishment get diluted if the criminal justice system is characterised by endemic delays during both the pretrial and trial phase. If the criminal gets to enjoy a normal life by virtue of being out on bail for several years before proven guilty, then the severity of punishment as a deterrent is seriously threatened. Again, with considerable time that the courts take to finish the trial process, most often than not weakens a case, thus diluting the certainty of punishment.

The traditional political cost of neglecting judicial reforms has a direct bearing on the economic sphere. Efficient and transparent legal systems reduce transaction costs for economic factors, including foreign investors. Since transaction costs increase the costs of direct investment, foreign investors should be averse to investing in countries with such higher costs and, thus, will gravitate towards states with more 'effective' or 'efficient' legal regimes.

Most developing countries, including India, suffer from a huge backlog of cases. This apparently insurmountable problem increases inefficiencies in the system, apart from putting a question mark with the efficacy over other legal reform measures initiated. Inefficiency in the judicial system also leads to higher litigation with harassment and delays as the primary motive, crowding out genuine litigants and forcing them to seek solutions in a quasi-legal framework.

India differs from its South Asian neighbours in many respects. India is a large democracy where rule of law exists, characterised by a fiercely independent judiciary. There is considerable political stability as well as freedom of expression, freedom of political association, freedom of political opposition and dissent. The central institutions of the legal system are reasonably fair. Yet in the rule of law index, it barely gets a positive score.[4] The primary reason is the low score it invariably secures, courtesy the outdated and complex procedural and institutional characteristics of the country's legal system, and which perhaps is more important, as is argued in this chapter. Despite having a wellestablished and laid out judiciary, the courts have got caught up in a quagmire of huge pendency. In addition, the police force desperately is in need of reforms, as there exist many bottlenecks through which the criminal justice system in India operates and which limits the efficacy of this institution. The prisons are overflowing and function in a pitiable state.[5] So the need of the hour is procedural reforms and simplification, apart from reforms in the institutions that delivers justice, especially in the criminal side. In the remaining portion of the chapter we focus on the issues pertaining to such reform measures.

The Agendas for Reforms

The two major problems besieging the criminal justice system are huge pendency of criminal cases along with the inordinate delay in disposal of criminal cases on one hand and the low rate of conviction in cases involving serious crimes on the other. In other words, any agenda for reforms need to address the judiciary on one hand, and the police on the other. Prison reforms are also important. Simplifying judicial procedures and practices, bringing about synergy among the Judiciary, the prosecution and police, making the system simpler, faster, cheaper and people-friendly, improving the pitiable conditions of the over-flowing prisons and restoring the confidence of the common man are the need of the hour.

With regard to the judiciary, the problem of arrears involving criminal cases is particularly acute in the district and subordinate courts of the country or in the trial courts. Around two-thirds of total pending cases in the district and subordinate courts are criminal cases. Of these, the Magisterial Courts alone has more than 90 per cent of all criminal cases and over 60 per cent of the total cases that are pending in the District and Subordinate Courts.[6] While the overall figure is huge in itself, it was found that supply side measures to rid the courts of congestion are highly

4. The primary aggregate indicator for rule of law is countries' point estimates ranging from -2.5 to +2.5 according to the World Bank. For details see Daniels and Trebilcock (2004).

5. For a detailed discussion see Hazra, Arnab Kumar (2004). "Institutional Reforms in the Enforcement of Criminal Justice in India", in Bibek Debroy (ed.) *Agenda for Improving Governance*, Academic Foundation, New Delhi.

6. There are also pending cases in various tribunals. However, the precise number in the tribunals is not known.

realistic.[7] At the current rate of disposal, it was found that if no new cases were instituted then it would take only 18 months or one-and-a-half years for all pendency to be over. Alternatively, if the strength of judges were to increase by 100 per cent, it would require only 18 months to resolve all pending cases at the 1998 disposal rate. The pendency figures broken down into civil and criminal cases reveals that for civil cases alone the time required is 20 months, with 25 months for District Courts and 17 months for Subordinate Courts individually. For Criminal cases alone the time required is 17 months, with 16 months for Sessions Courts and 17 months for Magisterial Courts individually. Surely, the situation is quite redeemable.

Large backlogs of cases and delays may affect both the fairness and the efficiency of the judicial system, which in turns weakens democracy, the rule of law, and the ability to enforce human rights. To solve the problem, the Indian government has launched a number of judicial reforms. The problem has been, however, the lack of systematic data on court congestion, performance and efficiency. The lack of relevant data and solid empirical analysis has hampered policy prescriptions, which then invariably tended to lose focus. As a result, the attempts to solve the problem of court congestion have produced half-hearted results. Except for the Supreme Court, where arrears have decreased significantly, the other tiers of justice have only been strained further.

The literature related to court congestion unanimously identifies inadequacy of judge strength, delay in filling up of vacancies and unsatisfactory appointment of judges as the main contributing causes for the accumulation of arrears in the courts.[8] In India, lack of judges has generally been cited as the main reason for court congestion and delays.[9] Indeed, the number of judges per capita has been low compared to other countries. For instance, data on 30 selected countries from the World Bank, *Justice Sector at a Glance,* database indicate that in 2000 the average number of judges per 100,000 inhabitants was 6.38 globally, while the corresponding number for India is about 2.7.[10]

---

7. For details see Hazra, Arnab Kumar (2003). *The Law and Economics of Dispute Resolution in India,* Bookwell, New Delhi.
8. *ibid.*
9. The number of judges per 100,000 inhabitants ranged from 0.13 in Canada to 23.21 in the Slovak Republic, not showing significant correlation with GDP per capita. It should be noted, however, that for some of the countries the statistics covered only the federal court system.
10. The 'actual' number of judges is even lower since the calculation is based on the sanctioned judge strength, not accounting for vacancies.

Table 13.5

Judge Strength, Vacancy, and Disposal Rate in the Lower Courts (1997 and 1998)[11]

State	*1997*					*1998*				
	A	*B*	*C*	*D*	*E*	*A*	*B*	*C*	*D*	*E*
Andhra Pradesh	700	-	0.00	1545	1545	771	-	0.00	1383	1383
Assam	200	4	2.00	559	570	216	12	5.56	449	475
Bihar	1664	222	13.30	199	230	1653	281	17.00	201	242
Delhi	352	134	38.10	1050	1695	352	118	33.52	1043	1568
Goa	38	7	18.40	698	855	43	5	11.63	562	635
Gujarat	622	58	9.30	3133	3455	621	78	12.56	2707	3096
Haryana	266	40	15.00	913	1074	266	43	16.17	984	1174
Himachal Pradesh	83	10	12.00	1705	1939	84	10	11.90	1764	2002
Jammu & Kashmir	128	2	1.60	1002	1018	128	2	1.56	1041	1057
Karnataka	632	180	28.50	1053	1473	629	151	24.01	1264	1663
Kerala	339	-	0.00	2231	2231	339	-	0.00	2359	2359
Madhya Pradesh	965	100	10.40	955	1065	943	187	19.83	966	1205
Maharashtra	1234	176	14.30	1591	1856	1269	109	8.59	1450	1586
Orissa	378	88	23.30	769	1002	384	88	22.92	480	623
Punjab	281	-	0.00	1120	1120	301	25	8.31	1024	1117

contd....

11. The recent data on the number of judges and vacancies are under processing.

...contd....

State	*1997*					*1998*				
	A	*B*	*C*	*D*	*E*	*A*	*B*	*C*	*D*	*E*
Rajasthan	591	-	0.00	863	863	624	-	0.00	847	847
Tamil Nadu	702	6	0.90	1926	1942	692	4	0.58	2014	2026
Uttar Pradesh	1711	271	15.80	1054	1252	1797	317	17.64	1112	1350
West Bengal	544	24	4.40	1784	1866	544	41	7.54	1120	1211
All-India Avg.	**11924**	**1327**	**11.13**	**1179**	**1327**	**12151**	**1479**	**12.17**	**1121**	**1276**

Source: Hazra (2003).

Note: A – Sanctioned Strength B – Vacancies C – Vacancy Percentage D – Disposal per Sanctioned Strength E – Disposal per Sanctioned Strength

Infrastructure in the courts has also failed to increase proportionately and there is an urgent need to increase it. Table 13.5 shows the high degree of vacancies prevalent in the lower courts in a number of states during 1997-98. As a result, the caseload per judge substantially increases, hampering the efficiency significantly.

The problem of court congestion in India has been a historical one and the inefficiency of the system has contributed to the problem. The huge arrears in turn further erode efficiency. So it has been a circular problem. The solution does not entirely lie in supply side economics of building more courts and appointing more judges. Substantial reforms in law as well as increasing the resource availability with the system are equally important.

The issue of police reforms is equally important, if any meaningful revamp of the criminal justice system is to be attempted.[12] Considerable government literature already exists in this regard and there is practically very little to add to them. So in effect, this section serves as a survey of the available official literature on Police Reforms. This is indeed very vital, for most of the reports are not strictly in the public domain and are quite old too (although extremely relevant). Moreover, it is easier for the government to implement measures that has been suggested by its own machinery. However, given the vastness of the subject, a detailed discussion is beyond the scope of this chapter.

The police force in India is known for the wrong reasons—inefficiency, high-handedness, brutality, corruption, and being politicised. However, the police function with a lot of constraints too. As a result the issue of police reforms assumes significance especially because the poor and the not-so-well-politically-connected people are invariably at the receiving end of the police action and inaction. The subject of police reforms is vast and covers many issues and concerns that is not just restricted to strengthening and improving the istructural and administrative aspects of the police force, but also includes issues like changing the culture and ethos of policing. The police have an obligation to function within the Constitution, law and democratic aspirations of the people. With significant changes taking place in the country since the inception of the police as an

12. For a detailed overview of the issues in police and prison reforms, see Hazra (2004) *op. cit.*

organisation and more so since Independence, the complimentary changes and reforms have been absent within the law enforcement agency. Those who control and run the system have abused it beyond repair. There are problems concerning every aspect of the system, right from the stage of recording the First Information Report to investigation of the case (which often involves search, arrests, detention and interrogation), prosecution, trial, conviction, imprisonment, parole, review, remission and rehabilitation, not to mention recidivism and relapse.

Report of the National Police Commission, 1979-1981

The first report after Independence that looked into the issue of 'police reforms' at large was the National Police Commission. Most of the recommendations have not been implemented although the report remains in a way the *Bible* for police reforms in India.

The National Police Commission was formed in 1977 to look into the role of the police. The National Police Commission submitted its report in eight parts, between 1979 and 1981. Each of the reports dealt with different aspects related to the police force and reforms pertaining to its image as well as functioning. A detailed summary of the recommendations of the National Police Commission on the various issues is in Appendix A-13.1.

The National Police Commission looked into issues like arrests, detention in police custody, interrogation of women and delay in investigation (which contributes to undue detention in custody of non-convicted persons). Besides highlighting the need to adhere to law, it made wide-ranging suggestions for amendment of the law and procedures to cut down delays at the investigation and trial stages and to obviate custodial violence and lock-up irregularities. The National Police Commission favoured a system of periodic visits to inspect and report on police lock-ups. It also laid down detailed guidelines for the organisational restructuring of the police force, including promotions, role, duties, functions, code of conduct, punitive measures and accountability of the police force.

The National Police Commission also acknowledged the extraneous pressures on the police. One needs to stop political interference in the process of investigation and also in the transfer of officers.

Too much distrust of the police is in-built in our system. The statements recorded by police officers during investigations of witnesses or the accused should be admissible in court. It should be left to the courts to rely on them or reject them. The National Police Commission recommended that the laws and procedures relating to arrest, search and seizure, recording of statements of the accused and witnesses by police officers, police remand, bail provisions, regulatory powers, and economic offences, specially sections 161 and 162 of the Criminal Procedure Code should be amended keeping in view the changed role of the police and public interest.

The National Police Commission also recommended that Section 151 of the Criminal Procedure Code should be amended to facilitate remand to preventive police custody for a few days by a magistrate. This will help in a truthful record of First Information Reports (FIR) and avoid registration of false cases for investigation. The police may be empowered in law to compound offences even at the stage of investigation in certain situations when both parties to a dispute are themselves keen to settle the matter. Public grievance and complaint cells, outside the police department, should inquire into complaints against police officers. The Commission recommended the creation of these cells to make the police more accountable and responsible.

Another reform that is long overdue is the separation of investigation from the police officers deployed in law and order duties. Successive police commissions including the National Police Commission have made this, recommendation but owing to misplaced priorities and strong internal opposition from the police department, the recommendations have not been implemented.

Corruption adversely affects police performance. The Report went into this aspect in great details. Misuse of discretionary powers by a police officer is the main form of corruption in the police department. Obviously, the remedy lies in putting a check on these discretionary powers. This can be achieved in two ways—through procedural changes, and through tight supervision and inspections. The Police Rules provide for an elaborate system of inspections at all levels but unfortunately, the system is in disuse. The responsibility rests squarely with the senior officers who spend far too much time in their offices when they should be touring and inspecting their subordinate offices. Some procedural changes about arrests, searches and seizures should reduce the scope for the misuse of these powers.

The legal wing of the police system needs to be strengthened by a Directorate of Prosecution as an integral part of the system. Co-ordination between the investigating wing and the legal wing would ensure thoroughness and fairness of investigation.

In the case of offences under the 'Social Legislations' the new concept of 'conditional cognizance' as recommended by the National Police Commission, giving all the essential powers of investigation to the police except the power of arrest, needs to be introduced in the Criminal Procedure Code.

The role, training and the status of the Constable need upgradation. To make the police more sensitive and responsive to public criticism, public grievances cells should supplement the efforts of vigilance cells within the department. Both training and equipment also need upgradation. Modernisation of the police cannot be achieved without funds. The National Police Commission details the areas where upgradation of equipment and modernisation is urgently required. It also calls for more financial powers to the Chiefs of the State Police.

The 1861 Police Act has become outmoded. It should be replaced by a new Act to meet today's needs such as the new model Police Act, the National Police Commission had in its report.

The Ribeiro Committee Report

In 1996, a civil writ petition was filed in the Supreme Court (Civil Writ Petition No. 316 of 1996) by two retired IPS officers, praying for issue of orders to the Government to implement the recommendations of the National Police Commission. The petition is pending with the Supreme Court. In pursuance of the directions issued by the Court in the above case, the Central Government (Ministry of Home Affairs) set up in July 1998 a Committee on Police Reforms under the chairmanship of J. F. Ribeiro.

Besides visiting states and interacting with government officials, the Ribeiro Committee collected the views of different persons and organisations through a questionnaire. The Ribeiro Committee submitted its report in two parts. The highlights of the Ribeiro Committee Report are given in Appendix A-13.2

The Ribeiro Committee finalised its report regarding the establishment of the State Security Commission; setting up of proper procedures to select the chiefs of police forces and providing a minimum secure tenure to them; and insulating the investigating wing of the police from its law and order functions. The Ribeiro Committee Report is pending with the Supreme Court.

The Ribeiro Committee has more or less approved the recommendations of the National Police Commission except for minor changes. However, where it departs from the recommendations of the National Police Commission in a major way is *vis-à-vis* in the establishment of the State Security Commission as a statutory body. While the National Police Commission has recommended that the State Security Commission should be a statutory body, the Ribeiro Committee has recommended that it should be a "non-statutory, advisory and recommendatory" body.

Padmanabhaiah Committee Report on Police Reforms

In January 2000, the Government of India announced the setting up of another Committee on Police Reforms under the chairmanship of Mr. Padmanabhaiah. The terms of the reference assigned to the Committee were very wide, covering different aspects of police organisation, structure, functioning and problems. The Committee completed its report in August 2000. The broad recommendations of the Padmanabhaiah Committee Report are given in Appendix A-13.3.

The Padmanabhaiah Committee Report went into the issues of police reforms in greater details then perhaps what the Ribeiro Committee did. Padmanabhaiah Committee Report tried to define the perspective roles of Centre and States in developing capabilities in the police including funding. It also recommended a system of planned induction based on proper manpower planning and career planning of individual group of officers.

The Padmanabhaiah Committee Report emphasised on a greater need to recruit more Sub-Inspectors instead of Constables. Incidentally the National Police Commission recommended the opposite. The Padmanabhaiah Committee Report also recommends career planning at the level of constables and says that it is very important. The Report laid special emphasis on the need for specialisation in police.

The report also went into issues like political interference from outside and corruption within. The Padmanabhaiah

Committee Report laid greater emphasis on forensic science and the role it can play in investigation or murder, sexual assault and terrorist cases, besides drug offences, vehicle crime and burglary. It recommended that the police manual must be amended to make it mandatory to collect samples and to obtain expert forensic opinion in all such serious crimes. This report is the first report that goes into issues like cyber crime and crimes related to terrorism.

The Padmanabhaiah Committee Report observes that the present classification of offences into cognizable and non-cognizable, made 150 years ago, is not very relevant today. It recommends that the Law Commission of India should review the entire classification and the powers of the police to investigate.

The Report also recommends a mandatory judicial inquiry into all cases of alleged rape of a woman or death of any person in police custody.

Reports of the Law Commission of India

Several reports of the Law Commission of India went into issues that fall within the ambit of Police Reforms or issues that the National Police Commission dealt within its report. Specifically two reports are discussed here.

The 78th Report of the Law Commission of India on "Congestion of Under Trial Prisoners in Jails", which was submitted in 1979, made the following recommendations with regard to release on bail:

- Release a person on bond without sureties, where such a release is permitted by court.
- Provide for release on bond without sureties in cases under Sections 395 (30 and 439 (1) (a) Criminal Procedure Code.
- Release on bond without sureties even in regard to non-bailable offences under Section 437 (1) Criminal Procedure Code.
- Create a new offence in the Indian Penal Code for punishing the failure of a person to appear and surrender to custody in conformity with a bond executed by him. However there are two caveats. There should be due regard, before the bail is granted, for: (i) the likely effect on public order and public

peace by the release of such a person, and (ii) his conduct after release on bail on a previous occasion.

The 142nd Report of the Law Commission of India, submitted in 1994, was on "Custodial Crime". In the report the Law Commission noted that the victims of Custodial Crimes and deaths usually belong to the weaker sections of society. The poor, the downtrodden and the ignorant with little or no political and financial power are unable to protect their interests (page 2).

Section 56 of the Criminal Procedure Code contains a mandatory provision requiring the police officer making arrest without warrant, to produce the arrested person before a Magistrate, without unnecessary delay. If the police want to detain the person further, then an order from of the Magistrate following the procedure as prescribed under Section 167 of the Criminal Procedure Code has to be obtained.

By Section 167 of the Criminal Procedure Code the police is further required to make entry of his arrest in several documents under the Police Act and Police Manual, which includes information to the District Magistrate and the Sub-Divisional Magistrate about the date and time of arrest. In order to avoid these rigours of law, the police make informal arrest without making any entry into the records. Instances are not lacking where the police has arrested a person without warrant in connection with the investigation of an offence and the arrested person is subjected to, torture to extract information from him for the purpose of further investigations or for recovery of weapons or goods and also for extracting confession in violation of the statutory law. The torture and the injury caused on the body of the prisoner sometimes results into his death. The death in custody is not generally shown in records.

Consequently, even if the victim or the kith and kin launch a formal prosecution, no direct evidence is available to substantiate the charge of torture or causing hurt resulting into death. This is because in the police lock up the sole witnesses are either policemen or co-prisoners who are highly reluctant to appear as prosecution. The Law Commission of India was of the opinion that "it is essential to make appropriate provisions in the Indian Penal Code, the Criminal Procedure Code, and the Indian Evidence Act to foreclose torture in custody by public servants and to protect the interest of the victims of custodial crimes" (page 51).

This difficulty was considered by the Supreme Court also in a series of cases and it observed that the situation required amendment of law relating to burden of proof in such cases. It is a matter of regret that in spite of the Law Commission's recommendations and the Supreme Court's observations in several cases the requisite amendment in the Law of Evidence has not been made.

National Human Rights Commission

The National Human Rights Commission (NHRC) in all its Annual Reports since the first one in 1993-94 expressed deep concern on the state of affairs afflicting the police in India. In particular it made the following points in relation to a case in the Supreme Court, which was reiterated in the Annual Report of 1997-98.

- Separation of the Investigation Wing of the Police with executive crime detection duties so as to insulate the investigation wing from extraneous pulls and pressures.
- Constitution of the 'Police Security and Integrity Committee' as a recommendatory and advisory authority, to begin with, who would recommend on: (a) broad policy guidelines and directions for the performance of preventive tasks and service oriented functions by the police, and (b) illegal transfers, promotion orders, illegal or irregular orders in the performance duties, no premature transfers and by a competent authority only.
- District Police Complaints Authority to look into misuse of power and abuse of authority including wrongful arrests, detentions, custodial violence, etc.
- Institution of 'lay visitors' to Jails and police lock-ups by respectable and independent members of the public without interfering in any manner.
- Improvement in the mode of appointment of prosecution personnel.

On prison reforms, the concern encompasses on one hand issues relating to diet, wages, buildings, sanitary conditions, and medical care; while dealing with issues like undertrials, segregation of women and children, issues of corruption, charter of relevance for prisoners and the need for more prisons on the other.

In the case of *Ramamurthy vs. State of Karnataka,*[13] the Supreme Court discussed the complete case law on the subject of prisons. The Court concluded that there are nine major problems, which afflict the system and which needs immediate attention. These are: 1) overcrowding, 2) delay in trial, 3) torture and ill-treatment, 4) neglect of health and hygiene, 5) insubstantial food and inadequate clothing, 6) prison vices, 7) deficiency in communication, 8) streamlining of jail units, and 9) management of open air prisons.

An all India Committee on Jail Reforms (1980-1983), headed by Justice A. N. Mulla, (popularly known as the Mulla Committee Report) had submitted a detailed report on the issue of prison reforms. The Mulla Committee had noted that a majority of the persons lodged in prisons, especially the undertrials, consisted of people belonging to the underprivileged sections of society, and that the majority of the prison population was from a rural and agricultural background.[14] First offenders involved in technical or minor violations of law accounted for a large number of them.

The reasons for overcrowding in jails are many. Inordinate delay in trials is the most important (as seen from Table 13.3), and results in many undertrials having to be detained in jail for unduly long periods—in many cases extending up to 10 years. The hardships that they face can surely be mitigated. There is a four pronged solution: (a) releasing the undertrials lodged in jail for sufficiently long periods of time, on bail and easing the procedure for procuring a bail; (b) expediting the process of trial. This entails reducing backlogs in courts; (c) reducing the number of arrests on mere suspicion without any substantial evidence; and (d) improving the conditions of the jails and also building more prisons. There has been no organised or systematic effort to bring about reforms in a sustained and institutionalised manner because of a variety of reasons like lack of formal policy, want of commitment by the government, budget inadequacies and the non-availability of the required number of professionals among jail administrators.

The legal system in most developing countries, including countries in South Asia, follow complex legal procedures, use written procedures, have dates for case hearings which are hardly continuous,

---

13. 1997 (2) SCC 642.

14. This has also been observed by the National Human Rights Commission, *Annual Report 1999-2000*, New Delhi, pp. 19.

suffer from resource constraints and have almost no database. All these render the working of the deterrence mechanism, an effective tool to ensure rule-of-law in a country, quite weak. The cross-state analysis of India, as attempted in the current paper, hardly finds any evidence of such mechanism. On the contrary, the huge court congestion serves exactly the opposite purpose. Therefore, India is in the dire need of implementing judicial reforms apart from police and prison reforms, long overdue.

Bibliography

Alvi, Naziya (2005). "Tihar Jail Stares at HIV Scare", *Hindustan Times*, September 25.

Becker, Gary S. (1968). "Crime and Punishment: An Economic Approach", *Journal of Political Economy*, 76, pp. 69-217.

Becsi, Zsolt (1999). "Economics and Crime in the States", *Economic Review*, Federal Reserve Bank of Atlanta.

Brookings Institution (1990). *Justice for All: Reducing Costs and Delay in Civil Litigation*, Brookings Institution, Washington, DC

Brunetti, Aymo, Gregory Kisunko and Beatrice Weder (1998). "Credibility of Rules and Economic Growth: Evidence from a Worldwide Survey of the Private Sector", 12, *World Bank Economic Review*.

Buscaglia, E. and M. Dakolias (1996). "Judicial Reform in Latin American Courts: The Experience in Argentina and Ecuador", *World Bank Technical Paper 350*, World Bank, Washington DC

Carothers, Thomas (1998). "The Rule of Law Revival", 77, *Foreign Affairs*.

Cooter, R. and T. Ullen (2003). "Law and Economics", *Addison Wesley Longman*, Fourth Edition Massachusetts.

Dakolias, Maria (1999). "Court Performance Around the World: A Comparative Perspective", *World Bank Technical Paper No. 430*.

Daniels, Ronald J., and Michael. Trebilcock (2004). "The Political Economy of Rule of Law Reform in Developing Countries", *www.wdi.bus.umich.edu/global_conf/papers/revised/Trebilcock_Michael.pdf*

Ehrlich, Isaac (1973). "Participation in Illegitimate Activities: A Theoretical and Empirical Investigation", *Journal of Political Economy*, 81, pp. 521-65.

———. (1996). "Crime, Punishment, and the Market for Offenses", *Journal of Economic Perspectives*, 10, pp. 43-67.

Glaeser, Edward L. and Bruce Sacerdote (1996). "Why Is There More Crime in Cities?" *Working Paper No. 5430*. National Bureau of Economic Research.

———. (1979-81). "Report of the National Police Commission", Ministry of Home Affairs", Government of India, New Delhi

———. (1980-83). "All India Committee on Jail Reforms Report", Ministry of Home Affairs, Government of India, New Delhi.

———. (1997). "Report of the Committee on Rationalisation of Classification of Prisoners in Tihar Jail", Government of Delhi, New Delhi.

———. (2001). "Crime In India, 2000", National Crime Records Bureau, Ministry of Home Affairs, Government of India, New Delhi.

———. (2004). "Crime In India, 2002", National Crime Records Bureau, Ministry of Home Affairs, Government of India, New Delhi.

———. (1994). "The One Hundred and Forty Second Report on Custodial Crime", Ministry of Law, Government of India, Delhi.

(1988). "The One Hundred and Twenty Fourth Report on High Court Arrears: A Fresh Look", Law Commission of India, Ministry of Law, New Delhi.

———. (1979). "Seventy Eighth Report on Congestion of Under Trial Prisoners in Jails", Law Commission of India, Ministry of Law, New Delhi.

Hazra, Arnab Kumar (2004). "Institutional Reforms in the Enforcement of Criminal Justice in India", in *Agenda for Improving Governance* Bibek Debroy (ed.), Academic Foundation Press, New Delhi., pp. 485-562.

Hazra, Arnab Kumar (2003). "The Law and Economics of Dispute Resolution in India", Bookwell, New Delhi.

Hewko, John (2002). "Foreign Direct Investment: Does the Rule of Law Matter?" *Working Paper* No. 1, Rule of Law Series, Democracy and Rule of Law Project, Carneige Endowment for International Peace.

Imrohoroglu, Ayse, Antonio. Merlo and Peter Rupert (1996). "On the Political Economy of Income Redistribution and Crime", *Working Paper* No. 9609, Federal Reserve Bank of Cleveland.

Kaufmann, Daniel, Aart Kraay and Pablo Zoido-Lobatón (1999). "Governance Matters" *World Bank Policy Research Working Papers No. 2196.*

Köhling, Wolfgang K. C. (2000). "The Economic Consequences of a Weak Judiciary: Insights from India", Centre for Development Research, University of Bonn.

Levitt, Steven D (1998). "Why do Increased Arrest Rates Appear to Reduce Crime: Deterrence, Incapacitation, or Measurement Error?" *Economic Inquiry*, 36, pp. 353-372.

Messick, Richard (1999) "Judicial Reform and Economic Development: A Survey of the Issues", 14(1), *The World Bank Research Observer*, pp. 117-36.

Micevska, Maja B. and Arnab Kumar Hazra (2004). "The Problem of Court Congestion: Evidence from Indian Lower Courts", *ZEF-Discussion Papers on Development Policy* No. 88, Centre for Development Research, University of Bonn, Germany.

National Human Rights Commission, *Annual Report 1999-2000*, New Delhi.

Oliver, Alison (2002). "The Economics of Crime: An Analysis of Crime Rates in America", *The Park Place Economist*, X, pp. 30-35.

SK (2000). "Police and Courts: Perpetuating Insecurity", *Economic and Political Weekly*, September 30, pp. 3561-63.

Soares, Rodrigo, R. (2004). "Development, Crime and Punishment: Accounting for the International Differences in Crime Rates", *Journal of Development Economics*, 73, pp. 155-184.

Srivastava, Ravi and Sasikumar, S. K. (2003). "An Overview of Migration in India, its Impacts and Key Issues", presented at the Regional Conference on *Migration, Development and Pro-Poor Policy Choices in Asia*, jointly organised by the Refugee and Migratory Movements Research Unit, Bangladesh, and the DFID, UK, 22–24 June Dhaka, Bangladesh. Available at: *www.livelihoods.org.*

Tamanaha, Brian (1995). "The Lessons of Law and Development Studies", 89, *American Journal of International Law.*

Weder, Beatricem (1995). "Legal Systems and Economic Performance: The Empirical Evidence" in Rowat, Malcolm, Waleed H. Malik, and Maria Dakolias, *Judicial Reform in Latin America and the Caribbean, Technical Paper* 280, World Bank., Washington, D.C.

White, Ann (1980). "Estimating the Economic Model of Crime with Individual Data", *Quarterly Journal of Economics*, 94, pp. 57-84.

Wolpin, Kenneth (1978). "An Economic Analysis of Crime and Punishment in England and Welsh: 1894-1967", *Journal of Political Economy*, 86, pp. 815-40.

World Bank (2002). *World Development Report 2002: Building Institutions for Markets*, Oxford University Press, New York.

———. (1999). "Reducing Court Delays: Five Lessons from the United States", *PREM notes 34*, World Bank, Washington, DC.

———. (1997). *World Development Report 1997: The State in a Changing World*, Oxford University Press, New York.

Appendix A-13.1

Some Selected Recommendations from the Report of the National Police Commission on Police Reforms

The First Report

The Indian Police System and structure as presently organised is based on the Police Act 1861. The previous report before that of the National Police Commission was in 1902-03, by the Indian Police Commission. The Commission had concluded "the police force throughout the country is in a most unsatisfactory condition, that abuses are common everywhere, that this involves great injury to the people and discredit to the government, and that radical reforms are urgently required".[1] The National Police Commission remarks "what the Police commission said in 1903 appears to be more or less equally applicable to the conditions obtaining in the police force today" (Para 1.2, page 7).

Constabulary

The First Report of the National Police Commission confined itself to a detailed discussion on the Constabulary, who constitutes a large majority of the staff and form the foundation of the entire police structure. So any meaningful attempt at police reform has necessarily to start at their level since no restructuring of the system will be practicable or enduring unless the mass base of the system is redeemed healthy and efficient. The Report focused on aspects of the constable's personality, status and role in the police.

The quintessence of efficient policing is the effective and amiable street presence of a well-trained and motivated constable. However the present position of the constables is a far cry from this position. The First Report of the National Police Commission accordingly also went into issues of pay, housing, supply of essential commodities, removal of orderly systems, a machinery for redressal of grievances of the constables, recruitment, training and career planning.

Complaints against the Police

However the most significant reforms and recommendations pertained to a detailed structure of modalities for inquiry in to complaints against the police. Unfortunately, the follow up action and implementation of these recommendations is still in doubt.

1. Quoted in the First Report of the National Police Commission, page 7.

According to the National Police Commission, any arrangement for inquiry into complaints against police should be acceptable both to police and public as fair and just. The Commission, therefore, suggested arrangements, which would include inquiries conducted by departmental authorities and those conducted by an independent authority outside the police. The Commission felt that a large number of complaints against police should be looked into and disposed of by the supervisory ranks in the police hierarchy. The Commission however recommended that a judicial inquiry should be made mandatory following complaints of alleged rape of a woman in police custody, death or grievous hurt caused while in police custody, and death of two or more persons resulting from police firing in the dispersal of unlawful assemblies, against the police. It will also be mandatory, on the part of the government, to publish the report of the inquiry into these complaints, and the subsequent decisions taken thereon within two months of receipt of the report.

The Second Report

Appointment of the Criminal Justice Commission

According to the National Police Commission, the police cannot achieve complete success in their work unless all wings of the criminal justice system operate with simultaneous efficiency. It is therefore necessary to set up a body, which would comprehensively monitor the performance of all agencies and apply corrective measures from time to time. The existing Law Commission may be enlarged to function as a Criminal Justice Commission on a statutory basis. Such arrangements at the centre should be supported by similar arrangements at the state level.

Police Role, Duties, Powers and Regulations

The crux of police reforms in this country is to secure professional independence for the police to function truly and efficiently as an impartial agent of the law of the land, and at the same time to enable the government to oversee the police performance to ensure its conformity to law. A supervisory mechanism without the scope for illegal, irregular or *mala fide* interference with the police functions has to be devised. This is what the Second Report of the National Police Commission deals with.

The report went into several welfare measures to cover housing, education, medical care, recreational facilities, financial aid and special retirement benefits in distress situations arising from death or physical disability caused by service conditions, etc.

The National Police Commission remarked "there is an urgent need for a comprehensive reform in the procedural laws relating to investigation and trial in our system".[2] Further it commented that the "huddling together of a large number of undertrials with convicted prisoners and the mixing together of old and hardened criminals with the young first offenders tend to promote in the minds of all inmates feelings of criminalisation instead of remorse and regret for their previous conduct and a desire to reform".[3] The rules that govern the present accusatorial system of criminal trials make various demands from and place various restrictions on the prosecution so that the defendant gets all the help he can to defend himself. At the end of the trial the prosecution must prove their case beyond reasonable doubt, but the accused may, however, only raise a doubt and get its benefit to secure his acquittal. The severe limitations placed on the admissibility of evidence from the prosecution side and norms for determining the value of the admitted evidence make it difficult for the police as the investigating agency to carry forward all the material uncovered during the investigation to the final point of success in getting the offender convicted under the law.

The National Police Commission was of the view that the need for effective interaction between the police and the prosecuting agency at the stage of court trial for proper marshalling and presentation of all the evidence uncovered during investigation. The need for such interaction should also be suitably recognised in law instead of being left as a mere administrative arrangement.

There is considerable scope for exercise of discretion at various stages in the discharge of police functions, particularly in regard to preventive policing measures before a crime occurs, as distinct from investigation which starts after the occurrence of the crime (the responsibility of which is spelt out in the Police Act). The National Police Commission was of the view that the exercise of discretion in all such situations should be based on the assessment and judgment of the police functionaries concerned only. To prevent freakish or whimsical decision in such matters some broad guidelines should be laid down to cover all such conceivable situations. Police Manuals, which do not contain such guidelines at present, should be appropriately amplified. These guidelines should be set out in clear terms and also made known to the public.

The Second Report of the National Police Commission recommends the constitution of a Statutory Commission in every state, which can be called

---

2. Para 18.29, Page 47, the Second Report of the National Police Commission.
3. *ibid.*, Para 18.31, page 47.

the State Security Commission. This Commission can lay down broad policy guidelines for efficient functioning, evaluate the performance of the State Police, look into complaints of extraneous pressures in the form of illegal or irregular orders, look into discrepancies regarding promotions and transfers, and act as a forum of appeal. This can help considerably in making police performance politically neutral.

Extraneous Political Pressures

The Second Report also deals extensively with "Interference and misuse of police by illegal or improper orders or pressure from political executive or other extraneous sources". The Report noted that the influence is very strong.

The threat of transfer/suspension is the most potent weapon in the hands of the politician to bend the police down to his will. The National Police Commission recommended that the superintendence of the state government over the police should be limited to ensure that police performance is in strict accordance with law. In the performance of its tasks, the police should be subject to overall guidance from the government, which should lay down broad policies for adoption in different situations. There should however be no instructions in regard to actual operations in the field. In regard to investigation work, in any case, the police are beyond any intervention by the executive or politicians.

To help the state government discharge their superintending responsibility in an open manner under the framework of law, a State Security Commission should be set-up through law in each state. The State Security Commission should (a) lay down broad policy guidelines and directions for the performance of preventive tasks and service-oriented functions by the police; (b) evaluate the performance of the State Police every year and present a report to the State Legislature; (c) function as a forum of appeal to dispose of representations from officers regarding their being subjected to illegal orders and regarding their promotions; and (d) review the functioning of the police in the state.

The selection of Chief of Police should be from a panel of three Indian Police Service officers of that state cadre. A committee headed by the Chairman of the Union Public Service Commission should prepare the panel. The chief of police should also be assured of a fixed tenure of office. The tenure may be for four years or for a period extending up to retirement, whichever is earlier. The removal of the chief of police from his post before the expiry of the tenure should require approval of the State Security Commission.

Police officers should also be effectively protected against whimsical and *mala fide* transfer/suspension orders. There should be a provision in the Police

Act, specifying the authorities competent to issue such orders regarding different ranks. Any such orders passed by any authority other than those specified in the Act will be rendered null and void.

Gram Nyayalayas

The National Police Commission also recommends the setting up of *Gram Nyayalayas*. The working of *Nyaya Panchayats,* though well conceived in principle, suffered in practice, mainly because of the lay members of the *Panchayats* being subjected to local influences and pressures, which defeated the purpose. The report also pointed out that a *Nyaya Panchayats* were solely made up of lay members, who were unable to handle the judicial process. It was further recommended that *Nyaya Panchayats* would function far more efficiently if they were manned by trained persons with a certain minimum knowledge of law, rules and procedure.

The Third Report

Weaker Sections of the Society

The Third Report of the National Police Commission defines weaker sections of the society as those "who are subjected to social injustice and different forms of exploitation on account of poverty or ignorance besides age old traditions, customs, beliefs and the interplay of vested interests that have grown around them".[4] The recommendations were as follows:

- The State Governments may set up Special Courts under section 15 A (2) (iii) of the Protection of Civil Rights Act, 1976, to bring down the large pendency of cases in Courts.
- The Ministry of Home Affairs may issue comprehensive guidelines for classifying crimes as 'atrocities' to ensure proper recording and analysis of all such offences over a period of time on a countrywide basis.
- Special cells may be set up in the Police Department in each state to, besides other thing, (i) monitor the progress of investigations of cases under the Protection of Civil Rights Act, 1976 or other atrocities against Scheduled Castes/Scheduled Tribes registered in district police stations; (ii) make enquiries or investigations into complaints from Scheduled Castes/Scheduled Tribes or other weaker sections of the

---

4. Third Report of the National Police Commission, Para 19.1, page 1.

people that may be received directly in the cell; and (iii) discuss with the prosecuting staff the progress of cases pending Trial to ensure satisfactory marshalling and presentation of evidence in Court.

- Importance should be given to causes for dissatisfaction of the weaker sections of society about lack of police response to their plight in certain situations and to the deficiencies in the scheme of allotment of land to the landless poor who include a large number of Scheduled Castes, cases related to motor vehicles accidents, etc.
- Strengthening of the Village *Chowkidar*/Police.

Corruption

The Third Report of the National Police Commission looks at the crucial issue of corruption in great details. The following recommendations were made:

- Insulate the police system from political interference.
- Systems of surprise checks, inspections and effective supervision by honest and well-motivated officers, at different levels of command within the hierarchy itself.
- Posting of police officers be the exclusive responsibility of the Deputy Superintendent of Police (DSP), and likewise the Chief of Police for the DSPs.
- The provisions in the service rules for compulsory retirement after completion of 20 years of service should be restored to weed out Officers with corrupt reputation. A suitably constituted high-level committee in the police should assess evidence regarding this reputation. There can be one appeal against the recommendations of the committee and after the disposal of the appeal the matter will be closed.

Arrests

It is an accepted fact that the police make far too many arrests that is actually warranted. The low prosecution rate is, therefore, a natural corollary (although there are a host of other reasons too, which contribute to such a low rate). There is a clear case for reducing the number of arrests in police work. This will also reduce the scope for allied corruption. The Third Report of the National Police Commission made the following observations/ recommendations:

- Several policemen are under an erroneous impression that an arrest is mandatory under the law while investigating a cognisable offence.
- Section 2 (c) and 2 (l) Criminal Procedure Code should be amended to remove the emphasis on arrests in the definition of cognisable offences.
- Departmental instructions may insist that a police officer making an arrest should also record the reasons for making the arrest.
- The recommendations of the 78th Report of the Law Commission of India titled "Congestion of Under Trial Prisoners in Jails", on release of an arrested person on bail, should be implemented.

Economic Offenses and Modernisation

The report deals with economic offenses like tax evasion, manipulation of stocks and shares, frauds in licences and permits, black marketeering, hoarding, adulteration of drugs and food stuff, etc. in Chapter XXIII.

The Report also deals with the issue of modernisation of law enforcement especially in transport, forensic science labs, scientific instruments, and wireless equipment, etc. in Chapter XXIV.

The Fourth Report

Investigation

In the first chapter of the Fourth Report of the National Police Commission, matters related to 'Investigation' was discussed. The following recommendations were made:

- The Cadre of investing officers must be increased.
- Provision of adequate transport, strengthening of forensic laboratory facilities and scientific aids to the detection of crime must be provided with the police force.
- Section 37 of the Criminal Procedure Code needs to be amended to facilitate the conduct of identification parades by the police themselves as an aid to investigation.
- Section 100 of the Criminal Procedure Code may be amended to facilitate the admission of search list as a piece of evidence without having to call upon search witness to depose in court, and further to facilitate public servants to function as search witness in certain situations.

- A new Section—50 A—may be added to Chapter V of the Criminal Procedure Code requiring the police to give intimation about the arrest of a person to anyone who may be reasonably named by him/her for sending such intimation, to avoid agonising suspense for the members of his family about his whereabouts.
- Surprise visits to the police stations by senior officers would help the immediate detection of persons held in unauthorised custody and subjected to ill treatment.
- A magistrate or judge before whom an arrested person is produced by the police for remand to custody should be required by administrative rules of criminal practice to specifically question the arrested person if he has any complaint of ill treatment by the police.
- To check third degree methods from being adopted, there should be a scheme for mandatory judicial inquires into complaints of death or grievous hurt caused while in police custody.
- By sub-sections (3) and (4) of Section 167 of the Criminal Procedure Code remand to police custody is exceptional and is actually dependent if the Investigating Officer pleads that the accused has already made a confession and his continued custody with the police is necessary. This is sometimes falsely made. These two sub-sections should be deleted and a new sub-section (3) may be added to facilitate remand to police custody in the interest of investigation whenever required.
- Section 2 Criminal Procedure Code may be amended to facilitate the establishment of special police station to deal with particular cases or classes of cases.

Court Trial

The Fourth Report of the National Police Commission has been especially critical of the way court trials are held and its fall out. It noted that "protracted proceedings in courts followed by acquittal in heinous crimes tend to generate a feeling of confidence among hardened criminals that they can continue to commit crimes with impunity and ultimately get away with it all".[5] This can have a cascading effect on the poor who generally bear the brunt of lawlessness being the farthest from the corridors of power and protection.

---

5. Fourth Report of the National Police Commission, Para 34.24, page 48.

The Fourth Report of the National Police Commission further mentions badly delayed trials arising from causes like non-appearance of witnesses, lack of preparedness of the prosecuting or defence counsel to get on with the day's work in court, frequent adjournments granted on the slightest of pretexts, prolonged cross examinations without regard to its relevance or need, taking unduly long time for perusing records or otherwise getting prepared for the case at different stages of trial, etc. The National Police Commission accordingly raised the following broad points, which can lessen the present predicament affecting court trials to a significant extent.

- The Commission felt that several of these causes (listed above) could be eliminated "if the presiding Magistrate/Judge adopts a positive approach to the daily proceedings in every case and adequately uses his powers under the Criminal Procedure Code and Section 165 of the Indian Evidence Act for expeditious disposal of the cases".[6]
- The National Police Commission suggests a whole time functionary at the rank of a Senior District and Sessions Judge who is qualified for appointment as High Court Judge may be attached to each High Court to inspect the District Courts periodically. A similar functionary of the rank of Additional Sessions Judge may be entrusted with the inspections at the district level.
- The Commission also suggests that summary trial procedure should be made mandatory for offences specified in Section 260 of the Criminal Procedure Code. Accordingly, the words 'may, if he thinks fit' can be substituted by the word 'shall' in this Section.
- An adult who is proved to have organised a gang of juvenile criminals or otherwise abetted the commission of crime by a juvenile, should be held punishable under Chapter V of the Indian Penal Code which should provide for a more severe punishment than that stipulated for the main crime by the juvenile. A new Section may also provide for the mandatory award of a minimum punishment, except for special reasons to be recorded by the court.
- The National Police Commission also favours the institution of a Criminal Justice Commission at the Centre supported by a similar arrangement at the State level with special emphasis on the correctional services *vis-à-vis* the Protection of Offenders Act, and the Children Act.

---

6. *ibid.*, Para 34.33, page 49.

- Cooperation between the public prosecutors and the police at various levels aided by suitable additions to the Criminal Procedure Code to specify this rule.

Social Legislation

The Fourth Report of the National Police Commission discusses in detail the problem of social legislation. The normal role of the police as expected by the people is in the field of laws pertaining to the protection of life and security of property. The Indian Penal Code is the basic criminal law of the country for the police to perform this role. However, the police, as the premier law enforcement agency in the country, is frequently involved in the enforcement of a variety of laws aimed at social reforms. The National Police Commission categorises social legislation into five groups, as follows.[7]

- The First Group covers laws regulating social institutions like marriage, divorce, adoption, inheritance, etc. Here there is no role of the police that is envisaged in the enforcement of these laws.
- The Second Group pertains to laws dealing with social problem like prevalence of dowry, discrimination against women, begging, vagrancy, etc. The police should not have much role to play in the enforcement of these laws excepting some cases like enforcing the law prohibiting begging which is solely from the point of view of maintaining public order at a specified place.
- The Third Group deals with laws aimed at prohibiting the deterioration of the health of the people. Offences under these laws which involve commercially organised activity (e.g. drug trafficking) or disturbance of public order, should be made fully cognizable by the police. Offences which do not have any such angle but involve individual behaviour and conduct without creating any public disorder may be made cognizable by the police only on a specific complaint from a person alleging annoyance or injury caused to him/her by such behaviour and conduct and not on any intelligence gathered by the police themselves.
- The Fourth Group of law is aimed at prohibiting or regulating certain pastimes, which are likely to operate to the detriment of the earnings of the poor and their families. Laws that regulate gambling, horse racing, lotteries, etc., fall under this category. Police cognizance of

7. *ibid.*, Para 32.12 to Para 32.17, pages 39-40.

offences under these laws should be limited to those that have a public aspect.

- The Fifth Group consists of laws that are meant for protecting and rehabilitating the handicapped and the weaker sections of society and preventing their economic exploitation. Police should be fully involved in the enforcement of these laws. Protection of Civil Rights Act and the Suppression of Immoral traffic Act are examples of laws under these groups. Offences under these laws should be made cognisable and the general police should have full powers of enforcing them.

Prohibition

The Fourth Report of the National Police Commission comments that "the arrest of a large number of persons year after year and their passing through police custody for their involvement in prohibition offences alone would tend to 'criminalise' persons who are not perceived a criminal in the normal sense of the term by society at large" (Page 59). The prohibition law was conceived as a legislation primarily meant to benefit the ill informed and poorer sections of the community. Most of these, in jail under this law are in prisons (and in large numbers) for their involvement in illicit liquor trade. However, most of them are the consumers of illicit liquor and thus belong to the poorer sections of the society. Illicit distillation of liquor is carried out in remote areas and safe hideouts, but is easily available. The profits from this business far outweigh the economic losses from punishment and provides for big business and consumption. This results only in consumers getting caught and languishing in jails. Consequently, the Fourth Report of the National Police Commission recommended the following:

- Cognizable offences under the prohibition law should be limited to manufacturer, transport and sale of liquor.
- Offences relating to possession of liquor and drinking of liquor or being found in a state of drunkenness should be made non-cognizable.

The Fifth Report

Recruitment and Training of Police Personnels

The Fifth Report of the National Police Commission starts with a detailed discussion of recruitment and training of police personnels, especially for the constables. Some of the important points raised and recommendations made are as follows:

- Limit recruitment at two levels only–Constables and officers in Indian Police Service. The recruitment in the other levels should be eliminated in a phased manner.
- Recruitment of constables only at the district level, to ensure adequate representation.
- A qualitative change in police perspective and approach is needed so as to result in a total change in the police culture. Much greater effort is required in training and education to develop greater professional competence, at the level of constables.
- This should be complemented with intelligent supervision, purposeful inspection, favourable environmental conditions, mutual trust and willingness to delegate.
- Training material and basic instructional literature should be easily made available.
- Better planning and trainee manpower release is required.
- Attractive pay and other amenities are required.
- Recommendations of the 1973 Committee on police training should be implemented.
- Greater attention to the nature of the constable's interaction with the public is needed.
- The constable has to be made aware of the prospects of promotion.
- Constables like Sub-Inspectors should be attached to some social service organisation.
- Periodical exposure is required by way of refresher courses to increase the sensitivity and understanding of psychology, management techniques and behavioural sciences.
- Special courses at all levels for constables, sub-inspectors and inspectors.
- Deputy Superintendent of Police should go through the training imparted to the Indian Police Service Officers at the National Police Academy in Hyderabad.

District Police and the Executive Magistracy

The next aspect (of relevance here) discussed in the Fifth Report of the National Police Commission pertains to the role of the District Police. The District Police and the Superintendent of Police are subjected to two kinds of control—a hierarchical control exercised by the officers in the police and an operational control exercised by the Chief Executive of the District or the District Magistrate (DM). The arrangement contemplated in law for the administration of the police in the district is set forth in paragraph 2 of Section 4 of the Police Act, 1861. The "general control and direction" of the District Magistrate mentioned in Section 4 governs the relationship between the police and the magistracy in most parts of the country. However the words "general control and direction" have been left undefined in the law.

Police functions fall under two broad categories—investigative and preventive. The manner in which the investigative functions of the police are performed is described in details in the Criminal Procedure Code. On the other hand, the maintenance of public order is in a way part of the preventive function. Most actions of this type are justifiable in courts and should not be considered as left to unfettered executive discretion. However the District Magistrate has come to acquire considerable authority to interfere with the internal management of the district police organisation. Such control is not exercised only in the areas of drill, arms and discipline of the police force. The ground position of total subordination of the police to the executive magistracy is not contemplated under the law. This can only lead to distortion of police performance and dilution of police accountability to the law of the land. Consequently the following recommendations were made:

- Any police rule or regulation which unnecessarily or without purpose subordinates the police to the District Magistrate should be removed or amended. The requirements of administrative and public interest should alone be kept in view.
- Suitable amendments to Section 4 of the Police Act, 1861, should be incorporated. All the provisions in the State Police Acts should also be suitably amended.
- The police should have a distinct identity, adequate competence and operational independence to play an effective role in the administration.
- The Superintendent of Police should be adequately armed under the law to deal with situations independently.

Code of Behaviour for Police Personnels

The report proposes a Code of Behaviour for Police personnels which includes the non-occurrence of the following:

a) neglect of Duty, b) disobedience to orders without sufficient cause, c) discreditable conduct which is likely to bring discredit on the reputation of the police, d) misconduct towards a member of the police force without sufficient reasons, e) falsehood or pre-fabrication, f) corrupt or improper practice, g) abuse of authority, h) neglect of his health, i) improper dress and untidiness, j) reporting to duty in a state of drunkenness, k) be an accessory to a disciplinary offence, l) damage the unity of the police force especially on the grounds of religion, caste or community, and m) indulge in anti-national conduct.

Police Public Relation

According to the Fifth Report of the National Police Commission, police–public relations are in a very unsatisfactory state, essentially due to police partiality, corruption, brutality and failure to register cognisable offences.[8] Police do in fact harass even those who try to help them. The public in general does not think that the police is efficient. Again people who appear in courts as witnesses have to undergo considerable inconvenience and hardship and for this they blame the police more than the law courts because their appearance in a court of law is a consequence of their involvement in a police investigation. On the other hand even though criminogenic factors are not under the control of police, the forces, which generate disorder, are confused with normal dissent and the police is blamed squarely for rise in crime and spread of disorder.

The Indian Police Commission of 1902-03 in Para 26 concluded, "what wonder is it that the people are said to dread the police, and to do all they can do to avoid any connection with a police investigation".[9] Hundred years on, the conclusion is still very much true. Policemen in general do not believe that very much is at fault and blame the system, which even according to some is beyond improvement. The recommendations to improve the police – public relations, were as follows:

- The major recommendations are in the directions of content of training in all orientation programmes and in the process of imparting the training wherein attitudinal changes can be brought about. The police service is a service dedicated to the protection of the common citizen and they should decide how best they could render the help sought and not how through subterfuge of law and regulation, evade their legitimate responsibility. They should also understand that dissent

8. Fifth Report of the National Police Commission, See Para 43.110 to Para 43.123, page 74-76.
9. *ibid.*, page 74.

on the part of the citizen is not to be construed as a threat to law and order unless there is an apprehension of breach of peace.

- The police should place greater emphasis on service-oriented functions like rendering first aid to the injured, or helping in the distribution of food and clothing. Youth counselling should be made a regular feature.
- There should be the provision of a 'visitor's room' in the police stations.
- There should be high visibility in traffic policing and patrolling.
- The police should give up to a considerable extent the secrecy that surrounds their functioning.
- News of crime is of considerable interest to the people and therefore the press is interested in it. The police should establish a system of communication through which authentic facts relating to the crime and disorder can be quickly given to the press.

Victim Compensation

The police functions in the context of a punishment-oriented judicial system. As a sub-system of the criminal justice system, the role of the police also becomes punitive and therefore negative. On paper, this is balanced by the right of every victim of crime to claim damages in a civil court but it is common knowledge that very few can afford the excessively lengthy processes of civil courts, the end result of which are often uncertain and unsatisfactory. So there is little, even for the victim of a crime to motivate him/her to co-operate with the police except a wish to impose retribution. Although the National Police Commission recommends in its Fifth Report, to have a legislation of a Criminal Injuries Compensation Act, precious little on this subject was deliberated upon.

Women Police

Regarding the women police in the police force the Fifth Report of the National Police Commission makes the following recommendations:

- There should be a larger intake of women police especially in the ranks of Assistant Sub-Inspectors and Sub-Inspectors.
- The women police should be involved more in investigation related work especially relating to children and women.
- Delinquency among girls is a more serious problem than delinquency among boys. So women police can play a more useful role on both the spheres of investigation and prevention.

- Greater presence of women police in the police stations is required.
- Women police is essential for cities, urban police stations and in thickly populated areas.

The Sixth Report

Indian Police Service

The first chapter of the Sixth Report of the National Police Commission deals with Indian Police Service. The National Police Commission calls for the equality in the pay scales and prospects of the Indian Police Service with the Indian Administrative Service. The Kothari Committee also recommended this. Most of the other recommendations of the National Police Commission for the Indian Police Service have more or less been implemented, except to an extent, the issue of equality of pay.

Police and Students

The Sixth Report of the National Police Commission, in view of the problems that the police face *vis-à-vis* the students and also regarding its image at large, devoted a chapter to this cause and had the following recommendations to make:

- The police should be kept out as far as possible from administrative problems in universities and colleges and their campuses. The primary responsibility for resolving and mitigating campus problems of indiscipline involving students shall be that of the academic authorities. Police intervention should be restricted to situations wherein the prevention of grave crime and other unlawful activities are needed, in the detection and investigation of a crime already committed and in cases where the authorities request for police intervention provided the police is satisfied that the situation is serious and is likely to result in a breach of law and order.
- The police should take actions as per law in off campus situations where violence can erupt or has erupted.
- Police interaction in non-conflict situations needs encouragement, as it will remove the impression among the students that the police are generally hostile to them.

Urban Policing

The National Police Commission with respect to urban policing envisaged a greater role for it in preventive and regulatory action. However modernisation along with greater manpower was urgently called for. The Report's other recommendations were for control room, single digit bureau, increasing use of computers especially for registration of motor vehicles and checking antecedents of persons with doubtful character, separate homicide squad, economic offences and forgery squad, auto thefts squad, etc. for all cities with over five lakh population. Although these measures have been implemented in most big cities, there are still cities with over five lakh population without these police facilities.

The Seventh Report

Organisation and Structure of Police

The National Police Commission made the following comments/ recommendations:

- The police stations need restructuring and a facelift. The buildings, housing the police stations need improvement throughout the country. They need to be strengthened and made more effective.
- Should be free from political interference.
- Police stations in the rural areas are few and far between. They also have a very vast jurisdiction, which dilutes police presence and effectiveness. More police stations are required. The jurisdiction need to be delimited and made more compact and manageable.
- The criteria for creating police stations should be the number of crimes to be investigated, the area in which law and order has to be maintained and the population which they need to serve.
- The lock-ups are like dungeons with very poor sanitary conditions. These need improvement.
- Manpower commensurate with the volume of work should be available to the police stations and a committee should be constituted to work out suitable norms.
- An operative 'job content' needs to be developed for each rank.
- There should be a promotion scheme for every rank within the police structure. For example, a constable should be able to become a Head Constable after eight years of service provided he does not have unsatisfactory records and so on. However a bright constable should be able to become an Assistant Sub-Inspector of police through a competitive examination without necessarily having to become a Head Constable.

- Regarding the 'State Armed Police Battalions' and 'District Armed Reserve', the National Police Commission notes that these have not been accorded the importance they deserve.
- Transfer from armed police to civil police for constables should be allowed after three years.

Delegation of Financial Powers to Police Officers

The Report of the National Police Commission calls for the delegation of financial powers to police officers, essentially more powers to the Chief of State Police, equivalent to the Director General, BSF or the Director General, CRPF. For example,

- Chief of State Police should be authorised to create temporary posts from the rank of Constables to Deputy Superintendent of Police for a period of two years.
- Chief of State Police should be authorised to make financial sanctions for the purchase and repair of motor vehicles, wireless equipment, etc. upto a certain amount.

Ministerial Staff and other Administrative Work

- The ministerial staff should be brought under the purview of the Police Act, 1861. They should be integrated with the rest of the policemen in respect of the terms and conditions of service, discipline, etc.
- In order to enhance the career prospects of the ministerial staff, they should be provided with openings in to regular police force.
- The Chiefs of State Police should take personal interest in making more effective use of computer both in operational matters and administrative matters.

Home Guards

Home Guards are a statutorily backed organisation that fills the gap between organised policing and individual self-policing in a society and consists of individuals who voluntarily organise themselves or who offer voluntarily their services. The National Police Commission noted the following:

- The Home Guards can employ a sizeable number of unemployed people if used more effectively.
- The Home Guards are used too infrequently and they should be utilised on many more occasions.

- If the regular use of Home Guards for patrolling proves to be more cost effective and commands greater public acceptability, then this could as well be made a regular feature and this will also promote the idea of self-policing.
- The Home Guards could be made to play a significant role in protecting the weaker sections of the society.
- Deficiencies in training staff, living accommodations, and apparatus must be removed wherever they exist.
- The daily allowance paid to the Home Guards should be realistic and not be unreasonably discriminatory.

Performance Appraisal of the Police Personnel

The National Police Commission makes the following recommendations in this issue.

- Use of annual confidential reports should be treated as a source of information for administrative purposes and for organisational development through improving the performance of the employee.
- The employee should be made aware of the quality of his performance, his shortfalls and failures, if any, so that he/she can correct himself/herself.
- The proximity between the officer reported upon and the reporting officer should increase.
- Monthly or quarterly counselling sessions should be carried out systematically.
- A superior inspecting officer should record their assessments.
- Annual performance appraisal report must contain an integrity column.
- A cell at the district and the state level be made responsible for follow up action both on the continuos appraisal as well as the annual appraisal.

Disciplinary Action

The Fifth Report of the National Police Commission detailed a 'Code of Conduct' for the Police. In breach of this code, certain disciplinary action was outlined in this report.

- Prompt and effective disciplinary action should be taken when departmental norms are broken.
- There should be a foolproof grievance redressal machinery for the police personnel.

- Major punishments under the department involve: (i) dismissal, (ii) removal, and (iii) reduction in rank. These should be awarded only after drawing up of regular disciplinary proceedings.
- Minor punishments include: (i) censure, (ii) withholding of increment, and (iii) withholding of promotion. These can be awarded through a shorter procedure, in which, the delinquent officer should be confronted in writing with the facts of the case and the penalty proposed against him/her. He/she may then be asked to furnish his/her representation against the same within a specified period and the final order may be passed after taking the representation into consideration.
- Petty punishments may be awarded to the member of the constabulary in the orderly room and these may include: (i) reprimand, (ii) confinement to quarter-guard for a period not exceeding 15 days, (iii) punishment drill, extra guard duty, fatigue or other punitive duty, not exceeding 15 days, with or without confinement, and (iv) fine not exceeding one month's pay in a month.
- Against any of the major punishments awarded to a police official, there should be a provision of only one appeal to the authority just above the punishing authority, followed by one revision if necessary to an authority just above the appellate authority. There should be one appeal but no revision against minor punishments. There can be no appeal against petty punishments.
- Major punishments must be given after careful consideration and should not be resorted to in a routine manner.
- Suspension should not normally be ordered without getting the complaint looked into through a preliminary inquiry. Further suspension should not be resorted to unless facts and circumstances of the case indicate that the punishment will be a major one. Suspension should not be ordered for extraneous considerations.
- The charge must be furnished to the delinquent police official within a period of 15 days from the date of suspension, failing which, the incumbent would be entitled to automatic reinstatement.
- Time limits should be prescribed for completing various stages of disciplinary proceedings. In case such time limits have to be exceeded, specific approval should be sought from the next higher authority.

The Eighth Report

Accountability of Police Personnel

The responsibility should be squarely fixed on the officers of the level of Superintendent of Police and above to carefully watch the reputation of the SHOs and take appropriate measures whenever warranted. Any failure on their part in this regard should be seriously viewed. In those circumstances where the supervisory officer may either fail to assess the reputation of the SHO or fail to take appropriate action in a particular instance, the people have a right to petition to the State Security Commission. In the event of such complaints, the State Security Commission should gauge the reputation of the SHO concerned and take such actions as may be required.

Section 132 and Section 197 of the Criminal Procedure Code, 1973 provides protection to various categories of public servants against any prosecution brought against them relating to performance of official duties. The protection available to the police officers under these sections should be withdrawn so that the private complainant is free to press his complaint against police official for a judicial pronouncement without there being a provision to obtain prior permission of the competent authority for such prosecution. However, the police officer against whom a complaint is brought in a court of law should be defended at the cost of the Government.

High Courts may impress upon subordinate courts that complaints against police officials should be disposed of on priority basis. The High Court may further draw the attention of the lower courts to the provisions of Section 202 Criminal Procedure Code, and advise them generally to ask for a report from the District Superintendent of Police on the complaint filed before them, It would be the responsibility, of the District Superintendent of Police to either make an inquiry himself or have it made by a sufficiently senior officer and submit a factual report to the court before the latter decides to proceed further with the case. On mere filing of a complaint, unless there is a *prima facie* case and justification for the same, transfer of the concerned official should not be ordered.

Functionaries in the department at each level should be held accountable only with respect to the functions and duties assigned to him and accountability should not extend to duties over which he has no direct control. Therefore, police functionaries from SHO to that of Chief of Police cannot be held accountable for each isolated incident in a particular region in their respective jurisdiction, however serious it may be unless it is proved that the particular incident occurred because of act of omission or commission on the part of the police functionary or such incidents have been widespread and the official has failed to react adequately.

The sanction of fixing unreasonable or impossible targets, which cannot be achieved except through illegal or irregular means, should be effectively discouraged.

Police Act

- It is necessary to replace the existing outmoded Police Act of 1861. The recommendations made in the eight reports of the National Police Commission should be incorporated in the new legislation.
- The Central Government may enact the necessary legislation for the constitution of a Central Police Committee; define its role and such other details in terms of matters relating to:
    a) police organisation and police reforms of general nature
    b) grants and loans to the state police forces for their modernisation and development, and
    c) budgetary allocations to the state police forces.

Appendix A-13.2

Salient Features of the Ribeiro Committee's Recommendations on Police Reforms[1]

First Report (October 1998)

- A Security Commission should be setup in each state consisting of the minister in charge of police as the Chairman, the Leader of the Opposition, the Chief Secretary of the State, a sitting or retired judge nominated by the Chief Justice of the State's High Court and three other non-political citizens of proven merit and integrity as members. These three citizens should be chosen by a committee to be setup by the Chairman of the National Human Rights Commission, which has taken much interest in the establishment of this proposed institution. The name of the Commission should be "The Police Performance and Accountability Commission." (PPAC)
- The four non-political members of this Commission excluding the Chief Secretary should hold office for three years after which persons of equal merit chosen in the same manner will replace them.
- The Security Commission will have advisory and recommendatory powers for the present. The State's Director General of Police will be its Secretary and Conveyor.
- The Security Commission will oversee the performance of the Police and ensure that it is accountable to the law of the land. Its functions will be as is spelt out by the National Police Commission in Para 15.48 of their report. In addition, Security Commission will ensure that no premature transfers of officers of the rank of Superintendent of Police and above are made without prior clearance from the Security Commission and that transfer are made only by the authority competent under the rules to do so.
- Besides the Security Commission, a District Police Complaints Authority will be set up in each Police District as a non statutory body to examine complaints from the public of police excesses, arbitrary arrests and detention, false implications in criminal cases, custodial violence, etc and to make appropriate recommendations to the Police Performance and Accountability Commission, as well as to the

1. A part of these comments were made by the Commonwealth Human Rights Initiative, India.

Government and to the State or National Human Rights Commission. The Principal District and Sessions Judge, the Collector of the district and the SSP would constitute this authority.

- In every state, a Police Establishment Board should be constituted with the Director General of Police (DGP) and his four seniormost officers, borne on the IPS cadre of the State but who are immediately junior to the DGP, as members to monitor all transfers, promotions, rewards and punishments as well as other service related issues. The Board should be given the legal authority to discharge its duties by amending the relevant rules.
- Rules should be framed by the Government on transfers, tenures, promotions, rewards and punishments and the police authorities designated to administer these rules. Any departure from these norms and rules will be brought to the notice of the PPAC.
- The Director General of Police will be selected by the Chief Minister of the State from a panel of three names prepared by a Committee headed by the Chairman of the UPSC and consisting of the Union Home Secretary, the Director of Intelligence Bureau, the State's Chief Secretary and the State's incumbent DGP. This Selection Committee may consult the Chief Vigilance Commission before drawing up a panel. The DGP will have fixed tenure of three years. He can be removed within the period of tenure only on the recommendations of the PPAC and for specified reasons, made in writing to the Government.
- The investigation wing of the police will be insulated from undue pressure if the DGP is selected in the manner prescribed above and given a tenure and also if the PPAC discharges its role of overseeing police performance and ensuring accountability. All investigating officers should be specially trained in scientific methods of investigation and not utilised for law and order duties, except in small rural police stations where it may not be possible to strictly demarcate the two important police functions. The investigating officers should not be shifted to law and order or other duties for five years at least.

Second Report (March 1999)

- The National Police Commission had recommended that there should be a State Security Commission at the Centre. There is no need for such an institution at the central level. In case of CBI, the Supreme Court has already given directions. The Intelligence Bureau is an intelligence organisation and the BSF and the CRPF are paramilitary outfits that do not involve themselves with local politics and politicians.

- The Central Police Committee as recommended by the National Police Commission in its Seventh Report, should be constituted.
- The old Police Act of 1861 needs to be replaced by a new Police Act.
- The recommendations of the Law Commission about insulating the investigative functions of the police from its law and order work should be implemented urgently.
- The recommendations of the National Police Commission about recruitment, training and welfare of the constabulary should be implemented.
- The minimum educational qualifications for recruitment to the level of constable should be higher secondary.
- The National Police Commission had recommended the reorganisation of the hierarchy of the police, with an increase in the strength at middle levels of Assistant Sub-Inspectors/ Sub-Inspectors /Inspector to be offset by reducing numbers at the lower levels of constabulary. This would improve promotion opportunities of lower ranks. We endorse the recommendations of the National Police Commission.
- Every state should establish an independent Police Recruitment Board and entrust to it, the task of recruitment of all non-gazetted ranks.
- A qualitative change in the training being imparted in police training institutions is imperative to improve performance and behaviour of the police.

Appendix A-13.3

Salient Features of the Padmanabhaiah Committee Report on Police Reforms[1]

- To define perspective roles of Centre and States in developing capabilities in the Police including funding.
- A system of planned induction based on proper manpower planning and of career planning of individual group of officers. The Padmanabhaiah Committee on Police Reforms mentioned in Para 7.6, "we are yet to see a police department which has a well-thought-out and researched manpower plan for next five years and which knows what its growth rate should be".
- There should be a greater recruitment of Sub-Inspectors instead of Constables. This can be seen to be the opposite of the view taken by the National Police Commission. Recruitment to constabulary should be restricted till a teeth-to-tail ratio of 1:4 is achieved as against present ratio, which ranges from 1:7 to 1: 15 in different states.
- Ban the recruitment at the level of Inspectors and Deputy Superintendent of Police.
- Constables should be recruited young. Boys/girls, who have passed 10th standard examination and are below 19 years in age, should be eligible to appear in a common competitive qualifying examination. The successful candidates should be put through a rigorous two-year training programme and qualify for appointment as constables only after passing a final examination.
- The existing constabulary should be re-trained to enable them to imbibe right attitudes to work. Those who do not successfully complete training should be compulsorily retired.
- A constable should be classified as a 'skilled worker' in view of the skills required and risks involved in the job.
- There should be a career plan in the police department. The career plan should take into account: (a) promotional avenues and prospects, (b) the needs of specialisation, (c) the training needs, and (d) posting policy.

---

1. A part of these comments were made by the Commonwealth Human Rights Initiative, India.

- Career planning at the level of constables is very important. Today only less than 25 per cent of constables ever get any promotion. The remaining constables usually retire in the same rank in which they were recruited.
- The eligibility criteria for recruitment to the level of Sub-Inspectors should be 12th class pass and an upper age limit of 21 years. They should be recruited on the basis of a common written qualifying examination. The successful candidates must pass a final examination after undergoing a three-year training programme. Fifty per cent of vacancies of Sub-Inspectors should be filled by direct recruitment and 50 per cent reserved for promotions.
- Promotions up to the level of Deputy Superintendents of Police should be based on undergoing certain mandatory training programmes and passing certain examinations.
- A constable would be eligible to appear for Assistant Superintendent of Police post in 3 years service and Superintendent of Police in 6 to 9 years of service and Inspector in 14 to 16 years of service. The average age of promotion to the post of Inspector therefore would be 35 to 40 years, which is young enough to hold SHO-ship of a Police station, but old enough to be mature and still energetic. In theory, an intelligent and lucky constable can hope to be a Deputy Superintendent of Police by 45 years and Additional Superintendent of Police by 52 to 55 years of age.
- Police Training Advisory Council should be set up at the Centre and in each state to advise the Home Ministers on police training matters.
- All promotions should be subject to completing the mandatory training programmes and passing of promotional examinations.
- There should not be more than one Director General post in the police department and that the Director General should have the right of writing the confidential reports of all officers at the level of Additional Director Generals and Special Director Generals.
- Special emphasis on the need for specialisation in police. After a policeman, whether he is from the constabulary or from the officer ranks, spends the first eight years of service, his aptitude and potential for development in a particular area of specialisation, like investigation, crime prevention, community policing, intelligence gathering, traffic, various branches of forensic work, fire arms, security, etc., should be assessed.

- The Indian police should adopt the philosophy of community policing. The Government of India should support this by bringing out a handbook on the subject, providing training inputs and funding pilot projects.
- Lack of a proper tenure policy for posting of officers at different levels and arbitrary transfers have been used by politicians to control and abuse the police for their own ends. To deal with this problem, following action is required: a) A body headed by the Chief Justice of the State High court as Chairman, State Chief Secretary and an eminent public person as members should be constituted to recommend a panel of two names for appointment to the post of the Director General of Police. b) A Police Establishment Board, consisting of DGP and three other members of the police force selected by him should be constituted to decide transfers of all officers of the rank of Deputy Superintendent of Police and above. c) The minimum tenure of all officers should be two years. d) Another Committee under the Chief Secretary, with Home Secretary and the DGP as members, should be constituted to hear representations from police officers of the rank of Superintendent of Police and above alleging violation of rules in the matter of postings and transfers.
- To deal with the problem of corruption in the police, which leads to the criminalisation of the force, the committee has recommended a more serious enforcement of the code of conduct and simpler but more effective procedures for removing corrupt officers.
- Since police work cannot be organised on an eight-hour shift basis, police personnel should be given a weekly off and compulsorily required to go on earned leave every year. Holiday homes may be constructed for police personnel.
- Investigation should be separated from law and order work. In the first phase, this separation should take place at police station level in all urban areas. An Additional Superintendent of Police should be exclusively responsible for crime and investigation work.
- Sections 25 and 26 of the Indian Evidence Act should be deleted and confessions made to police officers of the rank of Superintendent of Police and above should be made admissible in evidence.
- Forensic science can play extremely dramatic role in investigation or murder, sexual assault and terrorist cases. It can play a very significant role in drug offences, vehicle crime and burglary. The police manual

must be amended to make it mandatory to collect samples and to obtain expert forensic opinion in all such serious crimes.

- The Government should create separate Department for Forensic Science and constitute an All India Forensic Science Service.
- Every police station should be equipped with 'investigation kits' and every sub-division should have a mobile forensic science laboratory.
- There has to be a two-phased programme for improving the upkeep of police stations. In the first phase, the minimum requirements should be provided. There should also be a conscious effort to locate new police stations, in residential and commercial areas, to make them easily accessible; incidentally such locations would act as a check on malpractice, third degree and violation of human rights, etc. at the station.
- The police leadership, through proper manpower and career planning, improved training, effective supervision and by inculcating a sense of values amongst the members of the force, can play an important role in encouraging specialisation, promoting professionalism and increasing morale in the force.
- In each district, there should be a crime prevention cell manned by officers who have specialised in crime prevention work.
- To deal with cyber crime effectively, police capabilities in various areas need to be developed. Capabilities of some police institutions, like the National Police Academy in the field of training, CBI in investigation, Intelligence Bureau in cyber surveillance and the National Crime Records Bureau in cyber technology/forensics should be enhanced.
- The present classification of offences into cognisable and non-cognizable made 150 years ago is not very relevant today. The Law Commission of India should review the entire classification and the powers of the police to investigate.
- At present, investigative officer wastes a lot of time in Court, where due to the prevailing backlog, their cases do not come up for hearing even though they might have been present in court for an entire day. As such, it is suggested courts should be advised to, as a rule, list cases police station-wise on each day. If this is done, investigative officer will be attending court only on the days the cases of his police station are listed.

- The concept of VIP security has been grossly, blatantly and brazenly misused. The entire concept of personal security needs a careful review and dismantling.
- Certain offences having interstate, national and international repercussions should be declared 'federal offences' to be investigated by the Special Crimes Division of the CBI, which should function under the administrative control of the Ministry of Home Affairs.
- Taking into account the wide ramifications of the terrorist crime, there have to be different norms regarding the burden of proof, degree of proof and the legal procedures in regard to trial of terrorist cases. There is a need for a special and a comprehensive law to fight terrorism.
- There should be a national counter-terrorism coordinator to prepare a comprehensive counter-terrorism plan and budget.
- A statutory independent body of police should be set up to carry out annual as well as thematic inspections of the police force and to report to the State Government whether the police force is functioning efficiently and effectively.
- A non-statutory District Police Complaints Authority (DPCA) should be set up with the District Magistrate as the Chairman and a senior Additional Sessions Judge, the District Superintendent of Police and an eminent citizen nominated by the DM as members. Investigations into public complaints against the police should in the first instance be done by the police department itself. Those who are not satisfied can approach the DPCA.
- There should be a mandatory judicial inquiry into all cases of alleged rape of a woman or death of any person in police custody.
- The Government of India should establish a permanent National Commission for Policing Standards to lay down norms and standards for all police forces on matters of common concern and to see that that the State Governments set up mechanisms to enforce such standards.
- The release of central grants for modernisation or upgradation of funds should be dependent upon compliance by State Governments with certain basic issues, like each State having a manpower and career planning system, a transparent recruitment, promotion and transfer policy and meeting certain minimum standards for training.

- The Government of India should play a much more active role in:
  1. all aspects of training like setting norms and standards for training for various levels of hierarchy, setting standards for training institutions and, in general, supporting and monitoring all training activities;
  2. providing infrastructures and specialised support services, like communications and computers, forensic science, etc;
  3. providing intelligence support;
  4. maintaining crime records and data banks;
  5. supplies of critical equipment, like night vision devices, BP jackets, BP cars and weaponry; and
  6. funding of various innovative and pilot projects.
- The Police Act of 1861 should be replaced by a new Act.
- The State Government must give high priority to the allocation of resources to the police.
- There should be a permanent National Commission for Police Standards and (NCPs) to set standards and to see that state governments set up mechanisms to enforce such standards.

Index

D

E

F

G

H

I

J

K

Some of the poems from this collection have appeared in the following print and on-line magazines:

Arson, The Bitter Oleander, Borderlands: Texas Poetry Review, Fire (U.K.), *House Organ, Hunger, The Iron Horse Literary Review, New Millennium Writings, Oyez Review, Pearl, Pemmican, Rattle, Red River Review, Sulphur River Literary Review, Sierra Nevada College Review, Square Lake, Unarmed, Ur-Vox* and *Wandering Hermit Review..*

Some poems were also included in the anthology *Corresponding Voices,* Point of Contact & Syracuse University, and in the chapbook, *Where Thirsts Intersect*, published in a limited edition of 30 copies by Bernardo Juaregui's Bagatela Press of Ciudad Juárez, Mexico. "San Fernando Valley Suite" was published as an artist's book by Jean-Claude Loubieres & AdeLeo Editions of Paris. "Literary History" also appeared on-line on the *Red River Review*, and was translated into Spanish by Alberto Blanco, & published in *Critica* of The University of Puebla, Mexico. "Cabal" and "The Lovers of Nephilim" and "Narrative of a Wolf With No Teeth," were translated into Spanish by César Silva Márquez and published in the journal *Parque Nandino* of Guadalajara, Mexico, and in *La Valquiria* of Xalapa, Veracruz.

TABLE OF CONTENTS

THERE IS A RIVER

INTRODUCTION

"I will write how you breathe," Anthony Seidman tells us in his remarkable new collection, *Where Thirsts Intersect*, a bold explosion of language that mines the depths of "[e]ach minute," which as the poet describes in "The Perfect Mosquito" is "pregnant with the tastes of a century." Journeying to Juárez, to the chthonic landscapes of his Latin American poetic forebears, Seidman poignantly takes us across borders of consciousness and returns us to new yet familiar places deep inside the psyche.

This is indeed a marvelous book—in the sense of its blistering imaginative and emotive reach, as well as in its embrace of the Surrealist search for the "marvelous" in the everyday. Seidman's associative net is wide, its arc rippling with the intensity of sun-glint fish lifted at dawn from the depths. Within just a few lines he tosses that net seamlessly from "the sleep of the reader where totemic wombs are swollen with the moon" to "[b]ulls, bearded with ringlet shags" to "vermilion that threads through a crackle of saffron and Mercurochrome."

Seidman's abundance of prose poems in this collection attests to his place as one of our premier prose poets, and his cast of characters—the likes of Federico García Lorca, Willem de Kooning, Chaim Soutine, Jack Kerouac, and Hart Crane—works to revitalize our consciousness, newly stunned-awake. His work possesses the tenderness yet ferocity of Neruda, the primordial reach of Aimé Césaire, and the fast-snapping discourse of jazz—but a jazz burning with the leaves of some shamanic plant embedded in the light dark keys of a soul blazing to understand the source of all that is.

The core conceit of Seidman's poems is that this source must be uncovered—*recovered*—by any means possible, and he steadies us through a kind of reciprocal dreaming to help us recognize that this source is to be seen, inhabited, and ultimately embraced not in hallucination but in the marvelous of the everyday, primarily through thepractice of intimate attention. "What the old man poured into buckets and sought out block after block," the poet tells us, "was the source—the enzyme itself—for workers with rough hands and mothers giving milk."

Workers, mothers, lovers of milky rough-handed poetry: "gather around entrails of sacrificed goats, in the sparks snapping and rising from the altar bonfires"; it is by this light that Seidman's poems are best read.

— George Kalamaras

for my father,
for Daniel and Leah,
for Estrella del Valle

el agua es la única eternidad de la sangre.
water is the sole eternity of blood.

—José Joaquín Pasos

I will write how you breathe: burgeoning of grape, feet pressing into dusk, teeth that have kissed the river of Narcissus, and steppes where horses rise from dust. I will write how you burn, scorpion pinned to ray through a magnifying-glass, shriveled quince in a drawer, plums falling onto grass; this is the thirst that expands, the man asleep with an erection, the woman crazed by red spiders in her last months before menopause, the adolescent who stares at a young woman, his pores opening like the pink roof'd and black gum'd maws of savannah cats, the boy playing with his girl cousin, and the adulterous couple, satiated, and each a distillation of their daytime liquids. My bones sweat words, writhing in the furnace that bubbles with the seasons and squeezing of lemons, the beetle in its mud, the poet astride her stallion. I feel the wind that drags fish from their depths and hangs them as fruit before delirious wasps, turn back the pages of my skin, make the shadows of my room a temple, and the crushed pomegranate an altar.

BOOK OF THE DISQUIET

La poesía te rompe la boca...
Poetry shatters your mouth...

— Martín Camps

OCTAVIO PAZ ADDRESSES MARIE-JOSÉ

Listen to me as one does the evening rain:

I have tried to image streets, tamarind
trees, the garden of my youth, the wind & its dominion, all
in the white mirror of a page.
Do not move; unbutton your blouse, let fall
your skirt which is wheat the wind combs; that
is our world.

I have choked on politics, watched
money rasp, ashes up chimneys, and sat
in the white atrium of silence.
Do not speak; undo your hair, let fall
your dress which is water tempting the moon; that
is our parliament.

The calendar has turned full
circle, fusing the gods of water & smoke.
But I am with you as a draft of syllables,
an echo that knocks, and fades, and I am
indifferent to the dying world because here
I sleep without you.

Without you, dark orchard,
tree of my blood, blade of noon.
Two birds took flight in your eyes:
the one without wings, the other on fire.

THUS, BLINDED

from an excess of light, man,
sitting at desk or filling pot-holes, sighs
in evenings or on holiday
and walks from life exhibit to exhibit:
gleam of asphalt after rain,
wasp tongues flickering over papaya,
pendant breasts heaving beneath
the blouse of a woman who has just run,
ochre-tinged calluses on his toes;
and the ringing in his ears like
moist finger circling the crisp
crystal of a wine goblet, as he tosses
and turns in bed, his conscience
a Torah scroll unrolled, rolled up repeatedly.
At last, cancer gluts on the plum
of prostate, and blood tires at netting the bright
trout pushing up through sadness and salt
to a meager orgasm; and he steps onto
that beach-strip between two blazing estuaries
where all he sees he can only see
dripping with light, covered in light, not
filaments of matterlessness, the gaps
through which he will drop like a letter
into a mail-slot, and be carried
in hands of time to a darkness, amen,
where light has petrified.

ISSA

Brine-print of the moon
in the morning sky; slowly,
a salt dissolving.

PEDRO MIR AND HIS COUNTERSONG TO WALT WHITMAN

He who was everyone and no one at once:

fishmonger swatting at flies in an open market,
machinist rolling up his sleeves, arm-hair
glistening with axle grease,
bridegroom and the bride, even
beached sailor, crab edging from out his slack jaw,

I see in them and myself the same old law...

So that the form would be in the air, lemon
on the bough, so that
in the Antilles, precisely *en suelo quisqueyano*
son of a Puerto Rican woman and Cuban worker
would grow on an island
its shores in the same trajectory as the sun,
an archipelago of sugar and alcohol,
four cardinal cordilleras, a shimmer
of vertical rivers,
and land,
land beneath trees and land
at the hills, since the cock's crow,
land across the pupils and marigolds of dusk, land
pouring into every clay pitcher,
land beneath the map and land
beneath the soil itself;
so that this
Dominican
writing from the same *cueva* as his peers,
noting the fecund drool of the oxen,

gnarled fingers of the campesino among cane
he would see
that the land, the mountain of origin
belonged to the sugar refinery, the *ingenio*;
that the road and its two scars
were the ingenio's,
the throng of rails and smoke
were the ingenio's,
the dirt and the mortar
were the ingenio's,
the white teeth and the peeled mango
were the ingenio's,
and the arms of the peasant
were the ingenio's,
and their veins of virile caliber
were the ingenio's,
and the cane and the grass and the baskets full of fish
were the ingenio's,
with the blood the sweat the saltpeter
and the ants and the drizzle
were the ingenio's...

all were the ingenio's!

All for a dollar,
spittle of blood,
coin under tongue
and the transubstantiation
of inflation into a pissed kidney stone; the dollar,
meat in cash nailed to a telegraph pole,

the cables zipping by
at the velocity of currencies passing through
the stubby fingers of moneylenders,
sanctity on the installment plan,
investment in arsenic, arson of interest,
syntax asunder cinders, and bones of vultures;
so the campesino had no land,
the campesino

had no word
but the vertigo of fermented cane,
had no gold
but the guitar mistaken for a butterfly,
had no güirra,
but the gnashing of teeth.

And this Dominican
of impeccable dress,
this professor of aesthetics
who also saw the veins throbbing on the temples
of a Haitian clearing a field of charred cane,
who published his poems at an age
when Neruda was a vastness of pines
but not the sluggish rivers where the odor
of death is as strong as that of lavenders;

this man whose poems
were the awaited social poems, and also the algebra,
un viaje al muchedumbre
so that Juan Bosch,

the voice Lyndon B. Johnson strangled,
Juan Bosch of the molten word: *Pentagonism,*
could say that at last the people were uttered.
And it was a voice Mir heard,
a countersong,
germinated in the I of Whitman
who was everyone and no one sieved through that I,
who cast the ballot of the compost,
who was the fuse for Mir exiled
from the land pushing the clouds toward the sea off Puerta Plata,
from the milk in a wood bucket, and the uterus of a rose,
who was exiled
while *el chivo* reigned
with his riding crop and leather boots,
the Trujillo
who fed miscreants to razors,
and bleached the black soil of the Diaspora with *lo hispano* yet
harnessed the *merengue* as propaganda,
the Trujillo
who was simply a monster excelling at the murder of butterflies.

So that exiled
in Cuba, in the green atrium of Mexico,
Mir knew it was the denouement of Christliness on his island,
and that murder,
a beast with its tail on fire,
a beast that in a metallic night
had been engendered in the yolk of gunpowder and oil,
with a vertebra called Slavery,
with another vertebra called Debt,

and hundreds of vertebrae called the Sugar Refinery,
and a dorsal vertebra called the Monroe Doctrine,
murder would run unrestrained
through the hard azure of the dog-days,
through the season of hurricane,
across the dirt patios with chickens and children playing,
across the dust the workers raise walking to the mill;
yet that poet
who was born sprawled *en suelo quisqueyano*,
who had apprehended the Pronoun emitted through a beard full of butterflies,
that Dominican who was also a kosmos,
didn't hear the word I.

Exiled, he strangled the dawn, wine, the workday,
he wandered the factories, marketplaces, the docks,
dreamt in the mines, and rose in celestial elevators,
and he found a black piano, tightened
the wires to the point of snapping,
ripped the hammers,
smashed the silent harp,
and threw it over the bridge of dusk,

and did that not once,
but repeatedly, exiled
in the brothels of Cuba, in Guatemala,
in the green shade of Costa Rica,
until he heard a word resound,
a countersong,
a word that opened his breath exponentially so that

he spoke that island and
addressed every lawyer silent in the capital,
every prostitute straggling to a room of dripping pipes,
every embryo blossoming, every man weeping or
drunk in the red patio where confessions are mandatory,
every woman on her wedding night, every worker,
and not only did he speak his island
but the Americas entire,
in one elbow-swoop,
with the word We
against those who soiled the luminous beard,
who mistook Walt's hair for the axle and the assembly line,
his eyes for silver coins,
a pound of his blood payment for the serpent and bulldozer.

To hear the word We
resound at the well's bottom,
in each doorway, at the threshold of water,
in the fine dust of chalk, in the steps of worm and stallion;
to hear it where man and furrow sleep so that
we too might follow the grooves of the cart's wheels,
and reach where distance dissolves into dusk,
and the sound of dogs barking in the village,
and then nothing but pollen in every palm, arms
heavy with wheat and the greenness of wind and We.

Faustino, starving in Juárez, had walked over the bridge to El Paso to donate plasma once again, and returned to a shack where the roaches scurried, where Maricela, who made a few bucks hustling American tourists as a "fichera," cursed him for his uselessness. A boy kicking in her womb, while her two year old daughter ate an egg for her day's meal. I was there when, after having pawned a necklace, and no work found, his voice cracked: What do you want?...and he pulled up his sleeves, veins needle-tracked from the Red Cross where, despite everything, he would recite lines of unedited amber, liquid doors, and memorize them while his blood swirled up tubes the transparency of a jellyfish's nematocyst.

CABAL

"It didn't have a name; therefore, it didn't exist."
— Bernardo Jaúregui

The absence of unnamed things. Coffee acridly tepid, piano keys yellowing, even the dough of stale pastries, do not crumble into that vacancy plicking with static and specks of treble, like the white-noise on the outer reaches of the A.M. dial. That absence, more pressing than the folded sleeve of the amputee, of un-invented utensils and unborn beasts, balls of wet fur, black noses sniffing light, before imploding, without blood or yelp, the way the roof of a convertible folds into itself, leaving no crease in the blue air. Because there is a solitude that weighs on my blood in the slippage between hours: awake at dawn and hearing rain race across my darkened roof. If a man walked up the stairs at that moment, and paused before my door as if to check the apartment number, then struck his fist against the wood with four thumps, would my fingers turn open the knob, or would I be at the threshold, raincoat dripping on mat, fist offering a coin to the cupped hands of another man praying?

HART CRANE IN THE ISLANDS

Rum bottle on mahogany desk. All day, the Victrola blasted Ravel's *Bolero*, while the curtains rippled from the window facing plantains. In his reveries, salt of a sailor stung his lips, as his tongue licked for that taste, the dark phallus in a rocking hammock, tears, and teeth; while composing, the rigging of metaphors pulled palms and flotillas, Ohio parlors, and the smoke and lachrymae of the Americas into his estuary.

Mornings on the sundazzled shore. Peeling mangos in an esplanade; and then, colors of the aquatic dusk. There was a lover, a cane-cutter tart with liquor & sweat, and bonfires on the sands. At night, he would correct sheaves containing *Voyages* and *The Bridge*, then sleep like a Faust cleansed of all knowledge-lust, shadows of birds passing across his face with the softness a boy feels as he sobs against an apron. And for the first time his body felt as if it was weightless, as the sea opened her drapes, revealing her bones.

The Yiddish poets are all gone,— volumes of Mani Leib in mildew. An old man persists in New York where last century those from Die Yunge movement wrote a poetry that was meant to chisel the bastard tongue into Parnassian precision. No longer a Karl Shapiro or Arthur Gregor who might translate his strophes and their imagery of autumn and crumbling stone. Soon, he will be a breath siphoned into the penumbra where dialects are exchanged for oblivion.

JEAN TOOMER DOWN SOUTH

Pine needles on the ground bent beneath his shoes, as he walked into woods with their rumors of Juju men; the cane-juice made him dizzy. Sharecroppers from their cabins discerned his color from the chalk and brittle songs of the white folk, yet they saw his plum neck-ties, and heard the drive of the city in his speech. Jean had passed for white in New York: skin the color of bleached-dry corn husk, and hair combed straight. Each evening, the sawmill would close, and the sweetness of lumber saturated the coolness. Then the young women would sit on their porches awaiting their lovers; women, dusky and humming, with rounded thighs and breasts full of nightwebbed rivers. They were like afternoons that push away the sun. The men drank, and by coal heaters, grandfathers narrated the Diaspora of time, bumper crops, girls who ripened too quickly, and the knife-fights. Once, while sitting on the steps of his lodging, Jean heard a man singing far off:

There's a basement with a window where the light's all brown;
there's a basement with a window where the light's all brown, —
sometimes I sit there all night when I feel like I'm gonna drown.

The new journals from New York became wind in fields of tin-cans and rats rattling bones. Where the nymphs had abandoned London, where Helen was a ghost on the pavements of Manhattan, Jean felt the flowers in his blood blossom, and heard the spirituals, tasted the wet air at dawn, and the region was a brown nipple at the mouth of that poet.

There's a basement light with a window...
'cause a man can't never drown...

And one twilight, while walking back from the woods, he saw men huddled round a bonfire by the sawmill. Fermented cane in a bottle, faces all his color, yet lit up by firelight. They noticed him, and invited him to a drink: the city boy who spent his time writing. Yet there was never a poem he wrote about that hour, while he spat and gossiped work and women with names like Karintha. Like his companions, he would swig at the bottle, shake his head then guffaw, tasting the smoke in the liquor, and all the while savoring it.

FOR TI JEAN, FOR KEROUAC

If anything, you're not bloated on port wine,
not spit-foaming about the protocol of Zion's cabal,
but sky-eyed, drunk with road-going, heart
pocket with notepad scribbles of cigar father, & love
for the brown parlors of boyhood gloom, gravy,
& riverrumble. With your body spry for spooling between
line-backers, you climb into a boxcar, hear
the whis-whissing & steel clank from smokenetted tracks, as
train lurches forward with release of brakes, rust-squeals of wheels
clicking across the Dakotas, your pupils dilated, your bones biting
for America, canvas duffle bag still heavy with dew.

JEAN-JOSEPH RABEARÍVELO ADDRESSES HIS MUSE OF SUICIDE

I

The poem is evisceration,
the poem is a discharge, puss,
rat-fangs flashing in the boneyard of Malagasy.
The poem is
formaldehyde diluting my daughter's rigor mortis,
vertigo of dice games,
backwash of liquor the black of a lemur's gums.

Because I write
and a knife stabs out from my gut & chest,
lungs belch a rose of bubbles through
this cavity where plasma is the consistency of steam, and
like pupae roosting in a cow's wound
the lexicon,
the spelling-primer,
the French alternately
sitting heavy on my tongue or
swarming with the lice of Villon,
through the fly-infested orifice of Rimbaud's vowel,
the Rose and Ronsard,
Parnassian marble & the thin lips of Baudelaire, all
aureate & astral,
the majestuousness of a lunar footprint,
the slow swift velocity of a frozen ammonia shard in Jupiter's atmosphere,
the words are charged,
lightning-bolted back to my bowel,
and transmogrify into
a maggot-writhe on my quotidian bile,
atoms & light woven with muscle & entrails.

I am

the poem's uterus, its hive,
words embryonic & gelling,
yet the poem is also I,

my doppelganger.

The poem

has glutted on my innards,
slashed open a lip to plop from my stomach,
placenta shredded, tossed
on the floor like a bricklayer's shirt
after hours of sweat and not enough centimes for beer.
The poem with my fingers
recognizing the archipelagos in my cursive writing,
but the words upchucked with brine, vinegar,
words doused with the turpentine of this island,
and the poem wears out my shoes as
he walks from clerk job to tavern to urban bench,
the poem with handkerchief stopping nostrils as
he regards a peasant family in a stubble field
where they exhume a relative for the annual rites, and
ply horse-tooth'd smile with wine.

II

And early this morning, the poem donned my fedora, tied on my one cravat, walked to the corner café where natives are allowed, sharpened my pencil, wrote of the black glassmaker, the leper, peopling pages with jeremiads of this island bereft of the white utopias, negritude, the ateliers of Paris, the primitive chic, and then he sat in a stifling bus passing the shore where the colonists bathe, their teeth burning, their arms glistening, and the hatred mushrooming within them, the anthill smoldering, eyes stiff in the colonial latrine, the tourniquet ripped from a stump oozing flies, and he gagged on this stomach inching up his throat, and he opened the door to this hovel, looked at his double in the mirror, lay awake in bed as the ceiling fan spun, and the poem ruptured, too long muzzled,

burst bladder,
ripped gut & cirrhosis,
skewering nerves,
pushed,
seared its way out,
until the poem was
a disembowelment,

blade carving into the numinous

for Will Alexander

"Would to God were I still-born, "Borges thought, as he continued to write his cramped fables wherein the Buenos Aires suburbs, the streetcars, and his miserable librarian salary were sucked through the teeth of an Aleph, while all the pages of a 17th century atlas published in Antwerp were revealed simultaneously, and the bones of a wren were apprehended in the shape of a puddle in an empty lot somewhere in Indiana.

COMPRESSION

I

Lisbon in the 1920's: baroque façades of buildings dating from the blood and silver of colonial expansion have become heavy, on the point of imploding. During a drizzle, Pessoa eats his plate of liver and rice at a tavern, and writes on loose pages from an open file. The omnibus makes its rattle, yet the beaches of Estoril with their cafés serving platters of sardines, bottles of tart red wine, are the smoke and flash of summer: a season that always seems distant, even at the start of May. Better to stay in and write, after unbuttoning one's collar, and putting away the blotter and ledger.

Outside, the sun burning off the haze colored like boiled mutton; Pessoa looks up from his page, and notices that his plate has been taken away, yet his white napkin remains crumpled by the wine glass. Through the window, an old woman in a black shawl sweeping the sidewalk; it looks as if she could shrivel any instant into that skein of moth-tattered cloth. Her husband owns the tailor shop occupying part of the ground-floor of the building erected during the glitter of the Empire; a miracle that the structure survived the great earthquake. Like a palimpsest, the tailor's sign is discolored by stains of what was another sign advertising a tavern where sailors drank after returning from the tropics, their teeth black, and their faces red. Debris, withered flowers; Pessoa feels that malaise whenever he ponders time and human institutions. He thinks: Should a waiter place a glass of milk beside me, it would curdle instantly.

And at that stained table, he jots down an entry for his *Livro do Desassossego*; an observation on his atheism of nationality and social egoism. It is the briefest yet, and by legerdemain of the right simile, he is able to sum up his works, his childhood, paving stones and spectacles in three lines. Had it survived, and had he time to reread it, he might have stopped writing, knowing that he had written the key, the aperture.

His waiter is polite to the point of being meek. Pessoa, though, is oblivious to him, as he starts a new poem on a clean sheet of paper; beside his glass, crumpled paper, a sheet with a crossed-out line, and another page with that entry... True, it briefly shimmered, yet has now been set aside until he finishes a few strophes. The waiter clears his throat, picks up the napkin, inquires if he can take the goblet, and clear the trash; Pessoa waves his hand impatiently...

And an hour later, the sky outside the window reddened with dusk, the street dry, and the tailor shop locked, Pessoa puts away some pages, without noticing what was thrown away, and would be tossed that night into the flames of the incinerator.

II

The haiku suggests that seventeen syllables are enough to transfix a season, cherry blossoms, the ochre of a fountain apprehended through dark water, and all that is transient with a few images, yet each effort, as Issa penned, is a writing in dew in order to describe a world of dew. Without any success, I have sought what might compress the immutable and the mundane in a single dactyl or juxtaposition, yet all of my poems are botched.

Somewhere, on a neighboring block perhaps, a poet has been writing, documenting the jacarandas and wasps, sunlight on stucco, and the empty parking lots of my city. He is carving an image of my loneliness, and with each poem he attempts to incarnate that truth by way of one poem or word. One night, he dreams of speaking to a man dressed as a scrivener, with pointed chin, thin mustache, and round spectacles. He doesn't remember a word, but awakens the next morning intent on writing, on resuming the cycle, the reams upon reams of lost or burning paper, those revelatory words that have gone, like a puddle drying, and leaving no stain.

LORD BYRON, AT 29, WITNESSES HIS FIRST BEHEADING

The thief had pissed his rags, and ripped out his nails by clawing at the cell door and walls. Manicured, Byron had been carousing: "tooling" and drinking. Now bloated, he was on his regimen of soda water and bread. The priest and half-naked executioner found out that the thief's neck was too large for the aperture, and so an assistant held him down by the hair. Barking a *Domine...* over the man's cries, the priest flayed the air with holy water. Starved, Byron shook as he stared through an opera-glass at the guillotine and thief. A rattle, and the blade shimmied down. The head was lopped off close to the ears; blood splashed on the wood, a red miasma plopped from the skull. Byron could admit to being left hot and thirsty, yet later attended other executions with indifference. However, in Greece, while aiding against the Turks, bones sweating fever, and a cloud encroaching his light, Byron saw that condemned one who perhaps had not committed any greater aberrations than he. And he whispered a strophe for that man gazing at the planks, —a matter witnessed by the boy who wiped Byron's brow with a moist cloth, emptied his bed-pan, and could speak demotic Greek, but not English.

ANDALUSIA AFTER THE ASSASSINATION OF GARCÍA LORCA

I

Red wheat, green wheat,
fruit of stone, fruit of heat;
the olive turns green, the oleander red.

Beneath the shadow of a rock,
the cricket forgets its voice.
At the river the women are bathing,
and the bass string of a guitar is plucked as
seawater swells in the hearts of children playing
with wooden pistols.

Green wheat, red wheat,
fruit of stone, fruit of heat;
the oleander turns green, the olive red.

II

No one heard the mare gallop beneath the hot moon,
no one saw orange blossoms burn
in a contortion of daggers and water while
lips burnt lemon, and the sea swallowed the voices.
No one sang the hosanna
of thighs bearded with river and roses.

But now the shrill pink of a carnation
strangles the sleep of desire,
now stars cut the palms which cradled them,
now young men on balconies toss dice
in the dizzying game of gravity.

Darkness beneath the eyes of widows,
(the morning sky is purple).
Darkness dripping from the hands
of men choking violins,
(the evening sky is black).

III

Alone at night in the plaza
a blind boy was singing his *cante jondo:*
The cricket looking for its voice
took up residence in his blood.

THE HORSE'S MOUTH AND BARON SAMEDI*

The *loa*** is fed up with being muzzled: with the tight, frantic stomps of a man putting out a small flame, he percolates then flares across the forest. He is a fire clacking in a barn, sparks above the reddening hay. He is beer frothing, and the cranium of a newborn visible through the bleeding dilation, pushed out. The *loa* is rushing across the cane fields, across the dirt roads along which cinderblock huts, re-bar jutting like the antennae of locusts, are painted with propaganda of *kreole* smoking from the teeth of Toussaint L'Ouverture and his heart like a jacaranda abloom. The *loa* is a dust-demon, a hurricane, and he bursts through the door of the *hougan,* where the congo ratatatats, machetes shimmy air glistening with liquor, men writhe, and the women with white kerchiefs dance, pivot and squat, flowering as the *loa* finds his horse: the woman whose daughter died in the flood... her eyes roll back, jaw slackens, as a voice barks out from her, demanding rum and tobacco and his top-hat, before he narrates the graveyard, thunder, and red roads of the dead.

* *Baron Samedi: Voodoo deity of the dead.*

** *Loa: A Voodoo deity; the loas "mount" believers and speak through them, —hence, the expression to "hear it straight from the horse's mouth."*

STILL LIFE

Only the conceptualizing mind repeats, the senses never do.
— Duane Locke

Mind-forged manacles.
— William Blake

I

While the Danaans sack Ilium, spears skewer shoulders of matrons fleeing, guts glut swords of men with bronze helmets, their teeth glistening, daggers rip bellies, smoke blots out the arcades and atriums, while adolescent boys and men torn from sleep on hearth-pelts, scramble to defend a walled splendor where generations officiated before the altar fires and scent of myrrh, and milk and barley sated every stomach.

Aeneas, son of Anchises and Venus, sees his mother appear before him in a pillar of cerulean rain and sparks, and she admonishes him from rushing out to certain death, as the Danaan frenzy increases. And to convince him of the futility in defending Ilium, she tears off the conceptualizing cloud of his mortal consciousness, the word-forged manacle that from his infancy substituted every thing with conventional language, losing the sense-apprehended particulars, and the divine. Stopping his mortal time, she rubs the film from his sight so that he may distinguish, as towers tumble, that Neptune himself is shaking the walls, and that Juno with teeth serrated, swipes at a citadel, while from between her thighs, like a fetus evacuated, hemorrhages another phalanx, shields glistening, and Gorgons circling above the clanging swords.

Aeneas knew then that Ilium was falling:

as when an oak is ax-taken, each chop ringing through the woods, treetop nodding to the left, and again, and further to the left, until a groan resounds, and the oak topples, leaves trembling, dust billowing above the thump, and blueness streaming where once was shade.

II

Once, when reading Pound, I felt words in the same manner as when a carpenter runs his fingers along a plank. Body exhausted, yet thoughts coasting at the velocity of light, I read the *Pisan Cantos* in the courtyard of Toledo's library in Oaxaca. Moist air mottled with dark wind, as a summer storm approached; I sat at a wood table, my nerves biting at my lips, each word wholly its own ardor, and as I heard the voice, even the weather petrified... nothing breathed but language itself....

Unlike that protagonist in a fable by the blind librarian, a gaucho who perceived each minute transmogrification of an apple on a table, the skin on a farm girl carrying a bucket of water, the splashed water on paving stones, the world as a *naturaleza muerta*, yet in accelerated mutation and putrefaction, I now read the words of Pound in succession, but not each as a traversable microcosm replete with its own gravity and texture. Yet, from time to time, whether in poetry or life, there have been openings to the stasis outside of comprehension.

And so I ask, what other moments did my senses apprehend, if only for one instant, later to be registered and abstracted by memory, and conventional language? That first ejaculation, when on a toilet seat after having masturbated, I stared terrified at the semen spluttering, chlorine-like pungency pinching my nostrils? Or the neon and blaze of a Juárez summer carnival, seeing a woman approach me, black hair and whitest teeth, and a tug within me that she would bear my son, and share both poverty and bread?

Because this morning of unrepeatable clouds has dissolved just as this tracery of pen on paper is fleeting. Virgil will never see the vindictiveness of the Gods as he when he dictated those hexameters rendering the fall of Ilium; for in a poem, the conjunction of image and rhythm, and words, is revealed once to the man, before becoming an utterance that will endure or perish in burning libraries and other vagaries of time. Centuries later, and in a different language, Bashō wrote of a cricket chirping from under a helmet, for life cools to normalcy after the burial of a warrior, after the plum blossoms fall, after the death of children. All to be sung or bled. Though the senses never repeat, I catalogue each transience by way of a faith only poetry can endure.

The Hungarian wrote of butterflies on a scrap of paper between fits of coughing up blood; quarantined, he never set foot in Manhattan. Sometime during his final night, he etched "cocoon" on the wall with a nail. His fingers brittle as he carved his epitaph. Enduring for that word which is the bread and the chalice, the vessel of the horror and the verb, without the insignia, or the leather bag clinking with the ransom.

LITERARY HISTORY

When the first
poet sang
it was
in a scale only
whales could lift
from steepest floors.
The scale oozed
fingers of rain
from ears of the deaf and
stillborn; the scale
rippled over
swamps of cyanide where
submerged tigers
hunted red elephants
in their scalding dreams.
It was a scale
the woman heard when
the pit of a plum
petrified
in her womb; it was
in the key of wind
after silence gels,
and sentries fall
asleep by their spears.
It was the sound
of shock absorbers
silently pumping
over unpaved roads,
or a morning so
dark it stabs

your eyes, or the
bar after broken
bottles have been swept.
The first poet sang
in a scale that
had to be
whispered so
that an egg
was heard
hatching.

NARRATIVE OF A WOLF WITH NO TEETH

I fell in love in an ugly city.

The buses were rattle-bags,
growling retread tires salvaged from junkyards
where dust tinkles over beer cans, weeds, while wind
creaks stripped sedans looming
in ziggurats of iron-oxide.

Acetate, saline, a hook
stuck my tongue, dragging me
through streets where homes concealed
wet violins & trumpets, beans smoking in vats
large enough to boil the stomachs of a cow,
while I searched for lime
rinsing tequila, in order to
smash the window dividing the parlor
of polite conversation from the padded cell
of laughter.

And a metaphor gunned me
through the market where acne boys fried pig brain,
through the summers & dust.

The metaphor was a goblet carved from ice
that wouldn't shatter beneath the blade of noon,
it was a protein never burped,
it was oil that doesn't dry into chunks
the consistency of chopped liver,
it was the promise
of night cleansing the heat in violet waters.

And so I fell in love with an ugly city.

At first with the shadow that trailed after cars
speeding to greener latitudes; and then
with the sun needling its rays
and wrinkling steel.
But I was filled with a light
and my fingers hummed with minute pueblos of wattle & clay,
warmth bubbled beneath my skin like
air-pockets in leavened dough.
Silver coins in my pocket clinked while
snails left their cool trails across my thoughts.

And one afternoon
I walked into a stand where
goat meat simmered red, and sat
at the counter. And the waitress served me;
her hips jerked my stallions from their sleep,
her voice blossomed butterflies from
faucets dripping rust into teeth of
girls bullied into prostitution.
Her breasts held a sacrament beneath each nipple,
and they nourished my afternoon of stone.

And together we left for a desert town,
one road running through a stretch of cantinas,
mud-matted dogs, and boarded-up windows.
We found a hotel, and the bald proprietor showed us
our room: tile floor, fly buzzing round a bare bulb.
A mattress yellow-streaked and the window open.

She had left her job serving goat soup, abandoned her
fat brother & asthmatic mother.
We had left the ugly city,
the bars, the roads never reaching a meadow.
We would use all my money
and settle at the edge of the wind.

That night, I left a silvery trail with my spit
from her sweat-tang'd toes, through a black
frazzle of hairs cupped into a V,
and penetrated her as she clawed my back, bit
my ear, hissing:
Spill over into my mouth.

That night, my hunger was glutted.
That night, I fancied myself
a lion in the fields, sated.

The next morning
my hand reached out and groped
a crumple of paper. She had scribbled a note:

We exhumed stars from mud,
and I love you with your talk of the road,
but you are not the metaphor I carry
like the moon swollen &
shivering over the waters of my skin.
Take care. I left some money.
Kisses, X.

And I returned to that city
while she made it to the coast to suck
sweetness of shrimp from their shells and
drink brown-tinted bottles of beer.
I learned to trace my thirsts
over paper, that no two metaphors
look out the same mirror;
and that no matter what
the doorman must be tipped & dismissed
after the threshold has been crossed.

ALLEGRO SCHERZANDO

I am steam rising from coffee in a chipped cup on a diner counter where
truck drivers, dressed in red flannel shirts and denim vests, hair
slick with bathroom faucet water, sit and smoke. Outside, frost
nests in the rust of parked cars. The road is wet and salted; vapor
and ice-mist web the air.
I am the night sky studded with chipped bottles coalescing in the iris of a
grazing cow. The farmhouse windows are dark; blonde wheat
burns in the dreams of the father, his right arm hugging the waist
of his wife.
And I glow in the sleep of the reader where totemic wombs are swollen
with the moon. Bulls, bearded with ringlet-shags, fornicate with
the evening star, and vermilion that threads through a crackle of
saffron and Mercurochrome, while ciphers are branded on the milk
of genesis, an Aleph opens its teeth, and I am sieved through
the silver pointer on Torah parchment where six-wing'd seraphim brim over
with light, tongs pinch red coal, are pressed against my lips, as I arise
on a green stage, exhaling a shimmy of scales into a tenor sax. Bass, piano
and snare-rattle stops...cigarette smoke petrifies midair...
and my saliva, plasma, and sperm saturate each pitch, the way a seed is ripe
with tree, and the skylark embodies the sky.

SAN FERNANDO VALLEY SUITE

each porch, each door ere this,
an ark, a tabernacle is.

— Robert Herrick

I wake up some mornings and write about the edge of the Valley. There, shade hunkers beneath awnings of surplus stores selling scrap, gas-masks, and ripped tarpaulin. Desert pulls skin over skull, and stretches out its chaparral skin of railroad tracks, fields the dun of dry turd flecked with burr. I write about the last ware-house, cinder-blocks the gray of dung, the last billboard of malt liquor. And by writing, I hear the thrum of the inter-state, and the growl decrescendo of trucks hauling frozen beef beneath the unblinking sun, and all the cars abandon-ing this region where air is stagnant. By writing about this threshold to the desert, I find myself on a sidewalk leading to the last house on a block where sand serrates the wind crackling like a needle pacing the outermost groove of an L.P. I stagger, eyes clenched in the heat, one arm shielding my gaze, the other akimbo, and I mount warped steps, open the splintered door, and slam it shut, —beams shaking, foundation sinking an inch.

— for Robert Lopez

At first the poem is indistinguishable from my skin, or my libido expanding like water freezing. Then, after several months, I no longer recognize the traces of my self in the poem, and I am left with a matrix of words, a legible shadow or flame, whose meaning always had something that had little to do with me, yet a lot with salt, lemons, the shrubs of these hills, and the asphalt of these empty boulevards.

* * *

Billboards, palm trees, and telephone poles in the San Fernando Valley tend to punctuate the flat horizons tapering Roscoe Boulevard and Sherman Way to a vanishing point of smog: like pillars in a renaissance painting that showcase the newly discovered trick of perspective.

* * *

When Ed Ruscha painted the angular and jutted marquee of *Norm's* aflame, perhaps he meant to emphasize how unique is such ugliness, a singularity that must be illumined, even if by fire, for the resident to appraise what happened to this region which, a mere two hundred years ago, was populated by a flora and fauna of chaparral, sage-brush, along with possums and emaciated coyotes.

* * *

But no, —I think that he was suggesting how we are not inhabiting a movie-set; even this assemblage of stucco apartment buildings, parking lots and more parking lots are material, they are all we have, and they too can burn, like Chicago, a lover's last note, the secrets of our great-grand-parents, like Carthage.

* * *

I had to live in Mexico—in its rawest border town in the Chihuahua desert—and spend four years writing about its potholes and stray dogs, its young women, those brooders of dark severity who stir the plastic vats of melon and lime juice on hot avenues, and its neon and brothels, its beauty as haphazard as the flight of a dragonfly; I had to write of all of that, before coming back home and realizing that the corner quick-stop with its rows of candy bars and aisles of beer was also poetry, as well as the blue light outside embossing the paint of new cars being filled with gas, or the corner buffet where, yesterday, an obese couple deftly piled a pyramidal stack of fried chicken, corn & rice, pineapple & ham pizza, and home fries on their plates, leaving me only a thigh in the steaming, stainless-steel bin.

* * *

The sight of a bus stop, plastic bench and black graffiti scrawled across an advertisement for a woman's clinic, on Sherman Way, among warehouses, adult bookstores, taco shacks, no pedestrians, and semis growling, and the white sunlight in a zone the color and taste of cinderblock, —the sight of a bus stop, without a bus in sight, without anyone waiting, is the closest metaphor I have to describe the absence of God in my life, the absence of history in my poetry, the absence of any redeeming infrastructure in the San Fernando Valley, especially everything past Oxnard Boulevard.

* * *

Kitsch is the denial of the existence of shit, and having seen the promenade of Universal City—close to the studios where movies are mass-assembled—and the marble-floored malls, the cake-icing colors glazing our architecture and our amusement parks, I know this city is plastic.

Yet, to say that this city is a simulacrum of a simulacrum, one must have never smelled the urine-ripe stench of tripe frying, felt one's teeth crackle into fried bits, in a *taquería* by Tujunga and Vanowen, where the local men, who make livings dry-walling or painting houses, cure their Sunday morning hangovers by slurping stew.

* * *

This city has the dubious distinction of never having produced a world poet; no Pessoa from this Lisbon, no Eliot from this London, no Borges from this Buenos Aires. Los Angeles is proof that America is no melting poet; this is a caste society, and, centerless, each neighborhood for each ethnicity, an urban zone is jaggedly pieced together, while the freeways, with their monotonous murmur like *the noise of water making moan*, are our many rivers. And by the banks of the 101 Freeway, yea, I sat down and wept, thinking of the impossible Zion, and my lamentations poured forth for the motel and mini-mart scriveners and dreamers scattered in the metropolises that form this region.

* * *

No one will believe this of vast import to the nation, wrote Williams when talking about abandoned mattresses and chicken wire in the yards of the poor. I bypass the glitzy miles of Ventura Boulevard, the homes on the hills and the cafés, and cut to the mortal heart of this region, where the steadfast heat of summer never ceases, because the grape-sized turds of possums in vacant lots, weeds peppered with red ants, eucalyptus and hibiscus, all are honey to me. And never does the sky aspire to anything other than the categorically blue.

*   *   *

Praxilla of ancient Sicyon was derided for a verse celebrating cucumbers along with the moon and sun. The catalogue in the three lines that survive also mentions pears and apples as the sweet shards that would cut him as he passed from this world into shadow. When water seals these boulevards, and smog and stucco are crushed in the mortar of the last day, I ask that some citizen sing of the Pacific and desert in a dirge. But before I choke on age, before my nails dig into this lip of earth, I will recall orange trees, gas stations, these boulevards shimmering at night, the coffee while I stared at a diner's empty parking lot.

*   *   *

And if I had to write a litany or an ode for the Valley, from what, from whom would I beseech inspiration? From the white, steady-pounding feet of the Muses dancing? No, something different. I would invoke the deity of 99 cents stores, the deity of empty parking lots, the deity of silver-flash hubcaps and low-riders, the deity of liquor stores, of chili burgers and empty mini-marts where every employee has skin the color of wilted lettuce and frowns when a client walks in, and the deity of dry trees and traffic islands, of lunch-trucks, and cocktail lounges with juke boxes, and the deity of public libraries with their odor of wet wool, the deity of sad parks, the deity of black-top playgrounds half-melted beneath the sun, and the cream-colored public schools, and the deity of gentlemen clubs... a plethora of deities, tawdry Gods invoked by my prayers that not even I would know how to write so that a congregation might arise from the dust.

VITA NOVA

for Paul B. Roth, author of *Fields Below Zero*

I'm never speaking in my old language again.

Whenever I spoke, my heart grew teeth
and chewed the lull when my blood cooled
to the rhythm of rain bobbing fern leaves;
and I awoke to a suburb
chock-full of parking lots and liquor stores.

I'm never sleeping in my old language.
I'm never breathing in
my old language; it stunk of shoe-polish,
disinfectants, and tasted of asbestos and humidity.

Long before they provided me with that language;
long before the neon pavilions, the snapping crocodiles
of passports, and stairwells rising and
falling between landings made of water;
long before I assembled stone and milk with syllables
in that language which was also the language
of my grandparents and a village snoaring beneath loam,
a village with its supermarkets and electricity
illumining silken swimming pools, and trash;
long before that language became my own as well,
there was a brighter lexicon awaiting me, and I
was like a virtuoso who hissed into a harmonica in order to
compensate for the tango he heard only in his sleep.

And it is arduous to learn another language,
to find another language, your own
language, distinctly yours, and not the kingdom's

with its billboards, vacant lots sour with dog turds,
its dentures for the starving, its massage parlors
for the erotically malnourished, its temples.

Another language, that is, which is not
a language at all, but is like adding
with negative numbers, the palpable absence
an amputee feels in his sleeve, the sucking
intake through a zero, —yet, if you go that way,
you are sieved into a non-language,
a non-word, a logos that is deafening
because it has learned how to say everything
by having nothing to say, the way a stone
throbs with energy, hums with interior blueness so that
you might enter the stone and cusp its vista
of clouds and vines, or slide between the teeth
of the tides that wind themselves around the electricity
of saying nothing,
                                        pausing

before proceeding to talk in a new language.

Because there was an angelus interior, a muezzin confidant
who would not let me go deaf, and I arose
to walk streets where I could no longer read the billboards,
and I could no longer count my money: the bills burned
my fingers, and I could no longer bite into polished apples.
At night my wife opened her legs, urging me,
yet my penis was a bone thumping against bone,
and when I stopped to listen to the seasons change,
I could only hear my lungs rasp for breath.

And I knew it was time I needed a new language.

How terrifying it was to stand at bar
with a hated friend, in hours soured with tin beer and gossip,
and realize I only had words to barter for a scrap of fruit,
and that there was no blood that tasted sweeter
than the hours when I was blind to myself, snoring;
how maddening it was to stare at a woman,
to feel the knife-blades of my fingers cut into her skin
in search of milk, and yet realize that the semiotics
of skirts, thighs waxed of their hair, telephones,
were rotten, as her heels clacked into the sunlight and traffic.

No, not a single telephone wire crackled with the shrill
velocity of leaves falling through the weather of ice;
no newspaper spoke of the tumbling shadows
in the exploding barns just outside daily massacres;
no radio song, no graffiti scrawled in black across bus benches,
no movie theater ripe with the burps of soda and rustling
wrappers, no movie screen flickered a word that could encapsulate
the idiocy, the idiot's blabber of my days, freeways,
mini-marts and medical clinics, spiritually obese mechanics.

It was time for a covenant in a parking lot,
from shopping-mall escalators, within motel rooms.
It was time for awakening into desert fish and soft tractors;
for glue and feathers, and seashells which echo the birth of clouds;
gone, the heart growing teeth;
gone, the rooms full of toxic liqueurs;
gone, the porcelain music tinkling from papier-mâché moons.

Because I sat down in a corner far from
the latrines filled with thespians and antique collectors,
far from polar bears peeing in stifling cages, and children licking
pink cones, and men beating their bald heads against bathroom tile floors;
I sat down for a minute that slipped between the boulders of one
            hundred centuries,
and came through,
(see how I have come through!),
yes, I came through with a word
urging itself up, always up, through dust, through green stalks,
into a past perpetually present.

And I saw the shape of my own breath.
My fingers turned into ten trees,
and my brow a forest, my arms shovels,
and I began to plant a language, a new language, my own,
the vine and fruit of my crotch,
shadow-scent and mare of a hundred groves galloping
up the waterfall that is hair and cornfields, skin
of the Lady of Seeds who is myself and my language.

And words as heavy as bison, trout words, boulder words,
rain syllables slapping the paving stones
of coal-aged semantics, yet new and my own,
a clay of cooling spring, all, were woven into my new language,
and I raised these words above the billboards of clouds,
and my wife was the woman who glowed beneath her own skin,
and my friends were the syllables that once slipped from my grasp,
and my fingers cupped the pomegranate of each constellation,
and my heart had no teeth, it had hands that embraced
horizon and plantain leaf, and ushered
in the blue raptors that toppled my scarecrow.

POEMS FROM THE BONE MAP

for Heller Levinson

por dentro, muy adentro, ¡qué ancho soy!
Within, deeply do how vast I am!

— José Joaquín Pasos

ON DE KOONING'S "EXCAVATION"

the viewer unearths meat-flowers   fossils from crevices like cracks in plaster
        after an earthquake   red smudges   afterbirth   placenta stewing
in its juice   flame-shaped clusters that lick air before being snuffed   the
        viewer unleashes masturbators and saints in convulsions   blocks of
limestone   stalactites piercing the lily of gestation   tectonic plates folding
        into uterus   mouths swallowing blood-gorged appendages   beaks,
black eye-slits   anthropomorphic minerals secreting from cave walls
        snake jaws unlocking   fins flicking through a yellowness like urine,
snot thickened by hallucinogen of the Yanomami   fangs of an angler fish
        a myriad beasts all writhing in heat   shape-shifting   a lamprey
sucking the speckled egg of magpie   jellyfish that morphs into fingers
        coyote shit   follicles of pilobolus-fungi spores erupting   protein
tail of sperm whipping through an enzyme miasmas, everything   entrails,
        claws   sharks arrowing through smoke   spooling around a central
gash bleeding blueness   aperture through which the viewer glimpses
        the great helix,   the cipher within molar and plasma : word for
which each species is an exoskeleton   a disperser of genetic code   a parenthesis,
        a rung in evolution

RAISING THE WALL IN A RISING OF VOICE

I stop singing, and my breath petrifies;
bone-dun of cinderblocks, heat, vacant lot
empty reach of San Fernando Valley where
railroad tracks crisscross
miles of gas stations and intersections.

Crow in etiolated sky
flaps loose a feather, and
sun, the bronze of a Minoan cymbal.

Crow circles higher; above
first sphere of air & smoking water,
above second sphere, slivers
of ultraviolet light that catch on
living cells, puncturing them in
the flash it takes ice to burn cupped hands.
Final sphere, and crow
bursts into scalding helium,
orbiting the edge of my song.

Three thousand miles below,
the wall encloses a dust garden;
the bricklayer paid by charity,
locusts shedding their shells.
Freeway overpass sussurrates with commuters,
mouthwash and massage parlor billboards,
a dog streaks piss against the cinderblocks and
moistens sidewalk dirt, dark rivulets.

I stop breathing, and my song is
lifted into a wall, the lot is a tarmac,
and an hour turns into three centuries.
Crow burns in pale sky, bursts

from sight, and a feather drifts
into garden, touches ground...then naked,
bathed, eyes open, my body rises supine on that dust,
and clouds, black, weigh on the enclosure.

With a burst, rain like
minute scalpels, shaving me, skinning me
lovingly, washes away muscle & nerve until I am clean
again, opened cage of calcium & salt—
leaving no thirst, and all song falling up
to clouds from which this blood poured.

LETTER TO THELONIOUS MONK

for J.J. Blickstein

My Dear Friend Thelonious:

I'm a poet, father of one son, a gruff husband, a friend who returns calls, but prefers solitude. In my living room, I listen to your music while my four year old spins around in circles. Sometimes, I write a poem; when the Greeks asked for a god's favor at the bonfire, if a spark shot up, they knew their wish was granted. I like to think that your fingers are the tinder, and they leave my ears burning.

Some friends say your technique's percussive and quirky, percolating with the sour apples and parrots of random dissonance, but have they ever heard the lolling embarkation, a swirling of dark water and coolness, in the opening chords of *Crepuscule With Nellie*? And during the last bars of *Ruby My Dear*, when your fingers bunny-hop down the keys in a whole-tone scale, a thousand doors open where I only saw a wall. It would be nice were you here to play me one piece, preferably one that sounded like shock absorbers pumping over the pot-holes and dust of my purlieus.

Among the Sephardim of Morocco, it was an adage that if only one could see one's self from across the marketplace, there might be hope of profit and the messiah appearing. I have sat in restaurants eating alone, seen the desert through the moving window of a bus, made love and sat awake in the dark, and committed the treasons and robberies of every man, yet I have never seen my own self wave to me. But I sense that in the chords you would recycle, you would catch your shadow off guard, and watch the music that shimmers when one can see through one's own skin.

That's it. I also wanted to tell you that I still listen to *Off Minor*, and don't know how the soloists can follow the chord changes, and that were I able to transcribe *Nutty*, I would know the trajectory of pollen.

Know me your admirer,
Anthony Seidman

P.S. I also wish you the traffic of my poems and all of their itineraries, such as the clarity of water, and the teeth of children laughing.

THE HYACINTH GIRL SPEAKS

There are shards on which we step
when the glass dome shatters and we see
lucidly
that there is a last-
ditch chance to set our lands in order,
to splurge the wage
and buy a silver locket that gleams,
to fold the news,
and have faith enough
to glimpse the slowed light
fall
through the drizzle
while picking hyacinths.

Though the years ensuing
are blank as the pearl eyes of a drowned sailor,
though in our hearts
the Great Crab scratches, scratches,
and though we fear death by
any manner,
                              for a breath's pause
we are golden
in the throbbing silence,
the heart of light brims over,my arms are heavy with flower,
Milady spreads her embrace over us in
holie matrimonie,
while my eyes fail and
a wind blows us over the tropics
& ice-caps,
though time clicks like train wheels,
though the bridge will fall down,
and a dried root snaps
in the jaws of the black hound.

SOURCE

Everything is water: milk, my spit, starch and bone, the blade slicing through a tomato's skin, and the citron-tart bleed; even the hard sky of drought is water, even water so water *is* because of water. I see the tresses of rain whipping snap-dragons and bottle-brush on those nights in which the steam of ice embosses the windows of dark apartment buildings, and I reach into mirrors in order to touch the liquid my eyes secrete, as when I chop onions. Because water trickles between my cupped hands, knowing the riverbeds of my palms. Water is an oxygen I can't inhale. It beads my skin, licks my limbs when I splash through the heat of swimming pools with their chlorine-fumes smelling of semen. I have lost my state of being pure oxygen and hydrogen, those power-cables crackling with whiteness when snapped against one another. I am too much mud and meat, while sharks circling the ocean are cousins of my tears, henchmen against my blood, and conspire with water against my lungs. Only when I write will water open my mouth, and pour down my throat its vowel that is a drop on a fern's leaf, its consonant that is a current tugging at algae, my lips, fingers and brain into transparency.

CHAIM SOUTINE'S "RED GLADIOLI," 1919

Here is the darkness, brown of blood-sausage or
clay-red of uncooked liver.

Here is the night, his roach-basted atelier,
and his frost-pinched fingers.

But Chaim paints to extract the rain his ears bleed,
to taste the scabs mixed in with the porridge, to
sniff the yolk from a rotten egg while licking
the fossilized hunger of a tooth.

Here is the tin can, and the iron
door of nightmare clanging open, releasing
the crows, and the hail that rattles
across the roof; yet despite those shadows, I see

the red gladioli he paints in the night,
(heart-shaped and crackling, flames that erupt,
take flight from one stem to another, those
petals of incarnadine fire), I see

the red gladioli in the night, —
the only light by which that man can appraise himself
as more than pain ingested, or salt secreted.

CHAIM SOUTINE'S SELF-PORTRAIT, 1923

This "me so ugly," this
Soutine whose left shoulder & arm
plop forward like intestine tugged through
gash in the belly, and into the brownness
with mushed potato-colored stains on
sleeve, russet blotches, flecks the
darkblue & gray of pigeon-shit; swirls
like saffron stained with chicken's blood;
an intestine gorged and dangling
uselessly, an arm
tugged from bowels of *shtetl* dung
and turnip pails.

Nose like lump-sized erection, with
goat-colored foreskin, crooked up
between eyes; left nostril doubled
into shape of testis, patches like
coffee grounds wiped on starched apron; his
face, bread with olive-dun mold; idiot
eyes compressed black, suction-gust,
collapsed star sucking in light to
self-loathing center, outhouse
stewing with flies, and the mongrel left
in a barn while bombs eviscerate cows
a few kilometers away.

Yet there is also love, —the way the hair's
painted with sheen, kempt, as if Soutine
were consoling his simulacrum whose
lips quaver a grimace-smile, a boy

holding in the hurt, no sniffling. The right
arm & rest of body, folded from view,
snail slurking inside shell when fingers press
against antennae. Because the Chaim on canvas is
cautious; his ear curves forward to sniff
absolution for his Grotesqueness to
receive the anointment, enter the threshold
where the Self, once full of venom,
now brims over with mercy.

INSULATION

I awoke with two stones pressing down my eyelids.

Wood on fire turns to ash,
breath on fire turns to sand
the color of leather, & skin specked
with olive-brown cancer.
Stone in extreme heat turns to water.

Water transmogrifies
into the dust that smokes
around the moon as it sinks
into the dunes of my blackest word.

I awoke with a beetle tunneling my skull.

Ants crawled over
a bone in the gutter.
My word was passed from antennae
to antennae, heralding rounder hungers.

I awoke with my hands folded over my chest.

Air passes through everything porous,
including the walls of asbestos I raise
to insulate my language.
Mud is carved into lungs that channel light,
light takes on flesh and stretches to pluck stars.

I awoke between two parentheses.

The words *faith* and *poetry* suckled
at my chest and were nourished,
although no milk trickled from my nipples.

I awoke with ten tribes in each of my fingers,
I awoke with my hair on fire, and my body
submerged up to my waist in turpentine.
I awoke with the locomotive eating the horizon,
I awoke and swallowed a spoonful of salt.

By the time I opened my eyes and stepped outside,
winter had started. Frost glazed the windows
of my car warming up in the driveway. Inside &
in the driver's seat, I wrote

my name on the fogged windshield.

ON THE PAINTING BY POUSETTE-DART: "WHITE CIRCLE, TIME"

Porous circle surrounded by blackness
and pulsating flecks shaped like minerals jutting
from feldspar or burr on a
steel plate through which holes have been drilled;
circle like the human egg
in its plasma-webbed canal, —a target
for tail-flicking penetration of spermatozoa.

Gray-white circle whose curves are
intestinally braided as if with ribosome
wedged within their protein enclosure.

Blue-gray circle like the darkness inside testicles,
viscous yolks swelling with sperm, frazzle
of electricity from colon to brain,
dog sniffing female, black tongue
dangling, fangs biting air,
or the tarantula's mating dance, cat yowling,
the moment so moment, the man
alive for flood-swell of two seconds.

Because at the center of the circle,
an emptiness
neither imploding or exploding,
mastication & excretion, and ravenous flowering,
flakes of light falling up into the center
and drifting back to the circle,
around which radiate,
corymbulous,
the stars, the

galaxy inside a pigeon-bone,
equator across an orange-peel, ammonia
atom, a single hair on a
tarantula...

her book lungs pumping, her
fangs clacking, her chelicerae trembling &
dripping digestive enzymes, ready for the
smaller male who jigs back & forth,
his pedipalps gorged with sperm,
ready for the mounting, and her glutting
frenzy on his abdomen.

TONIGHT

I sleep with volcanic dust creased in my eyelids,
I drink from a cedar cup tethered to
the well of liquid desires. I gift-wrap
my breath, & knit a scarf for poets
freezing in the Dakotas. I receive a phone call
from a thousand butterflies the color
of a plum, and grow another inch as
a grass blade sprouts in my palm.
Tonight a rosebush burns, but is not consumed,
and there's a Tunisian garden adrift within;
sandalwood smolders and my lover,
brown nipples sharp beneath a peach blouse,
caresses my hardened blood as the word
is elevated and dropped with open parachute
into the rippling moonshine below.

— *After Alan Britt*

EXEGESES

I want so much to confuse the bible.
— Yehuda Amichai

And We Wait *Genesis 3 : 24*

...and the sword crackles in the cobalt evening, like the blue whorls of breath He exhales at the hour when ferns shiver and water clenches its fingers into a fist...

and the flaming sword guards the way to the Tree of Life, and we await the trespassing man who, after wandering the argent fields of the moon, might find his way here, reachable only by sleep or metaphor...

and we are many, so many, that when I look to my side I see a chain of cherubim, their wings the only light in this darkened garden, abandoned like an 18th century farmhouse overtaken by the forest, these groves where at times we hear the serpent hiss, overripe plums fall with a thump on loam, while a vagrant hound howls and scratches claws on the steel gate...

and we wait, as stupid as squid for the harvester who would never find his way here, or even hope to, knowing that death would shrivel into a rat turd in a kitchen drawer, just by biting into those blue plums the size of a lamb's heart... death would dry up, would be dead itself....

But when the poem is edged up against the shovel, the clod breaks, and a word sprouts in the darkness and is the shadow that lovers feel beneath one another's skin, the seed they crack between their teeth, the first water breaking through bruised dams of blood...

Because the poem strives for an inch after death, not to bypass it; who would want to eat from the Tree of Life, denying the milk of the word?

So we wait, whiskers having never breached our parchment-thin skin, saccharine water in our veins, wings combustible as paper lanterns, and, like sponges or fruit-flies regurgitating sucrose on an orange pulp, we are not inoculated with the slightest grain of poetry; even worse, we are deathless.

The Book of Leviathan

I want to write the book of Leviathan, of the gospel according to the beasts, serpents, swinish mammals of cleft toes, the bacteria which the high priests in their white robes and gold breast-plates encrusted with rubies and lapis-lazuli, slandered or overlooked as they edited the leather scrolls which nomads copied out, those strophes dating from the ragtag emancipated who followed the *shekinah* smoking on the horizon, and subsisted on desert bread.

The opening verse would taste of water soured with rust, of the rat's afterbirth crows pick: Why did I not come forth from the womb and die? Why was there rain to quench my thirst? Why do I bare my fangs and pump venom into the veins of men whose words have lifted great prayers? Why must I hunt the svelte gazelle? Why was I carved barnacle-scabbed and of moon-bloated girth so that I must sink to the ocean's floor and trawl plankton to piecemeal my protein? Why won't I glimpse the evergreening hills of *Sheol*?

It would be a short Book, thinner than the pages comprising Ruth. And no voice crackling from the green flames burning bramble, no privation of crops or offspring suffered, and no trek through sands to a covenant peopled with stars and a nation. Nothing but that litany and its answer arrowing straight as the glance of Lot's wife:

The Breath blew its words into your lungs and gave you the gift of breeding and excreting to use you as a curse to exact against those men and women raising their towers, glutting on meat and ego, their oaths and groans during mating so loud that even if that Breath hadn't been snuffed some millennia ago, he couldn't hear your questions, nor care to answer.

The Lovers of Nephilim *Genesis 6 : 4*

What did those angels see in our women? Lice-ridden, sex's scent like shadows moist with flies, rain so tart in the desert after the blaze of dog-days. What did they want from our women serving broth in wooden bowls to the toothless patriarchs with their hundred head of cattle, to husbands with hairy backs who clutched them at night when torches were snuffed and the desert sand blue?

To be a father, or a brother fattening up a heifer as a dowry, and to know that one of the Nephilim had visited the daughter's tent, had caressed her buttocks, rubbed olive oil over her hard feet, seen in half-light the nipples ripening firm and grape-brown, licked the peppery span of her armpits, the perfumes concocted from rose-water and ambergris; surely, the men, themselves secretly desirous of their own daughters and sisters, they must have spat curses at the sky, at a God deaf to their appeals, like a drunk celebrant wandering back to the finger-drums and pipes, but only to retrieve a misplaced saddlebag.

Moreover, it wasn't a just barter; we know what those angels saw in our women: the limbs swollen with both sweetness and decay; the hands pulling in the pumping torso to clutch pleasure for a blurring instant, a mutability so alien to those angels and their centuries peopled with dust and stone calendars.

Yet in exchange, they left us bastards destined to become swordsmen, merchants who owned camels loaded with spices, the scriveners of strophes, the quack priests reading entrails of ewes, beautiful women married to alcoholics and braggarts, all bogged in a botched divinity.

A Kiss from Lot's Eldest Daughter *Genesis 19 : 31*

The story isn't true. The city was a splendor of limestone temples, atriums sweetened with smoldering rosemary, handmaids shuttling through palace chambers, the shadows of their torches like black flowers blooming against the masonry. And the plaza, crowded with merchants from Zeboiim and Admah, their recalcitrant camels, and men glancing back at us. My sister and I lived in a stasis, hearts like feathers, palates tart, lime slaked with honey, breasts swelling with the moon, and we would open our lattices at twilight, and the young men pelted us with roses, while mother glanced back at our house and would wave, her smile flashing, before cutting down an alley.

But it was when *they* arrived, and father, who with arthritic hands would shake open the prayer scrolls each evening, greeted those two shades with eyes colored like egg yolk flecked with hen's blood. He was at the gateway crying out to that God who hissed him to sleep, soughing about the wormwood of courtesans, about drinking water from one's own cistern, while sweet mother cuckolded him, her sex thumped to dough each night, legs wrapped around the torso of a guardsman. And our father washed those Angels' feet, swept clean the threshold to our house before they entered, begged them to cleanse our beloved Gomorrah. Our Gomorrah of bitumen streets and gates of glazed brick. Gomorrah of lovers who knew the ways of mandrake. Gomorrah of the zither and verse composed over wine.

The priests had foreseen this destruction in the entrails of sacrificed goats, in the sparks snapping and rising from altar bonfires. So when hundreds of men, merchants and domestic slaves, guardsmen, noblemen and potters, came to our house, pounded on the thick door, my sister and I were ecstatic in our fright, hugged each other, hoping that they would burst the threshold, drag away father, his two strangers and their babble of desert thunder and a pillar-shaped cloud.

No such thing.

And so, after the rushed stacks of unleavened bread and mother crying; after the departure in the darkness, and the cauldron sky cracking open, mother looked back for her lover beneath that rain of phosphor, and—as you know—turned into a coarse column.

It was then I knew that expiation had to be exacted.

Thinking us the only ones left on the plain, that first night in our cave I plied father with wine, danced around the fire with my sister, our slippers slapping beside the red kernels that shot from his eyes and crackled on the dust. Lifting up my skirt, my lungs rasping, I felt my sex burst, a grape tongued against a palate, while stars spluttered through my limbs.

And then again, on the following night, my sister and I filled father with drink, and I watched him fumble with her cloak, and I partook in the act... and heard that man groan: an ox led to the butchering blades of our kisses, his seed flaring within us, burning us with pleasures we were denied in that city of righteous debauchery.

INTERSECTIONS

Like dust smoking over a dirt road Chihuahua town, as the bus slows down
        at the stop, letting on a woman with pointed breasts, and black
        hair streaked blue with sun;
like the concrete arches raising the Hollywood freeway alongside palm
        trees shaking in Richters, the shrub-dun hills dotted with houses
        the glaze of bubblegum, and the sea only miles away:
like a car starting in the dead of night;
like the beggar's plucked guitar string, and his voice that shatters the
        crystal buttons holding the moon's dress in one piece;
like the oil drenched finger of silence sealing these syllables;
                                                            there is always a bridge
connecting the pitch of an egg cracked with a nail being hammered,
the barren woman with the flooded arroyo,
the hot coffee sipped in a diner with the black spit of the vinegarroon,
there is always a bridge, there is always a bridge, as

        the border between the north and south is pliable
                                                                    like water.

THERE IS A RIVER

for Emilio Martinez and Bernardo Jaurregui

Dios no está ningún lado del río,
porque Dios es el río.

God is on neither side of the river,
because God is the river.

— Carlos Zamora

AWAKENING

First, the train's horn would slap him awake. The night with its streets of brick houses painted in shades of violet and turquoise mascara, the stumps and swells of dead-ends and hills jutting from the *colonia bella vista* up to the *alta vista*, and the buzz of telephone wires; that tightly-wound spring of ramshackle infrastructure would suddenly be released as the train's caterwaul punctuated the distance and sped his dreams over the desert miles.

Then he would fall asleep as quickly as a sun-dazed laborer lifts a bottle of water to his mouth. An hour later, at six o'clock, the church bells would crackle and fuzz in a dissonant scale. Instead of a bell, the church on *calle oro* had a loudspeaker that blared the same recording each dawn. While listening to the sour arpeggios, he would grow less numb from sleep; his mouth would smack from the dry nights. Screen doors would soon open with the sound of nails scraping a chalkboard; *maquila* workers and laborers who fried hamburgers or cleaned offices in El Paso would start their cars, engines turning over and coughing up one last wheeze of strength.

Soon after, in a whizzing of echoes, the propane delivery truck would speed while blaring its recording of *la cucaracha*, announcing that it was time to rent another tank for the oven and water heater. Its noise would fade, then increase as it drove up an adjacent alley. By this time, his feet had touched the warm tile floor. A shower, and then he would head off to English classes he taught, invariably passing the fruit vendor in his mule-drawn wagon with wasps circling around the hoard of prickly pear, watermelon, and slightly dented tomatoes rejected from *S-Mart*.

But before he arose from bed, he would spend a moment below time, his body heavy and sinking in the mattress, while he rearranged the people he knew and stories he heard with different faces and different names, with foils of the fantastic and journalistic, mixing incident with incident, inventing and transcribing stories from the heat smoldering in the violet desert mornings.

HER GLANCES COVER ME LIKE IVY

"Parcourir a loisir ses magnifiques formes."
— Charles Baudelaire

Celeste is the sound of water being poured into a glass; she's the sting of winter air, and the boundless jungles steaming in the irises of a cat; she is bread and coffee for breakfast; she is the scratch of a beetle digging into the forest floor made of wood chips. She is the unapprehended relation between things: the pitch of an ambulance's siren that fells a redwood in Northern California. The elevator in a mall in Syracuse, New York that lifts a wave above the trough of weaker currents off Sicily upon reaching the third floor.

I didn't meet her during radiant summers I spent on the beach in San Sebastian; nor, when still dripping with cool desires, did I encounter her when my pen first licked paper with syllables that soared and sprayed into clusters of bird and foam; nor was she the woman who pushed the shopping cart with a vat filled with corn which she would butter and dust with chile powder while my friends and I drank beer in the projects facing the sunburnt chaparral hills of San Fernando.

I met her—or rather, she accosted me—as I wandered the *Pronaf* district in Juárez. In cafés painted the colors of bubblegum and denim, the wives of doctors and their lovers played chess or had coffee. It was a summer evening, and all my friends had saved enough money to take trips to the coast, or to drink in the bright plazas of Guadalajara. As I walked, a wind began hissing around me, although the night had been devilishly still and hot. Dust gritted in my teeth; a woman flashed before me with the speed of light flickering on & off during a thunderstorm. Her face was an aperture that led to many faces simultaneously: the virgin in her first ecstacy. An Etruscan handmaiden. A girl in a field of snow. Mary, Ishtar with hair aflame and skin the color of pearl. A waitress pouring coffee in a diner outside Modesto, California. A queen wearing a red wig; a prostitute rolling up her skirt on a stained mattress. The vision dissolved in the air and left the smell of burnt wood, yet the wind whispered in my ear, and I opened my palm, and put her in my pocket.

Upon arriving home—after an impossible bus trip with her breath billowing my shirt and pants—I took her out of my pocket. At once, my papers flew, books were thumbed and tossed, my armoire fell with a crash, and the sheets on my bed rippled over the full shape of her body. I fumbled with my buttons and zipper, and then slipped into bed. That night, my nerves ripened; I became every man at the apex of orgasm. Soft teeth bit my breath, her words heavy with hemlock shot through my veins, and poured out my mouth in the shape of smoke.

The next morning I awoke in an empty bed, and with a tangle of sheets and a headache that usually follows the lucidity of drunkenness. In wet ash, she had written her name across the wall. I spent that day awaiting her; during the following weeks, I would search the streets. In the evenings, I wrote poem after poem, hoping to summon her through the necromancy of metaphor.

It is only now, after five years, I realize her door opens where thirsts intersect. From that encounter, my hunger has been sharpened; meat doesn't satisfy me. I want to devour all the rain of India, and drink starlight dry. She has inhabited me so that I might fashion her in this flimsy simulacrum and write of her arrival with a gust of wind at your door. Let her in.

LABOR

The old man was always crimped as he held the reins. His burro hauled a cart with sploshing buckets of pig slop. He would stop at the corner of each block, and then yell out for the grandmothers abandoned by men now trotting on ghost horses, and the younger pregnant women to usher him into their back patios where they kept the plastic buckets filled with left-over oatmeal, stale bread and tortillas, soft tomatoes and chilies, pork fat coagulated and scooped from frying pans, and hardened rice and beans. Every block, a few women flap out onto the sidewalk in their slippers, or a retired worker would whistle for the old man's attention. Then the pig slop collector would wake up his burro with a *¡Ya!*, and pour the bile-yellow concoctions into the buckets in his cart.

Watching this from my Saturday morning porch, I would think of the butcher section in the *mercado*: fish tanks were filled with fried pork skins or tripe. Behind the brilliant counter windows revealing trays of steak, *carnitas*, and cow tongues colored the gray of a faded violet, the white teeth'd women would smile as they wrapped the meat for customers. Flies circled. Caged canaries flapped their wings wildly. And there was the stench of blood drying in the heat, like the odor of stale beer and unwashed crotch.

What the old man poured into buckets and sought out block after block was the source—the enzyme itself—for workers with rough hands and mothers giving milk. The seed for many meals, and the juice that quenches thirst. But it was the burro, and not the old man, that I would study, and still remember: a creature with two mud-puddles for eyes, its body like a dirty coat matted on a stick. Its fur would twinge from gnats, and from the leather belt used to speed up its trot. Under some sky in a further desert there must be a dune awaiting the step of its hooves. May the burro, that laborer, sink in the sand and be swallowed, before the vultures circle above.

PRIORITIZING

The force that through the green fuse...
— Dylan Thomas

Apart from the smell of curdled milk and wilted lettuce, you visit the public market of this border town for its pork-skin the color of crystallized urine; jalapenos and tomatoes piled on pink towels beside stalls where boys fry tripe; and the sharp-teeth'd teenagers, and matrons in brown shawls, passing from shade into sunlight and into shadow. You, too, turn left into half-light where the blueness of cow's stomachs on a platter scratches at your throat as you stumble through flies. And instead of purchasing dried beef or writing of rattlesnake-skin boots, or kiosks, you stop to sketch words when you spot a rooster, rusty with carrot-colored streaks, beak bent, beneath the corrugated-iron counter of a stall, tar stains, burnt *Pacifico* cigarettes, a cockroach's husk, yet the rooster blinking, its days spent with one leg tied by green wire, while radios clang the cowbells of *cumbias*, pedestrians brush past you, —and that wire, though adulterated, the greenest.

FAITH IN THE MASKS THAT MAKE US

I never wrote on Sundays; instead, I went for walks through the *Plaza de las Americas* mall with its skylight, while students from the local *preparatoria* milled around the ice-skating rink or stopped to look at the jeans and American clothing inside display windows. The day would always end with a movie when, worn-weary with sweat from walking to a cheaper theater two miles from the mall, I would sink into my seat and let the screen flash colors of a softer reality.

One Sunday, I was too hung-over for my routine. I walked to the *menudo* joint across the street from the city gym where boxers trained during the day and stray pigeons flew across the high ceiling. The *Menuda Rivas* was crowded as usual; it was a small, walk-in stand the size of half an urban bus. The owner, mustachioed and loud, greeted me with a *¿Qué Hubole?*, as he sweated over two vats of bubbling broth, while his stalwart daughter chopped onions. After slurping down my meal, I slopped my bread in the onion-sweet dregs, then finished my coffee with the pace of a man lounging on a bench in a stone plaza awash with sunlight. After I had finished, the owner asked if I had any plans for the day, and, looking outside, I saw a long line at the box office outside the gym. Vendors had already arrived and were selling *tostadas* and photos of masked Mexican wrestlers with such appellations as El Kizz, or Jock Starr. Adults and children were thronging.

It was a hot morning; inside the gym, it was a steam-bath. Bleachers dwarfed the ring where a match had just finished. Children were sucking on mango candy dredged in hot sauce, or teeth-crackling fried pork skins. Everyone was sweating, and my shirt stuck to my chest. I sat down, while the crowd clapped a rhythmic 1-2-3... 1-2-3... Warm drops streaked the top of my head, and, looking back, I glanced at men who were throwing their cups of beer down into the ring. Over loud speakers, the announcer rolled his R's and stretched out his vowels into jaw-cracking O's and A's: Jock Starr and El Charro Eléctrico were taking the ring. More beer splashed, and feet began stomping; down by the ring, red and yellow siren lights were swirling in tempo to disco.

I then noticed—while the wrestlers continued with their chest-beating—the wrinkled women who would trot down to the aisle, boo the bad wrestler who took every advantage to break the rules and poke his opponent in the eye or try to pull off his silvery mask. Those matrons cheered for the hero who, despite such trauma, would get back up and battle against the odds. One woman, dressed in a floral pattern dress and slippers, hobbled to the bathroom to fill a cup with tap water, and chuck the malignant elixir into the ring to protest the aberrations of the dark wrestler. Whether she knew the game was a baroque spectacle in which gesture counted more than contact, and in which a mask revealed more than the sweat-slick brow and straining muscles, didn't matter; indignation wracked her.

I whistled and cheered. I understood the world as theater, and the slipshod art of *lucha libre*—with its hooded personae and Furies—as a commedia unleashing the humors for catharsis. The rowdy men with faces mud-red cursed, while their children stood on bleachers and jumped. I also yelled as the roles of lover, death and clown battled and committed feats of bravery in order that the play continue. And in those few hours in a rundown gym in the ruinous district of a border town, I didn't know which—my life, or the match reaching its climax—was the true reality.

HAD I BEEN ABLE TO CONVERSE, I WOULD HAVE RETURNED TO MY EGO

Perhaps I would have returned with a mere story about the Sierra Tarahumara if it weren't for six events: First, after a trip during which every passenger slept as the train ascended the sierra and unsaddled horses wandered across fields, and past log cabins, I got off at an empty wood-shack station, and the conductor said, *You're in the navel of the cosmos.* There was a dirt road, and I followed it for a mile before I found a family renting a cabin for the night. Second: After eating *chile rellenos* with the family in their cinder-block home, the eldest son said he hadn't read the newspaper for years, and wanted to know the weight of a horse on the moon. Third: I rented a tired mare, and trotted with a *mestizo* in a cowboy hat, and his farmhand, a Tarahumara dressed in jeans. I asked the farmhand how to say thank you, water and bread in his language; he responded with silence. The *mestizo* whistled and rolled his eyes: *Forget it, you can never get them to talk.* We passed cornfields and smoking huts, mist, and copper boulders. Fourth: Back in the village, I asked a girl for the time. She had just gotten off a bus, and having no watch, she offered me an apple instead; it was so crisp that when I bit into it, a crow flapped away from its fence. Fifth: I looked for this exact poem that night, while writing beneath a bare bulb, but could only list the shriek of train brakes, flies on oil-cloth, the shadow scent of horses: the brine of a woman's hair on a pillow. And sixth: In the morning, I heard a language all susurration and inflection, and looking out my window, I saw the Tarahumara farmhand talking to a woman wearing a calico dress and leather-strap sandals. She was either his sister or sweetheart, and both were standing in the same dirt road I had journeyed the previous day. They spoke at length, and smiled when they parted, almost pirouetting around one another, in order to provide enough room for the other to set off. I understood that by not having uttered a single diphthong in their language, I had learned how to apprehend the shimmer in an O's center, or the serpentine tail of an S, and I opened these words.

for Amaury Terrero

THE GIFT

We met by accident on a bus headed back downtown. There had been a shooting on my block, and in order to avoid any cross-fire, and to also find relief from the heat inside my room, I had decided to go to the air-conditioned theater in the new mall on the fashionable side of Juárez. The movie had started at 10:30—a Swedish film picked as part of the second annual film festival—and by the time it had finished and I had caught the rust-red *circunvalación* line en route to the main plaza, it was already one in the morning. The *avenida 16* was almost deserted, and the bus inched along with its creaking chassis and screeching noise of brakes whenever a teenage mother holding an infant, or two elderly couples flagged the bus down. I sat in darkness; fatigue throbbed warmly in my limbs as the night air shushed through the open windows.

With the growl of tires hitting unpaved stretches of the avenue, and with my eyes closed, I didn't notice the shadow that slid next to me as the bus rattled over a pothole. Smelling sweat, I opened my eyes to a man lit by staccato flashes of streetlamp-yellow: mid-thirties, receding hairline, Adam's apple making its ascent and descent in slow intervals, aquiline nose, and crestfallen chin. I sat up and pondered if I should call out *¡Bajan!* and lumber down the aisle and onto the sidewalk. There had been articles published in the newspaper of muggings taking place onboard buses at night, with other passengers too terrified to protest, and the driver indifferent or in league. But his hands squeezed my wrist with the amount of pressure one would use on a friend in order to hook his attention before informing him of marriage or illness. His lips unglued dryly, with bottom and upper crescents slowly unpeeling.

—*Compa'*, I'm headed up to *Anapra* so that I can cross the river without getting hassled...

His voice sounded as if it had been whittled with a rough blade, or filtered through grit and sandpaper. I would see such types as I walked over the bridge into El Paso. Those ones, the poorest of the poor with skin so brown from working beneath the sun it had crazed the red of old enamel. On the Santa Fe bridge, exhaust fumes enveloping them, and beneath the white-hard sky, they would sell flowers, carry trays of tamarind candy, jog alongside sedans wiping windshields, and dicing their palms into half-open windows for change.

—...three kids as well. We came up all the way from just outside of Fresnillo, but the only work I could get here was selling roses on the *Puente Libre.* My old lady told me to cross and hook up with my brother-in-law in Las Cruces. He's dry-walling and making thirty bucks a day. You look like *buena gente,* can you help me out with ten pesos?

And he squeezed my wrist again. No menace in his grip or stare; not even a desperation that triggers rage. I dug into my pocket just as the tires hit the cobblestones of downtown, throbbing like a muddy current that has leapt its bed and rises all night, turning fields into brown water, carrying off the chickens and cows.

Nothing, except the few pesos I was saving for lunch. *Lo siento,* and I felt his calloused palm release me as I called out my stop.

Instead of getting home that night, I saw a friend exiting a bar. It was one of those grottos with a swivel door and concrete floor. We shook hands and laughed at the chance meeting. Emilio insisted that I come back in for a quick beer, and I told him that I had to teach the following day at noon. He pulled out from his pocket a roll of motley bills, announced that the university had both given him his summer bonus and fired him for exceeding his allotted sick days. He was out to get drunk and tugged me by my arm back inside *El Recreo.*

After tall bottles of lukewarm beer, we stumbled to a taxi stand, and paid an exaggerated fare for our ride to the strip only ten blocks away. We wandered from empty disco to empty disco with their doormen and lazy bartenders, tinsel palm trees, mirrors and neon. Monday night, and no one was drinking; there was still a good hour before everything closed.

After a while, Emilio and I stopped talking and sat in the last open bar, listening to Jimi Hendrix scrape blue and white sparks from his guitar, while a teenage boy swept the floor.

The next morning I sat slurping beef stew after having called in sick. Through the restaurant window I watched firemen at the station across the street. They washed their trucks and then engaged in a ludicrous drill that involved jogging in place with each phalanx holding a ladder above their heads. I stuck my left hand into the broth in order to pluck a chunk of meat when I noticed the negative of the grip of that man I had encountered on the bus. It wasn't red or bruised. There was only the shape of his fingers and palm curving around my wrist in a reverse shadow, for the surrounding skin was darker than the print of his hand.

I stopped chewing, swallowed, and felt a large bolus inch down my throat. At first slowly with amazement, and then with panic and haste, I tried to rub it off. I threw my 20 pesos on the table and walked out with my left hand in my pocket so that no one might see that pale stigma. Then, walking down a side street, I began to methodically scratch it. The street spilled into downtown, and a car horn bleated as I jogged across an intersection. Passing dress stalls with women vendors ululating, past a cop probing his gums with a toothpick, I scratched at it until my skin turned raw.

And so, for days I exhibited the grip of that man from Fresnillo who now might be back in Juárez polishing shoes, assembling televisions in a *maquila,* picking tomatoes in Northern California, or in his hometown and in debt to the general store. The mark dissolved a little day by day, but it left something beneath the skin, like a thin strip of scar tissue where the shadow burned. To this day—and it has been five years—I rub it in penance every so often in order to recall a gift denied. Moreover, I now understand that the mark stays there as something I must bear during my lifetime: a branding that signifies original betrayal, while the less fortunate have only their faith to remind them.

THIRST

Before I met my wife, I lived in the ramshackle *colonia bella vista.* When I walked home in the evenings from teaching English, I would cut through *boys' town.* Taxi cab drivers leaning against their sedans would snap their fingers and shout: *Hey, you wanna see the girls*? Smothered in smoke and pink neon, the strip clubs would reverberate with the whistle and thump of dance music. At the doors, black-vested bartenders would grab the arms of teetering Americans and promise two beers for the price of one. But after several blocks, the noise would fade and then be drowned out by the grumble of buses down-shifting and grinding brakes at intersections. The streetlamps would buzz; stray dogs everywhere, and children sucking on tamarind candy dusted with spicy powder. The neighborhood matrons gossiped in slippers on the sidewalk and would greet me as I approached my block. The only frazzle to the peace were the rival gangs from downtown that would drive by, shooting bullets up in the air, but after the children were put to bed, and the only ones awake were the men drinking on their porches or on chairs set out in front of the screen doors. The doors were locked after the men turned in for the night; they were never tired, though, and they always had a bottle of brandy to share, although it would eventually be the death of them.

Ten *Caguamas*, 32 ouncer bottles of beer, was Pipi's daily dosage. In the white mornings, he would start drinking at the usual corners: Chuy's automotive repair, a vacant lot with a canvas roof nailed to wooden beams and legs. The porch of a neighbor who had already left to cross the bridge into El Paso to shop or work. Beto's re-tread tire stand: a garage that stank of oil and tar. But you could always find Pipi: two spindly legs snapping in jeans, and a paunch that proceeded the rest of his body by six inches; and his smile, a checkerboard of yellowed and missing teeth rooted in gums the color of beef jerky, spittle frothing when he cursed or laughed. All the *colonia* would say hello as he straddled the sidewalk and shifted directions, and sometimes a grandmother would stop him and give him a couple of bills to run some errands. When there were no windshields to wipe with newspaper, no tips to accrue by making deliveries, he would beg for his drinking money. Come on, he would tug at my sleeve, give me just five pesos. And when properly drunk, he would strut down the street, singing that name which had branded him as the neighborhood sot.

As Pipi drank, his sister stripped for American soldiers and hustled drinks and dollars. His mother fumbled with her rosary, walked to church each morning, and collected social security checks from a PO Box in El Paso, thanks to a dead husband who spent his days working in the States. The masks stuck to their faces. And whether they saw red in the sting of a scraped knee, in a bubbling vat of chile rojo, they also saw crows picking at tire-flattened dogs, entrails caked on asphalt. Their roles resumed each morning, as Pipi rinsed his thirst with the first sip of sweet beer, while others started their trucks in order to drive the long bridge over the river. Some prayed, while the abandoned mothers swept the dust from their front doors, and spat morning phlegm in the gutter.

CONDUIT

As I rolled up her skirt, she raised her hips so that the fabric would nestle in the curve at the base of her back. Though her arms and legs were dark, her thighs were pale and glowed against her black panties. She lay still without moving, yet when I began to unclothe her sex—in the drawn-out descent of a leaf—her stomach shook in short breaths with the randomness of sun shimmying on the surface of a lake. When her pubic tuft was uncovered, it blossomed suddenly with the frazzle of those garden bushes with pine-like leaves. In the slow light of her bedroom, softened by the mustard-colored drapes, her coiled hairs glistened like wet-black ink. I brushed my lips over those hairs, and she spread her legs wider. There was a squishing noise as she fanned her thighs back and forth. I stared at the aperture, visibly wet and expanding and contracting, between her vulva shaded the violet and gray of a polished conch's interior and, lightly matted with purplish hairs. Lubricant glistened thickly and almost milk-like, and with the slow-bleed of a pierced yolk. What I smelled to this day makes me dizzy with yearning, and sitting in restaurants, or riding the bus, my crotch stirs awake. It was coffee ground, mint crushed and whiffed between soiled fingers; it was blood, tar bubbling at noon, and a sweet bonfire of leaves; it was moisture beaded on cheese hardening, raw meat and merlot, brine, and rough bread. It was a ferment of everything that rots and rejuvenates: like a tree stripped of bark, then crusted anew with alligator-like skin; like cells that shrivel in alkaline, and then bloom again in a white froth.

After the act, she lay snoring lightly, with one shoulder bare, and the rest of her body wrapped toga-like in the bed sheet. I dressed, and stepped out into the street. Walking down the city block, I put my fingers to my nose and smelled her. An old man wearing a battered fedora walked by me and let out an *¡Ay!* that swept the street's litter. At an intersection, a young woman brushed against me as we waited for the light to change; against my shoulder blades I felt her erect nipples. I passed a cantina, and heard a shuffle, and looking back, I saw two red-faced tourists from the open door who sniffed the peppery aroma. It was then I put my hands into my pockets and walked to a park, always isolated, with little shade, and a pigeon-stained statue of Benito Juárez. I sat down on a bench, stretched out my legs and let the sun lick me. With my eyes closed, I pulled my hands out from my pockets, and raised them, open-fingered, to the blue. A rustle of wings, many wings, converged around me, cooing and splaying me with sharp shafts of light and shade. I felt innumerable beaks and rough tongues pick at my fingers, palms, my lips, and my crotch. And I kept my eyes closed as I was lifted to an even brighter region.

THROBBING LIKE A FAULTY STOPLIGHT

Faustino was lost in the *mercado público* at 3:00 am. He was talking to God again, and the darkness was like a plum crushed inside a velvet sack. The alley cantinas with tile walls the yellow of urine had emptied. He only had the journey home now, through a twisted gut-heap of neighborhoods with stilting stucco buildings, and drainage pipes coughing up mud into streets littered with newspapers, lettuce, and wet tortilla.

That's how I imagine him that night. Sketch him on the blankness of a page: smelling like old milk, roughly handsome and with a scratch-slash across his left cheek which his woman had given him. Long hair the brown of an autumn leaf. His thirsts had swallowed him; he walked down crooked streets with the cautious zigzag and shift of a crab. Broke, job lost because he rarely showed up, and a savagely beautiful woman now pregnant and tired about his nonsense about writing, he survived by donating plasma, and scraping together a few hundred pesos a month by helping his landlord strong-arm tenants into paying overdue rent and loans.

I met Faustino in a bar. At that time, his clothes purchased in Guadalajara were not yet frayed at the collars. He carried a dog-eared copy of Erasmus, and let me listen to him as long as I bought him drinks. His nervous soliloquy with arms gesticulating and chin slicing the air left and right became more intense with each brandy and soda water. Phrases from Michaux and Bataille, neologisms and similes, and drinking stories poured from his mouth. *I'm going home,* he would slur; it was a phrase that I didn't fully grasp until later. His family, I learned, was rich, and often wrote him, ordering him to stop his wandering, leave the desert and jagged barrios of the border, and return to the clean linen, family business, and gardens of the south.

We often ran into each other, and sometimes he would visit me. He would sit at my desk—a door teetering on legs made from bricks—and critique the poems I was writing. It was during these visits that he would describe how God's presence filled him with a presentiment of silence, throbbing like a faulty stoplight. The signal led him into a winding of language and streets, like the *mercado* where I found him that night.

I visited him once at his apartment and read his elliptical poetry swarming with soft skulls, arrivistes of blue wine, tires, oily teeth, and silence gelling. After five beers, he and Maricela began arguing about money. Roaches scattered as she threw and shattered a plate against the kitchen wall. I would have left, yet she had locked the door so that he wouldn't escape. The two wrestled in front of me, knocking over a night table. When they stopped, and she finally gave me the key to open the door, I looked back and saw the two kissing: she had grabbed him by the hair as if it were a rein, and while feeding on his lips, she held a fork, prongs pressing into his throat.

Yet the only time I saw him completely distraught was on the night before I found his body. He came to visit and unfolded a letter written by his father, signed with a flowery signature. His parents were not going to recognize the baby; it was the child of a *fichera*, a slut; they would cut Faustino from the family, unless he came back home. The path was winding around him, leading him to that which awaits in a stone atrium.

The following night, I tossed a ten peso coin on the bar counter, and finished my drink. Outside, a taxi sped by me, missing me by a foot. The street was always better for walking than the half-paved and littered sidewalk. After a few blocks, I passed a stray dog which growled as it jogged past me. I neared the corner and saw a body in the street. Upon reaching it, I got on my knees and recognized Faustino. Blood that had been thrown up covered his mouth and chin, and stained his shirt. A black puddle had cooled around his skull, and I understood that he had gone home in the guise of two white-hot eyes, and a rattling chassis.

THE PERFECT MOSQUITO

All that June, the fair glowed on the grounds facing the *río bravo,* only a mile from the glass towers and banks of the United States. Nightfall, and the ruby and champagne colored lights on Ferris wheels and merry-go-round would slowly spin. Undulant rows of couples and friends would rotate around the canvas-stalls where proprietors frothed beer into plastic mugs. The young women—those brooders of dark severity—for once smiled at the young men. A rush of flight, an ardor flooded the fair. Even the occasional cop seemed more tolerant, as he leaned outside the pissy, hot bathrooms, or stood guard by the hall where the curses thundered at the start and crescendo of each cock-fight.

I had invited a secretary working in the payroll department at the university to join me. Time dissolved, while fireworks and drums resounded from within the grounds. Stood up, bored, I decided to buy a ticket and go in by myself. This was in the days when I first moved to Juárez with the ambition of writing a Bildungsroman, having the border serve as its locus. While teaching English to Engineering students, I envisioned pages teeming with sugar skulls and guitars. The fair, I reasoned, might also provide a descriptive passage, or the backdrop for a pivotal scene.

Back then, I carried a pen and small notepad in my breast pocket, and I would word-sketch everything: a vacant lot before which a man wearing sandals pushed a cart of lemon and melon juice, wasps circling above. The yellow tiled interior of a restaurant with water stains on its ceiling. A girl in a stained, pink blouse sucking on tamarind candy. And so, I spent an hour wandering around the main stalls, drinking, and saw the fair as another vista saturated with the fantastic. My shirt was sweat-drenched and stuck to my chest, and, being so happy, I didn't take out my pen or paper to write. After I had tired of seeing the same stages and faces flushed with drunkenness, I walked down the path abandoned except for couples necking in the half-light. After five or six yards, there were no more stalls, and the din of the fair was swallowed by a throbbing silence. A cricket chirped once. The crackle, far off, of phosphor as a cigarette was lit. The laughter of a man and woman.

Around the bend of a path, I saw floodlights reveal a rodeo ring, and bleachers dotted with a few drunks or teenagers smoking marijuana. At the entrance of the ring was a stall illuminated by a single bulb around which circled moths. A man sat at the counter. I approached the stall out of curiosity, and noticed the shelves stocked with bottles. The bottles held a clear liquid; some were pickling chunks of browned meat or gobs of rot. The proprietor stood up and smiled when I reached his counter. He had large cheeks and a frazzle of black hair; an old undershirt was stretched to the point of transparency over his paunch.

"Are you getting much studying done?"

His Spanish had the singsong pitch and staccato rhythm of the way people speak in Chiapas or Oaxaca. He pointed to the notepad and pen jutting from my chest. I explained that I was a poet. At once, he recited a line by Amado Nervo, one of those maudlin refrains over-anthologized and dripping with syrup. Taking my cup of beer, he finished the dregs of warm foam, and tossed it into the trash can behind him. He then took down one of the bottles, and, with a knife, fished out some meat.

"It was fermenting with chicken. Makes it more potent. That'll be twenty Pesos."

I hesitated. But he leaned over the counter, cupped his hands over my ear, and whispered: *What you'll see is better than a thousand verses.* He pulled away from me slowly, as if painfully ungluing himself.

"Good choice."

And he took my money.

I found a corner in the bleachers overlooking the wet dirt of the rodeo ring. A wind carried the toy-box music and bells of the carnival. I put the jar to my lips and almost sneezed from fumes acridly wafting. I choked at the first sip, and coughed up phlegm. Taking a deep breath, I then forced down a long draught, and felt my throat and chest burn; without waiting, I forced down a second and third gulp so that my Adam's apple resounded loudly, as if I were finally drinking water after a day of intensive labor.

My sight failed me; for a long moment below time it felt as if I was tumbling, and then my eyes opened, as I heard a voice. It was as if I had been wandering down a fogwebbed path, until a confused blackbird struck me, flapping in my face, before soaring back up to its proper sphere with a caw. Although adjectives and the temporal nature of narration won't aptly describe what happened during that pause, I will set it down in words:

While passed out, or while truly awake, I saw the night: smoke-like, it writhed above me as a serpent, armored with small, black scales, between which were chinks the color of lapis lazuli, crushed grape, and dark water. There were no stars, and the bleachers and floodlights crumbled without a sound. The snake then flaked and dissolved, and the celestial vault, still without stars, rained soft phosphor; blue sparks cracked silently, and they exploded as they hit red flames miles below me. One of the scales landed on my lap without burning me. I looked up as I heard a monotonous whine. I saw a mosquito whose wings were its own source of light. It was the size of a fist, and hovered before me with a clear, syringe-like proboscis. It landed on the night-scale, and though its wings had stopped fluttering, it crackled with propane-blue light. It then began to suck a violet liquid from the scale; the liquid bubbled up its needle, and slowly began to gorge its belly. I was not afraid; awe filled me. The mosquito rose and, landing on my arm, stuck its needle in my vein and backwashed that violet. No pain, only an inexplicable release. As the intake of nightblood increased, the amount of light my eyes absorbed increased as well. Little by little, I once again noticed the bleachers, the light of dawn, and the cop shaking me awake, telling me that the grounds were closing.

How can I explain my life after that night? Each minute is pregnant with the tastes of a century. Though I still eat, teach, and make love, a sweet darkness courses through my veins. I was never able to thank my benefactor; his stall was empty by the time I stumbled out of the rodeo ring. I walked home that morning, my vision cleansed, and I felt a consanguinity with every bird, face, cloud, and stray dog. While passing a trashcan in a park, I tossed my notepad and pen, without despair, but with perfect equanimity. I haven't written a word since then.

MEMENTO

Au detour d'une sentier, une charogne
— Charles Baudelaire

Carrion of dog by a dirt pile and dried tree: littered bottles, meat-scraps, yellowed newspaper the color of jaundiced skin stretched over ribs. Traffic ten yards away, noon sun blinding, —a desert day in which air was packed to the seams with heat.

I'd seen other dogs bloated with eyes the color of halibut scales, or fur-strips of coyote whiskered with skid marks and oil on asphalt, yet this was once the perrenial border dog: trotting or limping with pendulant testicles or teats, fur the dun of coffee muddied with cream and ash, —those beasts no one feeds and yet they continue breeding, sniffing out for one another in fallen adobe houses, behind brick walls plastered with wrestling and beer ads, and lap gutter water with black tongues, nip fangs at coagulated lard smeared on *burrito* wrappers.

It had been dead for months: no fur, but soap-smooth hide, tar-colored, and which could be snapped like a pencil, and mandible-pick'd clean, as ants and cockroaches milled through a cavernous aperture in what was once the beast's belly. Organs a sponge-mass stewing in weeds. And trickling through this aspic, the marrowless vertebrae, each descending disk the yellow of piano keys in a mahogany parlor stinking of mildew.

A gaseous up-thrust of flies jarred my concentration, and my throat itched at my tongue. Yet I gazed on, coughed phlegm from the odor, like cow stalls moist with beetles, huge wheels of cheese beaded with grease, or breath and damp cotton on a humid bus. A single drop of cold sweat scurried down my back, and quickly warmed when it reached the base of my spine, as my skin absorbed its salt.

This pause on my way to a friend's house took only a minute, yet I now chop it into paragraphs, like a butcher who partitions vast sides of a pig or cow into protein which white teeth will later shred. Because this is my compost for tomorrow, words mushrooming in the miasma, just as my own marrow and sperm diluted in the July heat, while ants crawled between my legs, and a tree cast its shadow on a plot awaiting me.

SLEEP

The heat was like an immobile pendulum. There was never a breeze to cool off the sweat on the foreheads of men standing under store awnings, or above the lips of women carrying their grocery bags, or waiting on corners for the *rutera*, the city buses. Every color burned, whether it was the melon and lemon juices displayed in plastic vats, chrome on a car bumper, store-front windows, or the *Coca-Cola* advertisement painted on the market wall. As he would go on his way to meet a friend at a cantina with ceiling fans, or at a restaurant with starched tablecloths and white-vested waiters, he would walk through those streets, through those colors.

At times, he would spend the entire day harvesting: downy blackness, faint as smoke curling from sandalwood, above the lips of a teenage girl on an errand to the corner store; the rust stripe on the side of a bus; the disinfectant-blue stripe on a police car. And the fleckless, hard azure of sky. Miles of new districts with stucco buildings—all liquor stores and movie rental chains—painted egg-yolk yellow and turquoise. The sand in a vacant lot. Old side-streets with crumbling squat adobe homes the brown of chocolate frothed with milk. Fur on a stray dog the gray of coagulated lard.

Eventually, these colors would brim over his cupped hands and run down his arms, like thawing ice, and stain his shirt, pants, and shoes. But he would continue cradling this increasing load of vistas and shades in his arms; sweat would sting his eyes, and that motley bouquet would radiate like a sunset reddened through distance and dust. After walking for a long time, they would sear or dry like book-pressed petals. And still he would carry them, although the afternoon wind would blow some of the ash-light fragments away. Upon arriving at his street, he would walk to the wall of a fallen house facing his alley window. By then, all the colors had wilted to browned husks, and he would scatter them to the rising wind, so that they might inhabit the alley and broken walls. Soon the sandstorms would come, and erase those ashes, and a new day would start with its unique and perishable colors.

And as the sun set, he would return to his room to lie down and rest. He would fall asleep, with the faces, corners, and sunlight flashing and blurring into a disc that would spin slowly, falling over the edge of the violet, evening sand.

ABOUT THE AUTHOR

Anthony Seidman completed his B.A. in English & Textual Studies, & Spanish & Spanish American Literature at Syracuse University, before going on to the University of Texas at El Paso where he completed an M.F.A. in the bilingual creative writing program. While completing his M.F. A., he lived for several years in Ciudad Juárez; he worked as an English instructor at the Autonomous University of Ciudad Juárez. His first book, *On Carbon-Dating Hunger*, was published in 2000 by The Bitter Oleander Press.